CORTINA METHOD

CONVERSATIONAL
FRENCH
IN 20 LESSONS

Cortina Method Books

FRENCH IN 20 LESSONS
SPANISH IN 20 LESSONS
GERMAN IN 20 LESSONS
ITALIAN IN 20 LESSONS
AMERICAN ENGLISH IN 20 LESSONS
MODERN GREEK IN 20 LESSONS
RUSSIAN IN 20 LESSONS
INGLÉS EN 20 LECCIONES
FRANCÉS EN 20 LECCIONES
INGLÊS EM 20 LIÇÕES
CONVERSATIONAL BRAZILIAN PORTUGUESE
CONVERSATIONAL JAPANESE
SPANISH CONVERSATIONAL GUIDE
SPANISH IN SPANISH
FRANÇAIS EN FRANÇAIS
ENGLISH IN ENGLISH
DEUTSCH AUF DEUTSCH
ITALIANO IN ITALIANO

CORTINA METHOD

CONVERSATIONAL FRENCH IN 20 LESSONS

ILLUSTRATED

Intended for self-study and for use in schools

With a Simplified System of Phonetic Pronunciation

By

R. DIEZ DE LA CORTINA

UNIVERSITIES OF MADRID AND BORDEAUX
AUTHOR OF THE CORTINA METHOD
ORIGINATOR OF THE PHONOGRAPHIC METHOD OF
TEACHING LANGUAGES.

and Revised by

DOUGLAS W. ALDEN

PRINCETON UNIVERSITY

An Owl Book

HENRY HOLT AND COMPANY

New York

CORTINA LEARNING INTERNATIONAL, INC.
Publishers • WESTPORT, CT 06880

Cataloging Information

Cortina Method French in 20 Lessons, illustrated, intended for self-study and
    for use in schools; with a new system of phonetic pronunciation to en-
    able the student to speak correct French, by R. Diez de la Cortina and
    rev. by Douglas W. Alden. New York, R. D. Cortina Co., 1977.
        382 p. illus. 21 cm.
    1. French language—Grammar. 2. French language—
Conversation and phrase books. I. Title.
PC2111.C715 1977   448.242   55-4890
ISBN 0-8327-0003-7 (hardbound)
ISBN 0-8327-0011-8 (paperback)

Printed in the United States of America
HH Editions 9 8 7 6 5 4 3 2 1   *9009–12.5

INTRODUCTION

How a Knowledge of French Can Help You

There are many reasons why forward-looking Americans should want to know French at this time.

French is truly the "international language." No matter where you go in the world you can converse with cultured people if you speak French. French is the universal language of translation at the United Nations. It is the only sure means of communication in Europe, the Orient and Africa. It is the recognized medium of diplomatic intercourse. It is the mark of social polish . . . the language of etiquette in all countries.

Because it has been the "second language" of cultured people for so long a time—French has found its way into many parts of our own language. Our literature and polite conversation is often sprinkled with French expressions. French dishes are on the menus of most of our fine restaurants. French is an important part of the vocabulary in the world of fashion, art, science, theatre, opera, etc.

No trip abroad would be complete without some time spent *in the most visited of foreign countries* . . . France. And when you visit France, you will find your knowledge of the native tongue a source of unending satisfaction and pleasure. You will be able to become more intimate with the French people. You will be welcomed as a cultured friend—not merely a tourist.

5

You will be invited into French homes. Instead of finding your trip a dull procession of monument-visiting—you will have many thrilling experiences to relate when you return home. And you will find that your knowledge of French saves you money when you deal with tradespeople, hotel-keepers, ticket-sellers, and so on.

And even though you may not be planning a trip abroad at this time, you never know when you will have the opportunity. But apart from traveling, there are many other ways in which a knowledge of French can add to your happiness. You can dine in a charming restaurant and order from the elaborate menu without the slightest hesitation. Then suppose you have seats for the opera—*Thais, Faust, Manon,* or *Louise?* All these beautiful operas (whether you see them or hear them on radio, television, or recordings) become twice as enjoyable. And at home, in your easy chair, you can read French newspapers and fascinating Parisian magazines. Or you can enjoy the classics of French literature—Hugo, Moliere, de Maupassant, Balzac, etc.—*in the original French,* with all its sauce, humor and deep, human understanding. Discover these literary treasures for yourself and have *the real fun* of learning French as you do!

PREFACE

In 1882, The Cortina Academy of Languages was founded in the United States by Count Cortina. Besides engaging professors for all the modern languages (French, Spanish, German, Italian, Portuguese and English) Count Cortina himself gave language instruction for many years.

From this actual teaching experience, Professor Cortina developed a new simplified method that became an instant success. It has never been surpassed since. For the past 95 years the method has been constantly refined and improved from the Academy's long experience in teaching languages, and in terms of the changing needs of the present-day language student. It is now known all over the world as THE CORTINA METHOD.

Because of the success and the demand for the Cortina instruction from students who could not attend classes, The Academy was forced to publish Cortina lessons in book form. Well over two million Cortina books have been sold, and they are a clear testimonial to the ease with which students have learned a new language through THE CORTINA METHOD.

Many thousands of students have learned a new language by this method at home, in their spare time. Many others have used THE CORTINA METHOD in schools and colleges throughout the United States and South America.

You may ask: "What is the secret of THE CORTINA METHOD's success? How is it different from other ways to learn a language?" One of the main reasons is that the lessons are devoted to intensely interesting and every-day topics which encourage the student to learn. The lessons begin with subjects that we all used as children when we learned our native tongue. For instance, right from the start, the first lessons teach you the same words that a child first speaks: *Mother, father, brother, sister,* as well as every-day words relating to meals, drinks, clothing, footwear and so on. Not only are these words easily put to use at once; not only are they much more interesting than the usual abstract and academic words a student is asked to learn—but they also strike a deeply primeval chord in all of us. This adds color and excitement and arouses in the student a desire to learn the language.

Features of this New Edition

The Editors have included two new features in this edition which will also be found of great help to the student:

First, the format of the lessons has been changed to allow for carefully chosen illustrations which have been drawn by an excellent artist. The drawings have been arranged to highlight the subject matter of the lessons and thus will greatly aid the student in memorizing the foreign words through the graphic representation.

Second, a complete REFERENCE GRAMMAR has been appended at the back of the book so that the student may refer to any part of speech he wishes as he advances in his studies. The necessary grammar for the lessons is included in the footnotes, lesson by lesson, for the student's convenience.

HOW TO STUDY

Language is habit. We are constantly expressing thoughts and ideas in speech, from habit, without paying any particular attention to the words, phrases or idioms we use. When we say *"How do you do," "I've had a wonderful trip," "All right, let's go,"* we do so spontaneously. We are merely repeating a speech pattern that we have used so many times before it has become automatic, or, a habit. Repetition, therefore, is the basis of language learning, and so it is extremely important that the student acquire a correct pronunciation at the very beginning so that he learns *the right speech habits.*

For this purpose THE CORTINA METHOD provides a *Guide to French Pronunciation* on page 19. It explains how to pronounce French sounds, words and phrases through simplified English spelling (phonetic symbols) and also how to articulate those sounds which occur only in the French language. In Lesson 1 the entire French vocabulary and conversations are transcribed in these symbols. Using them as a guide the student will be able to read the entire lesson aloud, and he should do so as many times as necessary to read the French text aloud *easily and correctly.* Through this practice, not only will the student attain fluency, but he will eventually express his *ideas* in French just as easily and effortlessly as he does in English. Should any student wish to accelerate his progress and master spoken French in the easiest possible manner, the Cortina Company has recorded the French text of this book. The vocabularies and conversations are spoken by native French instructors whose voices have been chosen for their excellence of accent, clarity of speech and pleasing tonal quality. In classroom study too, *the phonograph method of learning languages* (originated by Cortina) has been found an invaluable aid to both student and teacher for oral practice and ear training.

LESSON ARRANGEMENT. The lessons are arranged so that the student can follow them easily. For each lesson there is (a) a vocabulary of important words of a general character, (b) a specific vocabulary covering the topic of the lesson and (c) conversations showing how these vocabularies are used in everyday conversations. To the right of each word or sentence is given the phonetic spelling so that the student can pronounce them correctly, and in the next column is given the English translation of the French text.

The student should start each lesson by memorizing as much of the general (active) vocabulary as possible. Then, in turning to the conversation that follows, he will complete his mastery of these words by actually using them *to express thoughts*. The CONVERSATION sentences should be read *aloud* using the pronunciation guide for this purpose, and at the same time making general reference to the translation of each sentence. *Learn the thoughts* that the French sentence conveys rather than a word for word translation. The lesson has been mastered when the student can read the lesson aloud without reference to either the PRONUNCIATION or TRANSLATION columns.

The special arrangement of columnizing the TEXT, PRONUNCIATION and TRANSLATION is for the student's convenience in checking his own progress. This is done by merely covering the TRANSLATION with a piece of paper to test if he knows what the French words and sentences mean, and in reverse, by covering the French text and translating aloud the English words into French. It cannot be emphasized too strongly that the student should read the French *aloud. Speak out clearly* and don't be embarrassed by the sound of your own voice. Let a friend take part in the conversation with you. *Go to a French restaurant*—or pretend you do—*do anything* just as long as it helps you to keep *speaking* French.

The grammatical explanations in the FOOTNOTES are of great importance to the student and close attention should be paid to them. They also clear up many of the idiomatic difficulties and are very helpful because they give other illustrations of the language in actual use. For more elaborate grammatical explanation of any particular lesson the student can refer to the cross-reference table (on page 190) which precedes the *Complete Reference Grammar*.

In conclusion there is no better way to learn a language than the way children learn *by speaking it*. THE CORTINA METHOD is based upon this principle with a few modifications to adjust *this natural method* to the adult mind. The first words a child learns are those necessary to satisfy his instinctive interests and desires. What are these first words? *Mother, father*, something to eat and drink, and after that something to wear and protect the body. After these wants are satisfied he grows in stature until he gradually builds up a vocabulary and speech patterns covering every conceivable subject, but his primary wants must be satisfied first. The Cortina lessons begin exactly this way, *mother, father*, eatables, clothing, footwear, etc. With a little application you will have a lot of fun learning French this way and what a satisfaction it will be to have *this important second language* at your command.

TABLE OF CONTENTS

VOCABULARIES AND CONVERSATIONS

REFERENCE GRAMMAR

* (§) is the symbol for paragraph.

THE ADVERB

THE PRONOUN

THE PREPOSITION

THE CONJUNCTION

THE VERB

FRENCH PRONUNCIATION

DICTIONARIES

GUIDE TO FRENCH PRONUNCIATION

Part I

The following discussion of French pronunciation is divided into two parts. The first describes the articulation of the sounds of the French language in terms of similar English sounds. The second part relates this information to the conventional spelling of the French language. Part II is on page 306.

GUIDE TO FRENCH SOUNDS

Although more "phonetic" than English, the French language still has a somewhat complicated spelling system. For this reason we shall indicate pronunciation by a system of simplified spelling and diacritical markings based as much as possible on the spelling of English. This Guide to Pronunciation generally follows the French word and is in parentheses.

Les Voyelles

THE VOWELS

(lay vwayèl)

In comparing French and English vowels, the basic principle to follow is that *all vowels in French are pure vowels.* Pronounce, for example, the English word *day.* It can easily be prolonged into *day-ee,* and even when the vowel is not prolonged you will realize *if you listen carefully* that the *ee* is actually present at all times. The normal English vowel is a diphthong, not a *pure vowel.* If you are to pronounce the corresponding French vowel correctly, you must strive to eliminate the second half of the diphthong; that is, you must say *day* with as short a vowel as possible and not *day-ee.* For English speaking people the problem of eliminating the diphthong arises in the case of most French vowels. How to pronounce French vowels will be described in the following pages.

In the study of phonetics (the science of human speech), it has been possible to observe scientifically the articulation of the vowels in the mouth. From these observations the following chart has been devised to show the relative position of the crest of the tongue as it moves about in the mouth. We shall study these vowels first in the order in which they occur naturally in the mouth.

19

Where Sounds Occur in Mouth

FRONT OF	*ee*	ü	*oo*	BACK OF
MOUTH	*ay*	e⁰	ô	MOUTH
	è	e	o	
	a	è⁰		
		â		

ee Similar to *ee* in tr*ee*. But the English vowel is not pure since it has a slight "eh" sound coming off the end. To make the French vowel pure, stretch corners of lips further back than in English.

ay Similar to *ay* in d*ay*, or better *a* in *a*te. Stretch corners of lips further back than in English; avoid saying "*ay-ee*."

è Similar to *e* in m*e*t. Stretch corners of lips back slightly more than in English. This is a short vowel, shorter than *ee* and *ay* in French (which themselves are shorter than their English equivalents).

a Between *a* in f*a*t and *a* in f*a*ther. A shorter sound than in English and not as "flat."

â Like *a* in f*a*ther or exclamation *ah*! Mouth is opened maximum amount. A simple sound to produce.

o As in *awe* or *ou* in *ou*ght. A shorter vowel sound than in English. Has slight rounding of lips not present in English vowel.

ô As *o* in n*o*te. French vowel has more lip-rounding than English. A pure vowel: avoid saying ô-*oo* as in English.

oo As *oo* in p*oo*p. French vowel has more lip-rounding than English.

ü This vowel has no English equivalent. It is similar to *ü* in the German word *ü*ber. The following exercise is useful in pronouncing the French sound: pronounce *oo*, then *ee*; now pronounce *ee* but round lips as though for *oo*; the result is the sound ü.

e Same as *e* in *the man*, if said normally with no stress on article. This is the easiest vowel to pronounce since it requires no force or muscular tension.

e⁰ Another vowel with no English equivalent. The following exercise will teach the articulation: Pronounce with force the vowel e and with the same lip-rounding as for ô. A second exercise will have the same result: pronounce *ay*, then ô; then pronounce *ay* while gradually rounding lips in the direction of ô; the final position will be the sound e⁰.

è⁰ Another vowel with no English equivalent. The following exercise will teach the articulation: pronounce e^o but open mouth wide with same opening as for *o*. A second exercise will have the same result: pronounce è, then o; now pronounce è but round lips in direction of o; the final position will be the sound è^o.

Les Voyelles Nasales
THE NASAL VOWELS   (*lay* vwayèl nazal)

Nasal vowels are vowels which have absorbed the nasal vibrations of an adjacent *m* or *n* when these consonants follow the vowel and are in the same syllable. Only four vowels in French are nasalized. To nasalize a vowel pronounce it through the nose. If you have difficulty doing this, squeeze the bridge of the nose slightly as you pronounce the simple vowel from which the nasal is derived.

â^n No English equivalent. Pronounce vowel â through nose.

ô^n No English equivalent. Pronounce vowel ô through nose. Note that ô^n has more lip-rounding than â^n.

è^n No English equivalent. Pronounce vowel è through nose.

e^n No English equivalent. Pronounce vowel e^o through nose.

Les Demi-Voyelles
THE SEMI-VOWELS   (*lay* d^{e}mee vwayèl)

Certain vowels lose their full force when they precede another vowel in the same syllable. These vowels then become semi-vowels which are really a type of consonant.

y   Same as *y* in *yes*.

w   Same as *w* in *wet*.

ü   No English equivalent. Pronounce ü rapidly in combination with another vowel as, for example: *üee*. The sound may also be described as a w with greater compression of lips.

Les Consonnes
THE CONSONANTS   (*lay* kô^{n}son)

b   Like English. Press lips tighter together and release more explosively in order to eliminate aspiration (the "huh" sound) of English.

d   Like English. Bring tip of tongue further down towards base of teeth.

f   Same as English.

g   Same as *g* in *g*uide or *g*et.

k   Same as *k* in *k*een or *c* in *c*at.

l   A more distinct sound in French. It is same as *l* in *l*ow, but it is not the *l* in English bi*ll*.

m   Same as English.

n   Same as English.

ny   French phoneticians consider this to be a single sound. It is same as Spanish *ñ* or *ny* in the English ca*ny*on which is borrowed from the Spanish.

p   Like English. Press lips tighter together and release more explosively in order to eliminate aspiration of English.

r   This sound is only remotely like English *r*. It is a gargling sound made by causing the uvula, an appendage in the back of the throat, to vibrate.

s   Same as *s* in *s*oap or *c* in *c*ity.

sh   As in English, this is in reality a simple consonant sound. Same as *sh* in *sh*ip, or *ch* in ma*ch*ine.

t   Like English. Bring tip of tongue lower down towards base of teeth.

v   Same as English.

z   Same as *z* in *z*ipper or *s* in ro*s*e.

zh   This diacritical spelling has been adopted to designate the simple consonant sound which is present in *z* of English a*z*ure. This sound can also be derived by vocalizing *sh*.

Part II of *Guide to French Pronunciation* appears in the Appendix (page 306) and it relates French sounds to *conventional (normal) French spelling.*

NORMAL SPELLING   (ortograf normal)

Alphabet Français

FRENCH ALPHABET   (alfabè frânsè)

The following are the letters, capital and small, of the French alphabet, with their French names and their pronunciation according to the diacritical system described on preceding pages:

Lettres Majuscules (lètre mazhüskül) Capital Letters	Lettres Minuscules (lètre meenüskül) Small Letters	Prononciation (pronônsyasyôn) Pronunciation
A	a	â
B	b	bay
C	c	say
D	d	day
E	e	eo, ay
F	f	èf
G	g	zhay
H	h	ash
I	i	ee
J	j	zhee
K	k	ka
L	l	èl
M	m	èm
N	n	èn
O	o	ô
P	p	pay
Q	q	kü
R	r	èr
S	s	ès
T	t	tay
U	u	ü
V	v	vay
W	w	dooble vay
X	x	eeks
Y	y	eegrèk
Z	z	zèd

ACCENTS FRANÇAIS

The accents in French are: the acute accent (*l'accent aigu*) (´), the grave accent (*l'accent grave*) (`) and the circumflex accent (*l'accent circonflexe*) (^).

L'ACCENT AIGU (´)

Is used only on the e and gives it a short, acute sound, as indicated by its name. The use of this accent cannot be defined by any particular rule.

L'ACCENT GRAVE (`)

1. It is used on the **a** and **u** in order to make the distinction between words which are spelled in the same way though having widely different meanings, as for instance:

a (a) (he) has   **à** (a) to or at   ç**a** (sa) that   ç**à** (sa) here
la (la) the (fem.)   **là** (la) there   **ou** (*oo*) or   **où** (*oo*) where

2. It is used on the **e** of a penultimate syllable whenever immediately followed by a final combination of letters the first of which is a consonant and the second a silent *e*, as in:

père (pèr) father   **frère** (frèr) brother

3. Also in adverbs and substantives the singular of which ends in *es*; e. g.:

progrès (progrè) progress   **après** (aprè) after

L'Accent Circonflexe (^)

This accent is always applied whenever a prolonged open and marked sound is to be given to a vowel. It is used:

1. As a substitute for a letter which may have been eliminated from a form of the word now obsolete, as in:

tête (tèt) head, instead of **teste** (obsolete)

2. Also to determine the difference of meaning between two words spelled in the same way:

du (dü) of the (masc.)   **sur** (sür) upon
dû (dü) owed   **sûr** (sür) sure

3. And lastly, in the first and second persons plural of the preterit of all verbs and in the third person singular of the imperfect tense in the subjunctive mood:

nous finîmes (noo feeneem) we finished
vous finîtes (voo feeneet) you finished
qu'il parlât (keel parlâ) that he should speak

PREMIÈRE LEÇON
First Lesson

Nouveau Vocabulaire Pour Cette Leçon

(Noovô vocabülèr poor sèt l^esô^n) • New Vocabulary for this Lesson

je désire[1] (*zh^e* d*ayzeer*)	I desire, I wish
désirez-vous (d*ayzeeray* v*oo*)	do you wish? do you want?
il désire (*ee*l d*ayzee*r)	he wishes; he wants
beaucoup[2] (bôk*oo*)	much, very much
parfaitement (parfètmâ^n)	perfectly
une automobile[3] (ünôtomob*ee*l)	an automobile
à quelle heure (a kèl*è*^{o}r)	at what time
un avion (*e*^{n}navyô^n)	an airplane
un voyage (*e*^{n} vwaya*zh*)	a trip
un[4] **bateau** (*e*^{n} batô)	a boat
demain (d^{e}mè^n)	tomorrow
seul (sè^{o}l)	alone
avec (avèk)	with
un peu, adv. (*e*^{n} p*e*^{o})	a little
prenez-vous (pr^{e}n*ay* v*oo*)	do you take
je prends (*zh^e* prâ^n)	I take
le[5] **train** (l^e trè^n)	the train
partir (part*ee*r)	to leave
bientôt[6] (byè^{n}tô)	soon
seulement (s*è*^{o}lmâ^n)	only

les affaires[7] (*l*ayzafèr)	business
intéressant (è^{n}tayrèsâ^n)	interesting
monsieur[8] (*m^{e}sye^o*)	mister, sir
un Français (frâ^{n}sè)	a Frenchman
mais (mè)	but
aussi (ôsee)	also
très (trè)	very
bien (byè^n)	well
le parler (l^e parl*a*y)	to speak it
pourquoi (p*o*orkwa)	why
parce que (parsk^e)	because
ou (*oo*), **où** (*oo*)	or; where
apprendre (aprâ^{n}dr)	to learn
habiter (abeet*a*y)	to live, to dwell
mon, masc. (mô^n)	my
ma, fem. (ma)	my
votre (votr)	your
aller (al*a*y)	to go
le matin (l^e matè^n)	the morning
qui (k*ee*); **que** (k^e)	who; what

LA FAMILLE
(la fam*eey*) • The Family

l'homme[9] (lom)	the man
le mari (mar*ee*)	husband
la femme[10] (fam)	woman, wife
les parents (parâ^n)	parents, relatives
la mère (mèr)	mother
le père (pèr)	father
le fils (f*ee*s)	son
la fille (f*eey*)	daughter
le frère (frèr)	the brother
la sœur (sè^{o}r)	sister
l'oncle (lô^{n}kl)	uncle
la tante (tâ^{n}t)	aunt
le cousin (k*ooz*è^n)	cousin (m.)
la cousine (k*oozee*n)	cousin (f.)
le beau-frère (bôfrèr)	brother-in-law
la belle-sœur (bèlsè^{o}r)	sister-in-law
un[11] **enfant** (e^nnâ^{n}fâ^n)	a child (m.)

un garçon (garsô^n)	boy
une enfant (ünâ^{n}fâ^n)	child (f.)
une jeune[12] **fille** (*zhè*^{o}n fe*ey*)	girl
une petite fille (p^{e}t*eet* f*ccy*)	little girl

LES NATIONALITÉS ET LES LANGUES

(l*ay* nâsyonale*etay ay* l*ay* lâ^{n}g) · The Nationalities and the Languages

un Italien (*ee*taly*è*^{n})	an Italian
un Anglais (â^{n}glè)	an Englishman
un Russe (rüs)	a Russian
un Espagnol (èspa*ny*ol)	a Spaniard
un Suisse (s*üee*s)	a Swiss
un Belge (bèl*zh*)	a Belgian
un Américain[13] (am*ay*reek*è*^{n})	an American (masc.)
une Américaine (am*ay*reekèn)	an American (fem.)
le français (frâ^{n}sè)	the French language
l'anglais (lâ^{n}glè)	the English language

FOOTNOTES: *1.* The INFINITIVE of this verb is *désirer*, a regular verb of the "first" *-er* conjugation. The French verb is more complicated than the English verb. The verb endings to express present time correspond to the subjects as

CONVERSATION

1 Je désire . . .

2 Que désirez-vous,[14] monsieur?

3 Je désire parler[15] français.

4 Qui désire parler français?

5 Il désire parler français.

6 Désirez-vous parler la langue anglaise?

7 Oui, monsieur, je désire la[16] parler.

8 Parlez-vous espagnol?

9 Je parle français et espagnol aussi.

10 Désirez-vous me[17] parler en français?

11 Je désire beaucoup vous parler, mais je ne parle pas[18] très bien[19] le[20] français.

12 Parlez-vous anglais parfaitement?

13 Non, monsieur, je le parle seulement un peu.

14 Pourquoi désirez-vous apprendre le français?

15 Parce que[21] je désire habiter en France.[22]

---

follows: *je* (I) *désire; tu* (thou) *désires; il* (he, it), *elle* (she, it) *désire; nous* (we) *désirons; vous* (you) *désirez; ils* (they, masc.), *elles* (they, fem.) *désirent.* Note that there is only one *present* tense in French, *je désire,* etc., whereas we say, "I wish," "I am wishing," "I do wish," etc.   **2.** *Beaucoup* means *much* or *very much.* Never place the word *très* (very) before it.   **3.** Also pronounced otomobeel.   **4.** The INDEFINITE ARTICLE is also an adjective and has the form *un* (masc.), *une* (fem.), *des* (masc. and fem. plural).   **5.** NOUNS in French are either masculine or feminine; there is no neuter. ADJECTIVES agree with their nouns in number and gender, that is to say, the form of the adjective varies according to the noun modified. For example, the ARTICLE *the* is an adjective and takes the forms *le* (masc.), *la* (fem.), or *les* (masc. and fem.

PRONUNCIATION	TRANSLATION
*1 zh*ᵉ *day-zeer . . .*	I wish . . .
*2 k*ᵉ *day-zee-ray voo, m*ᵉ*-sye*ᵒ*?*	What do you wish (*literally* what wish you), sir?
*3 zh*ᵉ *day-zeer par-lay frâ*ⁿ*-sè.*	I wish to speak French.
*4 kee day-zeer par-lay frâ*ⁿ*-sè?*	Who wishes to speak French?
*5 eel day-zeer par-lay frâ*ⁿ*-sè.*	He wishes to speak French.
*6 day-zee-ray voo par-lay la lâ*ⁿ*g â*ⁿ*-glèz?*	Do you wish (*lit.* wish you) to speak the English language?
*7 wee, m*ᵉ*-sye*ᵒ*, zh*ᵉ *day-zeer la par-lay.*	Yes, sir, I want to speak it.
8 par-lay voo(z)ès-pa-nyol?	Do you speak Spanish?
*9 zh*ᵉ *parl frâ*ⁿ*-sè ay ès-pa-nyol ô-see.*	I speak French and Spanish also.
*10 day-zee-ray voo m*ᵉ *par-lay â*ⁿ *frâ*ⁿ*-sè?*	Do you wish to speak to me in French?
*11 zh*ᵉ *day-zeer bô-koo voo par-lay, mè zh*ᵉ *n*ᵉ *parl pâ trè byè*ⁿ *l*ᵉ *fra*ˡˡ*-sc.*	I want very much to speak French to you but I do not speak French very well.
*12 par-lay voo â*ⁿ*glè par-fèt-mâ*ⁿ*?*	Do you speak English perfectly?
*13 nô*ⁿ*, m*ᵉ*-sye*ᵒ*, zh*ᵉ *l*ᵉ *parl sè*ᵒˡ*-mâ*ⁿ *e*ⁿ *pe*ᵒ*.*	No, sir, I speak it only a little.
*14 poor-kwa day-zee-ray voo(z)a-prâ*ⁿ*-dr*ᵉ *l*ᵉ *frâ*ⁿ*-sè?*	Why do you wish to learn (*lit.* the) French?
*15 pars k*ᵉ *zh*ᵉ *day-zeer a-bee-tay â*ⁿ *frâ*ⁿ*s.*	Because I wish to live in France.

plural) to agree with the noun modified.   6. This is actually two words, *bien* and *tôt;* therefore *en* keeps pronunciation it had before being combined and does not become â ⁿ.   7. Note that *business* in French is plural.   8. Note unusual pronunciation of first syllable.   9. Observe elision of article *le* which becomes *l'* before vowel or *h* mute. Examples: *l'enfant, l'homme, l'heure.*   10. Note unusual pronunciation.   11. Normally the pronunciation of an "*n*" in linking after a nasal vowel destroys nasalization; monosyllables *un, en,* and *on* are exceptions. 12. The word *fille,* when used to mean *girl* instead of *daughter,* must be modified either by *jeune* (young) or *petite* (little).   13. As a true adjective the adjective of nationality is not capitalized. However, when used as a noun to designate a person of that nationality, it is capitalized. In the masculine the adjective of nationality is also used as a noun to designate the language of that nationality; in

16 Est-ce que[23] votre[24] famille habite aux[25] États-Unis?

17 Non, monsieur, ma famille habite au[25] Canada.

18 Où est-ce que[23] votre sœur habite?

19 Ma sœur et mon frère habitent[26] en Belgique.

20 Est-ce que votre femme est française?[27]

   21 Non, monsieur, ma femme est américaine.[27]

   22 Est-ce que votre fils est français?

   23 Oui, monsieur, mon fils est français.

   24 Qui est italien?

   25 Mon cousin est italien.

   26 Est-ce qu'il désire aller en Italie?

   27 Non, il désire aller en Suisse.

   28 Prenez-vous le train pour[28] aller en France?

   29 Non, pour aller en France, je prends[29] un bateau ou un avion.

   30 Est-ce que votre père désire faire[30] un voyage en automobile?

31 Oui, monsieur, le voyage en automobile est très intéressant.

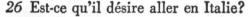

that case it is not capitalized.   **14.** Note that with pronoun subjects other than *je* interrogative order is simple: the pronoun subject is placed after the verb and joined by a hyphen.   *15. Parler* means *to speak.* No preposition is used after many verbs (example: *désirer*) to introduce a dependent infinitive; some verbs require *à* or *de* in sense of *to.*   **16.** Most PRONOUN OBJECTS go before the verb of which they are the object. Third person pronoun objects have same form as definite article (see note 5 above).   **17.** Another pronoun object before verb; *me* means "me" or "to me."   **18.** A verb is made negative in French by placing *ne* directly in front of the verb and *pas* after it.   **19.** Normal place for ADVERB is after the verb. Note literal translation.   **20.** Up to sentence *11* notice that the article is omitted before the name of the language. The article *is always used in*

16 ès-k^e vo-tr^e fa-*meey* a-*beet* ô-*zay*-ta-zü-*nee*?

Does your family live in (*lit. is it that* your family lives *to*) the United States?

17 nôⁿ, m^e-*sye*^o, ma fa-*meey* a-*beet* ô ka-na-da.

No, sir, my family lives in (*lit.* to the) Canada.

18 oo ès-k^e vo-tr^e sè^or a-*beet*?

Where does your sister live (*lit.* where *is it that* your sister lives)?

19 ma sè^or *ay* môⁿ frèr a-*beet* âⁿ bèl-*zheek*.

My sister and my brother live in Belgium.

20 ès-k^e vo-tr^e fam è frâⁿ-sèz?

Is your wife French?

21 nôⁿ, m^esye^o, ma fam è-ta-*may*-ree-kèn.

No, sir, my wife is American.

22 ès-k^e vo-tr^e fees è frâⁿ-sè?

Is your son French?

23 wee, m^esye^o, môⁿ fees è frâⁿ-sè.

Yes, sir, my son is French.

24 kee è-*tee*-ta-lyèⁿ?

Who is Italian?

25 môⁿ koo-zèⁿ è-*tee*-ta-lyèⁿ.

My cousin is Italian.

26 ès-keel *day-zeer* a-*lay* âⁿ-*nee*-ta-*lee*.

Does he want to go to Italy?

27 nôⁿ, eel *day-zeer* a-*lay* âⁿ süees.

No, he wants to go to Switzerland.

28 pr^e-*nay* voo l^e trèⁿ poor a-*lay* âⁿ frâⁿs?

Do you take the train to (*lit.* in order to) go to France?

29 nôⁿ, poor a-*lay* âⁿ frâⁿs, *zh*^e prâⁿ eⁿ batô oo eⁿ-na-vyôⁿ.

No, to go to France, I take a boat or an airplane.

30 ès-k^e vo-tr^e pèr *day-zeer* fèr eⁿ vwa-ya*zh* âⁿ-nô-to-mo-beel?

Does your father want to take an automobile trip (*lit.* in automobile)?

31 wee, m^esye^o, l^e vwa-ya*zh* â^unô-to-mo-beel è trè-zèⁿ-*tay*-rè-sâⁿ.

Yes, sir, the trip by automobile is very interesting.

French with the name of the language (contrary to English use) *except* when the name of the language is preceded by the preposition *en*. After the verb *parler* the use of the article is optional; generally it is omitted.   *21*. Note that CONJUNCTION *parce que* (because) is in two parts.   *22*. Countries ending in *e* are feminine. As in the case of languages, you expect to use the article before the name of the country. But with feminine countries the word for "in" is *en* after which the article is omitted.   *23*. The simplest way of formulating a question is to place *est-ce que* (is it that) before normal declarative word order. If the sentence already contains an interrogative word, place *est-ce que* in same position that *is it that* would occupy if the English sentence were reorganized.   *24*. This is a POSSESSIVE ADJECTIVE, agreeing with its noun; some of its forms are *mon*

32 Quand est-ce que le train part?[31]

33 Le train part le[32] matin.

34 Pourquoi désirez-vous aller en[33] Angleterre?

35 Je désire y[34] aller pour affaires.

36 Quand est-ce que votre mère part?

37 Ma mère désire partir bientôt.

38 Désirez-vous y aller seul?

39 Non, je désire y aller avec ma famille.

40 Pourquoi voulez-vous aller avec votre famille?

41 Parce que je ne désire pas voyager seul.

42 Mon oncle habite en Angleterre.

43 Est-il anglais?

44 Non, monsieur, il est espagnol.

45 Ma tante est russe.

46 Est-ce qu'elle parle la langue russe.

47 Oui, elle la parle. Parlez-vous la langue russe?

48 Non, monsieur, mais elle est très intéressante.

49 Je désire apprendre l'anglais.

(my, masc.); *ma* (my, fem.); *mes* (my, masc. and fem. pl.); *votre* (your, masc. and fem. sing.); *vos* (your, masc. and fem. pl.).   25. Contraction of *à* + *les* = *aux* and *à* + *le* = *au*. With masculine countries the preposition *à* (normally meaning *at*) is used in sense of *in* and article remains.   26. As a verb ending -*ent* is unpronounced.   27. Adjectives form their feminine by the addition of an *e* to the masculine singular.   28. If *to* can be replaced by *in order to* without changing sense of English, use *pour* (*lit.* for) with the infinitive.   29. The infinitive of this verb is *prendre*, the ending -*re* being the sign of the *third* conjugation. But it is an *irregular* verb of this conjugation; that is, it does not always follow the normal pattern of such verbs. *Prendre* is conjugated in the following manner in the present tense: je prend*s*, tu prend*s*, il prend, nous pren*ons*, vous

32 kâⁿt ès-kᵉ lᵉ trèⁿ par?	When does the train leave?
33 lᵉ trèⁿ par lᵉ ma-tèⁿ.	The train leaves (in) the morning.
34 poor-kwa day-zee-ray voo(z)a-lay âⁿ-nâⁿ-glᵉ-tèr?	Why do you wish to go to England?
35 zhᵉ day-zeer ee a-lay poor a-fèr.	I wish to go there for business.

36 kâⁿ-tès-kᵉ vo-trᵉ mèr par?	When is your mother leaving?
37 ma mèr day-zeer par-teer byèⁿ-tô.	My mother wishes to leave soon.
38 day-zee-ray voo ee a-lay sèᵒl.	Do you wish to go there alone?
39 nôⁿ, zhᵉ day-zeer ee a-lay a-vèk ma fa-meey.	No, I wish to go there with my family.
40 poor-kwa voo-lay-voo-za-lay a-vek vo-trᵉ fa-meey?	Why do you wish to go with your family?

41 parsᵉ-kᵉ zhᵉ nᵉ day-zeer pâ vwa-ya-zhay sèᵒl.	Because I do not wish to travel alone.
42 mo-nôⁿ-kl a-bcet âⁿ-nâⁿ-glᵉ-tèr.	My uncle lives in England.
43 èt-eel âⁿ-gle?	Is he English?
44 nôⁿ, mᵉsyᵉᵒ, eel èt ès-pa-nyol.	No, sir, he is Spanish.
45 ma tâⁿt è rüs.	My aunt is Russian.

46 ès-kèl parl la lâⁿg rüs?	Does she speak the Russian language?
47 wee, èl la parl. par-lay voo la lâⁿg rüs?	Yes, she speaks it. Do you speak the Russian language?
48 nôⁿ, mᵉsyᵉᵒ, mèz-èl è trèz èⁿ-tay-rè-sâⁿt.	No, sir, but it is very interesting.
49 zhᵉ day-zeer a-prâⁿdrᵉ lâⁿ-glè.	I wish to learn English.

---

prenez, ils prennent. The endings are the same as for a regular verb of the third conjugation, but it is obvious that the stem changes. Compare this with the regular verb *vendre* which is conjugated as follows in the present tense: je vends, tu vends, il vend, nous vendons, vous vendez, ils vendent. 30. Another irregular -re verb (3rd conj.). 31. An irregular verb of -ir (2nd conjugation). 32. With days of the week or parts of the day no word is used for "in": le matin, "the morning" or "*in* the morning." 33. With feminine countries en not only means *in* but also *into* or *to*. 34. This is called an ADVERBIAL PRONOUN because of its various functions. It is most often translated by English "there." Note that, like pronoun objects *le* and *me*, it also precedes verb.

2 DEUXIÈME LEÇON
Second Lesson

Nouveau Vocabulaire Pour Cette Leçon
(Noovô vocabülèr poor sèt l^{e}sô^n) • New Vocabulary for this Lesson

la salle à manger[1] (sal a mâ^{n}zhay)	the dining room
de bonne heure[2] (d^e bon è^{o}r)	early
généralement (zhaynayralmâ^n)	ordinarily
accompagner (akô^{n}panyay)	to accompany
il y a (eelya)	there is, there are
par contre[3] (par kô^{n}tr)	on the other hand
merci (mèrsee)	thanks, thank you
je suis désolé (zh^e süee dayzolay)	I am sorry
voulez-vous (voolay voo)	will you, do you want
je dois (zh^e dwa)	I must, I have to
tard (tar)	late
le théâtre (tayâtr)	the theater
je bois[4] (zh^e bwa)	I drink
manger (mâ^{n}zhay)	to eat
le verre (vèr)	the glass
la rue (rü)	the street
vendre (vâ^{n}dr)	to sell
le chapeau (shapô)	the hat
plus (plü)	more

aimer (èm*ay*)	to like, to love
avant (avâ^n)	before
après (aprè)	after
maintenant (mè^{n}tnâ^n)	now
offrir (ofr*ee*r)	to offer
préférer (pr*ay*f*ay*r*ay*)	to prefer
tendre (tâ^{n}dr)	tender
assez (as*ay*)	enough
sucré (sükr*ay*)	sweet
amer[5] (amèr)	bitter
la tasse (tâs[6])	the cup
le goût (g*oo*)	the taste
acheter (a*sh*t*ay*)	to buy
bon, masc. (bô^n)	good
bonne, fem. (bon)	good
au lieu[7] **de** (ô ly*e*^{o} d^e)	instead of
d'abord (dabor)	at first
je peux (*zh*^{e} p*e*^{o})	I can, I may
le prix (pr*ee*)	the price

LA NOURRITURE ET LES REPAS
(la nooreetür ay lay r^{e}pâ) · Food and Meals

le boeuf[8] (b$\grave{e}^o$f)	the ox, beef
le pain (pè^n)	bread
le petit pain[9]	roll
le dessert (d$a$ysèr)[10]	dessert
un fruit[11] (frü*ee*)	a fruit
le petit déjeuner[12]	breakfast
le déjeuner (d$a$yzhè^{o}nay)	lunch
le souper (soopay)	supper
le repas (r^{e}pâ)	meal
le poulet (poolè)	chicken
le veau (vô)	the veal
la viande (vyâ^{n}d)	meat
l'agneau (l$a$nyô)	lamb
le mouton (mootô^n)	sheep, mutton
la côtelette (kôtlèt)	chop
le jambon (zha^nbô^n)	ham
le porc (por)	pork
le petit lard (p^{e}t*ee* lar)	bacon
le rôti (rôt*ee*)	roast
rôti	roasted
un oeuf (à la coque)[13] (è^{o}f a la kok)	an egg (soft-boiled)

la poule au riz (*pool* ô *ree*)	chicken fricassee
à des prix raisonnables	reasonably priced
(a d*ay* pr*ee* rèzonabl)	
de très bonne qualité	of very good quality
(d*e* trè bon kal*ee*t*ay*)	
le potage (pot*azh*)	the soup
le dîner (d*ee*n*ay*)	dinner
le beurre (b*è*^{o}r)	butter
les légumes (l*ay*güm)	vegetables
le poisson (pwasô^n)	fish
le gâteau (gâtô)	cake
frit (fr*ee*)	fried
bien cuit (byè^n k*üee*)	well cooked
dur (dür)	tough
la tarte (tart)	the pie
le fromage (from*azh*)	cheese
l'eau, fem. (lô)	water
le café (kaf*ay*)	coffee
le thé (t*ay*)	tea
le vin (vè^n)	wine
le chocolat (*sh*okola)	chocolate
le lait (lè)	milk
la confiture (kô^{n}f*eetür*)	jam

FOOTNOTES: *1*. Lit. *the hall for eating*. *2*. Idiom. (An *idiom* is an expression which is unique and to which the general rules of grammar do not apply.

CONVERSATION

1 Je prends mon petit déjeuner.

2 A quelle heure prenez-vous **votre** petit déjeuner?

3 Je le prends de bonne heure.

4 En^{14} quoi^{15} consiste^{16} votre petit déjeuner généralement?

5 Mon petit déjeuner consiste généralement en une tasse de café au^{17} lait ou de chocolat, et un petit pain avec de la^{18} confiture.

6 Allons^{19} dans^{20} la salle à manger.

7 Désirez-vous manger maintenant ou avant de^{21} partir?^{22}

8 Je préfère^{23} manger plus^{24} tard.

9 Que prenez-vous pour dîner?^{25}

10 Généralement, le mardi,^{26} je prends deux côtelettes de **veau** bien cuites.

11 Pour le déjeuner je préfère un œuf à la coque et du^{27} jambon avec de la salade.

12 Est-ce que vous n'aimez pas le^{28} porc?

Generally an idiom makes little or no sense when translated literally). **3.** Idiom: *Contre* means *against*. **4.** From irregular verb *boire*. **5.** Note that final consonant "*r*" is pronounced. **6.** Note that "*a*" is long. **7.** Lit. *in place of*. **8.** Both *bœuf* and *œuf* pronounce the "*f*" in the singular but not in the plural. **9.** Lit. *the little bread*. **10.** Note unusual pronunciation of first syllable. **11.** Collectively *the fruit* in French is plural: *les fruits*. **12.** *Déjeuner* means *to break fast*, but, since the noon meal also bears this name, the first meal of the day is called *the little breakfast*. **13.** Lit. *in the shell*. **14.** Idiom: *consister en*, to consist of (lit. *in*). **15.** After prepositions a special form of the pronoun is required called the DISJUNCTIVE PRONOUN. The word *what* as an interrogative pronoun, direct object, is *que*, but after a preposition, it becomes *quoi*.

PRONUNCIATION

1 zhᵉ prâⁿ môⁿ p(ᵉ)tee dayzhèᵒnay.

2 a kèl èᵒr prᵉnay voo votrᵉ ptee dayzhèᵒnay?

3 zhᵉ lᵉ prâⁿ dᵉ bonèᵒr.

4 âⁿ kwa kôⁿseest votrᵉ ptee dayzhèᵒnay zhaynayralmâⁿ?

5 môⁿ ptee dayzhèᵒnay kôⁿseest zhaynayralmâⁿ âⁿnün tâs dᵉ kafay ô lè oo dᵉ shokola ay eⁿ ptee pèⁿ avèk dᵉ la kôⁿfeetür.

6 alôⁿ dâⁿ la sal a mâⁿzhay.

7 dayzeeray voo maⁿzhay mèⁿtnâⁿ oo avâⁿ dᵉ parteer?

8 zhᵉ prayfèr mâⁿzhay plü tar.

9 kᵉ prᵉnay voo poor deenay?

10 zhaynayralmâⁿ, lᵉ mardee, zhᵉ prâⁿ deᵒ kôtlèt dᵉ vô byèⁿ küeet.

11 poor lᵉ dayzhèᵒnay zhᵉ prayfèr eⁿnèᵒf a la kok ay dü zhûⁿbôⁿ avèk dᵉ la salad.

12 èskᵉ voo nèmay pâ lᵉ por?

TRANSLATION

I take my breakfast.

At what time do you take your breakfast?

I take it early.

Of (lit. in) what does your breakfast consist (lit. of what consists your breakfast) generally?

My breakfast consists generally of a cup of coffee with milk, or chocolate and a roll with jelly (lit., some chocolate . . . some jelly).

Let us go into the dining-room.

Do you want to eat now or before leaving?

I prefer to eat later (lit. more late).

What do you take for dinner?

Ordinarily, on Tuesdays, I take two veal chops well done (lit. cooked).

For lunch (lit. the lunch) I prefer a soft-boiled egg (lit. an egg in the shell) and ham with salad (lit. some ham . . . some salad).

Don't you like (lit. is it that you do not like) pork (lit. the pork).

16. After certain interrogative words such as *quoi* or *où* (where), inversion may occur even with a noun subject. Compare with lesson 1, footnote 23. 17. The ingredients of which a food is made are generally put in a phrase beginning with "*à*." 18. The PARTITIVE CONSTRUCTION or PARTITIVE ARTICLE *du* (m.), *de la* (f.), *des* (m. and f. plural), meaning *some*. Frequently English does not use the word *some* where the French requires it. If, starting with the English, the noun is not modified by a definite or an indefinite article, try to insert the word *some*; if it fits in English, the French requires the *partitive construction*. The partitive consists of *de* + *definite article* (le, la, les). In some cases it will also help to consider the partitive as the *plural of the indefinite article*. If the sentence reads: *Frenchmen are men*, test this by reducing it to a singular: *The Frenchman is a*

13 Oui, monsieur, mais je préfère le[28] mouton.

14 Est-ce que je peux[29] vous offrir du poulet rôti? Ce[30] poulet est très tendre.

15 Merci, mais je prendrai[31] d'abord du potage au lieu de hors-d'œuvre.

16 Ce rôti de bœuf n'est pas très tendre.

17 Par contre le poisson est délicieux.

18 Que désirez-vous pour dîner?

19 De la viande, de la salade, du pain et du beurre.

20 Et ensuite?

21 Ensuite je prendrai du dessert.

22 Que préférez-vous comme dessert, du fromage, des fruits ou des gâteaux?[32]

23 Je préfère du fromage avec du pain.

24 Désirez-vous du thé?

25 Non, je préfère prendre du café après le repas.

26 Prenez-vous du vin avec vos repas?

27 Généralement je bois un verre de vin et un verre d'eau.

---

man. It is clear that the second half of the sentence requires an indefinite article in the singular; hence it also requires one in the plural. Example: *Les Français sont* des *hommes.* **19.** IMPERATIVE form of the verb. The imperative *Go!* in French is *allez*, with the same personal ending as would be necessary if the unexpressed subject *vous* actually were expressed. The French also has a FIRST PERSON PLURAL IMPERATIVE *allons* corresponding to *nous* which must be translated *let us go.* **20.** This is the common word for *in* or *into*. *En* is used only in special cases: for example, before feminine countries and before languages. **21.** When *avant* is used before an infinitive it requires *de* also. **22.** After a preposition (other than *en*), the INFINITIVE form of the verb is required, not the present participle as in English. Examples: *avant de prendre,* before taking; *pour manger,* in order to eat. **23.** Note change from "é" to "è" whenever the verb

13 wee, m^esye^o, mè *zh*^e prayfèr l^e mootôⁿ.	Yes, sir, but I prefer mutton (*lit.* the mutton).
14 èsk^e *zh*^e pe^o voozofreer dü poolè rôtee? s^e poolè è trè tâⁿdr.	May I offer you (*lit.* is it that I am able to offer to you) some roast chicken? This chicken is very tender.
15 mèrsee, mè *zh*^e prâⁿdra*y* dabor dü pota*zh* ô lye^o d^e ordè^ovr.	Thank you (*lit.* thanks), but I shall take some soup first instead of (*lit.* in the place of) hors d'oeuvre.
16 s^e rôtee d^e bè^of nè pâ trè tâⁿdr.	This roast beef (*lit.* roast of beef) is not very tender.
17 par kôⁿtr l^e pwasôⁿ è *daylee*sye^o.	On the other hand the fish is delicious.
18 k^e dayzeera*y* voo poor deena*y*?	What do you want for dinner?
19 d^e la vyâⁿd, d^e la salad, dü peⁿ a*y* dü bè^or.	Meat, salad, bread, and butter (*lit.* some meat, some salad ... etc.).
20 a*y* âⁿsüeet?	What next?
21 âⁿsücet *zh*^e prâⁿdra*y* dü daysèr.	Next I will take some dessert.
22 k^e prayfayra*y* voo kom daysèr, dü froma*zh*, da*y* früee, oo da*y* gâtô?	What do you prefer for (*lit.* as) dessert, some cheese, some fruit (*lit.* some fruits) or some cakes?
23 *zh*^e prayfèr dü froma*zh* avèk dü pèⁿ.	I prefer some cheese with bread.
24 dayzeera*y* voo dü ta*y*?	Do you want some tea?
25 nôⁿ, *zh*^e prayfèr prâⁿdr dü kafa*y* aprè l^e r^epâ.	No, I prefer to take some coffee after the meal.
26 pr^ena*y* voo dü vèⁿ avèk vô r^epâ?	Do you take wine with your meals?
27 *zh*aynayralmâⁿ *zh*^e bwâ eⁿ vèr d^e vèⁿ a*y* eⁿ vèr dô.	Ordinarily I drink a glass of wine and a glass of water.

ends in mute *e* (including the mute ending -*ent*). Example: *préférer*, but *je préfère*. **24.** Comparative form of adjectives or adverbs is made by placing *plus* (more) in front of them. Example: *plus tard*, later; *plus intéressant*, more interesting. **25.** Like *languages*, *meals* generally require the article; but this article is omitted after *pour*. **26.** To express *regular occurrence* with days of the week, the singular form of the noun is used with the definite article. **27.** Rules of CONTRACTION apply to the PARTITIVE. *De* + *le* = *du* and *de* + *les* = *des*. Contraction occurs only with *articles*, not with *pronoun objects*. **28.** *A noun in a general sense takes definite article* whereas the English has no article. Compare this with note *18* above. Example: *Frenchmen are men;* that is, "Frenchmen *in general—all* Frenchmen are men." The French therefore reads: *"Les*

28 Le café est-il[33] à votre goût, ou est-il amer?

29 Non, monsieur, il est assez sucré.

30 Voulez-vous[34] m'accompagner au théâtre après le dîner?

31 Je suis désolé de[35] vous quitter, mais je dois acheter un chapeau.

32 Dans cette rue il y a une bonne chapellerie.

33 Est-ce qu'on[36] y vend de[37] bons chapeaux?

34 Oui, monsieur, les chapeaux sont de très bonne qualité et on[38] les vend à des prix raisonnables.[39]

Français sont des hommes." 29. *Je peux* is from *pouvoir* (to be able). It also translates English auxiliary *can* or *may;* since the French has no such auxiliaries, *can* and *may* become the main verb *pouvoir* and the main verb of the English becomes a DEPENDENT INFINITIVE. Example: *I can go;* that is, *I am able to go: je peux aller.* 30. DEMONSTRATIVE ADJECTIVE: *ce,* masc. (this, that) becoming *cet* before vowel or *h* mute; *cette,* fem. (this, that); *ces,* masc. and fem. plural (these, those). 31. FUTURE TENSE. Formed with endings *(je)...ai;* *(tu) ...as;* *(il)...a;* *(nous)...ons;* *(vous)...ez;* *(ils)...ont* added to *entire* infinitive except in third conjugation where *e* of infinitive drops before future endings. Example: *j'aimerai* (1st conjugation); *je vendrai* (3rd conjugation). Future in English is expressed with auxiliary *"shall"* or *"will."* Observe again that French verb is in one piece. 32. Nouns ending in *"eau"* form their plural

28 le kafay èteel a votre goo, oo
   èteel amèr?

Is the coffee (*lit.* the coffee is it)
to your taste, or is it bitter?

29 nôⁿ, mᵉsyeᵒ, eel ètasay sükray.

No, sir, it is sweet enough (*lit.*
enough sweet).

30 voolay voo makôⁿpanyay ô
   tayâtr aprè lᵉ deenay?

Do you wish to accompany me to
the theater after dinner?

31 zhᵉ süee dayzolay dᵉ voo keetay, mè zhᵉ dwazashtay eⁿ
   shapô.

I am sorry to leave you, but I must
buy a hat.

32 dâⁿ sèt rü eelya ün bon sha-
   pèlree.

On (*lit.* in) this street there is a
good hat shop.

33 èskôⁿnee vâⁿ dᵉ bôⁿ shapô?

Do they sell (*lit.* is it that one sells
there) good hats there?

34 wee, mᵉsyeᵒ, lay shapô sôⁿ dᵉ
   trè bon kaleetay ay ôⁿ lay vâⁿ
   a day pree rèzonabl.

Yes, sir, the hats are of very good
quality and they are sold (*lit.*
one sells them) at reasonable
prices.

by adding "x." 33. Unless *est-ce que* is used (see lesson 1, note 23), apply the
following formula to form a question by inverting with a noun subject: *noun subject + verb + pronoun subject repeating noun subject.* See literal rendering in
translation above. 34. Distinguish *désirez-vous* (do you want) and *voulez-vous*
(do you want *and also* are you willing). 35. Infinitives depending on adjectives are most commonly introduced by *de.* 36. The INDEFINITE PRONOUN *on*
(*lit.* one) frequently translates English *they,* or even *you,* in an *impersonal* sense.
37. When an *adjective precedes a noun in a partitive construction* the partitive
consists only of *de* without an article. 38. The *on* construction (see note 36
above) is also used in French to avoid a passive. Note normal English translation
given for this sentence. 39. The normal place for the adjective in French is
after the noun; but certain short adjectives (example: *bon*) precede.

TROISIÈME LEÇON
Third Lesson

NOUVEAU VOCABULAIRE POUR CETTE LEÇON
(Noovô vocabülèr poor sèt l^{e}sô^n) • New Vocabulary for this Lesson

le feutre[1] (fe^{0}tr) — the felt, the felt hat
avoir besoin de[2] (avwar b^{e}zwè^n d^e) — to need
la soirée[3] (swar*ay*) — the evening, evening party
bien entendu[4] (byè^{n}nâ^{n}tâ^{n}dü) — of course
cher, masc. (*shè*r) — dear, expensive
chère, fem. (*shè*r) — dear, expensive
n'est-ce pas[5]? (nèspâ) — is it not so?
bon marché[6] (bô^n mar*shay*) — cheap
l'argent, masc. (larz*hâ*^{n}) — the money
coûter (koot*ay*) — to cost
combien (kô^{n}byè^n) — how much
bonjour (bô^{n}z*hoo*r) — good-day, hello
bonsoir (bô^{n}swar) — good evening
la nuit (nü*ee*) — the night
le magasin (magaz è^n) — the store
la semelle (s^{e}mèl) — the sole
le talon (talô^n) — the heel
assorti (asort*ee*) — matching
la couleur (koolè^{0}r) — the color
le soir[3] (swar) — the evening

la marche (marsh)	walking
étroit (*a*ytrwa)	narrow, tight
haut (ô)	high, tall
bas (bà)	low
court (k*oo*r)	short
le coton (kotô^n)	the cotton
la laine (lèn)	the wool
long, masc. (lô^n)	long
longue, fem. (lô^{n}g)	long
pareil (parèy)	same
différent (d*ee*f*a*yrâ^n)	different
élégant (*a*yl*a*ygâ^n)	elegant
quelques-uns (kèlk^{e}z*e*^{n})	some (masc.)
quelques-unes (kèlk^{e}zün)	some (fem.)
dedans (d^{e}dâ^n)	inside
trop (trô)	too much
il faut (*ee*l fô)	it is necessary
foncé, masc. (fô^{n}s*a*y)	dark, deep
foncée, fem. (fô^{n}s*a*y)	dark, deep

VÊTEMENTS ET CHAUSSURES
(vètmâ^n *ay sh*ôsür) • Clothing and Footwear

le costume (kostüm)	the suit
le veston (vèstô^n)	coat (suit)
le manteau (mâ^{n}tô)	coat
le gilet (*zhee*lè)	vest
le pantalon (pâ^{n}talô^n)	trousers
le pardessus (pard^{e}sü)	overcoat
le chapeau (*sh*apô)	hat
la casquette (kaskèt)	cap
la cravate (kravat)	the necktie
la chemise (*sh*^{e}mee*z*)	shirt
la manche (mâ^n*sh*)	sleeve
la manchette (mâ^n*sh*èt)	cuff
le mouchoir (m*oosh*war)	handkerchief
la chaussette (*sh*ôsèt)	sock
une paire (pèr)	a pair
le jupon[8] (*zh*üpô^n)	petticoat
le tissu (teesü)	the cloth (heavy material)
l'étoffe, fem. (*a*ytof)	cloth (light material)
la soie (swâ)	silk

le gant (gâ^n)	the glove
le sac à main[9] (sakamè^n)	handbag
la robe (rob)	dress
la jupe (zhüp)	skirt
la blouse (blooz)	blouse
la gaine (gèn)	the girdle
le bas (bâ)	stocking
le soulier (soolyay)	shoe
la pantoufle (pâ^{n}toofl)	slipper
le cuir (küeer)	leather
le porte-monnaie[10] (portmonè)	the change purse
le linge de corps[11] (lè^{n}zh de kor)	underwear
le caleçon (kalsô^n)	underdrawers, shorts
la combinaison (kô^{n}beenèzô^n)	slip
le tailleur, le costume tailleur (kostüm tayè^{o}r)	suit (for a woman)
la jaquette (zhakèt)	coat (of a woman's suit)
le soutien-gorge[12] (sootyè^n gorzh)	brassière

CONVERSATION

1 Bonjour, monsieur.—Bonsoir, madame.—Bonne nuit,[13] mon enfant.

2 De quoi parliez-vous[14] quand je suis entré?[15]

3 Nous parlions de vêtements et de chaussures.

4 Vous avez là un costume qui vous va[16, 17] très bien.

5 Oui, c'est[18] du[19] bon tissu, mais le veston est trop long et le gilet trop court.

6 Est-ce que le pantalon vous va?[17]

7 Oui, le pantalon me va très bien.

8 J'ai besoin d'un pardessus, d'un chapeau et d'une paire de gants.

9 Dans ce magasin vous pouvez[20] acheter tout ce[21] qu'il vous faut:[22] cravates, mouchoirs, chemises et chaussettes.

10 Avez-vous besoin aussi de linge de corps?

11 Oui, j'ai besoin de linge de corps.

12 Les manchettes de cette chemise de soie dépassent trop.

FOOTNOTES: *1.* Note *close* vowel instead of *open* vowel.   2. Idiom. Lit. *to have need of.*   3. *Soir* is used to indicate the time of the day known as *the evening. Soirée* is used in the sense of the duration of the evening, the events which take place in the evening. Example: *toute la soirée* (all evening). 4. *Entendre* means *to hear.* In "passive" it also means *agreed.*   5. Lit. *is it not?* Can be placed after any declarative sentence to make it interrogative.   6. Idiom. *Marché* means literally *market.*   7. Adjectives ending in é form feminine by adding *e* which does not change pronunciation.   8. The "on" ending is frequently a diminutive ending in French.   9. Lit. *bag for the hand.*   10. *Monnaie* means *change,* whereas *argent* (money) is a broader term.   *11.* Lit. *linen of (for) body.*   12. *Soutenir* means *to hold up.*   13. Said only to people

PRONUNCIATION

1 bônzhoor, mᵉsyeº. bônswar,
madam. bon nüee, monânfân.

2 dᵉ kwa parlyay voo kân zhᵉ
süeezântray?

3 noo parlyôn dᵉ vètmân ay dᵉ
shôsür.

4 voozavay la eⁿ kostüm kee voo
va trè byèⁿ.

5 wee, sè dü bôⁿ teesü, mè lᵉ
vèstôⁿ è trô lôⁿ ay lᵉ zheelè
trô koor.

6 èskᵉ lᵉ pâⁿtalôⁿ voo va?

7 wee, lᵉ pâⁿtalôⁿ mᵉ va trè byèⁿ.

8 zhay bᵉzwè deⁿ pardᵉsü, deⁿ
shapô ay dün pèr dᵉ gâⁿ.

9 dâⁿ sᵉ magazèⁿ voo poovay-
zashtay tooskeel voo fô: kravat,
mooshwar, shᵉmeez ay shôsèt.

10 avay voo bᵉzwèⁿ ôsee dᵉ lèⁿzh
dᵉ kor?

11 wee, zhay hᵉzwèⁿ dᵉ lèⁿzh dᵉ
kor.

12 lay mâⁿshèt dᵉ sèt shᵉmeez dᵉ
swâ daypâs trô.

TRANSLATION

Good-day, sir. Good evening, madame. Good night, my child.

What were you talking about (lit.
of what were you talking) when
I entered (lit. am entered)?

We were speaking of clothes and
footwear.

You have a suit there which fits
you very well.

Yes, it is good material, but the
coat is too long and the vest too
short.

Do the trousers fit you (lit. is it
that the trouser goes to you)?

Yes, the trousers fit me very well,

I need (lit. have need of) an overcoat, a hat and a pair of gloves.

In this store you can buy everything you need (lit. all that
which it is necessary to you):
neckties, handkerchiefs, shirts
and socks.

Do you need underwear also?

Yes, I need underwear.

The cuffs of this silk shirt (lit.
shirt of silk) are too long.

---

going to bed at bedtime. *14.* Example of IMPERFECT TENSE (French:
imparfait). In first conjugation remove infinitive ending *-er* and add endings
italicized in the following example: je donn*ais*, tu donn*ais*, il donn*ait*, nous
donn*ions*, vous donn*iez*, ils donn*aient*. *The imperfect tense expresses a state of
being in the past, or an action in the past that was continuous, habitual, or repeated, or going on when another action took place.* Examples: I *was speaking*
when he arrived: je *parlais* quand il est arrivé; I *used to go* to France every year:
j'*allais* en France tous les ans. *15.* Example of COMPOUND PAST TENSE
(French: *passé composé* or *passé indéfini*). In conversation this indicates a
completed action in the simple past. It is composed of the auxiliary *to have*
(*avoir*) or *to be* (*être*) plus a past participle. Example: j'ai donné (*I have given*

13 Je désire acheter un tailleur[23] pour ma femme.

14 Quel tissu préférez-vous?

15 Un bon tissu et pas[24] trop cher.

16 Désirez-vous une jupe et une blouse assorties?

17 Bien entendu. Je préfère une seule couleur foncée.

18 Nous avons des robes de soirée et des robes de ville qui[25] sont très élégantes.

19 Combien coûte ce feutre?

20 Ce chapeau est cher mais cette casquette est bon marché.

21 Mademoiselle Martin désire acheter une combinaison et des bas, n'est-ce pas?

22 Oui, et j'ai besoin aussi d'une gaine et d'un soutien-gorge.

23 Savez-vous où je peux acheter des souliers?

24 Au magasin de chaussures on trouve tout ce qu'il faut comme chaussures.[26]

25 Madame Blanc désire acheter des souliers de bal à talons[27] hauts et à semelle mince.

---

and also *I gave, I did give*). Most verbs use the auxiliary *avoir*. Reflexive verbs and a few other verbs like *entrer* are conjugated with *être* (for a complete list of such verbs see lesson XVIII, note *1*). *16.* From irregular verb *aller: je vais, tu vas, il va, nous allons, vous allez, ils vont.* *17.* Idiom. Note special use of *aller* in sense *to fit.* The pronoun before it is an *indirect* object. *18. Ce* is used for *it* with indefinite antecedent or when, after verb *to be*, there is a *modified noun*, a *pronoun* or a *superlative.* *19.* Observe exceptional use of *complete partitive* even though adjective precedes noun. *20.* From *pouvoir* (to be able): *je peux, tu peux, il peut, nous pouvons, vous pouvez, ils peuvent.* See lesson *2*, note *29.* *21.* Idiom: *tout ce que:* all that (*lit.* all that which). After *tout, ce*

13 zhᵉ dayzeer ashtay eⁿ tayèᵒr poor ma fam.

14 kèl teesü prayfayray voo?

15 eⁿ bôⁿ teesü ay pâ trô shèr.

I wish to buy a tailored suit for my wife.

What material do you prefer?

A good material and not too expensive.

16 dayzeeray voo ün zhüp ay ün blooz asortee?

17 byèⁿnâⁿtâⁿdü. zhᵉ prayfèr ün sèᵒl koolèᵒr fôⁿsay.

18 noozavôⁿ day rob dᵉ swaray ay day rob dᵉ veel kee sôⁿ trèzaylaygâⁿt.

19 kôⁿbyèⁿ koot sᵉ feᵒtr.

20 sᵉ shapô è shèr mè sèt kaskèt è bôⁿ marshay.

Do you want a matching skirt and blouse?

Of course. I prefer one (lit. a single) deep color.

We have evening dresses and street dresses (lit. town dresses) which are very elegant.

How much does this felt hat cost (lit. how much costs this felt)?

This hat is expensive but this cap is cheap.

21 madmwazèl martèⁿ dayzeer ashtay ün kôⁿbeenèzôⁿ ay day bâ, nèspâ?

22 wee, ay zhay bᵉzwèⁿ ôsee dün gèn ay deⁿ sootyèⁿ gorzh.

23 savay voo oo zhᵉ peᵒzashtay day soolyay?

24 ô magazèⁿ dᵉ shôsür ôⁿ troov tooskeel fô kom shôsür.

25 madam blâⁿ dayzeer ashtay day soolyay dᵉ bal a talôⁿ ô ay a sᵉmèl mèⁿs.

Miss Martin wishes to buy a slip and some stockings, doesn't she (lit. is it not so)?

Yes, and I need also a girdle and a brassière.

Do you know where I can buy some shoes?

In the shoe store one finds all that one needs in the way of shoes.

Mrs. Blanc wishes to buy some dancing slippers (lit. ball shoes) with high heels and a thin sole.

que must be used in sense of that. 22. Idiom. Note this construction: il vous faut un chapeau: there is necessary to you a hat, i.e., you need a hat. 23. Short for costume tailleur, tailored suit. 24. Without a verb not is merely pas in conversation, non in literary style. 25. RELATIVE PRONOUN: subject qui (who, which, that); object que (whom, which, that). 26. Observe literal translation of this idiom. 27. Descriptive phrase beginning with "with" in English begins with "à" in French. Note absence of partitives. 28. Adverb. Do not confuse with adjective petit. 29. CONDITIONAL TENSE (French: conditionnel). Formed with stem of future (see lesson 2, note 31) and endings of imperfect (see note 14 above). Example: j'aimerais: I should or would like; je vendrais: I should or would sell. Equivalent English tense has auxiliaries should and would. In case of vouloir, note irregular future stem voudr-.

26 Et nous voulons acheter aussi une paire de souliers pour la
    marche et des pantoufles.

27 Ces souliers sont un peu[28] trop étroits.

28 Désirez-vous un sac à main en cuir?

29 Oui, je voudrais[29] un sac avec un porte-monnaie pour mon
    argent.

26 *ay noo* voolôⁿza*shtay osee* ün pèr d^e *soolyay* p*oor* la mar*sh ay day* pâⁿ*toofl.*
And we also wish to buy a pair of walking shoes and some house-slippers.

27 *say soolyay* sôⁿ*te*ⁿ pe^o trôp*ay-trwa.*
These shoes are a little too tight.

28 d*ayzeeray voo e*ⁿ sak a mèⁿ âⁿ küee*r*?
Do you want a leather handbag?

29 *wee, zh*^e voodrè(z)*e*ⁿ sak avèk eⁿ portmonè p*oor* monarzhâⁿ.
Yes, I should like a bag with a change purse for my money.

QUATRIÈME LEÇON
Fourth Lesson

NOUVEAU VOCABULAIRE POUR CETTE LEÇON
(Noovô vocabülèr poor sèt l^{e}sô^n) • New Vocabulary for this Lesson

voici[1] (vwas*ee*)	here is, here are
faire[2] **enregistrer** (fèr â^{n}r^e*zhee*stray)	to check
demain matin (d^{e}mè^n matè^n)	tomorrow morning
retenir (r^{e}tn*ee*r)	to retain, reserve
s'il vous plaît[3] (s*ee*l v*oo* plè)	if you please
voulez-vous bien (v*oo*l*ay* v*oo* byè^n)	will you be kind enough
se trouver (s^e tr*oo*v*ay*)	to be, to be located
s'embarquer (sâ^{n}bark*ay*)	to embark, to sail
le départ (d*ay*par)	the departure
visiter (v*ee*z*ee*t*ay*)	to visit
vraiment (vrèmâ^n)	really, truly
vite (v*ee*t)	quickly
alors[4] (alor)	then
peser (p^{e}z*ay*)	to weigh
déjà (d*ay*zha)	already
pas encore (pâzâ^{n}kor)	not yet
le temps (tâ^n)	the time
à temps (a tâ^n)[5]	on time
le boulevard (b*oo*lvar)	the boulevard
atterrir (atèr*ee*r)	to land
décoller (d*ay*kol*ay*)	to take off (aviation)

un avion (avyô^n)	an airplane
valable (valabl)	valuable, valid
savoir (savwar)	to know (how)
la place (plas)	the seat, the square
il y a (*eel*ya)	there is, there are
y a-t-il? (yat*eel*)	is there? are there?
un kilo, un kilogramme (k*ee*logram)	a kilogram
monter (mô^{n}t*ay*)	to go up, to get (into)
le nord (nor)	the north
premier, mas. (pr^{e}my*ay*)	first
première, fem. (pr^{c}myêr)	first
tôt (tô)	soon
je sais[6] (*zhe* s*ay*)	I know
le jour (*zhoo*r)	the day
l'arrivée, fem. (lar*eev*ay)	the arrival
le pays (p*ay*ee)	the country
puisque (p*üee*sk^e)	since
prêt (prè)	ready
autre (ôtr)	other
une aile (èl)	a wing

MOYENS DE TRANSPORT
(mwayè^n d^e trâ^{n}spor) • Means of Transportation

la malle (mal)	the trunk
la gare (gar)	station
le billet (b*eey*è)	ticket
le guichet (*geesh*è)	ticket window
le wagon (vagô^n)	railroad car
l'horaire, masc. (lorèr)	time table
le vapeur (vap*è*^{o}r)	the steamboat
le bateau (batô)	the boat
la cabine (kab*ee*n)	cabin
le pilote (p*ee*lot)	pilot
le moteur (mot*è*^{o}r)	motor
le quai (k*ay*)	pier
le fuselage (füzla*zh*)	fuselage
le port (por)	port
le chemin de fer[7] (sh^{e}mè^n d^e fèr)	the railroad
le train (trè^n)	train
la valise (val*eez*)	suitcase

les bagages, masc. (baga*zh*)	the baggage
le bulletin (bültè^n) **de bagages**	baggage check
la salle (sal) **des bagages**	baggage room
le compartiment (k0^{n}parteemA^n)	compartment
aller et retour[8] (al*ay ay* r^e*toor*)	round-trip
un aérodrome (a*a*yrodrôm)	an airport
les hélices, fem. (l*ayzaylees*)	propellers
une agence (a*zh*â^{n}s) **de voyages**	a travel agency

FOOTNOTES: *1.* Lit. *vois-ici*, see here. *2.* Lit. *to cause to be registered.* Example of causal use of *faire. 3.* Lit. *if it to you is pleasing. 4.* Compare with *ensuite* which means exclusively *next* or *then* in sense of *next. 5.* Note that "*p*" is unpronounced. *6.* Note unusual pronunciation. *7.* Lit. *the road*

CONVERSATION

1 Où est la gare, s'il vous plaît?

2 Il y en[9] a une rue de Rennes et Boulevard du Montparnasse et une autre Place Denfert-Rochereau.

3 A quelle gare devez[10]-vous aller?

4 Pour aller à Bruxelles nous devons partir par[11] la Gare du Nord.

5 A quelle heure part le premier train?

6 Le premier train part très tôt le matin.

7 Alors il faudra[12] prendre un taxi pour aller plus vite.

8 Est-ce que vos bagages sont prêts?

9 Oui, les valises et les malles sont déjà à la gare.

10 Voulez-vous bien me dire où se[13] trouve le guichet?

11 Combien coûte un billet de troisième classe aller et retour pour Strasbourg?

12 Pour combien de temps est-ce que ce billet est valable?

13 Un aller et retour est valable pour dix jours.

14 Où est la salle des bagages? Je veux faire enregistrer mes malles.

---

of iron.   8. Lit. *going (to go) and return.*   9. The PARTITIVE PRONOUN *en* means *some, any, of it, of them.* When a number is used alone in a sentence the *partitive* pronoun is required before the verb.   10. From *devoir.* Compare with lesson 2, note 29.   11. Idiom. French says *by* rather than *from.*   12. Future of *il faut.*   13. Lit. *finds itself.* This is an example of a REFLEXIVE VERB. A

PRONUNCIATION

1 oo è la gar, s*eel* v*oo* plè?

2 eel yâ^n na ün rü d^e rèn *ay* bool-var dü mô^{n}parnâs *ay* ün ôtr plas dâ^{n}fèr ros*h^e*rô.

3 a kèl gar d^{e}v*ay* voo*z* al*ay?*

4 poor al*ay* a brüsèl n*oo* d^{e}vô^n part*eer* par la gar dü nor.

5 a kèl è^{o}r par l^e pr^{e}my*ay* trè^n?

6 l^e pr^{e}my*ay* trè^n par trè tô l^e matè^n.

7 al*or eel* fôdra prâ^{n}dr *e^n* taks*ee* poor al*ay* plü v*eet.*

8 èsk^e vô baga*zh* sô^n prè?

9 w*ee*, l*ay* val*eez ay* l*ay* mal sô^n d*ayzh*a a la gar.

10 v*oo*l*ay* voo byè^n m^e d*eer oo* s^e tr*oo*v l^e g*eesh*è?

11 kô^{n}byè^n k*oo*t *e^n* b*ee*yè d^e trwa-zyèm klâs al*ay ay* r^{e}t*oor* poor strâzb*oo*r?

12 poor kô^{n}byè^n d^e tâ^n èsk^e s^e b*ee*yè è valabl?

13 e^{n}nal*ay ay* r^{e}t*oor* è valabl poor d*ee zh*oor.

14 oo è la sal d*ay* baga*zh?* *zh^e* v*e^o* fèr â^{n}r^e*zh*ee*s*tr*ay* m*ay* mal.

TRANSLATION

Where is the station, please?

There is one (at the corner of) Rennes Street and Montparnasse Boulevard and another (at) Denfert-Rochereau Square.

To what station must you go?

To go to Brussels we must leave from the North Station.

At what time does the first train leave?

The first train leaves early in the morning.

Then it will be necessary to take a taxi to go more quickly.

Is your baggage ready?

Yes, the suitcases and trunks are already at the station.

Will you be kind enough to tell me where the ticket window is located?

How much does a third class ticket round trip to Strasbourg cost (*lit.* how much costs a third . . .)?

For how long (*lit.* how much time) is this ticket valid?

A round-trip is valid for ten days.

Where is the baggage room? I want to check my trunks.

---

reflexive verb is any verb with a reflexive pronoun object (reflexive pronoun in English is *myself, yourself,* etc.). Occasionally, as here, the French expression may be reflexive whereas the equivalent English is not. *14. Retenu,* past participle of irregular verb *retenir.* This is another example of *compound past tense* (see lesson 3, note *15*). *15.* With present participle *en* means *on* or *by.* (See lesson

15 Voulez-vous bien me donner mon
    bulletin de bagages?

16 Voici votre bulletin, Madame Blan-
    chard.

17 Combien pèse ma malle?

18 Votre malle pèse cinquante kilos.

19 Montons dans le train puisqu'il va
    partir.

20 Voici une bonne place dans un
    compartiment de troisième. Avez-vous l'horaire?

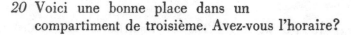

21 Non, mais je sais que le train arrive demain matin.

22 Alors nous arriverons à temps pour prendre le bateau.

23 Avez-vous retenu[14] votre cabine?

24 Pas encore, mais j'en[11] louerai une en[15] arrivant[16] au port.

25 Monsieur Bourgeois va à Londres
    par avion.

26 Vraiment? J'aimerais[17] faire un
    voyage en avion.

27 J'aimerais voir un aérodrome a-
    vant de nous[18] embarquer.

28 Très bien, nous visiterons l'aérodrome d'où partent les avions transatlantiques.

2, note 22).   *16.* With regular verbs the PRESENT PARTICIPLE is formed by adding *ant* to the same stem as for the present plural. The present participle is *never*
used to form a tense in French. The only preposition after which it is used is *en;*
all other prepositions take the infinitive form of the verb. (See lesson 2, note
22).   *17.* Example of CONDITIONAL TENSE (French: *conditionnel*), which is.

15 voolay v ϱ o byè^n m^e don$a$y mô^n bültè^n d^e bagaz$h$?	Will you be kind enough to give me my baggage check?
16 vwasee votr^e bültè^n, madam blâ^n s$h$ar.	Here is your check, Mrs. Blanchard.
17 kô^{n}byè^n pèz ma mal?	How much does my trunk weigh?
18 votr^e mal pèz sè^{n}kâ^{n}t keelô.	Your trunk weighs fifty kilograms.
19 mô^{n}tô^n dâ^n l^e trè^n püeeskeel va parteer.	Let's get on (*lit.* let us go up into) the train since it is going to leave.
20 vwasee ün bon plas dâ^{n}ze^n kô^{n}parteemâ^n d^e trwazyèm. av$a$y voo lorèr?	Here is a good seat in a third-class compartment. Do you have the timetable?
21 nô^n, mè zh^c say k^c l^c trè^n areev d^{e}mè^n matè^n.	No, but I know that the train arrives tomorrow morning.
22 alor noozareev^{e}rô^n a tâ^n poor prâ^{n}dr^e l^e batô.	Then we shall arrive in time to take the boat.
23 av$a$y voo r^{e}tnü votr^e kabeen?	Have you reserved your cabin?
24 pâzâ^{n}kor, mè zhâ^n loo^{e}ray ün â^{n}nareevâ^n ô por.	Not yet, but I shall get (*lit.* rent) one on arriving at the port.
25 m^{e}sye^o boorz$h$wa va a lô^{n}dr par avyô^n.	Mr. Bourgeois is going to London by plane.
26 vrèmâ^n? z$h$èm^{e}rè fèr e^n vwayaz$h$ â^{n}navyô^n.	Really? I should like to make a trip by (*lit.* in) plane.
27 z$h$èm^{e}rè vwar e^{n}na$a$yrodrôm avâ^n d^e noozâ^{n}bark$a$y.	I should like to see an airport before sailing.
28 trè byè^n, noo veezeet^{e}rô^n la$a$yrodrôm doo part l$a$yzavyô^n trâ^{n}zatlâ^{n}teek.	Very well, we shall visit the airport from which (*lit.* from where) the Transatlantic planes leave.

expressed in English with auxiliary *should* or *would* (but not *should* in sense of *ought* which is a form of *devoir* nor *would* in sense of *volition* which is *vouloir*). (See lesson 3, note *29*). *18.* Another *reflexive* verb with which *nous* means *ourselves*. See note *13* above.

CINQUIÈME LEÇON
Fifth Lesson

Nouveau Vocabulaire Pour Cette Leçon

à (a)	to
de (d^e)	from
même (mèm)	same
savez-vous? (sav*ay*-v*oo*)	do you know?
quel, m. (kèl)	which
quelle, f. (kèl)	which
souvent (s*oo*vâ^n)	often
plus (plü)	more
moins (mwè^n)	less
autant (ôtâ^n)	as much
le cahier (kay*ay*)	the notebook
là (la)	there
une fois (fwa)	once
à peu près (a pe^o prè)	about
une quinzaine (kè^{n}zèn)	a fortnight
double (d*oo*bl)	double
jusqu'à (*zh*üska)	until, up to, as far as
y (*ee*)	there (place already mentioned)
une centaine (sâ^{n}tèn)	about a hundred
compter (kô^{n}t*ay*)	to count; intend; expect
la première fois	the first time
la dernière fois (dèrnyèr)	the last time

LES NOMBRES ORDINAUX
(L*ay* nô^{n}br^e zord*ee*nô) · The Ordinal Numbers

1er.	premier, m. (pr^{e}my*ay*)	first
	première, f. (pr^{e}myèr)	first
2e.	second[1] (s^{e}gô^n)	second
	deuxième (de^{o}zyèm)	
3e.	troisième[2] (trwazyèm)	third
4e.	quatrième (katr*ee*èm)	fourth
5e.	cinquième (sè^{n}kyèm)	fifth
9e.	neuvième (n*e*^{o}vyèm)	ninth
21e.	vingt et unième (vè^{n}t*ay* ünyèm)	twenty-first

LES FRACTIONS
(L*ay* fraksyô^n) · The Fractions

la moitié (mwaty*ay*)	half
un tiers (tyèr)	a third
trois quarts (trwa kar)	three quarters
un douzième (*e*^{n} d*oo*zyèm)	a twelfth

NOMBRES CARDINAUX
(nô^{n}br^e kardeenô) · Cardinal Numbers

0. **zéro** (z$a$yrô)
1. **un** (e^n), **une** (ün)
2. **deux** (de^o)
3. **trois** (trwa)
4. **quatre** (katr)
5. **cinq**[3] (se^nk)
6. **six**[3] (sees)
7. **sept**[3] (sèt)
8. **huit**[3] (üeet)
9. **neuf**[3] (n$\grave{e}^o$f)
10. **dix**[3] (dees)
11. **onze**[4] (ô^{n}z)
12. **douze** (dooz)
13. **treize** (trèz)
14. **quatorze** (katorz)
15. **quinze** (kè^{n}z)
16. **seize** (sèz)
17. **dix-sept**[3] (deesèt)
18. **dix-huit**[3] (deezüeet)

19. **dix-neuf** (deezn$\grave{e}^o$f)
20. **vingt**[5] (vè^n)
21. **vingt et un** (vè^{n}tay e^n)
22. **vingt-deux** (vè^{n}t de^o)
23. **vingt-trois** (vè^{n}t trwa)
24. **vingt-quatre** (vè^{n}t katr)
25. **vingt-cinq** (vè^{n}t sè^{n}k)
26. **vingt-six** (vè^{n}t sees)
27. **vingt-sept** (vè^{n}t sèt)
28. **vingt-huit** (vè^{n}tüeet)
29. **vingt-neuf** (vè^{n}t n$\grave{e}^o$f)
30. **trente** (trâ^{n}t)
31. **trente et un** (trâ^{n}tay e^n)
40. **quarante** (karâ^{n}t)
41. **quarante et un**
    (karâ^{n}tay en)
50. **cinquant** (sè^{n}kâ^{n}t)
60. **soixante** (swasâ^{n}t)

70.	soixante-dix[6]	(swasâ^{n}t d*ees*)
71.	soixante et onze	(swasâ^{n}t*ay* ô^{n}z)
72.	soixante-douze	(swasâ^{n}t d*ooz*)
80.	quatre-vingts[7]	(katr^e vè^n)
81.	quatre-vingt-un[8]	(katr^e vè^n *e*^{n})
90.	quatre-vingt-dix[9]	(katr^e vè^n d*ees*)
91.	quatre-vingt-onze	(katr^e vè^n ô^{n}z)
100.	cent	(sân)
101.	cent un	(sâ^n *e*^{n})
150.	cent cinquante	(sâ^n sè^{n}kâ^{n}t)
200.	deux cents[10]	(d*e*^{o} sâ^n)
222.	deux cent vingt-deux	
900.	neuf cents	(nè^{o}f sâ^n)
1000.	mille	(m*ee*l)
2000.	deux mille	(d*e*^{o} m*ee*l)
1,000,000.	un million	(m*ee*lyô^n)
1949.	dix-neuf cent[11] quarante-neuf	
1951.	dix-neuf cent[11] cinquante et un	

FOOTNOTES: *1.* Generally, *second* is used only for the second of two. Example: *le second livre*, the second book (of two); *le deuxième livre*, the second book (of more than two). 2. With the exception of *premier* and *second*, the ordinals are

CONVERSATION

1 Savez-vous compter?

2 Oui, je sais compter.

3 Voulez-vous bien compter?

4 Un, deux, trois, quatre, cinq.

5 Vous avez compté de[12] un jusqu'à cinq.

6 Est-ce que Mademoiselle Lechevallier sait compter de un jusqu'à cent?

7 Oui, monsieur, je sais compter jusqu'à cent.

8 Quels[13] sont les nombres ordinaux[14], Monsieur de Sorbier?

9 Les nombres ordinaux sont: premier, deuxième, troisième, quatrième, cinquième, etc.

10 J'ai dix livres. Combien[15] de livres avez-vous?

11 J'en[17] ai la moitié; j'en[16] ai cinq.

12 Alors vous avez autant[15] de livres que moi, n'est-ce pas?

13 Non, j'ai moins[15] de livres que vous.[17]

14 Mademoiselle de Gorce a trois chapeaux et je n'en ai qu'[18] un.

15 Elle a plus de chapeaux que moi.[17]

---

formed by adding *ième* to the cardinals. Final *e* is dropped in *quatre; u* is inserted after *cinq; f* is changed to *v* in *neuf.*   *3.* If occasion for *linking* arises, normal rules of linking apply, *i.e.*, *six* is pronounced *seez*, etc. But, if these numbers come before a word beginning with a consonant, the final consonant of the number is not pronounced. Example: *six garçons*, (see garsô*n*).   *4.* There is never any *linking* or *elision* with *onze.*   *5.* Final *t* is unpronounced when word is used alone or before a consonant. Note that *t* is pronounced in compounds of twenty.   *6.* Lit. *sixty-ten, sixty-and-eleven, sixty-twelve*, etc.   *7.* Lit. *four-twenties.* Observe unpronounced *s* of this number and also fact that the succeeding numbers drop the *s* in

PRONUNCIATION

1 savay voo kôⁿtay?

2 wee, zhe say kôⁿtay.

3 voolay voo byèⁿ kôⁿtay?

4 eⁿ, deᵒ, trwa, katr, sèⁿk.

5 voozavay kôⁿtay de eⁿ zhüska
sèⁿk.

6 èske madmwazèl leshevalyay
say kôⁿtay de eⁿ zhüska sâⁿ?

7 wee, mesyeᵒ, zhe say kôⁿtay
zhüska sâⁿ.

8 kèl sôⁿ lay nôⁿbre(z) ordeenô,
mesyeᵒ de sorbyay?

9 lay nôⁿbre(z) ordeenô sôⁿ: pre-
myay, deᵒzyèm, trwazyèm, ka-
treeèm, sèⁿkyèm, èt sètayra.

10 zhay dee leevr. kôⁿbyèⁿ de leevr
avay voo?

11 zhâⁿnay la mwatyay; zhâⁿnay
sèⁿk.

12 alor voozavay(z)ôtâⁿ de leevr
ke mwa, nès pâ?

13 nôⁿ, zhay mwèⁿ de leevr ke voo.

14 madmwazèl de gors a trwa
shapô ay zhe nâⁿnay keⁿ.

15 èl a plü de shapô ke mwa.

TRANSLATION

Do you know (how) to count?

Yes, I know (how) to count.

Please count.

One, two, three, four, five.

You have counted from one up to
five.

Does Miss Lechevallier know how
to count from one to one hundred?

Yes, sir, I know how to count up
to a hundred.

What are the ordinal numbers,
Mr. de Sorbier?

The ordinal numbers are: first,
second, third, fourth, fifth, etc.

I have ten books. How many (lit.
of) books have you?

I have half as many (lit. the half
of them); I have (lit. of them)
five.

Then you have as many (lit. of)
books as I, don't you (lit. is it
not)?

No, I have fewer (lit. less of)
books than you.

Miss de Gorce has three hats and
I have (lit. of them) only one.

She has more hats than I.

---

spelling.   8. Observe that eighty-one, ninety-one, one hundred one do not have
et in them as twenty-one, etc. Note that t of vingt is unpronounced here.   9. Lit.
four-twenties-ten.   10. Note s here and absence of s in following example.
11. The word cent cannot be omitted in a date.   12. Note unusual case of failure
to make elision here.   13. In formula what + to be + noun, "what" is treated as
adjective.   14. Most nouns and adjectives ending in al form their plural in aux.
15. Example of an ADVERB OF QUANTITY. Corresponding to certain English adjectives (example: many, much) the French has only adverbs of quantity which,
being adverbs, do not agree and also require de. This de is actually a short parti-

16 Une fois j'ai acheté une centaine[19] de cahiers.

17 La prochaine fois vous ne devriez[20] pas en[16] acheter tellement.

18 La dernière fois que j'étais au Havre c'était mon troisième
voyage à cette ville.

19 J'y ai été vingt fois.

20 Cette fois j'irai à Genève.

21 Un billet de chemin de fer pour la
Suisse coûte deux fois plus cher
qu'un billet pour Dijon, n'est-
ce pas?

22 Oui, approximativement, et le voyage à Bordeaux coûte à
peu près la même chose qu'un voyage à Toulouse.

---

tive construction (see lesson II, note *18*).   *16.* With adverbs of quantity, numbers,
or other quantitative expressions standing alone in the sentence, the *partitive pronoun* is required before the verb (see lesson IV, note *9*).   *17.* Example of DIS-
JUNCTIVE PRONOUN. First person singular disjunctive is *moi* (*me* or *I,* depending
on construction); second plural disjunctive is *vous.* After *que* in sense *than*
always use disjunctive.   *18.* Special negative *ne . . . que* meaning *only.* Place *ne*
before verb and *que* in same place that *only* occupies in the equivalent English
sentence, provided that *only* is correctly placed in English. *Ne . . . que* cannot
refer to anything but the predicate of the sentence.   *19.* A COLLECTIVE NUMBER.

16 ün fwa *zhay* a*sh*tay ün sâⁿtèn·
d^e kay*ay*.

Once I bought about a hundred
notebooks.

17 la pro*sh*èn fwa *voo* n^e d^evr*eeay*
pâzâⁿna*sh*tay tèlmâⁿ.

The next time you ought not (*lit.*
of them) to buy so many.

18 la dèrnyèr fwa k^e *zh*aytè(z)ô
avr *s*aytè môⁿ trwazyèm vwa-
ya*zh* a sèt v*eel*.

The last time (that) I was at Le
Havre (it) was my third trip to
that city.

19 *zh*ee *ay* aytay vèⁿ fwa.

I have been there twenty times.

20 sèt fwa *zh*eeray a *zh*^enèv.

This time I shall go to Geneva.

21 eⁿ beeyè d^e *sh*^emèⁿ d^e fèr p*oor*
la *sü*ees k*oot* de° fwa plü *sh*èr
k^{en} beeyè p*oor* deez*h*ôⁿ, nès
pâ?

A railroad ticket for Switzerland
costs twice as much (*lit.* two
times more expensive) as a
ticket for Dijon, doesn't it?

22 wee, aprokseemateevmâⁿ, *ay* l^e
vwaya*zh* a bordô k*oot* a p*e*°
prè la mèm *sh*ôz k^{en} vwaya*zh*
a tool*ooz*.

Yes, approximately, and the trip
to Bordeaux costs about the
same (thing) as a trip to Toulouse.

The ending *aine* can be added to the numbers 8, 10, 12, 15, 20, 30, 40, 50, 60, 100
to form collective numbers. *Une dizaine* (note unusual spelling), for example,
means *about ten*. *Une douzaine*, meaning *twelve things of a kind*, gives us the English *dozen*. Collective numbers, like adverbs of quantity, take partitive *de* when
accompanied by a noun.   **20.** Conditional of *devoir*, the verb of obligation and
necessity. Like *pouvoir* (see lesson II, note 29), it is a main verb, not an auxiliary
verb, in French. *I must* or *I have to* in the present, it translates *I ought* or *I
should* in the conditional (see lesson IV, note 17).

SIXIÈME LEÇON

Sixth Lesson

Nouveau Vocabulaire Pour Cette Leçon

le froid (frwa)	the cold
la chaleur (*shalèʰor*)	the heat
aujourd'hui (ô*zhoor*düee)	today
demain (dᵉmèⁿ)	tomorrow
se diviser (sᵉ dᵉee*vee*zay)	to be divided
consister (kôⁿsees*tay*	to consist
commencer (komâⁿsay)	to begin
le repos (rᵉpô)	the rest
ni...ni... (*nee...nee*)	neither...nor
durer (düray)	to last
le soleil se couche[1] (solêy sᵉ *koosh*)	the sun sets
il fait mauvais[2] (*eel* fè movè)	the weather is bad
cela veut dire[3] (sᵉla veᵒ deer)	that means
d'une façon générale (dün fasôⁿ *zhay*nayral)	in a general way
une année[4] (ünanay)	a year (duration)
dernier, m. (dèrnyay)	last
dernière, f. (dèrnyèr)	last
après-demain (aprè dᵉmèⁿ)	day after tomorrow
avant-hier (avâⁿtyèr)	day before yesterday
se composer (sᵉ kôⁿpôzay)	to be composed

un jour de congé (*zhoor d^e kô^{n}zhay*)   a holiday
il fait froid (*frwa*)   the weather is cold
un après-midi (*aprèmeedee*)   an afternoon
le lever du soleil (*l^{e}vay dü solèy*)   the sunrise

LES MOIS DE L'ANNÉE[5]
(*Lay* mwa d^e lan*ay*) · The Months of the Year

janvier (*zhâ^{n}vyay*)	January
février (*fayvreeay*)	February
mars (*mars*)	March
avril (*avreel*)	April
mai (*mè*)	May
juin (*zhüè^n*)	June
juillet (*zhüeeyè*)	July
août (*oo*)	August
september (*sèptâ^{n}br*)	September
octobre (*oktobr*)	October
novembre (*novâ^{n}br*)	November
décembre (*daysâ^{n}br*)	December

Le Jour · L'Année · Les Saisons
(l^e *zhoo*r, lan*ay*, l*ay* sèzô^n) · The Day, the Year, the Seasons

le matin (matè^n)	the morning
la nuit (*nüee*)	the night
la semaine (s^emèn)	the week
le mois (mwa)	the month
un an (*e*^{n}nâ^n)	a year
le siècle (syèkl)	the century
le coucher du soleil	the sunset
(*kooshay* dü solèy)	
le printemps (prè^{n}tâ^n)	the spring
un été (*aytay*)	a summer
un automne (ôton)	an autumn
un hiver (*eevè*r)	a winter
l'aube, f. (ôb)	the dawn
midi, m. (m*eedee*)	noon
minuit, f. (*meenüee*)	midnight
il fait beau (bô)	the weather is good
il fait chaud (*shô*)	the weather is hot

LES JOURS DE LA SEMAINE[5]
(*Lay zhoo*r d^e la s^{e}mèn) • The Days of the Week

lundi (le^{n}dee)	Monday
mardi (mardee)	Tuesday
mercredi (mèrkr^{e}dee)	Wednesday
jeudi (*zhe*^{o}dee)	Thursday
vendredi (vâ^{n}dr^{e}dee)	Friday
samedi (samdee)	Saturday
dimanche (deemâ^n*sh*)	Sunday

FOOTNOTES: *1.* Lit. *goes to bed.* *2.* The impersonal *il fait*, meaning *it makes*, followed by an adjective or a partitive construction, is the preferred expression for the weather. *Il fait mauvais (temps)* translates then literally: *it makes bad (weather).* Observe that the English, as in sentence 30 of this lesson, occasionally

CONVERSATION

1 Comment se divise la journée?

2 La journée se compose du matin, de l'après-midi et du soir.

3 Le matin dure jusqu'à midi. L'après-midi dure plus ou moins jusqu'à la tombée de la nuit.

4 Quand est-ce que le soir commence?

5 Le soir commence d'une façon générale après le coucher du soleil.

6 Que signifie le terme "aube"?

7 L'aube veut dire le lever du soleil.

8 Combien de jours y a-t-il[6] dans la semaine?

9 La semaine se compose de sept jours.

10 Quel jour de la semaine est-ce aujourd'hui?

11 Aujourd'hui c'est lundi, qui est le premier jour de la semaine. Le dernier jour de la semaine est dimanche, qui est un jour de congé ou de repos.

12 Quel jour serons-nous[7] demain?

13 Demain ce[8] sera mardi et le jour suivant sera mercredi.

14 Est-ce que c'était hier mercredi?

15 Non, monsieur, hier c'était dimanche et avant-hier c'était samedi.

---

uses *"it"* for *the weather.* If, however, the English read: *it is cold,* with the word *water* as the antecedent of *it,* the French would read: *elle est froide.*   3. Lit. *that wishes to say.*   4. Roughly the feminine forms *journée* and *année* emphasize duration but actually the use of these words is idiomatic. In the expression *toute*

PRONUNCIATION

1 komân s^e deeveez la *zhoor*nay?

2 la *zhoor*nay s^e kôⁿpôz dü matèⁿ, d^e laprèm*eedee ay* dü swar.

3 l^e matèⁿ dür *zhü*ska *meedee.* laprèm*eedee* dür plü*zoo* mwèⁿ *zhü*ska la tôⁿb*ay* d^e la *nüee.*

4 kâⁿtèsk^e l^e swar komâⁿs?

5 l^e swar komâⁿs dün fasôⁿ *zhay*nay*ral aprè l^e *kooshay* dü solèy.

6 k^e *seenyeefee* l^e tèrm ôb?

7 lôb ve^o deer l^e l^ev*ay* dü solèy.

8 kôⁿbyèⁿ d^e *zhoor* ee ateel dâⁿ la s^emèn?

9 la s^emèn s^e kôⁿpôz d^e sèt *zhoor.*

10 kèl *zhoor* d^e la s^emèn ès ô-*zhoor*düee?

11 ô*zhoor*düee sè leⁿdee, kee è l^e pr^emy*ay zhoor* d^e la s^emèn. l^e dèrny*ay zhoor* d^e la s^emèn è deemâⁿsh, kee èteⁿ *zhoor* d^e kôⁿ*zhay* oo d^e r^epô.

12 kèl *zhoor* s^erôⁿ noo d^emèⁿ?

13 d^emèⁿ s^e s^era mardee *ay* l^e *zhoor* süeevâⁿ s^era mèrkr^edee.

14 èsk^e *sayt*è yèr mèrkr^edee?

15 nôⁿ, m^esye^o, yèr *sayt*è deemâⁿsh *ay* avâⁿtyèr *sayt*è samdee.

TRANSLATION

How is the day divided?

The day is composed of the morning, the afternoon, and the evening.

The morning lasts until noon. The afternoon lasts more or less until nightfall (*lit.* the falling of the night).

When does the evening begin?

The evening begins in a general way after sunset.

What does the term "dawn" signify?

Dawn means sunrise.

How many days are there in a week?

The week is composed of seven days.

What day of the week is it today?

Today is Monday, which is the first day of the week. The last day of the week is Sunday, which is a holiday or day of rest.

What day will it be tomorrow?

Tomorrow will be Tuesday and the following day will be Wednesday.

Was yesterday Wednesday?

No, sir, yesterday (it) was Sunday and day before yesterday (it) was Saturday.

---

l'année (the whole year) duration is clearly emphasized (see lesson III, note *3*). **5.** The days, the months, and the seasons are not capitalized in French. Study irregular pronunciation.   **6.** To invert a third person singular verb ending in a vowel, a "*t*" surrounded by hyphens must be inserted. Historically this *t* is a

16 Pouvez-vous me dire comment se divise l'année?

17 L'année se divise en douze mois.

18 Dans[9] quel mois sommes-nous[7]?

19 Nous sommes maintenant en[9] septembre, le mois prochain sera octobre et le mois dernier était août.

20 Quel est le premier mois de l'année?

21 Le premier mois de l'année est janvier.

22 Combien de saisons y a-t-il dans l'année?

23 L'année a quatre saisons: le printemps, l'été, l'automne et l'hiver.

24 Quels sont les mois de[10] printemps?

25 Les mois de printemps sont mars, avril et mai.

26 Est-ce qu'il fait beau ou mauvais en cette saison?

27 Au printemps il fait beau en général, ni trop froid ni trop chaud.

28 Quels sont les mois d'été?

29 Les mois d'été sont juin, juillet et août.

30 Est-ce qu'il fait froid en cette saison?

31 Non, monsieur; en été il fait toujours chaud.

32 Combien d'années y a-t-il dans un siècle?

33 Il y a cent ans dans un siècle.

---

survivor from the times when all third singulars ended in *t.*   7. Idiom (lit. fut. tense: *will we be?*; pres. tense: *are we?*).   8. Example of "*it*" without antecedent becoming *ce.* See lesson III, note *18.*   9. Compare this way of expressing question

16 poovay voo m^e deer komâ^n s^e deeveez lanay?

17 lanay s^e deeveez â^n dooz mwa.

18 dâ^n kèl mwa som noo?

19 noo som mè^{n}tnâ^n â^n sèptâ^{n}br, l^e mwa proshè^n s^{e}ra oktobr ay l^e mwa dèrnyay aytè oo.

20 kèl è l^e pr^{e}myay mwa d^e lanay?

21 l^e pr^{e}myay mwa d^e lanay è zhâ^{n}vyay.

22 kô^{n}byè^n d^e sèzô^n ee ateel dâ^n lanay?

23 lanay a katr^e sèzô^n: l^e prè^{n}tâ^n, laytay, lôton ay leevèr.

24 kèl sô^n lay mwa d^e prè^{n}tâ^n?

25 lay mwa d^e prè^{n}tâ^n sô^n mars, avreel ay mè.

26 èskeel fè bô oo movè â^n sèt sèzô^n?

27 ô prè^{n}tâ^n eel fè bô â^n zhaynayral, nee trô frwa nee trô shô.

28 kèl sô^n lay mwa daytay?

29 lay mwa daytay sô^n zhüè^n, zhüeeyè ay oo.

30 èskeel fè frwa â^n sèt sèzô^n?

31 nô^n, m^{e}sye^o; â^{n}naytay eel fè toozhoor shô.

32 kô^{n}byè^n danay ee ateel dâ^{n}ze^n syèkl?

33 eelya sâ^{n}tâ^n dâ^{n}ze^n syèkl.

Can you tell me how the year is divided?

The year is divided into twelve months.

What month is it now (*lit.* in what month are we)?

It is now September (*lit.* we are now in September), the next month will be October and (the) last month was August.

What is the first month of the year?

The first month of the year is January.

How many seasons arc there in the year?

The year has four seasons: (namely) spring, summer, autumn, and winter.

What are the spring months?

The spring months arc March, April, and May.

Is the weather good or bad at (*lit.* in) this season?

In the spring the weather is good in general, neither too cold nor too hot.

What are the summer months?

The summer months are June, July, and August.

Is it cold at this season?

No, sir; in summer it is always warm.

How many years are there in a century?

There are a hundred years in a century.

---

with construction in sentence 10. *10. Spring months:* lit., "months of spring." In French, a noun cannot function as an adjective, as it can in English. To modify a noun by another noun, the modifying noun is generally used in a prepositional phrase with *de. Office manager* is thus translated as "manager of office": *chef de bureau.*

SEPTIÈME LEÇON
Seventh Lesson

Nouveau Vocabulaire Pour Cette Leçon

quelle heure[1] est-il[2]? (kèl è^{o}r èt*eel*)	what time is it?
à moins (a mwè^n)	for less
nouveau, m. (n*oov*ô)	new
nouvelle, f. (n*oov*èl)	new
s'arrêter[4] (sarèt*ay*)	to stop
chez[3] Jean (*shay* zhâ^n)	at John's place
chez[3] lui (*shay* lü*ee*)	at his place
un ami, m. (e^{n}nam*ee*)	a friend
une amie, f. (ünam*ee*)	a friend
donner (don*ay*)	to give
un agent de police (a*zh*â^n d^e pol*ees*)	a policeman (city)
le gendarme (*zh*â^{n}darm)	the state policeman
s'appeler (sapl*ay*)	to be called, named
le reste (rèst)	the rest, remainder
encore (â^{n}kor)	again, still, yet
en effet (â^n*ay*fè)	in reality, in fact, indeed, to be sure
un état (e^{n}n*ay*ta)	a state, condition

il est une heure (*eel* ètün *è*⁰r)   it is one o'clock
il est deux heures (de⁰zè⁰r)   it is two o'clock
casser (kas*ay*)   to break
réparer (r*ay*par*ay*)   to repair
détraqué (d*ay*trak*ay*)   out of order
sale (sal)   dirty
indiquer (è*ⁿ*deek*ay*)   to indicate
examiner (ègzameen*ay*)   to examine
remplacer (râ*ⁿ*plas*ay*)   to replace
pardon (pardô*ⁿ*)   pardon (me)
nettoyer (nètway*ay*)   to clean
moins (mwè*ⁿ*)   less

L'HEURE · LA MONTRE · L'HORLOGER
(lè°r, la mô^{n}tr, lorlo*zhay*) · The Time, the Watch, the Watchmaker

une horloge (orlo*zh*)	a (public) clock
la pendule (pâ^{n}dül)	the (wall) clock
le bracelet-montre (brasl*ay* mô^{n}tr)	the wrist watch
un horloger (orlo*zhay*)	a watchmaker
une heure (è°r)	an hour
la minute (m*ee*nüt)	the minute
la seconde[5] (s^{e}gô^{n}d)	the second
la montre en or (â^{n}nor)	the gold watch
sonner (son*ay*)	to ring, strike
le ressort (r^{e}sor)	the spring
le mouvement (m*oo*vmâ^n)	the movement
le rubis (rüb*ee*)	ruby, jewel (of watch)
la montre (mô^{n}tr)	the watch
une aiguille[5] (èg*üeey*)	a hand (of a clock), needle
une horlogerie (orlo*zhree*)	a watchmaker's shop
le verre (vèr)	the glass, crystal
avancer (avà^{n}s*ay*)	to be fast, to gain time
retarder (retard*ay*)	to be slow, to lose time

FOOTNOTES: *1.* Time (*lit.* hour). *2.* observe that *il est*, in this type of expression, is invariable. *3.* The preposition *chez* has no English equivalent. It means *to* or *at a place belonging to someone*, the nature of the place not being

specified. Following the preposition is a noun or a pronoun designating the owner of the place. All prepositions require the *disjunctive* form of the pronoun (see lesson V, note *17*). The third singular disjunctive pronoun is *lui* (masc.), *elle*

CONVERSATION

1 Pardon, monsieur, pouvez-vous me dire l'heure?

2 Oui, monsieur, il est deux heures vingt.[6]

3 Est-il encore trois heures?

4 Oui, il est trois heures précises[7].

5 Il n'est pas encore plus d'[8]une heure moins le quart.[9]

6 En effet, il n'est pas encore trois heures.

7 Est-ce que quatre heures n'ont pas encore sonné?

8 Oui, Pierre, votre montre n'est pas à l'heure.[10] Je crois qu'elle avance de[10] cinq minutes.

9 Au contraire, ma montre retarde d'[10]un quart d'heure.

10 Est-elle cassée?

11 Je crois qu'elle est arrêtée; elle doit être détraquée et il me faudra la porter chez[3] l'horloger.

12 L'avez-vous remontée?[11]

13 Oui, mais elle est sale et il faudra la faire[12] nettoyer.

14 Où y a-t-il un bon horloger pas[13] trop cher?

(fem.). *Chez* is frequently translated *to* or *at the house of*, but it does not mean necessarily *house*; it may be a shop, office, or store. It also has a figurative sense: *chez les Américains* (among the Americans); *chez Balzac* (with Balzac).   **4.** In the intransitive sense *"to stop"* translates as a reflexive; in the transitive sense it is not reflexive. Example: *L'automobile s'arrête:* the automobile stops; but:

PRONUNCIATION

1 pardô^n, m^{e}sye^o, *p*oovay *v*oo
m^e deer lè^{o}r?

2 wee, m^{e}sye^o, eelè de^{o}zè^{o}r vè^n.

3 èteel â^{n}kor trwazè^{o}r?

4 wee, eelè trwazè^{o}r pr*ay*seez.

5 eel nè pâzâ^{n}kor plü dün è^{o}r
mwè^n l^e kar.

6 â^{n}nayfè, eel nè pâzâ^{n}kor trwa-
zè^{o}r.

7 èsk^e katr è^{o}r nô^n pâzâ^{n}kor
son*ay?*

8 wee, pyèr, votr^e mô^{n}ti nè pâza
lè^{o}r. zh^e krwa kèl avâ^{n}s d^e sè^n
meenüt.

9 ô kô^{n}trèr, ma mô^{n}tr^e r^{e}tard
de^n kar dè^{o}r.

10 ètèl kas*ay?*

11 zh^e krwa kèl ètarèt*ay*; èl
dwatètr^e daytrak*ay ay* eel m^e
fôdra la port*ay* sh*ay* lorlozh*ay.*

12 lav*ay v*oo r^{e}mô^{n}t*ay?*

13 wee, mè(z)èl è sal *ay* eel fôdra
la fèr nètway*ay.*

14 oo ee ateel e^n bonorlozh*ay* pâ
trô shèr?

TRANSLATION

Pardon (me), sir, can you tell me
the time (*lit.* the hour)?

Yes, sir, it is twenty minutes past
two (*lit.* two hours twenty).

Is it three o'clock yet?

Yes, it is exactly three o'clock.

It is not yet more than a quarter
to one (*lit.* one hour less the
quarter).

In fact it is not yet three o'clock.

Hasn't four o'clock rung yet?

Yes, Peter, your watch is not on
time. I believe it is five minutes fast (*lit.* advances by five
minutes).

On the contrary, my watch is a
quarter of an hour slow (*lit.*
retards by a quarter hour).

Is it broken?

I think it has stopped; it must be
out of order and I shall have to
take it (*lit.* it will be necessary
for me to carry it) to the watchmaker's.

Have you wound it up?

Yes, but it is dirty and it will have
to be cleaned.

Where is there a good inexpensive
watchmaker (*lit.* not too dear)?

J'arrête l'automobile: I stop the automobile.   5. Note exceptional pronunciation.
6. Note literal translation. To subtract minutes from next hour, say *moins* (less).
Example: *ten minutes to three:* trois heures moins dix (*lit.* three hours less ten).
7. English uses adverb whereas French uses adjective.   8. When the word *than*
occurs before a number or a fraction, it is translated as *de.*   9. For fractions of

15 Au quarante-cinq rue de Vaugirard.

16 Comment s'appelle cet horloger?

17 Il s'appelle[14] Greuzard.

18 Le quarante-cinq est près du Boulevard Raspail, n'est-ce pas?

19 Oui, monsieur, c'est entre le Boulevard Raspail et la rue d'Assas.

20 Monsieur Greuzard est-il là, s'il vous plaît?[10]

21 A votre service, monsieur, qu'est-ce que je peux faire pour vous?

22 Un de mes amis m'a donné votre adresse; voudriez[15]-vous me[16] réparer cette montre?

23 Oui, monsieur, mais je dois l'examiner d'abord.

24 Quand est-ce qu'elle sera prête? Combien est-ce que cela[17] coûtera?

25 Elle sera prête dans cinq jours et cela vous[18] coûtera cent cinquante francs.

26 Cela me semble un peu cher. Ne pourriez-vous pas le faire à moins?

27 Non, monsieur, c'est impossible; le ressort est cassé et je dois le remplacer.

28 Est-ce que le reste du mouvement est en bon état?

29 Oui, monsieur, mais je dois aussi remplacer le verre.

hour, say, for example: *a quarter past three:* trois heures et quart (*lit.* three hours and a quarter); *half past three:* trois heures et demie (*lit.* three hours and a half); *a quarter to four:* quatre heures moins le quart (*lit.* four hours less the quarter). *10.* Idiom. *11.* In compound tenses, past participles conjugated with *avoir* agree with the *preceding direct object;* past participles conjugated

15 ô karâ^{n}t sè^{n}k rü d^e vô*zh*eerar.

At (number) forty-five Vaugirard Street.

16 komâ^n sapèl sètorlo*zh*ay?

What is that watchmaker's name (*lit.* how does that watchmaker call himself)?

17 ee*l* sapèl gre^{o}zar.

His name is (*lit.* he calls himself) Greuzard.

18 l^e karâ^{n}t sè^{n}k è prè dü *b*oolvar raspay, nès pâ?

Number forty-five is near Raspail Boulevard, isn't it?

19 wee, m^{e}sye^o, sètâ^{n}r^e l^e *b*oolvar raspay *ay* la rü dasas.

Yes, sir, it is between Raspail Boulevard and Assas Street.

20 m^{e}sye^o gre^{o}zar èteel la, see*l* *v*oo plè?

Is Mr. Greuzard there, please?

21 a votr^e sèrvees, m^{e}sye^o, kèsk^e *zh*^{e} pe^o fèr poor *v*oo?

At your service, sir, what can I do for you?

22 e^n d^e m*ay*zamee ma don*ay* votr adrès; *v*oodree*ay* *v*oo m^e r*ay*par*ay* sèt mô^{n}tr?

One of my friends gave me your address; would you repair this watch for me?

23 wee, m^{e}sye^o, mè *zh*^{e} dwa lèg-zameen*ay* dabor.

Yes, sir, but I must examine it first.

24 kâ^{n}tèskèl s^{e}ra prèt? kô^{n}byè^n èsk^e s^{e}la *k*ootra?

When will it be ready? How much will it cost?

25 èl s^{e}ra prèt dâ^n sè^n *zh*oor *ay* s^{e}la *v*oo *k*ootra sâ^n sè^{n}kâ^{n}t frâ^n.

It will be ready in five days and it will cost you one hundred and fifty francs.

26 s^{e}la me sâ^{n}b*l* e^n pe^o *sh*èr. n^e pooree*ay* *v*oo l^e fèr a mwè^n?

That seems to me a little dear. Couldn't you do it for less?

27 nô^n, m^{e}sye^o, sètè^{n}poseeb*l*; l^e r^{e}sor è kas*ay* *ay* *zh*^{e} dwa l^e râ^{n}plas*ay*.

No, sir, it is impossible; the spring is broken and I must replace it.

28 èsk^e l^e rèst dü moovmâ ètâ^n bon*ay*ta?

Is the rest of the movement in good condition?

29 wee, m^{e}sye^o, mè *zh*^{e} dwa(z)ô-see râ^{n}plas*ay* l^e vèr.

Yes, sir, but I must also replace the crystal.

with *être* agree with the *subject*; past participles of reflexive verbs, although conjugated with *être*, agree with the *preceding direct object*. **12.** Causal use of *faire*. See lesson IV, note 2. **13.** See lesson III, note 24. **14.** *Appeler* means *to call*; *s'appeler* means *to call oneself*. Note English translations given for this expression. This verb doubles the "*l*" any time it is followed by a mute *e* verb

30 Très bien. Au revoir, monsieur, et à[10] jeudi.

31 Avez-vous des montres en[19] or?

32 Oui, et ma femme a un bracelet-montre en or.

33 Est-ce que les montres en diamants sont chères?

34 Une montre en diamants est tou-jours chère.

35 Pouvez-vous me dire combien de minutes il y a dans une heure?

36 Une heure se compose de soixante minutes et une minute de soixante secondes.

37 Qu'est-ce qui indique l'heure dans une pendule?

38 Les deux aiguilles indiquent l'heure, la grande aiguille[20] indique les minutes et la petite aiguille les heures.

ending. *15.* Conditional of *vouloir.* *16.* Indirect object frequently called DATIVE OF REFERENCE. The person *for whom* something is done is commonly expressed as an indirect object pronoun before the verb. *17.* Normally *it* with imprecise antecedent is *ce* (see lesson VI, note *8*), if it occurs before the verb *to be.* Before other verbs it becomes *cela.* *18.* Indirect object since *cent cin-*

30 trè byèⁿ. ôr(^e)vwar, m^esye^o, ay a zhe^odee.	Very well. Good day (*lit.* until seeing each other again), sir, and until Thursday.
31 avay voo day môⁿtr âⁿnor?	Have you any gold watches?
32 wee, ay ma fam a eⁿ braslay môⁿtr âⁿnor.	Yes, and my wife has a gold wrist watch.
33 èsk^e lay môⁿtr âⁿ dyamâⁿ sôⁿ shèr?	Are diamond watches expensive?
34 ün môⁿtr âⁿ dyamâⁿ è toozhoor shèr.	A diamond watch is always expensive.
35 poovay voo m^e deer kôⁿbyèⁿ d^e meenüt eelya dâⁿzün è^or?	Can you tell me how many minutes there are in an hour?
36 ün è^or s^e kôⁿpôz d^e swasâⁿt meenüt ay ün meenüt d^e swasâⁿt s^egôⁿd.	An hour is composed of sixty minutes and a minute of sixty seconds.
37 kèskee èⁿdeek le^or dâⁿzün pâⁿdül?	How does the clock indicate the time? (*lit.* what indicates the hour in a clock?)
38 lay de^oz ègüeey èⁿdeek lè^or, la grâⁿd ègüeey èⁿdeek lay meenüt ay la p^eteet ègüeey layzè^or.	The two hands indicate the time, the large hand for the minutes and the small hand for the hours.

---

quante francs is the direct object. Note this important principle: *a French verb will not have two direct objects; one of them must be indirect.* 19. The material of which a thing is made is put into a prepositional phrase beginning with *en* or *de.* The choice between the two is generally idiomatic. 20. *Grande aiguille* and *petite aiguille* are the technical terms for *hour hand* and *minute hand.*

HUITIÈME LEÇON
Eighth Lesson

Nouveau Vocabulaire Pour Cette Leçon

établir (*ay*tabl*eer*)	to establish, draw up
n'importe[1] quel (nè^{n}port kèl)	any, no matter which
comment va...? (komâ^n va)	how is...?
la procuration (prokürasyô^n)	the power of attorney
la restriction (rèstreeksyô^n)	the restriction
la transaction (trâ^{n}zaksyô^n)	the transaction
régler (r*ay*gl*ay*)	to settle, regulate
acheter (a*sh*t*ay*)	to buy
au comptant (ô kô^{n}tâ^n)	for cash
vendre (vâ^{n}dr)	to sell
le crédit (kr*ay*d*ee*)	the credit
à crédit (a kr*ay*d*ee*)	on credit
importer (è^{n}port*ay*)	to import
exporter (èksport*ay*)	to export
signer (s*ee*ny*ay*)	to sign
sans doute (sâ^n d*oot*)	without doubt
un bénéfice (b*ay*n*ay*f*ee*s)	a profit
le notaire (notèr)	the notary
le témoin (t*ay*mwè^n)	the witness
une espèce (èspès)	a kind
geler (*zh*^{e}l*ay*)	to freeze

espérer (èspayray)   to hope
la banque (bâⁿk)   the bank
l'argent, m. (larzhâⁿ)   the money
le guichet (geeshay)   pay-window
le tabac (taba)   the tobacco
le sucre (sükr)   sugar
les céréales, f. (sayrayal)   cereals
le pétrole (paytrol)   petroleum
l'étain, m. (aytèⁿ)   tin
partout (partoo)   everywhere
je vais² bien (mal)   I am well (ill)
  (zh^e vay byèⁿ – mal)
le raisin (rèzèⁿ)   the grape
la figue (feeg)   fig
la banane (banan)   banana
l'ananas, m. (anana)   pineapple
la cacahuète (kakaüèt)   peanut
l'huile, f. (lüeel)   oil
le blé (blay)   wheat
le cuir (küeer)   leather

LE COMMERCE
(l^e komèrs) • Trade

le marchand (marshâ^n)	the merchant
le taux (tô)	rate
le change (shâ$^n zh$)	exchange
la traite (trèt)	draft
le produit (prod$\ddot{u}ee$)	product
les affaires, f. (layzafèr)	business
les valeurs, f. (val$è^o$r)	the securities
la viande frigorifiée (freegoreefyay)	frozen meat
l'engrais, m. (â^{n}grè)	fertilizer
les chapeaux de paille	straw hats
(shapô d^e pây)	
le vin (vè^n)	the wine
vin blanc (vè^n blâ^n)	white wine
vin rouge (vè^n roozh)	red wine
la maison (mèzô^n)	the house, firm
la succursale (sükürsal)	branch (of a firm)
le pamplemousse (pâ^{n}pl^{e}moos)	grapefruit
la noix de coco (nwâ d^e kokô)	cocoanut
un échange ($ay sh$â$^n zh$)	an exchange (transfer)

FOOTNOTES: *1.* Idiom: *no matter which.* *2.* Idiom: *I go well.* *3.* See lesson II, note *35.* *4. Longtemps* is an adverb in French. Do not try to put an article in front of it. *5.* Idiom. *6.* See note *3* above. Nouns also normally introduce dependent infinitives with *de.* *7.* Normal expectation would be a partitive before

this adjective. Observe that partitive is not used with *certain*. *8.* With *de* in sense of *from* with feminine countries omit the usual article. *9.* See lesson II, note *11.* *10.* Future of *faire*. *11.* In spite of verb *être* construction is same as

CONVERSATION

1 Comment allez-vous? Je suis très content de³ vous voir.

2 Je vais très bien, merci; et vous?

3 Pas trop mal, merci.

4 Comptez-vous rester longtemps⁴ à Paris?

5 Non, monsieur, je suis venu pour quelques mois seulement pour affaires.

6 Et comment vont les choses en Afrique du Nord? Vous y serez sans doute avant le printemps.

7 Oui, monsieur, d'ici là⁵ j'espère pouvoir régler toutes mes affaires.

8 Avez-vous l'intention de⁶ faire de l'importation?⁵

9 J'aimerais importer le café, le tabac, le sucre, la laine et certaines⁷ espèces de fruits.

10 Est-ce que vous pensez importer ces produits de toutes les régions méditerranéennes?

11 De partout; d'⁸Egypte je recevrai du tabac, du coton, du sucre et des céréales, et, de⁸ Grèce, des raisins et des figues.

12 Et qu'est-ce que vous recevrez des colonies françaises?

13 Eh bien, d'Algérie je recevrai des fruits⁹, c'est-à-dire⁵ des oranges, des bananes, des pamplemousses; de Tunisie, de l'huile d'olive et du blé; du Maroc, du cuir; et du Sénégal des cacahuètes et des noix de coco.

---

that described in note 6 above.   12. A few cities in French have articles as part of the name: *Le Havre, Le Caire, La Haye* (The Hague, which has an article in

PRONUNCIATION

1 komâⁿtalay voo? zhᵉ süee trè kôⁿtâⁿ dᵉ voo vwar.

2 zhᵉ vay trè byèⁿ, mèrsee; ay voo?

3 pâ trô mal, mèrsee.

4 kôⁿtay voo rèstay lôⁿtâⁿ a paree?

5 nôⁿ, mᵉsyeᵒ, zhᵉ süee vᵉnü poor kèlkᵉ mwa sèᵒlmâⁿ poor afèr.

6 ay komâⁿ vôⁿ lay shôz âⁿnafreek dü nor? voozee sᵉray sâⁿ doot avâⁿ lᵉ prèⁿtâⁿ.

7 wee, mᵉsyeᵒ, deesee la zhèspèr poovwar rayglay toot mayzafèr.

8 avay voo lèⁿtâⁿsyôⁿ dᵉ fèr dᵉ lèⁿportasyôⁿ?

9 zhèmrè(z)èⁿportay lᵉ kafay, lᵉ taba, lᵉ süükr, la lèn ay sèrtènzèspès dᵉ früee.

10 èskᵉ voo pâⁿsay èⁿportay say produee dᵉ toot lay rayzhyôⁿ maydeetèranayèn?

11 dᵉ partoo, dayzheept zhᵉ rᵉsᵉvray dü taba, dü kotôⁿ, dü süükr ay day sayrayal, ay, dᵉ gres, day rèzèⁿ ay day feeg.

12 ay kèskᵉ voo rᵉsᵉvray day kolonee frâⁿsèz?

13 ay byèⁿ, dalzhayree zhᵉ rᵉsᵉvray day früee, sètadeer dayzorâⁿzh, day banan, day pâⁿplemoos; dᵉ tüneezee, dᵉ lüeel doleev ay dü blay; dü marok, dü küeer; ay dü saynaygal day kakaüèt ay day nwâ dᵉ kokô.

TRANSLATION

How are (lit. go) you? I am very glad to see you.

I am (lit. go) very well, thanks; and you?

Quite well (lit. not very badly), thanks.

Do you expect to remain a long time in Paris?

No, sir, I came for a few months only on (lit. for) business.

And how are things in North Africa? You will doubtless be there before spring.

Yes, sir, from now until then (lit. from here to there) I hope to be able to settle all my business.

Do you intend to do importing?

I should like to import coffee, tobacco, sugar, wool and certain kinds of fruit.

Do you think you will import (lit. to import) these products from all the Mediterranean regions?

From everywhere; from Egypt I shall receive tobacco, cotton, sugar, and cereals, and, from Greece, grapes and figs.

And what will you receive from the French colonies?

Well, from Algeria I shall receive fruit, that is to say oranges, bananas, grapefruit; from Tunisia, olive oil and wheat; from Morocco, leather; and from Sénégal peanuts and cocoanuts.

English also). The normal rules of contraction apply to the first two examples, in which case the capitalization of the article disappears. 13. The long RELATIVE

14 Avez-vous l'intention de vendre au comptant ou à crédit?

15 A certains marchands j'ouvrirai un crédit à courte échéance;[5] ou bien je ferai[10] un échange de produits.

16 Comment comptez-vous établir ce commerce?

17 Mon idée est d'[11]établir une succursale de ma maison au[12] Caire, à la tête de laquelle[13] il y aura un de mes frères.

18 Aura-t-il besoin d'une procuration de la part[5] de votre maison pour légaliser ses transactions?

19 Naturellement; il en[14] aura besoin pour acheter[15] et vendre au[5] nom de la maison.

20 Pour établir une procuration à qui[16] faut-il avoir recours?[5]

21 Il faut la faire établir par un notaire et devant deux témoins.

22 Quel est le taux du change aujourd'hui?

23 Le change est assez favorable.

24 Est-ce que je pourrais toucher une lettre de change en dollars?

25 A présent il y a des restrictions sur les valeurs et monnaies[17] étrangères; mais je crois que vous pourriez toucher en argent français une traite sur n'importe quelle banque française.

26 J'aimerais aussi faire de l'exportation en Turquie.

PRONOUN (*pronom relatif composé*): *lequel,* masc.; *laquelle,* fem.; *lesquels,* masc. pl.; *lesquelles,* fem. pl., having numerous functions. It is used to distinguish antecedents in the unusual cases where there is a possibility of ambiguity. Its use is obligatory, as in the example above, when a relative *referring to a thing* is placed *after a preposition.* The same forms are also used as the interrogative pronoun with an antecedent, translating the English *which* (*one*) or *which* (*ones*).

14 avay voo lèⁿtâⁿsyôⁿ dᵉ vâⁿdr
ô kôⁿtâⁿ oo a kraydee?

Do you intend to sell for cash or on credit?

15 a sèrtèⁿ marshâⁿ zhoovreeray
eⁿ kraydee a koort ayshayâⁿs;
oo byèⁿ zhᵉ fᵉray eⁿnayshâⁿzh
dᵉ produee.

For certain merchants I shall open up a short term credit; or else I shall make an exchange of products.

16 komâⁿ kôⁿtay voo aytableer sᵉ
komèrs?

How do you expect to establish this business?

17 moneeday è daytableer ün sü-
kürsal dᵉ ma mèzôⁿ ô kèr, a la
tèt dᵉ lakèl eelyôra eⁿ dᵒ may
frèr.

My idea is to establish a branch of my company at Cairo, at the head of which will be (lit. there will be) one of my brothers.

18 ôrateel bᵉzwèⁿ dün prokürasyôⁿ
dᵉ la par dᵉ votrᵉ mèzôⁿ poor
laygaleezay say trâⁿzaksyôⁿ?

Will he need a power of attorney on behalf of (lit. from the part of) your company to legalize his transactions?

19 natürèlmâⁿ; eel âⁿnôra bᵉzwèⁿ
poor ashtay ay vâⁿdr ô nôⁿ dᵉ
la mèzôⁿ.

Naturally; he will need one to buy and sell in the name of the company.

20 poor aytableer ün prokürasyôⁿ
a kee fôteel avwar rᵉkoor?

In order to draw up a power of attorney, to whom is it necessary to have recourse?

21 il fô la fèraytableer par eⁿ
notèr ay dᵉvâⁿ dᵉᵒ taymwèⁿ.

It must be drawn up by a notary and before two witnesses.

22 kèl è lᵉ tô dii shâⁿzh ôzhoordüee?

What is the rate of exchange to-day?

23 lᵉ shâⁿzh ètasay favorabl.

The exchange is rather favorable.

24 èskᵉ zhᵉ poorᵉ tooshay ün lètrᵉ
dᵉ shâⁿzh âⁿ dolar?

Could I cash a letter of exchange in dollars?

25 a prayzâⁿ eelya day rèstreek-
syôⁿ sür lay valᵉʳr ay monè-
(z)aytrâⁿzhèr; mè zhᵉ krwa kᵉ
voo pooreeay tooshay âⁿnar-
zhâⁿ frâⁿsè ün trèt sür nèⁿport
kèl bâⁿk frâⁿsèz.

At present there are restrictions on foreign securities and curren-cies; but I think you could cash in French money a draft on any French bank.

26 zhèmrè(z)ôsee fèr dᵉ lèksporta-
syôⁿ âⁿ türkee.

I should like also to do some ex-porting to Turkey.

---

14. *En* can also mean *of one* as it does here.   15. See lesson II, note 22.
16. INTERROGATIVE PRONOUN. For persons it is *qui*, subject; *qui*, object; *qui*, ob-ject of a preposition (translation *who* or *whom*). For things: *qu'est-ce qui*, subject; *que*, object; *quoi* object of preposition (translation *what*). For interrogative with antecedent, see note 13 above.   17. This is a technical use of *monnaie*. See lesson III, note 10.

NEUVIÈME LEÇON

Ninth Lesson

NOUVEAU VOCABULAIRE POUR CETTE LEÇON

mettre le couvert[1] (mètr^e l^e koovèr)	to set the table
saignant[2] (sèny$\hat{a}^n$)	rare
tout de suite[3] (tood süeet)	immediately
la pomme de terre[4] (pom d^e tèr)	potato
les pommes de terre en purée[5] ($\hat{a}^n$ püray)	mashed potatoes
la bisque de homard[6] (beesk d^e omar)	cream of lobster
le verre (vèr)	the glass
la tasse (tâs)	the cup
le filet (feelè)	the fillet
la carafe (karaf)	decanter
la salade (salad)	salad
la bouteille (bootèy)	bottle
le poivre (pwavr)	pepper
la moutarde (mootard)	mustard
la nappe (nap)	the tablecloth

glacé (glas*ay*)	iced
le plat (pla)	the course
le plateau (platô)	tray
la serviette (sèrvyèt)	napkin
le garçon (garsö^n)	waiter
le couteau (k*oo*tô)	the knife
la fourchette (*foo*rshèt)	the fork
la cuiller[3] (k*üee*yèr)	the spoon
une assiette (asyèt)	a plate
les poireaux, masc. (pwarô)	the leeks
l'assaisonnement, m. (asèzonmâ^n)	the seasoning
au contraire (ô kô^{n}trèr)	on the contrary
l'addition, fem. (ad*ee*syô^n)	bill
le café (kaf*ay*)	sidewalk restaurant
l'argenterie, fem. (lar*zh*â^{n}tr*ee*)	silverware
le poulet cocotte (p*oo*lè kokot)	chicken cooked in an earthenware dish

LE RESTAURANT · LA TABLE · LA NOURRITURE

(l^e restorâⁿ, la tabl, la nooreetür) · The Restaurant, the Table, the Food

le vinaigre (veenègr)	the vinegar
le sel (sèl)	salt
la laitue (lètü)	lettuce
la tomate (tomat)	tomato
le légume (laygüm)	vegetable
une omelette (omlèt)	an omelet
un appétit (apaytee)	an appetite

FOOTNOTES: *1.* Lit. *to put the cover.* *2. Saignant:* here an adjective but actually the present participle of *saigner,* to bleed. *3.* Note unusual pronunciation. *4.* Lit. *apple of the earth.* *5.* Lit. *potatoes in a thick sauce.* *6 Homard:* note *aspirate h* which is clearly indicated by the failure to make elision. *7.* An invariable adjective, *i.e.* vit does not change in feminine. *8.* Imperative form of the reflexive verb *s'asseoir.* The *vous* is direct pronoun object. With AFFIRMATIVE IMPERATIVE

le sucrier (sükree*ay*)	sugar bowl
le rognon (ro*nyô*ⁿ)	kidney
le pourboire (p*oo*rbwar)	tip
la carte du jour (kart dü zh*oo*r)	the menu (for the day)
le menu (mᵉnü)	menu
la carte des vins (kart d*ay* vè*ⁿ*)	wine list

only, pronoun objects come after verb and are attached to it by a hyphen. *9.* Very common idiom. *Venir de+infinitive* means *to have just . . .* Example: *Je viens de manger une omelette:* I have just eaten an omelet. *10.* In a passive construction many verbs take *de*, rather than *par*, in the sense of *by* or *with* when there is no action involved. *11.* Irregular adjective: *blanc*, masc.; *blanche*, fem. Color adjectives always come after their nouns. *12.* Observe that *que* is the

CONVERSATION

1 Voulez-vous me dire où je pourrai trouver un restaurant?

2 Sur le Boulevard Saint-Michel il y a plusieurs[7] restaurants où on mange bien.

3 Voudriez-vous m'accompagner?

4 Avec grand plaisir.

5 Asseyez-vous[8] à cette table. Le garçon vient de[9] mettre le couvert.

6 Cette table est couverte d'[10]une nappe blanche.[11]

7 Et qu'[12]est-ce qu'il y a sur la table?

8 Sur la table il y a l'argenterie: des fourchettes, des couteaux et des cuillers. Il y a aussi des serviettes, des assiettes, une carafe d'eau gla-cée et plusieurs verres.

9 Appelons le garçon.

10 Garçon, le menu et la carte des vins, s'il vous plaît.

11 Je désire une bisque de homard, un filet mignon[13] avec des pommes de terre en purée et des poireaux, et une salade.

12 Je n'aime pas la viande trop cuite.

13 On dit, n'est-ce pas, que la viande saignante est plus nour-rissante?

object of *il y a*, whereas in English it is a predicate nominative.   13. *Mignon*, masc., *mignonne*, fem., means *darling, pretty, delicate*. The term *filet mignon* is used also in English to designate a specially delicate cut of beef tenderloin. 14. See note 8 above. With AFFIRMATIVE IMPERATIVE, use disjunctive pronoun in first and second person singular. Otherwise pronoun objects have same form as

PRONUNCIATION

1 voolay voo m^e deer *oo zh^e* pooray troovay e^n rèstorâ^n?

2 sür l^e boolvar sè^n meesh$èl$ eelya plüzyè^{o}r rèstorâ^n oo ô^n mâ^{n}zh byè^n.

3 voodreeay voo makô^{n}pa$n$yay?
4 avèk grâ^n plèzeer.
5 asèyay voo a sèt tabl. l^e garsô^n vyè^n d^e mètr^e l^e koovèr.

6 sèt tabl è koovèrt dün nap blâ^{n}sh.
7 ay kèskeelya sür la tabl?
8 sür la tabl eelya larzhâ^{n}tree: day foorshèt, day kootô ay day küeeyèr. eelya ôsee day sèrvyèt, dayzasyèt, ün karaf dô glasay ay plüzyè^{o}r vèr.
9 aplô^n l^e garsô^n.
10 garsô^n, l^e m^{e}nü ay la kart day vè^n, seel voo plè.

11 zh^e dayzeer ün beesk d^e omar, e^n feelè meenyô^n avèk day pom d^e tèr â^n püray ay day pwarô, ay ün salad.
12 zh^e nèm pâ la vyâ^{n}d trô küeet.
13 ô^n dee, nès pâ, k^e la vyâ^{n}d sè$n$yâ^{n}t è plü nooreesâ^{n}t?

TRANSLATION

Will you (*lit.* are you willing) tell me where I can (*lit.* shall be able to) find a restaurant?

On Saint-Michel Boulevard there are several good restaurants (*lit.* where one eats well).

Would you like to accompany me?
With great pleasure.
Sit down (*lit.* seat yourself) at this table. The waiter has just set it (*lit.* comes from putting the cover).

This table is covered with a white tablecloth.
And what is on the table?
On the table is the silverware: forks, knives, and spoons. There are also napkins, plates, a decanter of ice water and several glasses.
Let's call the waiter.
Waiter, the menu and the wine list, please.

I wish some cream of lobster, a *filet mignon* with mashed potatoes and leeks, and a salad.
I do not like meat too well done (*lit.* cooked).
They say (*lit.* one says), don't they, that rare meat is more nourishing?

conjunctive pronoun objects which occur before verb. *15.* In compounds *demi* does not agree. But it does agree in *une heure et demie* where it is an adjective used as a noun. Any adjective used as a noun takes the gender of the noun which it replaces: *the red one* (assuming *one* to refer to *the book*) is in French *le rouge*. Note that in such an expression there is no word corresponding to the English *one*.

14 Apportez-moi[14] un poulet cocotte et une demi[15]-bouteille de vin rouge ordinaire.

15 Voulez-vous mettre du sel, de l'huile et du vinaigre sur votre salade?

16 A moins qu'elle ne soit[16] déjà assaisonnée.

17 Je n'ai pas d'[17]appétit parce que j'ai déjeuné assez tard, à onze heures, et j'aimerais une omelette aux rognons.

18 Ce plat est un peu salé.

19 Au contraire, je ne le trouve pas assez salé.

20 Voulez-vous bien me passer la cafetière? Je veux me servir du café dans cette tasse.

21 Voici le sucre, dans le sucrier.

22 Garçon, l'addition, s'il vous plaît. C'est combien?

23 Voici, monsieur; deux cent cinquante francs. Je vous apporte[18] la monnaie tout de suite.

24 Très bien. Laissons un pourboire au garçon.

25 Et après ce dîner succulent ne croyez-vous pas que nous devrions faire une promenade?[19]

26 Cela me plairait beaucoup.

----

16. PRESENT SUBJUNCTIVE of *être*. French subjunctive rarely corresponds to English subjunctive and no general rule governs its use. At the outset it is easier to note the specific cases in which the subjunctive *must* be used *automatically* in French. For example, certain conjunctions: *quoique* (although), *avant que* (before), *à moins que* (unless), *pour que* (so that), automatically take subjunctive. Furthermore *à moins que* requires a pleonastic (*i.e.* superfluous) *ne* which has no meaning whatever. There are several other constructions, not all of them subjunctive, in

14 aport*ay* mwa eⁿ pool*è* kokot *ay* ün d^emeeboot*èy* d^e vèⁿ roozh ordeenèr.

Bring me a *poulet cocote* and a half bottle of ordinary red wine.

15 vool*ay* voo mètr dü sèl, d^e l*üeel* *ay* dü veenègr sür votr^e salad?

Do you want to put some salt, oil and vinegar on your salad?

16 a mwèⁿ kèl n^e swa d*ayzha* asèzon*ay*.

Unless it is already seasoned.

17 zh^e n*ay* pâ dap*aytee* parsk^e zh*ay* d*ayzhè*^on*ay* as*ay* tar, a ôⁿz è^or, *ay* zhèmrè ün omlèt ô ron*yô*ⁿ.

I have no appetite because I breakfasted rather late, at eleven o'clock, and I should like a kidney omelet.

18 s^e pla èteⁿ pe^o sal*ay*.

This course is a little salty.

19 ô kôⁿtrèr, zh^e n^e l^e troov pâz-as*ay* sal*ay*.

On the contrary, I don't find it is salty enough.

20 vool*ay* voo byèⁿ m^e pâs*ay* la kaftyèr? zh^e veⁿ m^e oèrvoor dü kaf*ay* dâⁿ sèt tâs.

Will you kindly pass me the coffee pot? I want to serve myself some coffee in this cup.

21 vwas*ee* l^e sükr, dâⁿ l^e sükr*eeay*.

Here is the sugar, in the sugar bowl.

22 garsôⁿ, lad*ee*syôⁿ, s*eel* voo plè. sè kôⁿbyèⁿ?

Waiter, the bill, please. How much is it (*lit.* it is how much)?

23 vwas*ee*, m^esye^o; de^o sâⁿ sèⁿkâⁿt frâⁿ. zh^o voozapoit la monè tood süeet.

Here it is, sir; two hundred fifty francs. I will bring you the change immediately.

24 trè hyèⁿ. lèsôⁿ eⁿ poorbwar ô garsôⁿ.

Very good. Let's leave a tip for the waiter.

25 *ay* aprè s^e deen*ay* sükülâⁿ n^e krway*ay* voo pâ k^e noo d^evreeôⁿ fèr ün promnad?

And after this succulent dinner don't you think that we ought to take (*lit.* to make) a walk?

26 s^ela m^e plèrè bôk*oo*.

That would please me very much.

which *pleonastic "ne"* is required. *17.* SHORT PARTITIVE AFTER NEGATIVE VERB. Review first lesson II, notes *18* and *37* and lesson I, note *9. New rule:* after negative verb partitive construction consists only of *de*, not the usual *de* + *article*. *18.* Note special force of present here where English uses future. In a promise or a *threat* the present is used, rather than the future, to give greater vividness and inevitability to the idea. *19.* Idiom. Lit. *to make a walk.*

DIXIÈME LEÇON
Tenth Lesson

NOUVEAU VOCABULAIRE POUR CETTE LEÇON

meubler (mèᵒblay)	to furnish
choisir (*shwazeer*)	to choose
parfois (parfwa)	sometimes
quelquefois (kèlkᵉfwa)	sometimes
confortable (kôⁿfortabl)	comfortable
un invité (èⁿ*veetay*)	a guest
la banlieue (bâⁿlyeᵒ)	the suburbs
laver (lav*ay*)	to wash
la vaisselle (vèsèl)	the dishes
un escalier (èskaly*ay*)	a stairway
un ascenseur (asâⁿsèᵒr)	an elevator
la clef¹ (kl*ay*)	key
le jardin (*zh*ardèⁿ)	garden
la fontaine (fôⁿtèn)	fountain
la cour (k*oo*r)	(inner) court
la chambre à coucher³ (*shâ*ⁿbr a k*oosh*ay)	the bedroom
le rez-de-chaussée² (r*ay*d*sh*ôs*ay*)	ground floor
l'électricité, fem. (lay*l*èktr*eeseetay*)	electricity
allumer (alüm*ay*)	to light, turn light on
éteindre (*ay*tèⁿdr)	extinguish, turn light out

le miroir (meerwar)	the mirror
la table de toilette (tabl d^e twalèt)	dressing table
la glacière (glasyèr)	the refrigerator
la lampe (lâ^{n}p)	lamp
le tableau (tablô)	picture
la serviette (sèrvyèt)	towel
le matelas (matla)	mattress
le bois (bwa)	wood
un étage (aytazh)	a floor
la pièce (pyès)	room
le salon (salô^n)	living room
le cabinet (kabeenè)	the toilet
la baignoire (bènywar)	bath tub
la cuisine (küeezeen)	kitchen
un évier (ayvyay)	a kitchen sink
la porte (port)	dor
la feneêtre (f^{e}nètr)	window
le rideau (reedô)	curtain
le gaz (gâz)	gas
la lumière (lümyèr)	light

LA MAISON · LE MOBILIER
(la mèzôⁿ, lᵉ mobeelyay) · The House, the Furniture

le canapé *(kanapay)*	the sofa
la commode (komod)	bureau
le meuble (mĕᵒbl)	piece of furniture
une armoire (armwar)	a wardrobe
le tapis (tapee)	the rug
le lit (lee)	bed
la couverture (koovèrtür)	cover, blanket
le drap (dra)	sheet
un oreiller (orèyay)	a pillow
le fauteuil (fôtĕᵒy)	armchair
la chaise (shèz)	chair
la salle de bains (sal dᵉ bèⁿ)	bathroom
la cuisinière (küeezeenyèr)	kitchen range
la bibliothèque (beebleeotèk)	library

FOOTNOTES: *1.* Note unusual pronunciation. *2.* Lit. *on a level with the road.* In the European system the *first floor (premier étage)* is not the *ground floor (rez-de-chaussée)* but the first floor up, that is, the *second floor* in the American system. *3.* Lit. *the chamber for going to bed.* *4. Habiter* is used both transitively and intransitively, that is, with or without the preposition *dans. Demeurer,* meaning the

same thing, is intransitive only. 5. Idiom. 6. When the REFLEXIVE PRONOUN is used in apposition to another word, the reflexive is formed by taking the disjunctive pronoun and adding *même*. Observe that the word order is, in this case, the same as in the English. 7. *Aider* takes "à" to introduce a dependent infini-

CONVERSATION

1 J'habite[4] dans une ville. Où habitez-vous?

2 Nous habitons en banlieue.

3 Est-ce que votre maison a beaucoup d'étages?

4 Nous habitons[4] un immeuble à trois étages, c'est-à-dire sans compter le rez-de-chaussée.

5 Combien de pièces y a-t-il dans votre appartement?

6 Mon appartement est composé de sept pièces: le salon, la salle à manger, deux chambres à coucher, la cuisine, la salle de bains et la bibliothèque.

7 Est-ce qu'il faut monter l'escalier pour aller chez vous?

8 Pas du tout,[5] il y a un ascenseur.

9 Avez-vous meublé l'appartement vous-même?[6]

10 Oui, mais naturellement ma femme m'a aidé à[7] choisir le mobilier, qui est de style moderne.

11 Si cela ne vous dérange pas, j'aimerais beaucoup voir votre installation.

12 Au contraire, cela me ferait grand plaisir. Entrons d'abord dans[8] le salon.

13 Voici un canapé, deux fauteuils, plusieurs petites tables avec leurs lampes et une jolie collection de tableaux.

---

tive. See lesson I, note *15*.   *8. Entrer* is an intransitive verb and requires *dans: entrer dans,* to enter into.   *9.* See lesson VII, note *19*.   *10.* In a question *how* is *comment;* but in an exclamatory sentence *how* is *comme* followed by *normal*

PRONUNCIATION

1 zhabeet dâⁿzün veel. *oo* abeetay voo?

2 noozabeetôⁿ âⁿ bâⁿlyeᵒ.

3 èskᵉ votrᵉ mèzôⁿ a bôkoo daytazh?

4 noozabeetôⁿ eⁿneemèᵒbl a trwazaytazh, sètadeer sâⁿ kôⁿ-tay lᵉ raydshôsay.

5 kôⁿbyèⁿ dᵉ pyès *ee* ateel dâⁿ votr apartᵉmâⁿ?

6 monapartᵉmâⁿ è kôⁿpôzay dᵉ sèt pyès: lᵉ salôⁿ, la sal a mâⁿzhay, deᵒ shâⁿbr a kooshay, la küeezeen, la sal dᵉ bèⁿ ay la beebleeotèk.

7 èskeel fô môⁿtay lèskalyay poor alay shay voo?

8 pâ dü *too*, eelya eⁿnasâⁿsèᵒr.

9 avay voo mèᵒblay lapartᵉmâⁿ voomèm?

10 wee, mè natürèlmâⁿ ma fam ma èday a shwazeer lᵉ mobeelyay, kee è dᵉ steel modèrn.

11 see sᵉla nᵉ voo dayrâⁿzh pâ, zhèmrè bôkoo vwar votr eᵘ-stalasyôⁿ.

12 ô kôⁿtrèr, sᵉla mᵉ fᵉrè grâⁿ plèzeer. âⁿtrôⁿ dabor dâⁿ lᵉ salôⁿ.

13 vwasee eⁿ kanapay, deᵒ fôtèᵒy, plüzyèᵒr p(ᵉ)teet tabl avèk lèᵒr lâⁿp ay ün zholee kolèksyôⁿ dᵉ tablô.

TRANSLATION

I live in a city. Where do you live?

We live in the suburbs.

Does your house have many floors?

We live in a three-story apartment house, that is to say, without counting the ground floor.

How many rooms are there in your apartment?

My apartment is composed of seven rooms: the living room, the dining room, two bedrooms, the kitchen, the bathroom and the library.

Does one have to go up the stairs to go to your place?

Not at all, there is an elevator.

Did you furnish the apartment yourself?

Yes, but naturally my wife helped me to choose the furniture which is in modern style.

If it is no bother for you, I should like very much to see your establishment.

On the contrary, that would give me great pleasure. Let's enter the living room first.

Here are a sofa, two armchairs, several little tables with their lamps and a pretty collection of pictures.

---

declarative word order. Note literal translation of this expression. *11. Couverture* is feminine, but *drap* is masculine. Since, in case of conflict of gender, masculine predominates, *beaux* is masculine plural, inasmuch as it modifies both. *12.* If the

14 En effet. Et les meubles, comme vous pouvez voir, sont en[9] acajou, qui est un bois aussi beau que solide.

15 Quel est l'ameublement de la chambre à coucher?

16 Le lit, la commode, la table de toilette, l'armoire et la petite table de nuit sont en noyer. La table de toilette et la commode ont deux grands miroirs.

17 Est-ce que ce sont des tapis de Perse?

18 Non, ils sont de fabrication française, mais de bonne qualité.

19 Comme[10] le matelas de votre lit est confortable! Et les couvertures et les draps sont si beaux.[11]

20 Allons dans la salle à manger, s'il vous plaît. La table au centre est grande parce que nous avons parfois des[12] invités. Il y a, en tout, douze chaises et un buffet où[13] nous mettons le service de table et l'argenterie.

21 Comme votre cuisine est grande![10] Plus[14] je la regarde, plus je l'aime.

22 Vraiment! Elle est si spacieuse que nous y prenons parfois nos repas. Nous avons une glacière et une cuisinière électriques et un évier pour laver la vaisselle.

23 Est-ce que je peux voir la salle de bains?

24 Faites comme chez vous. Vous y trouverez du savon et des serviettes à gauche de la cuvette et à côté de la baignoire.

English equivalent of this word, *some*, were to be construed as *a few*, the translation would be *quelque*. See lesson VIII, sentence 5.   *13. Dans + relative pronoun*

14 âⁿnayfè. *ay lay* mèᵒbl, kom *voo* poovay vwar, sôⁿtâⁿnakazhoo, *kee* èteⁿ bwa ôsee bô kᵉ soleed.

To be sure. And the furniture, as you can see, is of mahogany, which is a wood both beautiful and strong (*lit.* as beautiful as strong).

15 kèlè lamèᵒblᵉmâⁿ dᵉ la *shâ*ⁿbr a *kooshay*?

What are the furnishings of the bedroom?

16 lᵉ *lee*, la komod, la tabl dᵉ twalèt, larmwar *ay* la p(ᵉ)*teet* tabl dᵉ *nüee* sôⁿtâⁿ nway*ay*. la tablᵉ dᵉ twalèt *ay* la komod ôⁿ deᵒ grâⁿ meerwar.

The bed, the bureau, the dressing table, the wardrobe and the little night table are of walnut. The dressing table and the bureau have two large mirrors.

17 èskᵉ sᵉ sôⁿ d*ay* tap*ee* dᵉ pèrs?

Are these Persian rugs?

18 nôⁿ, *eel* sôⁿ dᵉ fabreekasyôⁿ frâⁿsèz, mè dᵉ bon kal*eetay*.

No, they are of French manufacture, but of good quality.

19 kom lᵉ matla dᵉ votrᵉ *lee* è kôⁿfortabl! *ay lay* koovèrtür *ay lay* dra sôⁿ *see* bô.

How comfortable the mattress of your bed is (*lit.* how the mattress of your bed is comfortable)! And the covers and the sheets are so beautiful.

20 alôⁿ dâⁿ la sal a mâⁿ*zhay,* s*eel voo* plè. la tabl ô sâⁿtr è grâⁿd parskᵉ *noo*zavôⁿ parfwa d*ay*zèⁿv*eetay*. *eel*ya, âⁿ *too*, dooz shèz *ay* eⁿ büfè *oo noo* mètôⁿ lᵉ sèrvees dᵉ tabl *ay* larzhâⁿtree.

Let's go into the dining room, please. The table in the center is big because we sometimes have guests. There are, in all, twelve chairs and a buffet in which we put the table service and the silverware.

21 kom votrᵉ k*üee*zeen è grâⁿd! plü *zh*ᵉ la rᵉgard, plü *zh*ᵉ lèm.

How big your kitchen is! The more I look at it, the more I like it.

22 vrèmâⁿ! òlò *see* spasy*o*z kᵉ *noo*zee prᵉnôⁿ parfwa nô rᵉpâ. *noo*zavôⁿ ün glasyèr *ay* ün k*üee*zeenyèr *ay*lèktreek *ay* eⁿnayvy*ay* p*oor* lav*ay* la vèsèl.

Truly! It is so spacious that we sometimes take our meals in it. We have an electric refrigerator and range and a sink for washing the dishes.

23 èskᵉ *zh*ᵉ peᵒ vwar la sal dᵉ bèⁿ?

Can I see the bathroom?

24 fèt kom *shay voo.* v*oo*zee troovr*ay* dü savôⁿ *ay* d*ay* sèrvyèt a *gosh* dᵉ la küvèt *ay* a kôt*ay* dᵉ la bè*ny*war.

Make yourself at home (*lit.* do as in your house). You will find soap and towels to the left of the basin and beside the bathtub.

---

referring to thing (see lesson VIII, note *13*) is generally replaced by *où* (where).
14. Idiom: *plus ..., plus ... : the more ..., the more (the better) ...*

ONZIÈME LEÇON
Eleventh Lesson

Nouveau Vocabulaire Pour Cette Leçon

le courant d'air (koorâ^n dèr)	the draft
le souffle d'air (soofl^e dèr)	the breath of air
il fait du soleil (eel fè dü solèy)	the sun is shining
le temps est couvert (l^e tâ^n è koovèr)	the weather is cloudy
agréable (agra*y*abl)	agreeable, pleasant
s'approcher (de) (sapro*shay* d^e)	to draw near (to)
là-bas (labâ)	there, over there
le parapluie (parapl*üee*)	the umbrella
un imperméable (è^{n}pèrm*a*yabl)	a raincoat
les caoutchoucs[1], masc. (ka*ootshoo*)	the rubbers
la tempête (tâ^{n}pèt)	tempest, storm
l'humidité, f. (lüm*eedeetay*)	humidity
le thermomètre (tèrmomètr)	thermometer
brumeux, mas. (brüme^o)	foggy
brumeuse[2], fem. (brüme^oz)	foggy
il fait froid (frwa)	it is cold

attraper un rhume (atrapay e^n rüm)	to catch a cold
il fait beau (*eel* fè bô)	it is nice
il fait chaud (*eel* fè shô)	it is warm
indiquer (è^{n}deekay)	to indicate
la température (tâ^{n}püyratür)	temperature
centigrade (sâ^{n}teegrad)	centigrade
ressembler (r^{e}sâ^{n}blay)	to resemble
humide (ümeed)	humid
il fait humide (*eel* fè(t) ümeed)	it is humid
augmenter (ogmâ^{n}tay)	to increase, augment
craindre (krè^{n}dr)	to fear
je crains (*zh*^{e} krè^n)	I fear
fahrenheit (farènhaeet)	Fahrenheit
le souffle (soofl)	breath
le tonnerre (tonèr)	thunder
tonner (tonay)	to thunder

LE TEMPS QU'IL FAIT
(l^e tâⁿ keel fè) · The State of the Weather

il fait doux (doo)	it is mild
il fait du vent (vâ^n)	it is windy
étouffer (aytoofay)	to suffocate
il pleut (eel ple^o)	it is raining
à torrents (a torâ^n)	pouring
au-dessus (ôdsü)	above
au-dessous (ôdsoo)	below
en hausse (â^n ôs)	rising
en baisse (â^n bès)	dropping
approcher (aproshay)	to approach
le climat (kleema)	climate
la chaleur (shalè^{o}r)	heat
les éclairs, mas. (layzayklèr)	the lightning
il fait des éclairs (dayzayklèr)	there are flashes of lightning

FOOTNOTES: *1*. French uses the original Indian word. *2*. Adjectives ending in x in masculine singular form feminine by changing x to s and adding customary e. *3. Donc*, like *just* in English, is used to intensify the imperative. In other

un orage (ora*zh*)	a storm
la pluie (pl*üee*)	the rain
pleuvoir (pl*e*ºvwar)	to rain
la neige (nè*zh*)	the snow
neiger (nè*zhay*)	to snow
la glace (glas)	the ice
la boue (b*oo*)	mud
la gelée (*zh*(ᵉ)l*ay*)	frost
le baromètre (baromètr)	barometer
le degré (dᵉgr*ay*)	degree

senses it means *therefore*. *4.* The complete preposition is *au-dessous de* or *au-dessus de*. Without the *de* these are adverbs. *5.* Another function of the subjunctive (see lesson IX, note *16*). After many expressions of *emotion*, and particularly after

CONVERSATION

1 Quel temps fait-il?

2 Il fait un temps délicieux. Il fait très beau.

3 Ouvrez donc³ la fenêtre et voyez le temps qu'il fait.

4 Il fait beaucoup de soleil, mais il fait aussi très froid.

5 Qu'indique le thermomètre? Est-ce que la température est au-dessus⁴ ou au-dessous de zéro?

6 Le thermomètre indique quatre degrés au-dessous de zéro.

7 Je crois que nous allons avoir du mauvais temps; le baromètre indique la pluie.

8 Le baromètre est en hausse; je crains que nous ayons⁵ une tempête de neige.

9 Regardez comme il fait des éclairs! L'orage approche; il fait déjà beaucoup de vent. Il y a beaucoup de boue dans les rues.

10 Quelle est la température maximum⁶ en France?

11 D'⁷une façon générale le climat du nord de la France correspond à celui de New-York, mais il est plus doux.

12 Quel est le climat de la Bretagne?

13 En hiver il y fait souvent un temps brumeux comme en Angleterre; mais il ne pleut pas à torrents comme en Amérique.

---

expressions of *fearing*, noun clauses (a *noun* clause begins with *que* and serves as the object of a verb) require the subjunctive.   6. Note, exceptionally, all absence of adjectival agreement.   7. Idiom. Note that the preposition is *de* and not what English might suggest.   8. Note use of *de*. A similar expression is: *Le prix est*

PRONUNCIATION

1 kèl tâⁿ fɔteel?

2 eel fè(t)eⁿ tâⁿ dayleesyeᵒ. eel fè trè bô.

3 oovray dôⁿk la feⁿnètr ay vwaycy le tâⁿ keel fè.

4 eel fè bôkoo de solèy, mèzeel fè(t)ôsee trè frwa.

5 kèⁿdeek le tèrmomètr? eske la tâⁿpayratür etôdsü oo ôdsoo de zayrô?

6 le tèrmomètr èⁿdeek katre degray ôdsoo de zayrô.

7 zhe krwa ke noozalôⁿzavwar dü movè tâⁿ; le baromètr èⁿdeek la plüee.

8 le baromètr ètâⁿ ôs; zhe krèⁿ ke noozèyôⁿ(z)ün tâⁿpèt de nèzh.

9 regarday kom eel fè dayzayklèr! lorazh aprosh; eel fè dayzha bôkoo de vâⁿ. eclya bôkoo de boo dâⁿ lay rü.

10 kèl è la tâⁿpayratür makseemeⁿm âⁿ frâⁿs?

11 dün fasôⁿ zhaynayral le kleema dü nor de la frâⁿs korèspôⁿ a selüee de nooyork, mèzeel è plü doo.

12 kèl è le kleema de la bretany?

13 âⁿneevèr eel ee fè soovâⁿ eⁿ tâⁿ brümeᵒ kom âⁿnâⁿgletèr; mèzeel ne pleᵒ pâza torâⁿ kom âⁿnamayrcek.

TRANSLATION

What is the weather (like)?

The weather is delightful. It is very fine.

Just open the window and see what the weather is like.

There is a great deal of sun, but it is also very cold.

What does the thermometer say? Is the temperature above or below zero?

The thermometer shows four degrees below zero.

I think we are going to have some bad weather; the barometer indicates rain.

The barometer is rising; I am afraid that we may have a snow storm.

Look how the lightning is flashing! The storm is approaching; there is already much wind. There is a lot of mud in the streets.

What is the maximum temperature in France?

In a general way the climate of the north of France corresponds to that of New York, but it is milder.

What is the climate of Brittany?

In winter it is often foggy there as in England; but the rain does not pour down as in America.

---

de *vingt-cinq francs*: The price is twenty-five francs. *9. Ressembler* is an INTRANSITIVE VERB and requires "*à*" to introduce object. *10.* DEMONSTRATIVE PRONOUN: *celui*, masc., *celle*, fem. (this, this one, that, that one); *ceux*, masc. pl., *celles*, fem. pl. (these, those). *11.* This is the same impersonal *il* which is

14 Sur la Côte d'Azur la température est souvent de[8] vingt ou vingt-cinq degrés centigrade[6] même en hiver. C'est un climat qui ressemble[9] à celui[10] de la Floride.

15 En hiver, ce doit être très agréable là-bas.

16 Est-ce que vous croyez qu'il va pleuvoir?

17 Le temps est couvert, mais je crois qu'il fait trop froid pour la pluie. Il[11] va geler très probablement et le temps est à l'orage.[12]

18 En effet, il neige déjà. Vous devriez mettre votre imperméable, car un parapluie ne vous serait pas très utile.

19 Avez-vous des caoutchoucs?

20 Il n'a pas fait si froid pendant tout l'hiver.

21 Croyez-vous qu'il fasse[13] trop chaud pour cette saison?

22 La chaleur est étouffante. Il n'y a pas un souffle d'air.

23 Ici il fait très humide et l'humidité ne fait[14] qu'augmenter la chaleur aussi bien que le froid.

---

found in *il faut, il fait mauvais, il neige.* Compare this with *ce* in sentence *15* above where the word *it*, although indefinite, still has a vague antecedent. 12. Idiom. Also expressed as *à la pluie.* 13. Present subjunctive of *faire.* This is still another application of the subjunctive. After expression of *doubt* a noun

14 sür la kôt dazür la tân$_p$ayratür è soovân d^e vè^n oo vè^{n}tsè^n d^{e}gray sân$_t$eegrad mèm ân$_n$eevèr. sète^n kleema kee r^{e}sân$_b$l a s^{e}lüee d^e la floreed.

15 ân$_n$eevèr, s^e dwatètr^e trèzagrayabl labâ.

On the French Riviera the temperature is often twenty or twenty-five degrees centigrade even in winter. It is a climate which resembles that of Florida.

In winter, it must be very pleasant there.

16 èsk^e voo krwayay keel va plè^{o}vwar?

17 l^e tâ^n è koovèr, mè zh^e krwa keel fè trô frwa poor la plüee. eel va zh^{e}lay trè probabl^{e}mâ^n ay l^e tâ^n èta lorazh.

18 ân$_n$ayfè, eel nèzh dayzha. voo d^{e}vreeay mètr votr è^{n}pèrmayabl, kar e^n paraplüee n^e voo s^{e}rè pâ trèzüteel.

19 avay voo day kaootshoo?

20 eel na pâ fè see frwa pâ^{n}dâ^n too leevèr.

Do you think it is going to rain?

It is cloudy, but I think it is too cold for rain. It is going to freeze very probably and it is stormy.

In fact, it is snowing already. You ought to put (on) your raincoat, for an umbrella would not be very useful to you.

Have you rubbers?

It hasn't been so cold all winter long (*lit.* during all the winter).

21 krwayay voo keel fâs trô shô poor sèt sèzô^n?

22 la shalè^{o}r ètaytoofâ^{n}t. eelnya pâze^n soofl^e dèr.

23 eesee eel fè trèzümeed ay lümeedeetay n^e fè kôgmâ^{n}tay la shalè^{o}r ôsee byè^n k^e l^e frwa.

Do you think that it is too hot for this season?

The heat is stifling. There is not a breath of air.

Here it is very damp and the dampness only increases the heat as well as the cold.

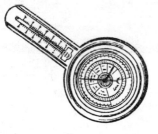

---

clause requires subjunctive. *Croire,* in the interrogative, counts as an expression of doubt.   *14.* Note translation. If, in the English, the word *only* modifies the verb, the verb of the English becomes a dependent infinitive in the formula *il ne fait que* + *infinitive.* Example: He only goes: *il ne fait qu'aller.*

DOUZIÈME LEÇON
Twelfth Lesson

Nouveau Vocabulaire Pour Cette Leçon

actuel, masc.	present
actuelle, fem. (akt*üè*l)	present
une étoffe (*a*ytof)	a material
la mode (mod)	the fashion, style
le ruban (rübâ^n)	the ribbon
précisément (pr*ayseezay*mâ^n)	precisely
porter (port*ay*)	to carry; to wear; to bear
ajuster (a*zh*üst*ay*)	to adjust
ajusté	close fitting
étroit (*a*ytrwa)	tight
la couture (k*oo*tür)	the seam, sewing
coudre (k*oo*dr)	to sew
couper (k*oo*p*ay*)	to cut
avoir la bonté de (avwar la bô^{n}t*ay* d^e)	to have the goodness to
neuf, masc. (nè^{o}f)	new
neuve[1], fem. (nè^{o}v)	new
flottant (flotâ^n)	loose
le patron (patrô^n)	the pattern
la garniture (garn*ee*tür)	the trimming

essayer (aysèyay)	to try, try on
mettre (mètr)	to put, put on
la dentelle (dâ^{n}tèl)	the lace
la broderie (brodree)	embroidery
la taille (tay)	waist
la ceinture (sè^{n}tür)	belt, waist (of body)
les ciseaux, masc. (seezô)	scissors
le crêpe (krèp)	crepe
la bonté (bô^{n}tay)	goodness
le veston (vèstô^n)	jacket, lounge coat
le mètre (mètr)	the meter
le tailleur (taye^{o}r)	the tailor
varier (varyay)	to vary
couvrir (koovreer)	to cover
employer (â^{n}plwayay)	to use, employ
ajouter (azhootay)	to add
la manche (mâ^{n}sh)	the sleeve
une variété (varyaytay)	a variety

LE TAILLEUR · LA MODISTE · LA MODE
(l^e taye^{o}r, la mod*ee*st, la mod) · The Tailor, the Dressmaker, the Style

le coton (kotô^n)	the cotton
la rayonne (rèyon)	rayon
le velours (v^{e}l*oo*r)	velvet
la soie (swâ)	silk
la flanelle (flanèl)	flannel
le bouton (b*oo*tô^n)	button
le corsage (korsa*zh*)	blouse
le col (kol)	collar
la mesure (m^{e}zür)	measure
une aiguille (ègü*ee*y)	a needle
le fil (f*ee*l)	the thread
la machine à coudre	the sewing machine
(ma*sh*een a k*oo*dr)	

FOOTNOTES: *1.* Adjectives ending in *f* change *f* to *v* before adding feminine ending *e. 2.* The adjective *actuel* is usually translated *present, present-day,* not as *actual.* Similarly the adverb *actuellement* means *now, at present,* and not *actually. 3. Dont* takes the place of *de+relative pronoun* referring either to a person or a thing. For that reason it will also frequently translate the English *whose. 4.* As

an ADVERB OF QUANTITY *bien* is interchangeable with *beaucoup,* but normally it takes after it a complete partitive, whereas *beaucoup* takes only *de.* Here, because of the adjective *autres, bien* also takes short partitive. 5. *Se connaître en*: idiom: *to know all about.* Note carefully this reflexive form of the verb. 6. *A l'aide de;*

CONVERSATION

1 Mademoiselle Duchâtel, auriez-vous la bonté de nous dire de combien de pièces se compose une robe de femme?

2 D'ordinaire elle se compose de deux pièces: le corsage et la jupe. Mais il y a aussi des robes en une seule pièce.

3 Très bien, Mademoiselle, et la partie de la robe qui couvre le bras s'appelle comment?

4 Elle s'appelle la manche. Le haut de la robe s'appelle le col et la partie ajustée à la ceinture s'appelle la taille.

5 Quelle est la mode actuelle² pour les manches?

6 Pour les manches la mode varie souvent. Parfois on les porte assez courtes ou bien assez longues; d'autres fois elles sont larges ou bien étroites.

7 De quoi est-ce que les robes sont faites?

8 Il y a une grande variété d'étoffes dont³ on peut les faire, mais les plus employées sont la soie, le crêpe, la rayonne, la flanelle, la toile, le coton, le velours et bien⁴ d'autres encore.

9 Vous vous connaissez⁵ en couture, n'est-ce pas?

10 Oui, monsieur, assez bien pour faire mes robes moi-même à l'aide⁶ d'un patron.

11 Voudriez-vous nous dire comment se fait une robe?

---

idiom: *with the help of.*   7. See lesson III, note 22.   8. From the irregular verb *coudre.*   9. *Soit . . . soit:* either . . . or. The *soit* is actually present subjunctive of *être* and means *be it.*   10. See lesson VII, note 16.   11. See lesson IX, note

PRONUNCIATION

1 madmwazèl düs*h*âtèl, ôree*ay*
voo la bôⁿt*ay* dᵉ noo deer dᵉ
kôⁿbyèⁿ dᵉ pyès sᵉ kôⁿpôz ün
rob dᵉ fam?

2 dordeenèr èl sᵉ kôⁿpôz dᵉ deᵒ
pyès: lᵉ korsa*zh* *ay* la *zh*üp.
mèzeelya ôsee d*ay* rob âⁿnün
sᵉᵒl pyès.

3 trè byèⁿ, madmwazèl, *ay* la
part*ee* dᵉ la rob kee koovrᵉ lᵉ
brâ sapèl komâⁿ?

4 èl sapèl la mâⁿ*sh*. lᵉ ô dᵉ la rob
sapèl lᵉ kol *ay* la part*ee*
a*zh*üst*ay* a la sèⁿtür sapèl la
tay.

5 kèl è la mod aktüèl poor l*ay*
mâⁿ*sh*?

6 poor l*ay* mâⁿ*sh* la mod var*ee*
soovâⁿ. parⁱwa ôⁿ l*ay* port
as*ay* koort oo byèⁿ as*ay* lôⁿg;
dôtrᵉ fwa èl sôⁿ lar*zh* oo byèⁿ
*ay*trwat.

7 dᵉ kwa èskᵉ l*ay* rob sôⁿ fèt?

8 eelya ün grâⁿd varee*ay*t*ay*
d*ay*tof dôⁿtôⁿ peᵒ l*ay* fèr, mè
l*ay* plüzâⁿplway*ay* sôⁿ la swâ,
lᵉ krèp, la rèyon, la flanèl, la
twal, lᵉ kotôⁿ, lᵉ vᵉloor *ay* byèⁿ
dôtr âⁿkor.

9 voo voo konès*ay* âⁿ kootür,
nès pâ?

10 wee, mᵉsyeᵒ, as*ay* byèⁿ poor
fèr m*ay* rob mwamèm a lèd
deⁿ patrôⁿ.

11 voodree*ay* voo noo deer komâⁿ
sᵉ fè ün rob?

TRANSLATION

Miss Duchâtel, would you be good
enough to tell us of how many
pieces a woman's dress is composed?

Ordinarily it is composed of two
pieces: the blouse and the skirt.
But there are also some dresses
in a single piece.

Very good, Miss (Duchâtel), and
the part of the dress which covers the arm is called what?

It is called the sleeve. The top of
the dress is called the collar and
the part fitted to the waistline is
called the waist.

What is the present style for
sleeves?

For the sleeves the style often
varies. Sometimes they are worn
rather short or else rather long;
other times they are wide or else
narrow.

Of what are dresses made?

There is a great variety of materials of which they can be made,
but the most used are silk, crepe,
rayon, flannel, linen, cotton, velvet and still many others.

You know all about sewing, don't
you?

Yes, sir, well enough (lit. enough
well) to make my dresses myself with the aid of a pattern.

Would you tell us how a dress is
made?

14. *12.* The SUPERLATIVE FORM of the adjective is made with definite article and
plus. If the superlative is placed after the noun, as it must be when the adjective
is one which must follow, there may even be two articles with the noun. Example:

12 Avec plaisir. D'abord, il vous faut[7] trois mètres ou plus d'étoffe, que vous coupez avec des ciseaux d'après le patron et les mesures, et ensuite vous la cousez[8] avec du fil et une aiguille, soit[9] à la main, soit à la machine.

13 Après cela je suppose que vous essayez la robe pour voir si elle vous va.

14 Précisément; et alors vous ajoutez la garniture qui consiste en dentelle, broderie, rubans et boutons de couleur.

15 Quand est-ce que votre mari aura besoin de cet argent?

16 Il en aura besoin immédiatement, car il doit s'[10]acheter un costume aujourd'hui.

17 Où a-t-il l'intention de faire faire son costume?

18 Chez le tailleur au coin de l'Avenue de l'Opéra et la rue Molière. Monsieur Clément est un bon tailleur.

19 Alors, allons-y[11]. Voici votre mari.

20 Bonjour, Monsieur Clément. Je désire me faire faire un costume.

21 Voulez-vous bien me montrer vos tissus les[12] plus neufs?

22 Je veux un costume sur mesure, car les costumes tout[13] faits ne me vont jamais très bien.

---

les livres *les* plus neufs: the newest books. But with a preceding adjective there is only one article. Example: *les* plus beaux livres, *the finest books.*   13. When it modifies an adjective *tout* is an adverb and does not agree except when the adjective is feminine and begins with a consonant (Example: *une réponse toute faite,*

12 avèk plèzeer. dabor, eel voo fô trwa mètr oo plü(s) daytof, k^e voo koopay avèk day seezô daprè l^e patrô^n ay lay m^ezür, ay â^nsüeet voo la koozay avèk dü feel ay ün ègüeey, swa(t)a la mè^n, swa(t)a la masheen.

With pleasure. First you need three meters or more of cloth, which you cut with scissors according to the pattern and the measurements, and then you sew it with needle and thread (*lit.* some thread and a needle), either by hand or with a machine.

13 aprè s^ela zh^e süpôz k^e voozayseyay la rob poor vwar see èl voo va.

After that I suppose that you try on the dress to see if it fits you.

14 prayseezaymâ^n; ay alor voozazhootay la garneetür kee kô^nseest â^n dâ^ntèl, brodree, rübâ^n ay bootô^n d^e koolè^or.

Precisely; and then you add the trimming which consists of lace, embroidery, ribbons and colored buttons (*lit.* buttons of color).

15 kâ^ntèsk^e votr^e maree ôra b^ezwè^n d^e sètarzhâ^n?

When will your husband need this money?

16 eel â^nnôra b^ezwè^n eemaydyatmâ^n, kar eel dwa sashtay e^n kostüm ôzhoordüee.

He will need it immediately, for he must buy himself a suit today.

17 oo ateel lè^ntâ^nsyô^n d^e fèr fèr sô^n kostüm?

Where does he intend to have his suit made?

18 shay l^e tayè^or ô kwè^n d^e lavnü d^e lopayra uy la rü molyèr. m^esye^o klaymâ^n ète^n bô^n tayè^or.

At the tailor's on the corner of the Avenue of the Opera and Molière Street. Mr. Clément is a good tailor.

19 alor, alô^nzee. vwasee votr^e maree.

Then, let's go there. Here is your husband.

20 bô^nzhoor, m^esye^o klaymâ. zh^e dayzeer m^e fèr fèr e^n kostüm.

Good day, Mr. Clément. I want to have a suit made for myself.

21 voolay voo byè^n m^e mô^ntray vô teesü lay plü nè^of?

Will you please show me your newest materials?

22 zh^e ve^o(z)e^n kostüm sür m^ezür, kar lay kostüm too fè n^e m^e vô^n zhamè trè byè^n.

I want a tailored suit (*lit.* a suit according to measure), for ready-made suits (*lit.* all made) never fit me very well.

a ready-made answer). *14.* Verbs ending -oyer and -uyer change y to i anywhere in the conjugation that they occur before a mute e. The e of the er infinitive used as the stem for the future or conditional is considered to be a mute e also. In -ayer verbs the change from y to i is optional. *15.* Idiom.

23 Permettez-moi[11] de prendre vos mesures. Voulez-vous le veston flottant ou ajusté?

24 Je le préfère flottant et confortable, et n'oubliez pas que j'en ai besoin pour la semaine prochaine.

25 J'essaierai[14] de l'avoir prêt pour vous sans faute mardi ou mercredi au plus tard.[15]

23 pèrmètay mwa de prândre vô mezür. voolay voo le vèstôn flotân oo azhüstay?

Allow me to take your measurements. Do you want the jacket loose (*lit.* floating) or tight?

24 zhe le prayfèr flotân ay kôn-fortabl, ay noobleeay pâ ke zhânnay bezwèn poor la semèn proshèn.

I prefer it loose and comfortable, and don't forget that I need it for next week.

25 zhaysèray de lavwar prè poor voo sân fôt mardee oo mèr-kredee ô plü tar.

I shall try to have it ready for you without fail Tuesday or Wednesday at the latest.

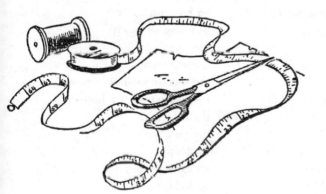

TREIZIÈME LEÇON
Thirteenth Lesson

NOUVEAU VOCABULAIRE POUR CETTE LEÇON

la pellicule (pèleekül)	film (negative)
la voiture (vwatür)	car (automobile)
se laver (s^e lav*ay*)	to wash (oneself)
s'habiller (sab*ee*yay)	dress (oneself)
se promener (s^e promn*ay*)	go for a walk, a ride
tant de (tâⁿ d^e)	so many, so much
la plage (pla*zh*)	the beach
le bord de la mer (bor d^e la mèr)	the seashore
le film (*f*eelm)	the motion picture
le cinéma (seen*ay*ma)	the motion picture house
le véhicule (v*ay*eekül)	the vehicle
le piéton (py*ay*tôⁿ)	the pedestrian
dormir (dorm*eer*)	to sleep
s'endormir (sâⁿdorm*eer*)	go to sleep
se coucher (s^e koo*shay*)	go to bed
se lever (s^e l^ev*ay*)	get up, rise
s'asseoir (saswar)	sit down
présenter (pr*ay*zâⁿt*ay*)	present

le bord (bor)	the edge
la place (plas)	the square
le trottoir (trotwar)	the sidewalk
le coin (kwè^n)	corner
une église (*aygleez*)	a church
le théâtre (t*ayâtr*)	the theater
le courrier (k*ooryay*)	mail
les gens, masc. (*lay zha^n*)	people

EN VILLE[1] (ân veel) · In Town

une école (aykol)	a school
le parc (park)	the park
un édifice (aydeefees)	a building
un hôpital (e^{n}nôpeetal)	hospital
le café (kafay)	the sidewalk café
la mairie (mèree)	town hall
la banque (bâ^{n}k)	bank
le marché (marshay)	market
le douanier (dwanyay)	the customs officer
la douane (dwan)	the customs house
un habitant (e^{n}nabeetâ^n)	an inhabitant
la connaissance (konèsâ^{n}s)	the acquaintance
l'amabilité, fem. (lamabeeleetay)	kindness
le bureau de poste (bürô d^e post)	the post office
un agent de police (azhâ^n d^e polees)	a policeman
un hôtel de ville (e^{n}nôtèl d^e veel)	city hall
le palais de justice (palè d^e zhüstees)	the court house
la préfecture (prayfèktür)	departmental capitol
la préfecture de police	police headquarters
la t.s.f. [télégraphic sans fil] (la tayèsèf)	radio
le poste de t.s.f. (post de tayèsèf)	radio set
la télévision (taylayveezyô^n)	television

CONVERSATION

1 A quelle heure vous êtes-vous[2] couché[3] hier soir puisque vous dormez encore?

2 Je me suis couché très tard et j'ai trop[4] dormi.

3 Je n'ai pas[5] pu m'endormir avant quatre heures du matin.

4 Ma bonne ne m'a pas appelé et je viens[6] de me réveiller.

5 Asseyez-vous, je vous en[7] prie; je vais me lever, me laver et m'habiller tout de suite.

6 Bien, je suis tout prêt, et je suis à vos ordres.

7 Partons quand vous voudrez.[8]

8 Où voulez-vous que nous allions?[9]

9 Si vous voulez, nous irons nous promener[10] au Bois de Boulogne.

10 J'aimerais mieux visiter des édifices publics tels[11] qu'une école, un bureau de poste, un marché, une église ou l'hôtel de ville.

11 Quelle idée magnifique! Et après nous irons au théâtre ou au cinéma. Sur cette place il y a un cinéma où on montre les meilleurs[12] films.

12 Plus je visiterai d'[13] édifices, mieux je connaîtrai la ville.

FOOTNOTES: *1.* La ville, *the town, the city,* pronounced veel, does not have the usual liquid *ll.* *2.* To invert compound tense, place pronoun subject after auxiliary. *3.* In all compound tenses reflexive verbs are conjugated with *être.*

PRONUNCIATION	TRANSLATION
1 a kèl è^{o}r voozèt voo kooshay yèr swar püeesk^{e} voo dormay â^{n}kor?	(At) what time did you go to bed last night (*lit.* evening) since you are still asleep?
2 zh^{e} m^{e} süee kooshay trè tar ay zhay trô dormee.	I went to bed very late and I slept too much.
3 zh^{e} nay pâ pü mâ^{n}dormeer avâ^{n} katr è^{o}r dü matè^{n}.	I wasn't able to go to sleep before four o'clock in the morning.
4 ma bon n^{e} ma pâzaplay ay zh^{e} vyè^{n} d^{e} m^{e} rayvèyay.	My maid didn't call me and I have just awakened.
5 asèyay voo, zh^{e} voozâ^{n} pree; zh^{e} vay m^{e} l^{e}vay, m^{e} lavay ay mabeeyay tood süeet.	Sit down, I beg of you; I am going to get up, wash and dress immediately.
6 byè^{n}, zh^{e} süee too prè, ay zh^{e} süeeza vôzordr.	Good, I am all ready, and I am at your orders.
7 partô^{n} kâ^{n} voo voodray.	Let's leave when you wish.
8 oo voolay voo k^{e} noozalyô^{n}?	Where do you wish us to go (*lit.* that we go)?
9 see voo voolay, noozeerô^{n} noo promnay ô bwa d^{e} boolony.	If you wish, we shall go take a walk in the Wood of Boulogne.
10 zhèmrè mye^{o} veezeetay daydaydeefees pübleek tèl kün aykol, e^{n} bürô d^{e} post, e^{n} marshay, ün aygleez oo lôtèl d^{e} veel.	I should prefer to visit some public buildings such as a school, a post office, a market, a church or the city hall.
11 kèl eeday manyeefeek! ay aprè noozeerô^{n} ô tayâtr oo ô seenayma. sür sèt plas eelya e^{n} seenayma oo ô^{n} mô^{n}tr lay mèyè^{o}r feelm.	What (a) magnificent idea! And afterwards we shall go to the theater or to the movies. On this square there is a moving picture house where the best films are shown.
12 plü zh^{e} veezeetray daydeefees, mye^{o} zh^{e} konètray la veel.	The more buildings I visit (*lit.* shall visit), the better I shall know the city.

4. In a compound tense adverb goes after auxiliary. Exception: time adverbs like *demain, aujourd'hui, hier* which follow the past participle. 5. To make a compound tense negative, place *ne ... pas* around auxiliary. 6. *Venir de* means *to have*

13 C'est merveilleux de voir un agent de police régler[14] la circulation. Il y a tant de véhicules dans les rues et tant de piétons sur les trottoirs et les passages cloutés[15] qu'il[16] doit être difficile de régler tout cela.

14 Paris a beaucoup d'habitants et avec ses larges avenues bordées d'arbres et ses nombreux parcs il rappelle la capitale américaine qui est pourtant moins grande et moins pittoresque.

15 Je dois aller à la banque pour faire changer mes dollars.

16 Le change est très défavorable. Je regrette de[17] ne[18] pouvoir[19] vous accompagner. Je vous attendrai chez le couturier.

17 Est-ce que vous auriez l'amabilité de me présenter à cette dame avant de partir?

18 Avec plaisir; je vais vous présenter tout de suite.

19 Ma chère amie, je voudrais vous présenter Madame Yvonnec.

20 Madame, je suis enchantée de faire votre connaissance.

21 Et moi aussi, Madame, car j'ai souvent entendu parler[20] de vous.

22 Allez-vous rester longtemps en ville?

just. 7. In this idiom, *en* means *de le faire:* to do it. 8. After *quand* (when) and *lorsque* (when), if the main verb of the sentence is future or imperative, verb of this clause will also be future. 9. Present subjunctive of *aller*. Subjunctive is required in noun clauses depending on an expression of *willing*. 10. *Se promener*

13 sè mèrvèye⁰ dᵉ vwar eⁿnazhâⁿ
dᵉ polees *rayglay* la seerkü-
lasyôⁿ. *eelya* tâⁿ dᵉ *vayeekül*
dâⁿ *lay* rü *ay* tâⁿ dᵉ *pyaytôⁿ*
sür *lay* trotwar *ay lay* pasa*zh*
k*lootay* keel dwatètrᵉ *deefeeseel*
dᵉ *rayglay too* sᵉla.

It is wonderful to see a policeman
control the traffic. There are so
many vehicles in the streets and
so many pedestrians on the side-
walks and the pedestrian crossings that it must be difficult to
control all that.

14 par*ee* a bôk*oo* dabeetâⁿ *ay* avèk
s*ay* lar*zhᵉ*zavnü bord*ay* darbr
ay say nôⁿbre⁰ park *eel* rapèl
la kapeetal ama*y*reekèn *kee* è
poortâⁿ mwèⁿ grâⁿd *ay* mwèⁿ
peetorèsk.

Paris has many inhabitants and
with its broad avenues bordered
with trees and its numerous
parks it reminds one of (*lit.* re-
calls) the American capital
which is, however, less big and
less picturesque.

15 *zh*ᵉ dwazal*ay* a la bâⁿk *poor*
fèr *shâⁿzhay may* dolar.

I must go to the bank to have my
dollars changed.

16 lᵉ *shâⁿzh* è trò d*ay*favorabl. *zh*ᵉ
rᵉgrèt dᵉ nᵉ *poo*vwar *voo*za-
kôⁿpa*nyay. zh*ᵉ *voo*zatâⁿdr*ay*
sh*ay* lᵉ kootüry*ay*.

The exchange is very unfavorable.
I regret that I cannot (*lit.* not
being able to) accompany you.
I shall wait for you at the dressmaker's.

17 èskᵉ *voo*zôr*yay* lamabeeleet*ay*
dᵉ mᵉ pr*ay*zâⁿt*ay* a sèt dam
avâⁿ dᵉ parteer?

Would you be kind enough to introduce me to that lady before
leaving?

18 avèk plèzeer; *zh*ᵉ v*ay voo*
pr*ay*zâⁿt*ay* t*oo*d süeet.

With pleasure; I am going to introduce you right away.

19 ma *shèr* am*ee, zh*ᵉ *voo*drè *voo*
pr*ay*zâⁿt*ay* madam eevonèk.

My dear (friend), I should like to
present to you Mrs. Yvonnec.

20 madam, *zh*ᵉ süeezâⁿsh*âⁿtay* dᵉ
fèr votrᵉ konèsâⁿs.

Madame, I am delighted to make
your acquaintance.

21 *ay* mwa ôs*ee*, madam, kar *zhay*
soovâⁿ âⁿtâⁿdü parl*ay* dᵉ *voo*.

And I too, Madame, for I have
often heard of you.

22 al*ay voo* rèst*ay* lôⁿtâⁿ âⁿ veel?

Are you going to remain in town
long?

---

is synonymous with *faire une promenade.* 11. *Such,* in the phrase *such as,* is an
adjective and therefore agrees. With the noun, English says *such a,* French *a such:*
un tel homme: a such man. 12. The irregular adjective *bon* has the comparative
meilleur and the superlative *le meilleur.* The adverb *bien* is compared: *bien, mieux,*

23 Pas longtemps, car je compte passer l'été au bord de la mer. On m'a dit que Deauville a de belles plages.

24 Et aussi beaucoup de divertissements. J'y vais aussi et cela[21] me plairait beaucoup de[22] vous servir de[23] guide.

25 Vous êtes bien aimable et je vous serai très reconnaissante.

26 Je serai à votre service et, en attendant,[24] je vous souhaite un bon voyage.

27 Au revoir,[25] Madame. A bientôt.[26]

le mieux.   13. The de is used here because of the adverb of quantity plus. 14. This use of the infinitive is exceptional in French and is possible only after a few verbs such as voir and entendre. It is impossible to translate with an infinitive: I want John to come; this must be expressed: Je veux que Jean vienne: I want that John come. With verbs which have an indirect object and which introduce their dependent infinitive with de, an infinitive construction must be used; example: Je demande à Jean de venir: I ask (to) John to come.   15. Passage clouté: literally: a nailed passage. So called because of the French method of marking pedestrian crossings with large brass knobs in the pavement.   16. Generally il is used in the formula it + to be + adjective + de + infinitive + object. Example: Il est facile de faire cela. Ce is used in the formula it + to be + adjective + à + infinitive. Example: C'est facile à faire. Note exceptional usage in: C'est merveilleux de voir un agent.   17. Regretter takes de to introduce a

23 pâ lôⁿtâⁿ, kar *zh*^e kôⁿt pâs*ay laytay* ô bor d^e la mèr. ôⁿ ma *dee* k^e dô*veel* a d^e bèl pla*zh*.

Not long, for I expect to spend the summer at the seashore (*lit.* at the edge of the sea). I have been told that Deauville has beautiful beaches.

24 *ay* ôsee bôkoo d^e deevèrteesmâⁿ. *zhee vay* ôsee *ay* s^ela m^e plèrè bôk*oo* d^e *voo* sèrveer d^e geed.

And also many amusements. I am going there too and it would give me great pleasure to be a guide for you (*lit.* to serve you as a guide).

25 voozèt byèⁿnèmabl *ay zh*^e *voo* s^eray trè r^ekonèsâⁿt.

You are very kind and I shall be very grateful to you.

26 *zh*^e s^eray a votr^e sèrvees *ay*, âⁿnatâⁿdâⁿ, *zh*^e *voo* swèt eⁿ bôⁿ vwaya*zh*.

I shall be at your service and, meanwhile, I wish you a good trip.

27 ô r(^e)vwar, madam. a byèⁿtô.

Good-bye, Madame. See you soon.

---

dependent infinitive. *18. Pouvoir* can be made negative with only *ne*. Ordinarily an infinitive is made negative by placing both *ne* and *pas* before the infinitive. Example: *Je lui demande de ne pas le faire:* I ask him *not* to do it. *19.* English will read: *I regret I am unable.* When subject of noun clause is same as subject of main verb, French will prefer to use an infinitive to avoid repeating same subject. This is especially necessary if a subjunctive is thereby to be avoided. Modern French never uses subjunctive when it can avoid it. *20.* Idiom: *entendre parler de quelqu'un:* to hear of someone (*lit.* to hear speak of someone). *21.* See lesson VII, note 17. *22. Plaire* takes *de* to introduce infinitive. *23. Servir de:* idiom: *to serve as.* Person served is indirect object. *24.* Idiom: *meanwhile* (lit. *while waiting*). *25.* Idiom. *26. A bientôt.* Similar to *à demain, à lundi:* until tomorrow, until Monday. Means: *until soon.*

QUATORZIÈME LEÇON
Fourteenth Lesson

NOUVEAU VOCABULAIRE POUR CETTE LEÇON

la sonnette (sonèt)	the bell (small bell)
se dépêcher (s^e d$a$ypèsh$a$y)	to hurry
se porter bien (s^e port$a$y byè^n)	to be well
la transpiration (trâ^{n}speer$a$syô^n)	perspiration
conduire (kô^{n}d$ü$$ee$r)	to conduct, drive; take
un tout petit peu (e^n too ptee pe^o)	a very little bit
toutes les heures (toot l$a$yz$è^o$r)	every hour
descendre (d$a$ysâ^{n}dr)	to go down, get off
la tête (tèt)	the head
avoir mal à la tête	to have a headache
(avwar mal a la tèt)	
le chauffeur (sh$o$fè^{o}r)	the driver
la cuillerée (k$ü$$ee$y^{e}r$a$y)	the spoonful
à domicile (a domeeseel)	at home
loin (lwè^n)	far
libre (leebr)	free
appuyez (ap$ü$$ee$y$a$y)	press
veuillez (vè^{o}yay)	please

attraper (atrap*ay*)	to catch
la portière (portyèr)	the car door
la salle d'attente (sal datâⁿt)	the waiting room
aller volontiers (al*ay* volôⁿty*ay*)	to go willingly
la pharmacie (farma*see*)	the pharmacy
une ordonnance (ordonâⁿs)	a prescription
combien (kôⁿbyèⁿ)	how much
demander (d*e*mâⁿd*ay*)	to ask, demand
pour (p*oo*r)	for, in order to
habiter (âb*ee*t*ay*)	to live
fermer (fèrm*ay*)	to shut, close
arrêter (arèt*ay*)	to arrest, stop
tâter (tât*ay*)	to feel, touch
tâter le pouls (tât*ay* l*e* p*oo*)	to feel the pulse
montrer (môⁿtr*ay*)	to show, display
la douleur (d*oo*le*o*r)	the pain, ache
revenir (r*e*v*e*n*ee*r)	to return
le médecin[1] (mètsèⁿ)	the doctor

CHEZ LE MÉDECIN
(shay l^e mètsè^n) · At the Doctor's

le docteur[1] (doktè^{o}r)	the doctor
le pouls (poo)	pulse
le rhume (rüm)	cold
la clinique (kleeneek)	clinic
la langue (lâ^{n}g)	the tongue
le vertige (vêrteezh)	dizziness
le symptôme (sè^{n}ptôm)	symptom
la pilule (peelül)	pill
les honoraires (layzonorèr)	the fee
la consultation (kô^{n}sültasyô^n)	consultation, visit
la fièvre (fyèvr)	fever, temperature
le médicament (maydeekamâ^n)	medicine
la médecine (mètseen)	medicine (profession)
avoir bonne mine (avwar bon meen)	to look well
souffrir (soofreer)	to be unwell

FOOTNOTES: *1.* Frequently *médecin* and *docteur* are interchangeable. But only *docteur* may be used with the doctor's name or in addressing him. *2.* Cardinal numbers, rather than ordinals, are used in dates. *3. Special sense of avoir:* to have something wrong. *4. Aller bien (mal)* and *se porte bien (mal)* are used interchangeably in sense of *to be well or to be ill. 5. Ne...plus* special nega-

tive meaning *no longer* and functioning same as *ne . . . pas.* 6. Note irregular
plural of *monsieur.* Similarly *madame* becomes *mesdames* in the plural. 7. Transitive use of *arrêter;* the term *la voiture* is understood. 8. A somewhat formal way
of saying *please. Veuillez* is one of the two subjunctive forms of *vouloir* used as the
imperative; see note on p. 304. 9. Note special use of present with *depuis.* In

CONVERSATION

1 Quel jour du mois sommes-nous?

2 Nous sommes le vingt-deux² septembre.

3 Qu'avez-³vous? Vous n'avez pas très bonne mine.

4 Je ne vais⁴ pas bien. Je n'ai plus⁵ d'appétit et j'aimerais voir un médecin.

5 Combien demande le docteur Bellanger pour une consultation à domicile?

6 Je ne sais pas, mais comme il habite assez loin, ses honoraires seront élevés.

7 Dans ce cas nous prendrons un taxi pour aller à sa clinique.

8 J'irai volontiers avec vous. Voici une voiture.

9 Chauffeur, votre voiture est libre?

10 Oui, messieurs,⁶ où voulez-vous aller?

11 Conduisez-nous au soixante-dix-neuf rue Quentin-Bauchard. Fermez la portière, s'il vous plaît.

12 Dépêchez-vous et vous aurez un bon pourboire.

13 Arrêtez⁷ ici; voici l'adresse et nous allons descendre.

14 Appuyez sur la sonnette.

15 Le docteur Bellanger, est-il là?

French an action begun in the past but continuing in the present is expressed by the present tense with *depuis* (or a similar construction, of which there are several). Example: *I have been here for three days;* but I am still here, so the French says: *I am here since three days* (*je suis ici depuis trois jours*). 10. *Sortir* is conjugated with *être*. 11. This is the same *dative of reference* mentioned in lesson

PRONUNCIATION

1 kèl *zhoo*r dü mwa som n*oo?*

2 n*oo* som l^e vè^{n}tde^o sèptâ^{n}br.

3 kav*ay* v*oo?* v*oo* nav*ay* pâ trè bon m*ee*n.

4 zh^e n^e v*ay* pâ by*è*^{n}. zh^e n*ay* plü dap*ay*tee *ay* z*h*èmrè vwar e^n mètse^n.

5 kô^{n}by*è*^{n} d^{e}mâ^{n}d l^e doktè^{o}r bèlâ^{n}z*hay* p*oo*r ün kô^{n}sültasyô^n a dom*ee*seel?

6 z*h*^{e} n^e s*ay* pâ, mè kom *eel* ab*ee*t as*ay* lw*è*^{n}, s*ay*zonorèr s^{e}rô^n-(t)*ay*lv*ay*.

7 dâ^n s^e kâ n*oo* prâ^{n}drô^n(z)e^n taks*ee* p*oo*r al*ay* a sa kl*ee*n*ee*k.

8 z*hee*r*ay* volô^{n}ty*ay* avèk v*oo*. vwas*ee* ün vwatür.

9 *sh*ôfè^{o}r, votr^e vwatür è l*ee*br?

10 w*ee*, m*ay*syc^o, *oo* v*oo*l*ay* v*oo* (z)al*ay?*

11 kô^{n}düeez*ay* n*oo* ô swasâ^{n}t deeznè^{u}f rü kâ^{n}tè^n bô*sh*ar. fèrm*ay* la portyèr, s*ee*l v*oo* plè.

12 d*ay*pè*shay* v*oo* *ay* v*oo*zôr*ay* e^n bô^n p*oo*rbwar.

13 arèt*ay* *ee*s*ee*; vwas*ee* ladr*è*s *ay* n*oo*zalô^n d*ay*sâ^{n}dr.

14 apüeey*ay* sür la sonèt.

15 l^e doktè^{o}r bèlâ^{n}z*hay*, èt*ee*l la?

TRANSLATION

What day of the month is it?

It is the twenty-second (of) September.

What is the matter with you? You don't look well.

I am not well. I have no more appetite and I should like to see a doctor.

How much does Dr. Bellanger ask for a house visit?

I don't know, but as he lives rather far (away), his fees will be high.

In that case we shall take a taxi to go to his clinic.

I shall gladly go with you. Here is a car.

Driver, is your car free?

Yes, gentlemen, where do you wish to go?

Drive us to (number) 79 Quentin-Bauchard Street. Please close the door.

Hurry up and you will have a good tip.

Stop here; here is the address and we are going to get off.

Ring (*lit.* press on) the bell.

Is Dr. Bellanger there?

VII, note *16*. When some action is performed to a part of the body, the owner of that part is expressed as an indirect object of reference and not as a possessive adjective as in English. Example: je *me* lave *les* mains: I wash *my* hands. *12.* See lesson XI, note *13.* *13. Fièvre* is used in French in sense of *temperature* and also in stronger sense of *fever.* *14.* This idiom can be changed to locate the hurt (*le*

16 Entrez dans la salle d'attente, s'il vous plaît. Le docteur va
venir.

17 Bonjour, monsieur, veuillez[8] passer
par ici.

18 Depuis quand souffrez[9]-vous?

19 Depuis hier soir. J'étais en transpiration quand je suis sorti[10] du
théâtre et j'ai attrapé un gros
rhume.

20 Laissez-moi vous[11] tâter le pouls.
Montrez-moi votre langue.

21 Croyez-vous, docteur, que les symptômes soient[12] graves?

22 Non, monsieur, le thermomètre
montre que vous avez un tout peuit
peu de fièvre.[13]

23 J'ai très mal à la tête[14] et j'ai des
vertiges.[15]

24 Prenez ces pilules pour calmer la
douleur.

25 Vous vous sentez[16] mieux?

26 Au contraire, cela[17] va plus mal.

27 Dans ce cas faites préparer cette ordonnance à la pharmacie
et prenez une cuillerée de ce médicament toutes[18] les deux
heures.

28 Si vous n'allez pas mieux, revenez me voir dans trois jours.

---

mal) in another part of the body. Example: *avoir mal aux dents:* to have a toothache; *avoir mal à la gorge:* to have a sore throat.   15. In singular *vertige* means
dizziness due to being on high place; in plural it means dizziness due to physical
condition.   16. As transitive verb *sentir* means *to smell* or *to feel;* as intransitive
it means *to feel* and, in French, is reflexive.   17. *Cela va mal* means *je vais mal.*
It might also mean in another context: *things are going badly.*   18. *Tout,* with

16 ântray dân la sal datânt, seel
voo plè. lᵉ doktèᵒr va vᵉneer.

Enter the waiting room, please.
The doctor will be here in a
minute (*lit.* is going to come).

17 bônzhoor, mᵉsyeᵒ, vèᵒyay pâsay
par eesee.

How do you do, sir; please come
this way (*lit.* pass by here).

18 dᵉpüee kân soofray voo?

How long have you been ill (*lit.*
since when suffer you)?

19 dᵉpüee yèr swar. zhaytè ân
trânspeerasyôn kân zhᵉ süee sortee dü tayâtr ay zhay atrapay
eⁿ grô rüm.

Since last night. I was in a perspiration when I came out of
the theater and I caught a bad
(*lit.* big) cold.

20 lèsay mwa voo tâtay lᵉ poo.
môⁿtray mwa votrᵉ lâⁿg.

Let me feel your pulse. Show me
your tongue.

21 krwayay voo, doktèᵒr, kᵉ lay
sèⁿptôm swa grav?

Do you think, Doctor, that the
symptoms are grave?

22 nôⁿ, mᵉsyeᵒ, lᵉ tèrmomètrᵉ
môⁿtr kᵉ voozavay eⁿ too p(ᵉ)-
tee peᵒ dᵉ fyèvr.

No, sir, the thermometer shows
that you have a very slight temperature.

23 zhay trè mal a la tèt ay zhay
day vèrteezh.

I have a bad headache and I feel
dizzy.

24 prᵉnay say peelül poor kalmay
la doolèᵒr.

Take these pills to stop (*lit.* to
calm) the pain.

25 voo voo sâⁿtay myeᵒ?

You feel better?

26 ô kôⁿtrèr, sᵉla va plü mal.

On the contrary, I feel worse.

27 dâⁿ sᵉ kâ fèt prayparay sèt or-
donâⁿs a la farmasee ay prᵉnay
ün küeeyᵉray dᵉ sᵉ maydeeka-
mâⁿ toot lay deᵒzèᵒr.

In that case have this prescription
filled at the drug store and take
a spoonful of this medicine
every two hours.

28 see voo nalay pâ myeᵒ, rᵉvnay
mᵉ vwar dâⁿ trwa zhoor.

If you are not better, come back
to see me in three days.

---

basic meaning *all*, occasionally has sense of *every*. As an adjective, *tout* and its
variants are always followed by an article in sense of *all*. *Tous les hommes:* all the
men, all *of* the men; *toute la leçon:* all the lesson, *the whole* lesson. *Every* in
the sense of *each*, is translated in the singular without an article: *toute femme,*
every woman. *Every* in a repetitive sense, as first noted, is translated in the plural
with an article: *every hour: toutes les heures.*

QUINZIÈME LEÇON
Fifteenth Lesson

NOUVEAU VOCABULAIRE POUR CETTE LEÇON

l'eau courante, fem. (lô koorâ^{n}t)	the running water
donner sur (donay sür)	to face, to look out on
quinze[1] jours (kè^{n}z zhoor)	two weeks
cela m'est égal[2] (s^{e}la mètaygal)	that is all the same to me
prévenir (prayvneer)	inform, to warn
dès maintenant (dè mè^{n}tnâ^n)	beginning now
le confort moderne (kô^{n}for modèrn)	modern conveniences
déménager (daymaynazhay)	to move away
louer (looay or lway)	to rent
le chauffage (shôfazh)	the heating
par semaine (par s^{e}mèn)	per week
la quinzaine (kè^{n}zèn)	the fortnight
à l'avance (a lavâ^{n}s)	in advance
aujourd'hui même (ôzhoordüee mèm)	this very day
la vue (vü)	the view
comprendre (kô^{n}prâ^{n}dr)	understand

FOOTNOTES: *1*. In common parlance, two weeks, exactly fourteen days, are called *quinze jours*. Similarly a week is called *huit jours*, especially in the expression *d'aujourd'hui en huit*: a week from today. *2*. *Egal* means literally *equal*. *3*. *La pension* means *board* and *boarding house*. *4*. This is subjunctive although it is spelled the same as indicative in this person. After *expressions of necessity*

promettre (promètr)	promise
le paiement (pèmâⁿ)	the payment
le reçu (rᵉsü)	receipt
la brosse (bros)	brush
s'installer (sèⁿstalay)	move in
munir (müneer)	furnish, supply

a noun clause takes the subjunctive. 5. The interrogative pronoun *what* becomes *ce qui* (subject), *ce que* (object) in a declarative sentence. 6. Subjunctive since it is required in a noun clause after *peu m'importe* which vaguely expresses an emotional attitude. 7. Idiom: by the month; by the week. 8. See lesson XII.

POUR LOUER UNE CHAMBRE ·ARTICLES DE TOILETTE
(poor looay ün shâ^{n}br, arteekl d^e twalèt) · To Rent a Room, Toilet Articles

la douche (doosh)	the shower
une éponge (aypô^{n}zh)	a sponge
le lavabo (lavabô)	wash basin
la cuvette (küvèt)	wash basin
un bail (bay)	a lease
la pension complète[3] (pâ^{n}syô^n kô^{n}plèt)	board and room
le loyer (lwayay)	the rent
une serviette de bain (sèrvyèt d^e bè^n)	a bath towel
la pâte dentifrice (pât dâ^{n}teefrees)	the tooth paste
le rasoir (râzwar)	razor
la lame (lam)	blade
la brosse à dents (bros a dâ^n)	tooth brush
la crème (krèm)	the cream, cold cream
le peigne (pèny)	comb
le parfum (parfe^n)	perfume
la poudre (poodr)	powder

note 14. 9. See lesson III, note 21, and compare note 5 above. 10. The adjective tel discussed in lesson XIII, note 11. French says, "Mr. a Such," for English, "Mr. So and So." 11. Archaic legal terminology. Past participle of seoir from which asseoir is derived. 12. The twenty-four hour clock is used in official an-

nouncements in France and in time-tables to avoid ambiguity; it is not used much in conversation. *13.* Since *voici* means *see here,* the subject of the English becomes the object of the French. Example: *Here it is:* French: See it here: *La voici.* Similarly: *la voilà,* there it is.

CONVERSATION

1 Il faut que je déménage[4] de cet hôtel aujourd'hui même.

2 Voulez-vous une chambre meublée ou non meublée?

3 J'aimerais mieux trois pièces non meublées: un salon, une chambre à coucher et une salle de bains.

4 Veuillez entrer et je vous montrerai ce que[5] vous voulez.

5 Aimeriez-vous mieux un salon qui donne sur la rue ou sur la mer?

6 Si c'est possible, je prendrai celui avec la vue sur la mer.

7 Peu m'importe que la chambre à coucher donne[6] sur la rue ou sur la mer.

8 Quel est le prix de cette chambre?

9 Quel est le prix de cet appartement?

10 Est-ce que vous louez au mois[7] ou à la semaine?[7]

11 Combien est la pension complète?

12 Est-ce que les repas sont à la carte?

13 Je veux louer une grande chambre meublée.

14 Je dois vous prévenir qu'on paie[8] à l'avance.

15 Je comprends, mais je préfère vous payer à la semaine.

16 Je suis désolé, mais tous mes arrangements sont au mois, et je ne peux pas louer à d'autres conditions.

17 Dans ce cas je vous paierai[8] tous les quinze jours à l'avance; c'est tout ce que[9] je peux vous promettre.

PRONUNCIATION

1 eel fô kᵉ zhᵉ daymaynazh dᵉ
sètôtèl ôzhoordüee mèm.

2 voolay voo(z)ün shâⁿbr mèᵒblay oo nôⁿ mèᵒblay?

3 zhèmrè myeᵒ trwa pyès nôⁿ
mèᵒblay: eⁿ salô, ün shâⁿbr a
kooshay ay ün sal dᵉ bèⁿ.

4 vèᵒyay(z)âⁿtray ay zhᵉ voo
môⁿtrᵉray sᵉ kᵉ voo voolay.

5 èmryay voo myeᵒ eⁿ salôⁿ kee
don sür la rü oo sür la mèr?

6 see sè poseebl, zhᵉ prâⁿdray
sᵉlüee avèk la vü sür la mèr.

7 peᵒ mèⁿport kᵉ la shâⁿbr a
kooshay don sür la rü oo sür
la mèr.

8 kèl è lᵉ pree dᵉ sèt shâⁿbr?
9 kèl è lᵉ pree dᵉ sètapartᵉmâⁿ?

10 èskᵉ voo looay ô mwa oo a la
sᵉmèn?

11 kôⁿbyèⁿ è la pâⁿsyôⁿ kôⁿplèt?
12 èskᵉ lay rᵉpâ sôⁿ(t)a la kart?
13 zhᵉ veⁿ looay üⁿ grâⁿd shâⁿbr
mèᵒblay.
14 zhᵉ dwa voo prayvneer kôⁿ pay
a lavâⁿs.
15 zhᵉ kôⁿprâⁿ, mè zhᵉ prayfèr
voo pèyay a la sᵉmèn.

16 zhᵉ süee dayzolay, mè too
mayzarâⁿzhmâⁿ sôⁿ(t)ô mwa,
ay zhᵉ nᵉ peᵒ pâ looay a dôtrᵉ
kôⁿdeesyôⁿ.
17 dâⁿ sᵉ kâ zhᵉ voo pèray too lay
kèⁿz zhoor a lavâⁿs; sè tooskᵉ
zhᵉ peᵒ voo promètr.

TRANSLATION

I must move from this hotel this
very day.
Do you want a furnished or unfurnished room?
I should prefer three unfurnished
rooms: a living room, a bedroom and a bathroom.
Please come in and I will show
you what you want.
Would you prefer a living room
which looks out on the street or
on the sea?

If it is possible, I shall take the
one with the view of (*lit.* on)
the sea.
It makes no difference to me (*lit.*
little does it matter to me)
whether the bedroom looks out
on the street or the sea.
What is the price of this room?
What is the price of this apartment?
Do you rent by the month or by
the week?

How much are board and room?
Are the meals à la carte?
I want to rent a large furnished
room.
I must warn you that the rent is
paid (*lit.* one pays) in advance.
I understand, but I prefer to pay
you by the week.

I am sorry, but all my arrangements are by the month, and I
cannot rent under (*lit.* at) other
conditions.
In that case I will pay you every
two weeks in advance; that is
all I can promise you.

18 La chambre a, bien entendu,[7] **un** lavabo et une salle de bains?

19 Oui, monsieur, nos chambres **ont** tout le confort moderne: gaz, électricité, chauffage central, eau courante froide et chaude.

20 Très bien, je veux m'installer le plus tôt possible, et, si vous voulez bien, je vais prendre la chambre dès maintenant.

21 Dans une heure mes bagages seront ici.

22 Voici le paiement de la première quinzaine. Voulez-vous bien me donner un reçu?

23 Voici le reçu signé.

24 Je vous prie de le lire.

25 "Reçu de Monsieur un Tel[10] la somme de 1500 (mille **cinq** cents) francs pour loyer et pension pendant quinze jours dans un immeuble sis[11] rue Madame, numéro 58 (cinquante-huit). Paris, le 1er (premier) juin, 1950 (dix-neuf cent cinquante)."

26 Heures des repas: petit déjeuner de 7 h. 30 (sept heures trente) à 9 (neuf) heures; déjeuner de midi à 13 (treize[12]) heures; et dîner de 17 (dix-sept) heures jusqu'à 21 (vingt et une) heures très précises.

27 Veuillez me montrer la salle de bains.

28 La[13] voici. Comme vous pouvez voir, elle est munie d'une douche, d'une éponge, **de ser**-viettes de bain et d'une petite armoire pour le peigne, **la** brosse, le parfum, la crème, la poudre, la pâte dentifrice, etc.

18 la shânbr a, byènnântândü, eⁿ
lavabô ay ün sal de bèⁿ?

19 wee, mᵉsyeᵒ, nô shânbr ôⁿ too
le kôⁿfor modèrn: gâz, aylèk-
treeseetay, shôfazh sântral, ô
koorâⁿt frwad ay shôd.

20 trè byèⁿ, zhᵉ veᵒ mènstalay le
plü tô poseebl, ay, see voo voolay byèⁿ, zhᵉ vay prândrᵉ la
shânbr dè mèntnâⁿ.

21 dânzün èᵒr may bagazh sᵉrôⁿ-
(t)eesee.

22 vwasee le pèmâⁿ de la prᵉmyèr
kèⁿzèn. voolay voo byèⁿ mᵉ
donay eⁿ rᵉsü?

23 vwasee le rᵉsü seenyay.

24 zhᵉ voo pree de le leer.

25 rᵉsü de mᵉsyeᵒ eⁿ tèl la som de
meel sèⁿ sâⁿ frâⁿ poor lwayay
ay pâⁿsyôⁿ pândâⁿ kèⁿz zhoor
dânzeⁿneemèᵒbl see rü madam,
nümayrô sènkâⁿt üeet. paree,
le prᵉmyay zhüèⁿ, deez nèᵒf
sâⁿ sènkâⁿt.

26 èᵒr day rᵉpâ: p(ᵉ)tee dayzhèᵒnay de sètèᵒr trâⁿt a nèᵒvèᵒr;
duyzhèᵘnay de meedee a trèz
èᵒr; ay deenay de deesètèᵒr
zhüska vèⁿtay ün èᵒr trè pray-
seez.

27 vèᵒyay mᵉ môⁿtray la sal de
bèⁿ.

28 la vwasee. kom voo poovay
vwar, èl è münee dün doosh,
dün aypôⁿzh, de sèrvyèt de bèⁿ
ay dün pᵉteet armwar poor le
pèny, la bros, le parfeⁿ, la
krèm, la poodr, la pât dântee-
frees, èt saytayra.

Of course the room has a wash basin and a bathroom?

Yes, sir, our rooms have all modern conveniences: gas, electricity, central heating, cold and hot running water.

Very well, I wish to move in just as soon as possible (lit. the soonest possible), and, if you are willing, I am going to take the room beginning now.

In an hour my luggage will be here.

Here is the payment for the first fortnight. Will you please give me a receipt?

Here is the signed receipt.

Please read it (lit. I beg you to read it).

"Received from Mr. So and So the sum of 1500 francs for board and room (lit. rent and board) for two weeks in an apartment house located Madame Street, number fifty-eight. Paris, June 1, 1950."

Meal hours: breakfast from 7:30 to 9, lunch from 12 o'clock to one; and dinner from 5 P.M. to 9:00 P.M. sharp.

Please show me the bathroom.

Here it is. As you can see, it is provided with a shower, a sponge, bath towels and a little cabinet for comb, brush, perfume, cold cream, powder, tooth paste, etc.

SEIZIÈME LEÇON
Sixteenth Lesson

NOUVEAU VOCABULAIRE POUR CETTE LEÇON

le papier à lettres (papy*ay* a lètr)	the letter paper
en pleine[1] ville (â^n plèn v*eel*)	in the center of the city
récemment[2] (r*ay*samâ^n)	recently
un exemplaire (*a*ygzâ^{n}plèr)	a (duplicate) copy
le connaissement (konèsmâ^n)	the bill of lading
le représentant (r^{e}pr*ay*zâ^{n}tâ^n)	representative, agent
la marchandise (mar*sh*â^{n}d*ee*z)	merchandise
la comptabilité (kô^{n}tab*eeleetay*)	accounting
la poste aérienne[3] (post a*a*yryèn)	air mail
par avion (par avyô^n)	by air mail
le bottin (botè^n)	the city directory
le papier carbone (papy*ay* karbon)	the carbon paper
le buvard (büvar)	the blotter
toucher (*tooshay*)	to touch, cash
au moins (ô mwè^n)	at least
gagner (ga*nyay*)	to earn, make, gain
occupé (oküp*ay*)	busy

FOOTNOTES: *1. Plein* means *full*. 2. Adverbs are formed by adding *ment* to the feminine singular of the adjective. Adjectives ending in *ent* in the masculine singular (example: *récent*) remove the *ent* and add *emment* (example: *récemment*). Adjectives ending in *ant* in the masculine singular (example: *indépendant*) remove the *ant* and add *amment* (example: *indépendamment*). Note that the end-

suffire (süf*eer*)	to suffice
la lettre (lètr)	the letter
la gomme (gom)	the eraser
le crayon[4] (krèyô^{n})	the pencil
la règle (règl)	the rule, ruler

---

ing *emment* is pronounced the same as the ending *amment*. *3.* Adjectives ending
in *el* or *en* in the masculine double the consonant before adding *e* for the feminine.
4. In a word of this type the *y* is actually pronounced twice. First it combines with
the *a* to form the vowel combination *ay* (or *ai*) which is pronounced *è*; then it

LES RELATIONS COMMERCIALES
(lay r^{e}lâsyô^n komèrsyal) • Commercial Relations

la machine à écrire (ma*shee*n a *ay*kreer)	the typewriter
la copie (kop*ee*)	copy
la brochure (bro*sh*ür)	pamphlet
la carte (kart)	map
la papeterie (paptr*ee*)	stationery store
le livre des recettes (*lee*vr^e d*ay* r^{e}sèt)	the cash book
la feuille de papier (fê^{o}y d^e papy*ay*)	sheet of paper
un agenda[5] (*e*^{n}na*zh*è^{n}da)	a journal
la bourse[6] (b*oo*rs)	stock exchange
une enveloppe (â^{n}vlop)	an envelope
la plume (plüm)	the pen
l'encre, fem. (lâ^{n}kr)	the ink
un encrier (â^{n}kr*eeay*)	an inkstand
le tampon (tâ^{n}pô^n)	the rubber stamp
le sceau (sô)	the seal

---

combines with the following vowel as a semi-vowel *y*. In this connection note the unusual word *pays*, pronounced *payee* or even *pèyee*. 5. Not the unusual nasal vowel in this word. Another word having such a vowel is the name *Benjamin:* bè^n*zh*amè^n. 6. Basic meaning of *bourse* is *purse;* it also means *scholarship*.

7. In the passive *occuper* takes *à* to introduce an infinitve; in the reflexive it takes *de*. *(S'occuper de* means *to concern oneself with).* 8. *La plupart,* meaning *most* in a quantitative sense, takes complete partitive after it. 9. See lesson XII, note 3. When English reads *whose,* paraphrase it as *of which* or *of whom* and

CONVERSATION

1 Qu'avez-vous fait aujourd'hui?

2 Avez-vous beaucoup travaillé?

3 Oui, nous avons été très occupés à[7] rédiger la correspondance avec nos agences à travers l'Europe et en Orient.

4 Avez-vous écrit vos lettres en français?

5 Bien entendu, car le français se parle dans la plupart[8] des capitales européennes, surtout dans les pays dont[9] la langue locale n'est pas connue à l'étranger:[10] par exemple la Roumanie, la Pologne, la Tchécoslovaquie, l'Egypte et la Perse.

6 Ecrivez-vous vos lettres à la machine?

7 Oui, généralement les maisons modernes tapent leurs lettres à triple exemplaire.[10]

8 Avez-vous des relations commerciales avec la Russie?

9 Oui, et nous faisons des affaires avec la Chine.

10 Je désire toucher une traite. J'ai besoin de dollars et je n'ai que des livres[11] sterling.[12]

11 A propos,[10] j'ai perdu mon carnet[13] de chèques.

12 Devons-nous aller à la banque immédiatement?

---

reorganize sentence, being sure to keep the relative at the head of the clause. Rearrange: *whose local language* as *of which the local language.* It is then clear that the French requires an article after *dont.* Furthermore, if, in English, *whose* modifies the object of the clause, there is a complicated inversion in the English whereas the French uses normal declarative order with *dont* still at the head of the

PRONUNCIATION

1 kavay voo fè(t)ôzhoordüee?

2 avay voo bôkoo travayay?

3 wee, noozavôⁿzaytay trèzokü-
pay a raydeezhay la korèspôⁿ-
dâⁿs avèk nôzazhâⁿs a travèr
lèᵒrop ay âⁿnoryâⁿ.

4 avay voo(z) aykree vô lètr âⁿ
frâⁿsè?

5 byèⁿnâⁿtâⁿdü, kar lᵉ frâⁿsè sᵉ
parl dâⁿ la plüpar day kapee-
tal(z) èᵒropayèn, sürtoo dâⁿ
lay payee dôⁿ la lâⁿg lokal nè
pâ konü a laytrâⁿzhay: parayg-
zâⁿpl la roomanee, la polony,
la tshaykoolovakoo, layzheept
ay la pèrs.

6 aykreevay voo vô lètr a la
masheen?

7 wee, zhaynayralmâⁿ lay mèzôⁿ
modèrn tap lèᵒr lètr a treepl
aygzâⁿplèr.

8 avay voo day rᵉlasyôⁿ komèrsyal avèk la rüsee?

9 wee, ay noo fᵉzôⁿ dayzafèr avèk
la sheen.

10 zhᵉ dayzeer tooshay ün trèt.
zhay bᵉzwèn dᵉ dolar ay zhᵉ
nay kᵉ day leevrᵉ stèrlèⁿ.

11 a propô, zhay pèrdü môⁿ karnè
dᵉ shèk.

12 dᵉvôⁿ noo alay a la baⁿk ee-
maydyatmâⁿ?

TRANSLATION

What did you do today?

Have you worked a great deal (*lit.* much)?

Yes, we have been very busy writing (*lit.* drawing up) the correspondence with our agencies throughout Europe and in the Orient.

Did you write your letters in French?

Of course, for French is spoken in most European capitals, especially in the countries whose local language is not known abroad: for example Romania, Poland, Czecho-Slovakia, Egypt and Persia.

Do you write your letters on the typewriter?

Yes, generally modern companies type their letters in three copies.

Have you business relations with Russia?

Yes, and we do business with China.

I wish to cash a draft. I need dollars and I have only pounds sterling.

By the way, I have lost my check book.

Must we go to the bank immediately?

clause. Example: *the man whose wife I met.* French: *the man of whom I met the wife:* l'homme dont j'ai rencontré la femme. *10.* Idiom. *11.* Livre in the sense of *pound* is feminine. *12.* Note failure to make agreement in the case of this borrowed word. *13.* Basic meaning of *carnet* is *memorandum book.* *14. Temps* means time spread over a *period of time;* to express the idea of a *point*

13 Oui, nous devons y aller tout de suite, parce que les banques ferment à trois heures précises.

14 Quand devez-vous envoyer ces articles?

15 Faut-il expédier la marchandise tout de suite?

16 Ne voudriez-vous pas câbler d'abord à votre représentant?

17 Non, une lettre par avion suffira. Il la recevra lundi.

18 Je dois aussi écrire à mon représentant à Stamboul.

19 Quand part le courrier pour la Turquie? Faut-il attendre longtemps?

20 Le bateau part au moins une fois[14] par semaine, mais il y a un service aérien tous les jours.

21 Est-ce que vous faites beaucoup d'affaires avec les Pays-Bas?

22 Récemment j'ai vendu beaucoup de marchandise en Hollande[15] et en Belgique.

23 Dans ce cas vous devrez ouvrir un nouveau bureau à Paris, n'est-ce pas?

24 J'ai l'intention d'établir mon siège social[16] en pleine ville près de la Bourse, le quinze de ce mois-ci.[17]

---

of time use *fois.* Example: *in the time of Louis XIV:* au temps de Louis XIV; but: *the first time:* la première fois. In the sense of *clock time* the word, however, is *heure.* Example: *what time is it:* quelle heure est-il?   15. Observe that *Hollande* has an aspirate *h.*   16. In this expression *siège social* (*lit.* company seat), the word *social* is an adjective derived from the common French word for company:

13 wee, noo d^evôⁿzee ala*y* too*d* süeet, parsk^e la*y* bâⁿk fèrm a trwazè^or pra*y*seez.

Yes we must go (*lit.* there) right away, because the banks close at precisely three o'clock.

14 kâⁿ d^eva*y* voo âⁿvwaya*y* sa*y*zarteekl?

When must you send these articles?

15 fôteel èkspa*y*dya*y* la marshâⁿdeez too*d* süeet?

Must the merchandise be shipped immediately?

16 n^e voodreea*y* voo pâ kâbla*y* dabor a votr^e r^eprayzâⁿtâⁿ?

Wouldn't you like to cable first to your representative?

17 nôⁿ, ün lètr^e paravyôⁿ süfeera. *eel* la r^es^evra leⁿdee.

No, an air mail (*lit.* by plane) letter will suffice. He will receive it Monday.

18 zh^e dwazôsee a*y*kreer a môⁿ r^eprayzâⁿtâⁿ a stâⁿbool.

I must also write to my representative at Constantinople.

19 kâⁿ par l^e koorya*y* poor la türkee? fôteel atâⁿdr lôⁿtâⁿ?

When does the mail leave for Turkey? Will (*lit* is) it be necessary to wait long?

20 l^e batô par ô mwèⁿ ün fwa par s^emèn, mèzeelya eⁿ sèrvees aayryòⁿ too la*y* shoor.

The boat leaves at least once a week, but there is plane service every day.

21 èsk^e voo fèt bôkoo dafèr avèk la*y* paye*e* bâ?

Do you do much business with the Low Countries?

22 ra*y*samâⁿ zha*y* vâⁿdü bôkoo d^e marshâⁿdeez âⁿ olâⁿd a*y* âⁿ bèlzheek.

Recently I sold a lot of merchandise in Holland and in Belgium.

23 dâⁿ o^e kâ voo d^evrya*y*zoovroor eⁿ noovô bürô a paree, nès pâ?

In that case you ought to open a new office in Paris, don't you think (*lit.* is it not so)?

24 zha*y* lèⁿtâⁿsyôⁿ da*y*tableer môⁿ syèzh sosyal âⁿ plèⁿ veel prè d^e la boors, l^e kèⁿz d^e s^e mwa se*e*.

I intend to establish my main office in the center of the city near the Stock Exchange, the fifteenth of this month.

---

société. The word *compagnie* is also used, however. 17. Since *ce mois* can mean either *this* or *that month*, it sometimes becomes necessary to make a distinction; -ci and -là are then added to the noun. Example: *ce livre-ci:* this book; *ce livre-là:* that book. In the example in sentence *24* above the same device is used for emphasis.

17 DIX-SEPTIÈME LEÇON

L'ARRIVÉE À PARIS

(La scène commence à la sortie du quai 8 à la Gare Saint-Lazare, puis[1] se déplace au fur et à mesure de l'action—puisqu'il s'agit[2] d'un film de cinéma plutôt que d'une pièce. Françoise de Nédélec, jeune Parisienne, surveille attentivement la foule des voyageurs qui débarquent d'un train transatlantique. Elle voit enfin celui[3] qu'elle cherche;[4] c'est Justin Lambert, jeune Américain, qui se met à lui faire des signes désespérés de l'autre côté de la barrière.)

FRANÇOISE, *s'approchant de la barrière et criant:* Ah! vous voilà, Justin. Je suis très contente de vous voir. Mais qu'avez-vous?

JUSTIN: Ah! bonjour, Françoise. Me voici, enfin. J'espère que vous allez pouvoir me tirer de ce camp de concentration, car j'ai perdu mon billet. N'est-ce pas qu'il faut le rendre à la sortie?

FRANÇOISE: Ne vous[5] inquiétez pas. Je vais expliquer à l'employé que vous n'êtes pas habitué aux us et coutumes des continentaux. *(S'adressant à l'employé à la sortie.)* Ce jeune Américain a égaré son billet, ne sachant[6] pas qu'il

---

FOOTNOTES: *1. Alors* may be used in all senses of *then; puis* and *ensuite* may be used only when *then* means *next. 2. It is a question of;* i.e., *we are dealing with. 3. The one who (whom); the ones who; he who; she who; they who; the one which; the ones which; those which* all translate by a demonstrative pronoun followed by a relative pronoun. 4. Observe that *chercher* is a TRANSITIVE VERB, which means that it takes a direct, instead of an indirect, object. 5. With NEGATIVE IMPERATIVE, pronoun objects come, as usual, before the verb. Compare lesson IX, note 8. 6. Present participle of *savoir.* 7. Imperfect tense of *falloir.* 8. Conditional tense of *pouvoir. Would you not be able;* i.e., *couldn't you?*

fallait[7] le garder. Ne pourriez-vous[8] pas le laisser sortir quand même?

L'Employé: Oh! ça va! Il a été contrôlé dans le train, son billet.[9]

Françoise, *se rapprochant de Justin*: Vous pouvez sortir. Votre billet a été contrôlé[10] dans le train. *(Justin une fois sorti,*[11]

elle poursuit.) C'est vrai. Je me rappelle. Le train transatlantique fait exception à la règle générale qu'on doit rendre les billets à la sortie.

Justin: Il fait bon respirer enfin l'air libre de Paris. . . . Merci d'être venue me chercher. Je crois[12] que j'aurais pu[13] me débrouiller tout de même. Si vous pouvez me guider jusqu'à la salle des bagages, j'ai une petite malle que je dois faire transporter d'abord à l'hôtel. Après cela je devrais passer à l'Hôtel Félix, rue Molière, pour être sûr d'avoir la chambre que j'ai

9. This repetition is colloquial.   10. Example of Passive Voice of verb. As in English, the passive is formed with the auxiliary verb *to be* and the past participle. In French this past participle agrees like an adjective with the subject. The tense of the passive is determined by the tense of the auxiliary. Hence *a été contrôlé* is Compound Past (*passé indéfini*) Passive; literally: *has been checked* although English would say merely *was checked*. French, in conversational style, must use *compound past* because action was completed (see lesson III, note 15).   11. *Once Justin has gone out.* Note use of past participle which

retenue par lettre il y a[14] deux mois. Je ne sais pas quels sont vos projets pour la journée ni si les convenances le permettent, mais j'aimerais bien[15] que vous puissiez[16] m'accompagner.

FRANÇOISE: Les convenances permettent bien[17] des choses ces jours-ci, depuis que les Françaises ont fait de la résistance[18] et ont obtenu le vote. On ne reçoit[19] pas d'Américains tous les jours et, si vous voulez bien, je vous consacre toute l'après-midi,[20] car je suis persuadée qu'il vous tarde de visiter Paris sous la conduite d'un guide expérimenté comme moi. A propos, maman vous invite à dîner ce soir.

JUSTIN: J'accepte avec plaisir et l'invitation et l'offre de vos services professionnels.

FRANÇOISE: Maintenant il faudra[21] récupérer vos bagages. J'espère que vous n'avez pas égaré aussi votre bulletin.

JUSTIN: Non, non, je l'ai toujours.

FRANÇOISE: Allons-y. . . . Voici la salle des pas perdus; l'escalier qui mène à la salle des bagages est au fond.

JUSTIN, *qui regarde les guichets:* Comme[22] c'est pratique cet appareil automatique qui livre les billets quand l'employé joue sur le clavier! C'est encore plus moderne que chez nous. C'est comme ces nouvelles voitures à impériale que j'ai remarquées sur des voies de garage quand notre train entrait en gare. Nos ingénieurs de chemin de fer pourraient apprendre bien des choses s'ils se donnaient la peine de traverser la mer.

---

in Latin is called an *Ablative Absolute;* Justin sorti: *Justin having gone out.* In such a construction the past participle is used without an auxiliary.   *12.* From *croire.* If doubtful about the forms of irregular verbs, consult the *Grammatical Appendix* which treats irregular verbs in detail.   *13.* Conditional of *pouvoir.* Literally: *I would have been able* but more correctly *I could have.* *14.* Special force of *il y a. Il y a deux mois:* two months ago.   *15. I should like.* *16.* Subjunctive of *pouvoir.* See lesson XI, note 5, and lesson XIII, note 9. *17. Bien des choses* is a more emphatic way of saying *beaucoup de choses.* *18. Have participated in the Resistance* (during the German occupation of France from 1940 to 1944).   *19.* Present tense of *recevoir.*   *20.* Although normally used in the masculine, this word may become feminine to emphasize the notion of duration.   *21.* Future of *falloir.*   *22.* In an exclamation *how* is expressed as *comme* or *que.* Note that these interjections take normal declarative order and not an inversion as in English.   *23.* This adjective has an alternate masculine form

FRANÇOISE: Oui, mais à côté de ces quelques innovations, il y a encore beaucoup de vieux[23] matériel qui roule encore, des voitures à quatre roues qui ne communiquent pas les unes avec les autres.[24] On pourrait encore supprimer son voisin en le poussant par la portière comme Lafcadio l'a[25] fait dans *les Caves du Vatican*.[26]

JUSTIN: En effet, j'ai vu ça aussi. . . . Mais nous voici arrivés.

(Après les formalités à la salle des bagages notre intrépide voyageur descend dans la cour de la gare et hèle un taxi.)

JUSTIN: Chauffeur, Hôtel Félix, s'il vous plaît.

CHAUFFEUR: Hôtel Félix. Connais[27] pas.

FRANÇOISE: Oui, vous savez, ce petit hôtel derrière la fontaine Molière.

CHAUFFEUR: Ah! oui; j'y suis.[28]

FRANÇOISE, *à Justin:* Je ne sais pas si vous pouvez vous orienter dans[29] Paris. Pouvez-vous me dire le nom de ce boulevard que nous traversons?

JUSTIN: Faites[30] comme si je ne le savais pas.

vieil to be used before a masculine noun *beginning with a vowel*. Feminine singular *vieille;* masculine plural *vieux;* feminine plural *vieilles*. 24. *With each other*. Each other may be the object of the verb, in which case it is a REFLEXIVE PRONOUN. *Nous nous aimons:* we love *each other. Ils se parlent:* they speak *to each other*. To distinguish from the normal reflexive, one may say: *Ils se parlent l'un à l'autre* for two people, or: *Ils se parlent les uns aux autres* for more than two. *Each other* may also be the object of a preposition, as: *with each other: l'un avec l'autre* or *les uns avec les autres*. 25. The verb *faire* generally cannot be used without an object. If the equivalent English has none, the French requires the pronoun object *le*. 26. Novel published by André Gide in 1914. This is the famous example of the Gidean "gratuitous act." 27. The omission of *je* before this verb is colloquial. 28. *I've got it*. 29. Generally *à* is used to translate *in* with the name of a city. *Dans* has the special meaning of *within the limits of*. 30. *Faites comme si* . . . : pretend I don't know. 31. Idiom: *in the 19th century*.

FRANÇOISE: C'est le Boulevard Haussmann. Il porte le nom de l'architecte qui a refait le plan de Paris au XIXe siècle.[31]

JUSTIN: C'est sur le Boulevard Haussmann, n'est-ce pas, que Marcel Proust[32] habitait dans sa fameuse chambre capitonnée de liège?

FRANÇOISE: Oui, mais derrière nous, dans la direction de l'Arc de Triomphe[33] qui n'est pas visible d'ici.

JUSTIN: Tiens! comme il est drôle, ce petit gendarme à la visière carrée! Il a l'air d'un porteur de chez nous doublé d'une fée, car son petit bâton blanc ressemble à une baguette magique.

FRANÇOISE: Vous êtes un poète doublé d'un railleur. Ne vous[5] moquez pas de notre petit gardien de la paix. Il appartient à la meilleure police du[34] monde. Pendant l'occupation sa conduite a été exemplaire; il a tiré d'un mauvais pas beaucoup de patriotes tout en[35] ayant l'air d'agir de complicité avec les occupants. D'ailleurs, il ne faut pas dire "gendarme" mais "agent." Un gendarme est une sorte de soldat; il fait partie de la police d'état qui fonctionne plutôt à la campagne.

JUSTIN: Excusez mon manque de respect. . . . Et voilà un autobus avec sa plate-forme ouverte à l'arrière. Il est plus grand que je ne[36] m'y attendais.

FRANÇOISE: Vous parlez de dimensions maintenant pour me faire plaisir. Les Américains semblent attacher tant de prix à

---

32. Famous French novelist (1871-1922), author of *A la recherche du temps perdu* (*Remembrance of Things Past*), a novel in sixteen volumes in the French edition.　33. The Arch of Triumph, which commemorates the victories of Napoleon, was completed in 1836.　34. After a SUPERLATIVE the English *in* translates by *de*.　35. The use of *en* with the present participle indicates that the action occurs at the same time as the action of the main verb. The adverb *tout* is sometimes used to intensify this notion of simultaneousness and is then untranslated. See lesson IV, note 15.　36. A pleonastic *ne* is required in a relative clause depending on a comparative. See lesson IX, note 16.　37. Allusion to the 1944

la grandeur. . . . Oui, les nouveaux autobus sont comme ça. Vous savez que les anciens ont fait la campagne de Normandie[37] avec les Chleuhs et qu'ils y ont laissé leur peau.

JUSTIN: Comment, les Chleuhs?

FRANÇOISE: C'est le nom qu'on donnait aux Allemands pour qu'ils ne sachent[38] pas qu'on parlait d'eux. . . . Chauffeur, passez directement par la Place de l'Opéra.

CHAUFFEUR: Bien, mademoiselle. Mais, vous savez qu'aux heures d'affluence il y a toujours de l'embouteillage là-bas?

JUSTIN: On n'est pas pressé. Dites-moi, guide, quel est ce grand bâtiment à gauche qui ressemble à l'abside d'une immense église romane?

FRANÇOISE: C'est l'Opéra que vous ne reconnaissez pas parce que vous le voyez de derrière. Je crois qu'on donne *la Reine de Saba*[39] de Gounod.[40] *Manon*[41] de Massenet[42] est à l'affiche de l'Opéra Comique.[43]

JUSTIN: Quelle est la différence entre l'Opéra[44] et l'Opéra Comique?

FRANÇOISE: C'est uniquement une différence de répertoire. Ce sont tous les deux des théâtres subventionnés. Du point de vue architecture et spectacle, il vaut mieux commencer par l'Opéra proprement dit qui est très impressionnant, surtout par[45] son escalier d'honneur et par son foyer où les spectateurs, pendant les entr'actes, se promènent et se regardent dans d'immenses glaces.

American campaign in Normandy.   38. Present subjunctive of *savoir*. See lesson IX, note *16*.   39. *Queen of Sheba*.   40. Charles Gounod (1818-1893).   41. Taken from the famous novel *Manon Lescaut* (1731) by the Abbé Prévost.   42. Jules Massenet (1842-1912).   43. Founded in 18th century. The present theatre was rebuilt in 1898.   44. Founded in 17th century. The present building was built in 1875.   45. English says *for*.   46. Originally a play written in 1892 by the Belgian poet-dramatist Maurice Maeterlinck.   47. Claude Debussy (1862-1918).   48. Originally a royal palace begun in 1204, finished in 1848.   49. The Council of State is the highest "administrative" court in France (administrative courts handle

JUSTIN: J'aimerais bien voir ça, mais, en fait de musique, j'aimerais mieux entendre *Pelléas et Mélisande*[46] de Debussy.[47]

FRANÇOISE: Nous passons maintenant devant la façade de l'Opéra. A droite vous voyez la terrasse du célèbre Café de la  Paix, rendez-vous des Parisiens élégants et des hommes d'affaires. A présent nous descendons l'Avenue de l'Opéra; tout au fond vous voyez un coin du célèbre musée du Louvre[48] où il faudra passer au moins une journée entière. Mais voici la rue Molière. Vous savez que vous logez à côté de deux édifices importants, la Bibliothèque Nationale et le Palais-Royal. Construit au XVIIᵉ siècle, le Palais-Royal comprend le Conseil d'État,[49] le Théâtre Français et puis une cour intérieure autour de laquelle se trouvent toutes sortes de boutiques qui ouvrent sur une arcade. C'est un endroit très curieux.

JUSTIN: Qu'est-ce que vous entendez par Théâtre Français?

FRANÇOISE: Je veux dire la Comédie Française fondée par Molière au XVIIᵉ siècle. C'est sur les planches de ce théâtre que le grand dramaturge est mort en 1673 en jouant le rôle du *Malade Imaginaire*.

JUSTIN: Est-ce que le Palais-Royal est plus vieux que le Louvre?

FRANÇOISE: Non. Certaines parties du Louvre actuel ont été construites[10] par le [50] roi François Iᵉʳ au XVIᵉ siècle.

JUSTIN: J'espère que vous pourrez m'accompagner au Louvre.

civil cases and are separate from judicial courts).   50. An article is necessary when a title, other than *monsieur, madame* or *mademoiselle*, precedes a person's name.   51. Another negative working the same as *ne . . . pas*. See Lesson I, note 18, and lesson XIII, note 5.   52. *Voilà* may be used without an object.   53. *Entrer* is an intransitive verb requiring the preposition *dans*.   54. The pronoun *personne*, which may be used either as the subject or the object of the verb, requires a *ne* before the verb. In a compound tense or with an infinitive it follows the entire

Mais j'aperçois l'Hôtel Félix. Il n'a pas l'air bien élégant. Je me demande même comment il tient debout.

FRANÇOISE: Oui, on ne peut guère[51] le comparer au Continental ni au Claridge. *(Le taxi s'arrête.)*

JUSTIN: Chauffeur, combien est-ce que je vous dois?

CHAUFFEUR: Le prix est indiqué au compteur. Soixante-dix francs s'il vous plaît.

JUSTIN: Voilà.[52] Vous pouvez garder la monnaie. *(Ils entrent dans*[53] *l'hôtel.)* Tiens! il n'y a personne.[54] Holà! Quelqu'un![55]

FEMME DE JOURNÉE *qui entre:* Vous désirez, monsieur?

JUSTIN: Je viens[56] d'arriver. J'ai déjà retenu une chambre.

FEMME DE JOURNÉE: Je vais appeler le gérant. *(Criant.)* Monsieur Muche! Y a[57] un client!

LE GÉRANT, *entrant:* Bonjour, monsieur.

JUSTIN: C'est pour une chambre retenue d'avance.

LE GÉRANT: Bien,[58] monsieur. A[59] quel nom?

JUSTIN: Justin Lambert.

LE GÉRANT: La chambre vous attend. Vous avez des pièces d'identité?[60]

JUSTIN: Voilà mon passeport.

LE GÉRANT: Voulez-vous remplir cette formule?

---

verb form (compare lesson XIII, note 5). Examples: *je n'ai vu personne; pour ne voir personne.*   55. The forms of this pronoun are *quelqu'un, quelqu'une, quelques-uns, quelques-unes* and derive from the adjective *quelque* (see lesson X, note *12*). In the singular, this pronoun presents no problem since it has only one translation, *someone.* In the plural it translates English *a few* or *some* in the sense of *a few* used as pronouns. Example: *Some (a few) of my friends: quelques-uns de mes amis.* Compare this with the partitive (lesson II, note *18*, and lesson IV, note *9*). Standing

JUSTIN, *après avoir écrit:* Il n'y a pas d'autres formalités?

LE GÉRANT: En tant qu'étranger il faudra vous faire inscrire au commissariat de police du quartier si vous comptez rester plus d'un[61] mois à Paris. —Maintenant, si vous voulez, je vous montrerai votre chambre. Le garçon montera vos affaires tout à l'heure.

JUSTIN, *à Françoise:* Voulez-vous m'attendre pendant que je visite ma nouvelle installation?

FRANÇOISE: Entendu. Je vous attends au salon.

alone as object of the verb, *quelques-uns* (*-unes*) would require the partitive pronoun *en* before the verb (see lesson V, note *16*).   56. *I have just arrived.* Idiom: *Venir de* (in the present tense) + infinitive, *to have just.*   57. Colloquial for *il y a.*   58. *Very good.*   59. English says merely: *What name?*   60. Even French citizens are required to carry a *carte d'identité.*   61. The word for *than* in a comparison is normally *que,* but *more than,* followed by a number, is *plus de.*

VOCABULAIRE POUR CETTE LEÇON

A

abside (apseed) *f.* apse

accepter (aksèptay) to accept

actuel, -le (aktüèl), *adj.* present-day

adresser, s'adresser à (adrèsay), to address

affaire (afèr) *f.* affair ...s *f. pl.* business, things

affiche (afeesh) *f.* bill (of a theatre)

affluence (aflüâns) *f.* heures d'... rush hour

ailleurs (ayèor) *adv.* elsewhere; **d'**... moreover

air (èr) *m.* appearance; **avoir l'air (de)** to look (like)

allemand (almân) *adj.* German

aller. ça va (sa va) that's O.K.

ancien, -ne (ânsyèn) *adj.* ancient, old, former

apercevoir (apèrsevwar) to perceive; **j'aperçois** I notice

appareil (aparèy) *m.* apparatus, device

appartenir (aparteneer) to belong

appeler (aplay) to call

architecte (arsheetèkt) *m.* architect

arrière (aryèr) *f.* à l'... in the rear

attacher du prix à quelque chose to set a value upon something

attendre (atândr) to await, wait for; **s'**... à to expect

attentivement (atânteevmân) *adv.* attentively

autobus (ôtobüs) *m.* bus

automatique (ôtomateek) *adj.* automatic

autour (ôtoor) *adv.* ... de *prep.* around

avance (avâns) *f.* à l'... ahead of time

B

baguette (bagèt) *f.* wand

barrière (baryèr) *f.* barrier, gate

bâtiment (bâteemân) *m.* building

bâton (bâtôn) *m.* stick, baton

blanc, blanche (blân, blânsh) *adj.* white

bon, -ne (bôn, bon) *adj.* good; **il fait bon** it is pleasant

bonne *f.* maid

boutique (booteek) *f.* shop

C

ça (sa) *pro.* (Contraction of cela) that

campagne (kânpany) *f.* country, campaign; **à la** ... in the country; **faire la** ... **de** to go through the campaign of

capitonner (kapeetonay) to pad

car (kar) *conj.* for

carré (karay) *adj.* square

cave (kav) *f.* cellar

célèbre (saylèbr) *adj.* famous

chercher (shèrshay) to look for, seek, get

chose (shôz) *f.* thing

clavier (klavyay) *m.* keyboard

client (kleeân) *m.* customer

comédie (komaydee) *f.* comedy

comme (kom) *prep. & conj.* as, like, since

commissariat (komeesarya) *m.* police station

communiquer (komüneekay) to communicate

comparer (kônparay) to compare

complicité (kônpleeseetay) *f.* **agir de** ... **avec,** to act in collusion with

comprendre (kônprândr) to understand, comprise

compteur (kôntèor) *m.* meter

conduite (kôndüeet) *f.* conduct

connaître (konètr) to know, be acquainted with

consacrer (kônsakray) to devote

conseil (kôⁿsèy) m. counsel, advice
construire (kôⁿstrüeer) to construct;
construit constructed
content (kôⁿtâⁿ) adj. happy
continental (pl. continentaux) m.
continental
contrôler (kôⁿtrôlay) to check
convenances (kôⁿvnâⁿs) f. pl. pro-
prieties
côté (kôtay) m. side; de l'autre ...
on the other side; à ... de, prep.,
beside
crier (kreeay) to shout
croire (krwar) to believe
curieux, curieuse (küryeº, küryeºz)
adj. curious

D

débarquer (daybarkay) to disembark
débrouiller (daybrooyay) to disen-
tangle; se ... to manage
demander (dᵉmâⁿday) to ask; se ...
to wonder
déplacer (dayplasay) to move; se ...
to move
depuis (dᵉpüee) prep. since; ... que
conj. since
derrière (dèryèr) prep. behind
désespéré (dayzèspayray) adj. desperate
devant (dᵉvâⁿ) prep. in front of
devoir (dᵉvwar) to have to, to owe; je
dois I must, I owe
dire (dᵉer) to say, tell
directement (deerèktᵉmâⁿ) adv. directly
doubler (dooblay) to double
dramaturge (dramatürzh) m. dramatist
droite (drwat) f. right (-hand) side
drôle (drôl) adj. funny

E

écrire (aykreer) to write; écrit written

égarer (aygaray) to mislay
embouteillage (âⁿbootèyazh) m. traffic
jam
employé (âⁿplwayay) m. employee
endroit (âⁿdrwa) m. place
enfin (âⁿfèn) adv. finally, in short
entendre (âⁿtâⁿdr) to hear, mean;
entendu agreed
entier, entière (âⁿtyay, âⁿtyèr) adj.
entire
entr'acte (âⁿtrakt) m. intermission
entrer (âⁿtray) to enter; ... en gare
enter the station (i.e., a train)
et (ay) conj. and; et ... et both ... and
étranger (aytrâⁿzhay) m.; étrangère
(aytrâⁿzhèr) f. foreigner
exception (èksèpsyôⁿ) f. faire ... to
make an exception
exemplaire (aygzâⁿplèr) adj. exemplary
expérimenté (èkspayreemâⁿtay) adj.
experienced
expliquer (èkspleekay) to explain

F

faire (fèr) to do, make, act
fait (fèt) m. en ... de as regards
falloir (falwar) to be necessary; il
faudra it will be necessary
fameux, fameuse (fameº, fameºz)
adj. famous
fée (fay) f. fairy
femme (fam) f. ... de journée charwoman
fonctionner (fôⁿksyonay) to function
fond (fôⁿ) m. au ... at the far end
fonder (fôⁿday) to found
fontaine (fôⁿtèn) f. fountain
formalité (formaleetay) f. formality
formule (formül) f. formula, form
foule (fool) f. crowd
foyer (fwayay) m. foyer (theatre),
lobby
fur (für) m. au ... et à mesure (de)
progressively (with)

G

garçon (garsôn) *m.* boy, waiter, bell-boy

garder (garday) to keep

gardien (gardyèn) *m.* guardian; ... de la paix policeman

gauche (gôsh) *f.* left (-hand) side

gendarme (zhândarm) gendarme (member of national militarized police)

gérant (zhayrân) *m.* manager

glace (glas) *f.* mirror

grandeur (grândèor) *f.* size, bigness

guide (geed) *m.* guide

guider (geeday) to guide

H

habitué (abeetüay) *adj.* accustomed

héler (aylay) to hail

heure (èor) *f.* hour; tout à l'... presently, just now

holà (ola) *interj.* hallo!

honneur (onèor) *m.* honor

hôtel (ôtèl) *m.* hotel

I • J

ici (eesee) *adv.* here

Ier (abbreviation for premier) first

impériale (ènpayryal) *f.* top-deck (of bus, etc.); voiture à ... double-decker car

impressionnant (ènprèsyonân) *adj.* impressive

ingénieur (ènzhaynyèor) *m.* engineer

inquiéter (ènkyaytay) s'... to become worried

inscrire (ènskreer) se faire ... to register

intérieur (èntayryèor) *adj.* interior

intrépide (èntraypeed) *adj.* intrepid

inviter (ènveetay) to invite

jeune (zhèon) *adj.* young

jouer (zhway) to play

journée (zhoornay) *f.* day

L • M

laisser (lèsay) to let, leave

liège (lyèzh) *m.* cork

livrer (leevray) to deliver

loger (lozhay) to lodge

magique (mazheek) *adj.* magic

malade (malad) *adj.* sick; ... imaginaire hypochondriac

maman (mamân) *f.* mama

manque (mânk) *m.* lack

matériel (matayryèl) *m.* equipment

mener (menay) to lead

mettre (mètr) to put; se ... à to begin

mieux (myeo) *adv.* better

moderne (modèrn) *adj.* modern

monde (mônd) *m.* world; tout le ... everybody

monnaie (monè) *f.* change

monter (môntay) to go up, carry up

montrer (môntray) to show

moquer (mokay) se ... de to make fun of

mourir (mooreer) to die; il est mort he died

musée (müzay) *m.* museum

N • O

nom (nôn) *m.* name

obtenir (opteneer) to obtain

occupant (oküpân) *m.* occupier

offre (ofr) *f.* offer

orienter (oryântay) to orient

ouvrir (oovreer) to open; ouvert open

P

paix (pè) *f.* peace

palais (palè) *m.* palace

parisien, parisienne (pareezyèn, pareezyèn) *adj.* Parisian

partie (partee) *f.* part; faire ... de to be part of

passeport (pâspor) *m.* passport

passer (pâsay) to pass; ... à to pass by; se ... to take place

patriote (patreeot) *m.* patriot
peau (pô) *f.* skin; **y laisser sa** ... not
to come out alive
peine (pèn) *f.* **se donner la** ... to take
the trouble
pendant (pândân) *prep.* during, for;
... **que** *conj.* while
perdre (pèrdr) to lose
permettre (pèrmètr) to permit
personne (pèrson) *f.* person; **ne** ...
pro. no one
persuader (pèrsüaday) to persuade
petit (petee) *adj.* little
peut-être (peotètr) *adv.* perhaps
pièce (pyès) *f.* play, room; ... **d'identité** identification paper
plaisir (plèzeer) *m.* pleasure; **faire** ...
to please
plan (plân) *m.* map (of a city)
planche (plânsh) *f.* plank, board
plate-forme (platform) *f.* platform
plutôt (plütô) *adv.* rather
poète (poèt) *m.* poet
point (pwèn) *m.* ... **de vue** point of
view
porteur (portèor) *m.* porter
poursuivre (poorsüeevr) to pursue,
continue
pousser (poosay) to push, grow
pouvoir (poovwar) to be able; **vous
pouvez** you can, you may; **je pourrai**
I shall be able
pratique (prateek) *adj.* practical
près (prè) *adv.* ... **de** near; **de** ...
close up
pressé (prèsay) *adj.* in a hurry
prix (pree) *m.* prize, price, value
professionnel, -le (profèsyonèl) *adj.*
professional
projet (prozhè) *m.* plan
propos (propô) *m.* word; **à** ... by the
way
proprement (propremân) *adv.* ... **dit**
properly so-called
puis (püee) *adv.* then

Q • R

quai (kay) *m.* platform (of a station)
quand (kân) *conj.* when; ... **même**
just the same
quartier (kartyay) *m.* quarter, section,
district
quelque (kèlke) *adj.* a few, few
railleur (râyèor) *m.* scoffer
rappeler (raplay) **se** ... to remember
rapprocher (raproshay) **se** ... **de** to
draw close to
recevoir (resevwar) to receive
reconnaître (rekonètr) to recognize
récupérer (rayküpayray) to recover
refaire (refèr) to remake
regarder (regarday) to look at; **se** ...
to look at oneself or at each other
reine (rèn) *f.* queen
remarquer (remarkay) to notice;
faire ... to call one's attention to;
se faire ... to attract attention
remplir (rânpleer) to fill
rendez-vous (rândayvoo) *m.* meeting
place
rendre (rândr) to give back; **se** ...
to surrender
répertoire (raypèrtwar) *m.* repertory
respect (rèspè) *m.* respect
respirer (rèspeeray) to breathe
ressembler (resânblay) to resemble
rester (rèstay) to remain
roi (rwa) *m.* king
rôle (rôl) *m.* part (in a play)
roman (român) *adj.* romanesque;
roman *m.* novel
roue (roo) *f.* wheel
rouler (roolay) to roll, run

S

salle (sal) *f.* ... **des pas perdus** waiting room
scène (sèn) *f.* scene, stage
sembler (sânblay) to seem
signe (seeny) *m.* sign

soldat (solda) *m.* soldier
sorte (sort) *f.* sort; **de ... que** *conj.* so that
sortie (sortee) *f.* exit
sortir (sorteer) to go out
spectacle (spèktakl) *m.* spectacle, show
spectateur (spèktatèᵒr) *m.* spectator
subventionner (sübvâⁿsyonay) to subsidize
suivre (süeevr) to follow
supprimer (süpreemay) to suppress, do away with
sûr (sür) *adj.* sure
surveiller (sürvèyay) to supervise, watch

T

tant (tâⁿ) *adv.* en ... que as
tarder (tarday) **il lui tarde de** he longs to
tenir (teneer) to hold, to keep; **tiens** I say; **... debout** to stand up
terrasse (tèras) *f.* terrace (also sidewalk area covered by tables in front of a café)
tirer (teeray) to pull; **... d'un mauvais pas** to get out of a bad fix
toujours (toozhoor) *adv.* always, still
tout (too) *adj.* all; **tous (toutes) les**

deux both; **... adv.** quite; **... de même** just the same; **... à fait** altogether
transatlantique (trâⁿzatlâⁿteek) *adj.* **un train ...** a transatlantic boat train
transporter (trâⁿsportay) to transport, carry
traverser (travèrsay) to cross

U • V

uniquement (üneekmâⁿ) *adv.* exclusively
us (ü) *m. pl.* **... et coutumes** (üzaykootüm) the ways and customs
valoir (valwar) to be worth, **il vaut mieux** it is better
vieux (vyeᵒ) *m.* **vieil** (vyèy) *m.* **vieille** (vyèyᵉ) *f.* old
visière (veezyèr) *f.* vizor
voie (vwa) *f.* way, track; **... de garage** side-track
voir (vwar) to see; **vous voyez** you see
voisin (vwazèⁿ) *m.* neighbor
voiture (vwatür) *f.* carriage, car, railway car
voyageur (vwayazhèᵒr) traveller, passenger
vrai (vrè) *adj.* true

18 DIX-HUITIÈME LEÇON

Une Conversation au Salon

(La scène se passe dans le salon de Madame de Nédélec, mère de Françoise. Quand le rideau se lève, Justin est seul.)

Madame de N., *qui entre:* Ah! bonjour, Justin. Je suis la mère de Françoise.

Justin: Je suis très heureux de faire votre connaissance, Madame.

Madame de N.: Vous m'excuserez, j'espère, de n'être[1] pas allée[2] à votre rencontre tout à l'heure. La nouvelle bonne qu'on vient de m'envoyer manque d'expérience et n'ose pas lever le[3] doigt sans que[4] je sois là pour lui donner des ordres. Il y

avait justement une petite crise à la cuisine quand vous êtes arrivé parce qu'elle ne savait pas faire marcher le fourneau à gaz.

Justin: Françoise me disait qu'on a des difficultés actuellement pour se faire servir.

Madame de N.: C'est malheureusement trop vrai. Comme je ne vois pas Françoise, je suppose

---

Footnotes: *1. For not having gone.* Excuser *takes* de *(in sense of* for*) to introduce a* Dependent Infinitive. *This infinitive, in its compound form, uses the auxiliary* être *because* aller *belongs to the list of verbs conjugated with* être *(see lesson III, note 15). The most common verbs conjugated with* être *are:* aller, arriver, descendre, devenir, entrer, monter, mourir, naître, partir, rentrer, rester, retourner, revenir, sortir, tomber, venir. *2.* In this example the past participle agrees with the implied subject of the infinitive (see lesson VII, note *11*). *3.* With parts of the body in the predicate of the sentence, French uses definite article instead of possessive adjective. Example: *Je lève la main:* I raise my hand. In other expressions the English possessive adjective becomes an Indirect Object of Reference: *Je me lave les mains: I wash my hands* (the hands with reference to

qu'elle est encore occupée à sa toilette. Je sais qu'elle voulait mettre sa nouvelle robe pour vous éblouir ce soir. Une nouvelle robe est si rare dans sa vie, pauvre chérie. Mes enfants ne connaissent pas la vie facile de mon enfance, enfin celle que vous connaissez encore dans la[5] libre Amérique. Mais ne parlons pas de cela.[6] Racontez-moi plutôt votre promenade de cet après-midi. Qu'avez-vous vu[7] de notre belle ville de Paris?

JUSTIN: Tout et rien. Nous avons fait comme si je n'avais qu'une seule après-midi à y passer, ce qui n'est pas vrai, car j'ai des semaines devant moi. Je voulais tout[8] voir en une seule fois sans rien[9] approfondir. Voulez-vous que je vous raconte[10] notre itinéraire?

---

me). See lesson XIV, note *11*.   4. Another conjunction requiring subjunctive (see lesson IX, note *16*). Observe the awkwardness of the English equivalent: *without my being there*.   5. When the adjective precedes the name of a country, an article is also required.   6. INDEFINITE DEMONSTRATIVE PRONOUN translated *this* (ceci) or *that* (cela) when there is no precise antecedent giving number and gender. See lesson XI, note *10* and lesson XVII, note *3*.   7. Past participle of *voir*.   8. *Tout* in the sense of *everything*, though really a pronoun, is treated as an adverb in compound tenses and with an infinitive. Examples: *j'ai tout vu; pour tout dire*.   9. *Sans* has a negative force. *Rien* must therefore be used after it instead of *quelque chose* (*something*). *Rien* is a pronoun requiring also a *ne* before the verb. It may be subject or object. As object, in a compound tense, it occupies the same position as *pas*, that is, it goes after the auxiliary. Example: *je n'ai rien vu*: I have seen nothing. Similarly with an infinitive, it works like *ne* . . .

MADAME DE N.: Volontiers. Je vous écoute avec plaisir.

JUSTIN: Après avoir quitté[11] mon hôtel rue[12] Molière, nous avons pris[13] par des rues étroites, nous avons traversé au pas de course le jardin du Palais-Royal, et nous avons fait halte au beau milieu de la Place du Carrousel pour jouir de la perspective extraordinaire. Il faisait un temps superbe. Autour de nous, en forme de fer à cheval, il y avait les ailes de ce vaste édifice qu'est[14] le Louvre; à l'ouest, à travers le jardin classique des Tuileries[15] avec ses statues et ses parterres pleins de fleurs, on voyait[16] d'abord la Place de la Concorde[17] avec ses fontaines et son obélisque au centre; plus loin encore, toujours en ligne droite, c'était l'Avenue des Champs-Élysées[18] qu'on voyait à peine, naturellement; et, tout au bout, se dressait majestueusement sur la hauteur l'Arc de Triomphe de l'Étoile.[19]

MADAME DE N.: Oui, c'est là[20] la plus jolie perspective de toute la ville. Le Paris moderne s'évanouit dans les lointains de cette perspective classique. Évidemment tout le Louvre, et notamment les parties qui entourent la Place du Carrousel, ne date pas du XVIIe siècle, mais on ne s'en douterait pas. De même les façades classiques à[21] arcade de la rue de Rivoli[22] ne datent que des premières années du XIXe siècle,

---

pas. Example: *pour ne rien dire:* in order to say *nothing.* (In the above example the negative *sans* absorbs the *ne*). Compare the word order with *personne* (lesson XVII, note 54). 10. See lesson XIII, note 9. Translation: *Do you want me to tell you?* In translating such an English sentence into French, this rule must be observed: *An infinitive in French cannot have a subject.* The infinitive phrase becomes a subordinate clause in the subjunctive. Note that the verbs *demander, ordonner, commander* take a construction which may seem to violate the rule. Example: *Je demande à Jean de le faire:* I ask John to do it. *John,* however, is indirect object in French, not direct object. Compare lesson XIII, note *19.* 11. *Quitter* means *to leave* a place which is mentioned. If the place is not mentioned, use *partir.* Example: *Je quitte Paris.* But: *Je pars maintenant.* The expression *partir de* can be substituted for *quitter.* Examples: *J'ai quitté Paris; je suis parti de Paris. Laisser* means *to leave behind.* Example: *J'ai laissé le livre sur la table.* 12. With the name of the street prepositions are frequently omitted. 13. Past participle of *prendre.* 14. Inversion in a relative clause is very common.

mais elles ressemblent à celles, plus anciennes, de la Place Vendôme que vous avez vue sans doute.

JUSTIN: Non. Françoise m'a seulement fait remarquer la colonne Vendôme[23] qui se voit[24] très bien des Tuileries. Qu'est-ce que c'est[25] au juste que la Place Vendôme?

MADAME DE N.: C'est une grande place octogonale, bordée de[26] bâtiments modernes ou modernisés, mais dont les façades sont l'œuvre de Mansart, architecte de Louis XIV. Mais où êtes-vous allés ensuite?

JUSTIN: Place de la Concorde—sans contredit la plus belle place du monde. Puis, demi-tour, en passant devant la Chambre des Députés[27]—peut-être dois-je[28] dire maintenant l'Assemblée Nationale[29]—et en suivant le quai jusqu'à l'Institut. Françoise m'a expliqué quelque chose que j'ignorais, c'est que ce qu'on appelle couramment l'Institut est l'Académie des Sciences Morales et Politiques et que l'Institut de France, proprement dit, comprend aussi la célèbre Académie Française, fondée par Richelieu[30] en 1634, ainsi que trois autres académies un peu moins connues.[31]

MADAME DE N.: Vous savez que pour un Français, pour qui l'activité intellectuelle prime tout, être élu membre de l'Académie Française est le plus grand honneur possible. C'est ainsi que la France honore ses grands intellectuels et écrivains.

Example: *la maison qu'a vue Jean:* the house which John saw. In *qu'est le Louvre, que* is an accusative, not a nominative form. English says: *It is I.* But French says: *C'est moi:* It is me. **15.** The Tuileries Palace was burned by the mob in 1871 because Napoleon III had lived there. **16.** Imperfect tense of *voir.* **17.** Built in 1748. **18.** *Elysian Fields.* **19.** *Star.* The square is called the *Étoile* because it is a hub from which radiate out twelve broad avenues. **20.** Idiom. Emphatic way of saying: *That is.* **21.** In a descriptive phrase *with* translates *à.* Example: *L'homme au chapeau:* the man with the hat. **22.** Italian village where Napoleon defeated the Austrians in 1797. **23.** Tall bronze column, 142 feet high, commemorating Napoleonic victories. **24.** *Can be seen* (lit. *is seen*). The French avoids a true PASSIVE (see lesson XVII, note *10*). In translating English passive, the following principles should be observed: If the *agent* is expressed with the English passive, the French cannot avoid a passive. *The music was composed by Debussy:* La musique a été composée par Debussy. If the agent is not expressed and if the subject is a thing, the passive may be avoided by use of the reflexive or

Évidemment, je sais que le choix de l'Académie n'a pas toujours été heureux et que certains de nos grands auteurs n'en ont jamais fait partie.

JUSTIN: En effet, je crois qu'André Gide, bien qu'ayant reçu[32] le prix Nobel, n'est pas membre de l'Académie.

MADAME DE N.: C'est sans doute qu'il n'y tient pas. Les honneurs ne lui disent pas grand'chose.[33]

JUSTIN: Par contre il y a l'exemple de Napoléon, je crois, qui, pendant la campagne d'Égypte, signait ses dépêches "général en chef et membre de l'Institut."

MADAME DE N.: Avez-vous traversé le Pont des Arts qui se trouve devant l'Institut?

JUSTIN: Voulez-vous dire cette passerelle? En effet. La vue est superbe, n'est-ce pas? Puis nous avons retraversé la Seine par le Pont Neuf. C'est le pont le plus ancien de Paris, n'est-ce pas?

MADAME DE N.: Oui, il date de la fin du XVIe siècle.

JUSTIN: Après avoir admiré[34] les deux maisons du temps de Henri IV[35] qui se trouvent au bout de l'Ile de la Cité,[36] nous avons pénétré dans la cour du Palais de Justice[37]—non sans

by using *on* as the subject of an active verb. Example: *French is spoken here:* Le français se parle ici; *or* On parle français ici. If the agent is not expressed and the subject is a person, the only way to avoid the passive is to use *on*. Example: *He was punished:* On l'a puni.   25. *Qu'est-ce que c'est que* means *what is* when the expected answer is a definition.   26. If the passive does not express a real action and has only a descriptive force, the *agent* in the passive (see note 24 above) is introduced by *de* instead of by *par*.   27. Until 1940 the legislative branch of the French government was divided into the *Chamber of Deputies* and the *Senate*.   28. When *peut-être* precedes the verb *there is an automatic inversion*. 29. The *Chamber of Deputies* has had its name changed to *National Assembly* by the Constitution of 1946. The same constitution abolished the senate and replaced it by a number of consultative bodies without legislative authority.   30. Armand-Jean du Plessis, Cardinal de Richelieu (1585-1642), prime minister of France under Louis XIII.   31. Past participle of *connaître*.   32. *Having received*.

avoir préalablement examiné les vieilles tours gothiques du côté nord, vestiges du château fort royal—et nous avons visité la Sainte-Chapelle de Louis IX.[38] Le soleil éclairait les vitraux quand nous sommes entrés. Jamais je n'ai rien vu d'aussi beau,[39] me semble-t-il.[40]

MADAME DE N.: Quand vous verrez[41] la cathédrale de Chartres où les bleus éclatants des vitraux font contraste avec l'obscurité de la nef et où les vastes dimensions ajoutent au caractère irréel de l'endroit, je crois que vous l'aimerez encore mieux que la Sainte-Chapelle. Avez-vous visité Notre-Dame?[42]

JUSTIN: Oui, tout de suite après la Sainte-Chapelle. Françoise m'a un peu gâté ma visite en parlant de Chartres. Il paraît que les statues du porche ne sont pas authentiques, que les vitraux sont moins beaux, et je ne sais quoi encore.[43] Comme c'était ma première cathédrale gothique, j'étais néanmoins très impressionné. Nous sommes même montés dans une tour pour profiter de la vue. De là on peut voir tous les monuments de Paris. C'est heureux qu'il n'y ait pas de gratte-ciel comme à Anvers;[44] cela gâterait tout.

MADAME DE N.: Il y a de grands bâtiments qu'on pourrait presque appeler des gratte-ciel,[45] mais en dehors de la ville, près du Bourget.[46]

---

33. Idiom: *Cela ne lui dit pas grand'chose:* That does not mean much to him.
34. See lesson II, note 22. The preposition *après* requires after it the COMPOUND INFINITIVE, never the simple infinitive.   35. *Henri Quatre.* With names of sovereigns cardinal numbers are used except with the first in a series. Example: *François Ier:* Francis I.   36. In the Middle Ages *cité* meant a walled city. The oldest part of London is still called the *City.* The *Ile de la Cité* is the oldest part of Paris.   37. The Paris Law Courts. In the Middle Ages it was the royal castle, parts of which are incorporated in the modern buildings.   38. The Holy Chapel, built by Saint Louis from 1242 to 1248.   39. When an adjective modifies *quelque chose* or *rien,* it takes the masculine form and goes into a prepositional phrase with *de.* Example: *quelque chose de beau:* something beautiful.   40. The inverted word order here is idiomatic.   41. Future of *voir.* See lesson XIII, note 8.   42. Our Lady of Paris, famous cathedral begun in 1163 and finished in 1230.   43. Idiom: *I don't know what else.*   44. Antwerp, Belgium.   45. This word is

JUSTIN: Comme j'avais voulu voir la petite église de Saint-Julien-le-Pauvre qui, d'après Françoise, est plus ancienne que Notre-Dame et qui était visible du haut de la cathédrale, nous avons de nouveau traversé la Seine pour la voir. Heureusement que[47] la Seine n'est pas très large! Mais j'abrège: ensuite ce furent[48] les ruines gallo-romaines des Thermes,[49] la Sorbonne[50] et le Collège de France,[51] puis la façade gothique de l'Hôtel de Cluny;[52] puis de nouveau, traversée de la Seine en passant par la pittoresque Ile Saint-Louis où nous nous sommes arrêtés devant l'Hôtel Lauzun,[53] décoré, m'a-t-on dit,[54] par les mêmes artistes que le château de Versailles. Le but de notre promenade était le Marais.[55]

MADAME DE N.: Pourquoi voir[56] le Marais quand, à deux pas de la Sorbonne, se trouvaient le Panthéon[57] et le Jardin du Luxembourg?[58]

JUSTIN: Je sais très bien que le Marais est considéré comme malsain et qu'on est en train de le démolir pour cette raison.

C'est pourquoi j'étais si pressé de le voir, comme s'il allait disparaître du jour au lendemain.[59]

MADAME DE N.: Il est difficile de s'imaginer que ce quartier délabré était le quartier aristocratique au XVIᵉ et XVIIᵉ siècles. La Place des Vosges,[60] l'ancienne Place Royale construite par Henri IV sur l'emplacement d'un ancien palais dans la cour duquel[61] le roi Henri II a péri dans un tournoi, la Place des Vosges, dis-je, a un air très coquet avec ses vieilles maisons Renaissance[62] en briques.

---

invariable and takes no *s* in the plural.   46. *Le Bourget* is an airport on the northern perimeter of Paris.   47. When *heureusement* begins the sentence it is followed by *que* in colloquial style.   48. This is in reality a literary expression. Hence the use of the *passé simple*, q.v.   49. *The Baths*, part of a Roman palace believed to have been built by the Emperor Constantius Chlorus about the year 300.   50. The Sorbonne is a large building housing the Faculties of Letters and Sciences of the University of Paris. The present Sorbonne was built about 1885

JUSTIN: Oui, mais j'aime autant l'imprévu du Marais. J'aime pousser une vieille porte cochère pour me trouver soudain dans la cour d'un vieil hôtel de l'ancienne noblesse, tels que l'Hôtel Lamoignon,[63] l'Hôtel de Sully,[64] l'Hôtel de Beauvais,[65] l'Hôtel des Ambassadeurs de Hollande,[66] sans parler de l'Hôtel de Sens[67] avec ses tourelles gothiques.

MADAME DE N.: Oui, tout cela est très curieux. Mais avez-vous vu au moins le Paris des grands boulevards?

JUSTIN: Oui, de la Bastille[68] nous avons pris[69] le métro jusqu'à l'Étoile pour nous replonger dans le Paris moderne, le Paris des grands boulevards et des Américains.

MADAME DE N.: Évidemment les Anglo-Saxons sont à éviter[70] si vous voulez perfectionner votre français.

JUSTIN: Je me suis pourtant[71] conduit comme un Américain dans le métro. Nous sommes descendus vers le quai quand le train y était déjà. Première gaffe: j'ai essayé de pousser le portillon automatique qui nous barrait l'entrée du quai, et pourtant il y avait un écriteau, comme  Françoise me l'a[72] montré ensuite, nous avisant qu'il était inutile de pousser. Elle s'est moquée[73] de moi. Le train parti, le portillon s'est rouvert[74] pour nous laisser passer. Deuxième gaffe: j'ai constaté que, pour descendre du train, les voyageurs ouvraient eux-mêmes les portes en tirant très fort. Une fois dans le train, je me suis retourné et j'ai fermé la porte. Tout le monde m'a regardé comme si j'étais fou, et j'ai vu un autre écriteau qui disait: "La fermeture des portes

but the chapel dates from 1629.   *51.* The Collège de France, founded in 1530 by Francis I to foster the new humanism of the Renaissance, is the highest institution of learning in France. Its forty professorships are occupied by the country's most brilliant minds. The courses are given as public lectures which anyone may attend; the College has no students and gives no degrees.   *52.* Originally a monastery of the order of Cluny, built in the 15th and 16th centuries.   *53.* Built in 1682 for the duc de Lauzun.   *54.* This inversion is similar to the one in this example: *"C'est mon ami," dit-il:* "He is my friend," he says. When all or part of

est automatique." Derrière moi j'ai entendu Françoise qui s'esclaffait.[75] Elle m'avait laissé faire[76] exprès.

MADAME DE N.: Donc vous allez garder un mauvais souvenir de votre premier voyage en métro?[77]

JUSTIN: J'avoue que je n'aime pas me faire remarquer. Mais ça n'a pas été si mal[78] que ça. Deux choses m'ont frappé dans le métro. D'abord le plan très détaillé du réseau du métro. Françoise m'a appris, par exemple, qu'ayant constaté que le terminus de la ligne passant par l'Étoile était le Pont de Neuilly,[79] il fallait suivre les écriteaux et flèches disant "Direction Pont de Neuilly" pour arriver au quai.

MADAME DE N.: Vous avez bien retenu votre leçon. Mais quelle a été votre deuxième impression?

JUSTIN: Eh bien, celle d'avoir voyagé dans un bocal puisque les fenêtres des voitures sont si larges. Et le bocal éclaire en passant les côtés du tunnel de sorte qu'on peut lire "Dubo-Dubon-Dubonnet"[80] qui se répète à l'infini.

MADAME DE N.: Vous avez vu, naturellement, le tombeau du

a direct quotation precedes the phrase "he says" (etc.), the phrase is inverted. 55. *Marais* means *swamp*. This is one of the oldest parts of Paris. 56. Idiom: *Why see?* 57. Shaped like the Pantheon of Rome, this building, completed in 1790, was originally a church. It now contains the tombs of famous people. 58. The Luxembourg Palace, until 1940 the seat of the French senate, was built in 1615-20 for Marie de Médicis, widow of Henri II. 59. Idiom: *from one day to the next.* 60. The Vosges are a mountain range in Alsace. 61. See lesson XVI, note 9. If *whose* or *of which* modifies a noun which in turn is introduced by a preposition, it is impossible to use *dont;* instead *de* plus the proper form of *lequel* must be used. If *whose* refers to a person, however, *qui* is more commonly used than *lequel*. 62. Generally a noun modifying another noun becomes a PREPOSITIONAL PHRASE with *de.* Example: *the history lesson:* la leçon d'histoire. This adjective use of the noun without a *de* is a modern French tendency. 63. Built in 1598 for Diane de France, duchesse d'Angoulême. 64. Built in 1624 for the duc de Sully. 65. Built in 1655 for the duchesse de Beauvais. 66. Built in 1655. 67. Built in 1507 for the archbishop of Sens. 68. An important square, site of the Bastille which was demolished during the Revolution. 69. Past participle of *prendre.* 70. In many cases the active infinitive has a passive sense as in the common expression: *C'est quelque chose à faire:* It is something to be done. 71. This adverb is placed in its normal position in the French sentence (see lesson XIII, note 4). 72. If there are two pronoun objects to be placed before the verb, they follow an intrinsic word order which is as follows: *me, te, se, nous, vous,*

soldat inconnu sous l'Arc de Triomphe; vous avez admiré la majestueuse Avenue des Champs-Élysées; et puis après . . . ?

JUSTIN: Nous voulions nous promener jusqu'au Trocadéro,[81] mais les jambes nous rentraient dans le corps.[82] Nous avons fini par reprendre le métro. Au Palais de Chaillot,[83] très style moderne,[84] nous avons joui du panorama sur le Champs de Mars[85] avec la vieille Tour Eiffel[86] au centre. C'est très beau, mais cela fait un peu décor Hollywood,[87] tandis qu'au Marais. . . .

MADAME DE N.: Mais vous y[88] tenez, à votre Marais! Ah! voilà Françoise qui est prête. On[89] va pouvoir dîner maintenant. Vous devez avoir faim.

before *le, la, les,* before *lui, leur,* before *y,* before *en.* With affirmative imperative (see lesson IX, note *14*) direct object precedes indirect except in the case of *y* and *en* which always come second. Example: *Donnez-le-moi:* Give it to me. Before *y* and *en,* with the affirmative imperative, *moi* and *toi* become *m'* and *t'.* Example: *Donnez-m'en:* Give me some. 73. For agreement of past participle, see lesson VII, note *11.* 74. This is really *re-ouvert.* Many intransitive verbs in English become reflexive in French. Example: *La porte s'ouvre:* The door opens. 75. Note special use of relative clause with *voir, entendre,* etc. Compare with English: *I heard Frances burst out laughing.* 76. Idiom: *She had let me go ahead and do it.* 77. *Voyage en métro,* as one says: *Voyage en automobile:* automobile trip. But one also says: *Voyage à bicyclette: bicycle trip.* 78. After *être* the adverbs *hien, mieux, mal,* etc., are used frequently instead of the expected adjective. 79. Neuilly is a suburb of Paris. 80. Dubonnet is the trade name of an appetizer. Their advertising is a feeble pun on the name. 81. A square on which was located the Palais du Trocadéro, built for the exposition of 1878. 82. Idiom: *We were too tired to stand.* 83. The most impressive modern building in Paris. Built on the site of the Trocadéro for the exposition of 1936. 84. *Modernistic.* 85. Originally a parade ground. 86. Built for the exposition of 1889. 87. *That gives the effect of a Hollywood setting.* 88. This repetition is colloquial. 89. The French frequently use *on* where a more precise pronoun might be expected.

158   THE CORTINA METHOD

VOCABULAIRE POUR CETTE LEÇON

A

abréger (abrayzhay) to cut short, be brief
activité (akteeveetay) f. activity
actuellement (aktüèlmân) adv. at present, nowadays
admirer (admeeray) to admire
ajouter (azhootay) to add
ainsi (ènsee) adv. thus. ... que conj. as well as
Amérique (amayreek) f. America
apprendre (aprândr) to learn, teach, inform. appris, past part.
approfondir (aprofôndeer) to go into deeply
après (aprè) prep. d' ..., according to
aristocratique (areestokrateek) adj. aristocratic
arriver (areevay) to arrive, reach
artiste (arteest) m. artist. ... adj. artistic
assemblée (asânblay) f. assembly
auteur (ôtèor) m. author
authentique (ôtânteek) adj. authentic
aviser (aveezay) to warn, inform
avouer (avway) to confess

B

barrer (baray) to block
bien adv. well. ... que conj. although
bleu (bleo) adj. blue
bocal (bokal) m. globe, goldfish bowl
border (borday) to border
bout (boo) m. end. tout au ... at the very end
brique (breek) f. brick
but (bü(t)) m. object, objective

C

caractère (karaktèr) m. character
cathédrale (kataydral) f. cathedral

centre (sântr) m. center. au ... in the center
château (shâtô) m. castle. ... -fort fortress
chef (shèf) m. chief
chéri, -e (shayree) m. & f., darling
choix (shwa) m. choice
classique (klaseek) adj. classical
colonne (kolon) f. column
conduire (kôndüeer) to conduct, lead, take
connaissance (konèsâns) f. acquaintance, knowledge
considérer (kônseedayray) to consider
constater (kônstatay) to ascertain, observe the fact that
contraste (kôntrast) m. contrast. faire ... to contrast
contredit (kôntredee) m. sans ... without question
coquet, -te (kokè, -èt) adj. dainty, trim
couramment (kooramân) adv. commonly, ordinarily. parler ... to speak with ease, rapidly
crise (kreez) f. crisis

D

décorer (daykoray) to decorate
dehors (deor) adv. en ... de outside
délabré (daylabray) adj. dilapidated
demi-tour (demeetoor) m. right about face
démolir (daymoleer) to demolish
dépêche (daypèsh) f. telegram, dispatch
détaillé (daytayay) adj. detailed
difficile (deefeeseel) adj. difficult, hard to satisfy
difficulté (deefeekültay) f. difficulty
disparaître (deesparètr) to disappear
doigt (dwa) m. finger
donc (dônk) conj. so, therefore

douter (*dootay*) to doubt. **se ... de** to suspect
dresser (*drèsay*). **se ...** to rise up

E

éblouir (*ayblweer*) to dazzle
éclairer (*ayklèray*) to light up
éclatant (*ayklatâⁿ*) *adj.* brilliant
écriteau (*aykreetô*) *m.* sign
écrivain (*aykreevèⁿ*) *m.* writer
élire (*ayleer*) to elect. **élu** elected
emplacement (*âⁿplasmâⁿ*) *m.* site
enfance (*âⁿfâⁿs*) *f.* childhood
entourer (*âⁿtooray*) to surround
entrée (*âⁿtray*) *f.* entrance
envoyer (*âⁿvwayay*) to send
esclaffer (**s'**) (*sèsklafay*) to burst out laughing
évanouir (**s'**) (*sayvanweer*) to faint, fade away
évidemment (*ayveedamâⁿ*) *adv.* obviously
éviter (*ayveetay*) to avoid
excuser (*èksküzay*) to excuse
exemple (*aygzâⁿpl*) *m.* example. **par ... for example
exprès (*èksprè*) *adv.* on purpose
extraordinaire (*èkstrordeenèr*) *adj.* extraordinary

F

facile (*faseel*) *adj.* easy
faim (*fèⁿ*) *f.* hunger. **avoir ...** to be hungry
fer (*fèr*) *m.* iron. **... à cheval** horseshoe
fermer (*fèrmay*) to close
fermeture (*fèrmetür*) *f.* closing
fin (*fèⁿ*) *f.* end
flèche (*flèsh*) *f.* arrow
fleur (*flèºr*) *f.* flower
forme (*form*) *f.* form. **en ... de** in the form of
fort (*for*) *adj.* strong. **... adv.** hard
fou (*foo*), **fol, folle** (*fol*) *adj.* crazy

fourneau (*foornô*) *m.* stove, range. **...
à gaz** gas stove
frapper (*frapay*) to hit, strike

G

gaffe (*gaf*) *f.* social error, blunder
gallo-romain (*galloromèⁿ*) *adj.* Gallo-Roman
gâter (*gâtay*) to spoil
gothique (*goteek*) *adj.* Gothic
gratte-ciel (*gratsyèl*) *m.* skyscraper

H

halte (*alt*) *f.* halt. **faire ...** to halt
haut (*ô*) *adj.* high **... m.** top
hauteur (*ôtèºr*) *f.* height
heureux (*èºreº*), **heureuse** (*èºreºz*) *adj* happy, fortunate
heureusement *adv.* luckily
honorer (*onoray*) to honor
hôtel (*ôtèl*) *m.* hotel, town-house

I

ignorer (*eenyoray*) to be unaware of
île (*eel*) *f.* island
imaginer (*eemazheenay*) **s'...** to imagine
impressionner (*èⁿprèsyonay*) to impress
imprévu (*èⁿprayvü*) *adj.* unforeseen
inconnu (*èⁿkonü*) *adj.* unknown
infini (*èⁿfeenee*) *adj.* infinite; **à l'...** ad infinitum
institut (*èⁿsteetü*) *m.* institute
intellectuel, -le (*èⁿtèlèktüèl*) *adj.* intellectual
interdit (*èⁿtèrdee*) *adj.* forbidden
inutile (*eenüteel*) *adj.* useless
irréel, -le (*eerayèl*) *adj.* unreal
itinéraire (*eeteenayrèr*) *m.* itinerary

J • L

joli (*zholee*) *adj.* pretty
jouir (*zhweer*). **... de** to enjoy

juste (*zh*üst) *adj.* just. **au** ... precisely, exactly
justement (*zh*üst^emân) *adv.* as it so happens, precisely
large (larzh) *adj.* wide
lendemain (lân^demèn) *m.* next day
lever (l^evay) to raise. **se** ... to get up, rise
ligne (leeny) *f.* line. **en** ... **droite** in a straight line
lire (leer) to read
lointain (lwèn tèn) *m.* distance

M

majestueusement (mazhèstüe^ozmân) *adv.* majestically
malheureusement (malè^ore^ozmân) *adv.* unfortunately
malsain (malsèn) *adj.* unhealthy
manquer (mânkay) to miss. ... **de** to lack
marcher (marshay) to walk. **le faire** ... to make it work
mauvais (movè) *adj.* bad, unpleasant
membre (mânbr) *m.* member
même (mèm) *adv.* even. **de** ... likewise. **de** ... **que** just as
métro (maytrô) *m.* subway
milieu (meelye^o) *m.* middle. **au beau** ... in the very middle
moderniser (modèrneezay) to modernize
monument (monümân) *m.* public or historic building

N • O

naturellement (natürèlmân) *adv.* naturally
néanmoins (nayânmwèn) *adv.* nevertheless
nef (nèf) *f.* nave
noblesse (noblès) *f.* nobility
notamment (notamân) *adv.* notably
nouveau (noovô) *adj.* **de** ... again
obélisque (obayleesk) *m.* obelisk

obscurité (opsküreetay) *f.* obscurity, darkness
octogonal (oktogonal) *adj.* octagonal
œuvre (è^ovr) *f.* work
oser (ôzay) to dare
ouest (wèst) *m.* west

P

paraître (parètr) to appear. **il paraît** it appears
parterre (partèr) *m.* flower-bed
pas (pâ) *m.* pace, step. **au** ... **de course** at a run
passerelle (pâsrèl) *f.* foot-bridge
pauvre (pôvr) *adj.* poor
peine (pèn) *f.* pain. **à** ... hardly
pénétrer (paynaytray) to enter
perfectionner (pèrfèksyonay) to perfect
périr (payreer) to perish
perspective (pèrspèkteev) *f.* vista
pittoresque (peetorèsk) *adj.* picturesque
plein (plèn), **pleine** (plèn) *adj.* full
plonger (plônzhay) to dive. **se** ... to immerse oneself
politique (poleeteek) *adj.* political
pont (pôn) *m.* bridge
porche (porsh) *m.* porch (church architecture)
porte (port) *f.* ... **cochère** carriage gateway
portillon (porteeyôn) *m.* wicket (gate)
pourtant (poortân) *adv.* however, nevertheless
préalablement (prayalable mân) *adv.* previously
prendre (prândr) to take. ... **par** to follow
près (prè) *adv.* ... **de** near
presque (prèsk) *adv.* almost
primer (preemay) to take precedence over
profiter (profeetay) to take advantage (of)
promenade (promnad) *f.* walk

Q • R

quai (k*ay*) *m.* embankment (street running parallel to a river), station platform

quitter (k*ee*t*ay*) to leave

raconter (rak*ô*n*tay*) to tell (about), relate

raison (r*è*z*ô*n) *f.* reason

rencontre (r*â*nk*ô*ntr) *f.* **aller à la ...de** to go to meet

répéter (r*ay*p*ay*t*ay*) to repeat

réseau (r*ay*z*ô*) *m.* network, system

retenir (r*e*tn*ee*r) to retain, remember (a lesson)

retourner (r*e*t*oo*rn*ay*) to return, go back. **se ...** to turn around

rien (ry*è*n) *pro.* nothing. **ne ... rien** nothing

ruine (r*ü*een) *f.* ruin

S • T

servir (s*è*rv*ee*r) to serve. **se faire ...** to get servants

soudain (s*oo*d*è*n) *adv.* suddenly

sous (s*oo*) *prep.* under

souvenir (s*oo*vn*ee*r) *m.* memory

suite (s*ü*eet) *f.* succession. **tout de ...** immediately

tandis que (t*â*nd*ee*(s)k*e*) *conj.* whereas, while

tel, -le (t*è*l) *adj.* such a

tenir (t*e*n*ee*r) to hold. **... à** to be anxious to, to value, care for

terminus (t*è*rm*ee*n*ü*s) *m.* terminal, end of the line

toilette (tw*a*l*è*t) *f.* dress, dressing (the act of)

tombeau (t*ô*nb*ô*) *m.* tomb

tour (t*oo*r) *f.* tower

tourelle (t*oo*r*è*l) *f.* turret

tournoi (t*oo*rnw*a*) *m.* tournament

train (tr*è*n) *m.* **être en ... de** to be in the act of, be engaged in

travers (trav*è*r) *m.* **à ...** across, through

traversée (trav*è*rs*ay*) *f.* crossing

V

vie (v*ee*) *f.* life

vitrail (veetr*ay*) *m.* (**vitraux,** *m. pl.*) stained-glass window

volontiers (vol*ô*nty*ay*) *adv.* gladly

DIX-NEUVIÈME LEÇON

APRÈS UNE JOURNÉE À VERSAILLES

(Françoise et Justin viennent de visiter le château et le parc de Versailles. Ils sont assis à la terrasse d'un café.)

JUSTIN: Qu'est-ce que vous allez prendre?

FRANÇOISE: J'aimerais prendre un bain de pieds, mais, comme cela ne se fait pas dans un café, je me contenterai d'une limonade.

JUSTIN: Garçon, une limonade pour mademoiselle et un bock pour moi.

GARÇON: Bien, monsieur.

FRANÇOISE: Enfin, c'est très beau, Versailles, mais le brave Roi Soleil[1] avait de la chance d'avoir une litière pour se promener au fond de son parc. Je le vois très bien s'y rendant

en procession pour prendre un bain de soleil au hameau.[2]

JUSTIN: Vous voulez dire, avec Marie-Antoinette, sans doute?

FRANÇOISE: Puis ils chanteraient *Malbrough s'en va-t-en guerre*[3] à l'ombre de la tour Malbrough[4] en trayant des chèvres.

JUSTIN: Je vois que vous êtes très forte en histoire de France. Comment a-t-on pu[5] vous recaler au bachot?

FRANÇOISE: Recaler? C'est pure médisance. Je n'avais qu'à faire les yeux doux[6] à la vieille barbe[7] qui m'examinait pour faire passer toutes mes balivernes sans la moindre protestation.

JUSTIN: Sans blague![8] Sérieusement, vous n'aviez pas le trac?

FRANÇOISE: Sérieusement, c'etait pis encore. Je bredouillais, je me sentais une moiteur dans les paumes. Ce n'est pas très gai, le bachot français.

JUSTIN: Où l'avez-vous passé?[9] A la Sorbonne?

FRANÇOISE: Oui. Le jury était composé de professeurs illustres qui étaient plus ironiques que méchants. Je ne leur en veux[10] pas maintenant que c'est fini.

JUSTIN: Mais vous vous vengez en embrouillant toutes leurs dates maintenant?

FRANÇOISE: C'est vous qui devenez méchant à présent. Vous trouvez sans doute que j'ai manqué de respect envers Louis XIV. Comment puis-je[11] réparer ma faute? En vous récitant des vers

FOOTNOTES: *1.* Name given to Louis XIV. *2.* The hamlet, in the park of Versailles, was built for Queen Marie-Antoinette. *3. Malbrough goes to war,* sung to the same tune as *The bear went over the mountain.* Marlborough was an English general who defeated the French in the Eighteenth Century. *4.* One of the buildings of the hamlet. *5.* Past participle of *pouvoir.* *6. To make sheep's eyes, to look sweetly.* *7. The old greybeard.* *8. No kidding!* *9. Passer un examen:* to take an examination. *10. En vouloir à:* to hold a grudge against. *11. Je puis* is the alternate form for *je peux.* It must be used in the interrogative.

de Racine[12] pour prouver mon admiration pour la littérature
du grand siècle?[13]

JUSTIN: Oui. Commencez. . . .

Oui, je viens dans son temple adorer l'Éternel.[14]

FRANÇOISE: Alors. . . .

Je viens, selon l'usage antique et solennel,
Célébrer avec vous la fameuse journée
Où sur le mont Sina la loi nous fut donnée.
Que les temps sont changés! Sitôt que de ce jour
La trompette sacrée annonçait le retour,
Du temple, orné partout de festons magnifiques,
Le peuple saint en foule inondait les portiques. . . .[15]

Allez,[16] continuez maintenant.

JUSTIN: Je ne saurais[17] pas, car je n'ai pas bonne mémoire. Je me rends.

FRANÇOISE: Si vous vouliez m'indiquer une pièce caractéristique du règne de Louis XIV, vous avez mal choisi votre passage, car *Athalie* date de la période où Racine, devenu historiographe du roi, avait abandonné le théâtre. La pièce n'a été jouée que pendant la Régence[18] après la mort de l'auteur et de Louis XIV.

JUSTIN: Cela est vrai. Mais rappelez-vous aussi que la pièce a été composée pour être jouée à Saint-Cyr à l'école de jeunes filles de Madame de Maintenon[19] et que les demoiselles de Saint-Cyr l'ont jouée sans costumes dans la chambre de Louis

12. Jean Racine (1639-1699), France's greatest dramatic poet. His most famous play is *Phèdre.*   13. The Seventeenth Century which was also the period of the reign of Louis XIV.   14. *Yes, I come into his temple to worship the Eternal God.* In French poetry mute *e*'s are pronounced except when they occur at ends of lines or before other words beginning with a vowel or mute *h.*   15. *I come, according to the ancient and solemn custom,/ To celebrate with you the famous day/ When on Mount Sinai the law was given to us./ How times have changed! As soon as of this day/ The sacred trumpet announced the return,/ Of the temple,*

XIV. La pièce n'a pas été représentée en public avant 1716, je crois.

FRANÇOISE: Comme vous êtes calé—j'allais dire "pour un Américain," mais ce n'aurait pas été très gentil. C'est moi qui me rends maintenant. Mais trêve de plaisanteries! Qu'est-ce que vous avez aimé le plus à Versailles?

JUSTIN: Voulez-vous que je vous dise[20] d'abord ce que je n'ai pas aimé? Ce sont ces deux pavillons à droite et à gauche de la Cour d'Honneur qui portent l'inscription "A toutes les gloires de France." Ils semblent appartenir à une autre époque que l'ensemble du château.[21]

FRANÇOISE: Je crois, en effet, qu'ils ont été ajoutés plus tard. Mais à part ces deux intrus, l'ensemble du château est exceptionnel par l'uniformité de son architecture et sa forme géométrique. N'avez-vous pas admiré les proportions harmonieuses de l'autre façade, celle qui donne sur les jardins?

JUSTIN: Oui, de loin, on a une impression de grandeur dont je n'ai jamais vu l'équivalent. On dirait que le souci de Louis XIV n'a pas été uniquement de faire grand,[22] comme un roi du pétrole américain, mais plutôt de faire quelque chose de royal où la dignité viendrait non seulement des dimensions harmonieuses mais aussi de l'échelle surhumaine de la construction. Évidemment, cela n'a rien à faire avec le Parthénon, mais je crois qu'on trouverait dans le temple grec la même alliance de gracieux et de surhumain.

---

ornamented with magnificent garlands,/ The holy people, crowding in, inundated the porticos . . .   16. Go ahead.   17. I couldn't possibly. Savoir is used instead of pouvoir in the sense of mental ability.   18. The Regency (1715-1723), during the minority of Louis XV.   19. Françoise d'Aubigné, marquise de Maintenon (1635-1719), morganatic wife of Louis XIV.   20. Subjunctive of dire (see lesson XIII, note 9).   21. The castle taken as a whole.   22. To do things on a big scale.   23. Conditional of aller.   24. Literally: which produce the result that. 25. On that account.   26. Idiom: perhaps so.   27. Character in the famous

FRANÇOISE: Louis XIV serait enchanté de vous entendre comparer son château au Parthénon. Cela irait[23] très bien avec le classicisme de son illustre siècle. Et je crois que vous avez bien saisi la nuance.  Il y a la même distance de l'architecture du Parthénon à celle de Versailles qu'il y a de la littérature grecque à la littérature française de l'époque classique. Il y a beaucoup de points de ressemblance, évidemment, qui font[24] que le grec et le français sont tous les deux classiques sans que le français soit pour cela[25] du néo-classicisme. Le classicisme français s'est affranchi de la tutelle de l'antiquité; c'est un mouvement intellectuel, littéraire et artistique qui a vraiment sa propre originalité.

JUSTIN: Excusez-moi de faire ici une observation critique. Vous parlez comme un cuistre. Est-ce que toutes les Françaises sont comme vous?

FRANÇOISE: Peut-être bien que oui.[26] Nous ne parlons pas ainsi par pédantisme mais—comme dirait le Bourgeois Gentilhomme[27] de Molière — "pour savoir raisonner des choses parmi les honnêtes gens."[28]  Une Française intelligente doit savoir tenir son salon[29] tout comme ces dames du temps de Louis XIV.

JUSTIN: Je vous vois[30] très bien à la Galerie des Glaces[31] en train de causer art et littérature avec des courtisans en habits brodés tandis que l'illustre duc et pair Saint-Simon[32] prend note à la

comedy by the same name. *Bourgeois* means middle-class; *gentilhomme* means gentleman (noble). *28. In order to know how to talk about things with respectable people.* 29. *Tenir son salon:* to have her drawing room. Since the Seventeenth Century certain noble or wealthy French ladies have received in their drawing rooms a select circle of literary, artistic, and political figures. In these *salons* conversation has become an art. 30. *I can imagine you.* 31. The *Hall*

dérobée pour pouvoir préserver vos paroles pour la postérité.
Avec votre particule[33] vos ancêtres ont dû[34] être à Versailles.

FRANÇOISE: Malheureusement pas. Dans mon cas il s'agit de
la toute petite noblesse de robe[35] qui remonte seulement au
XVIIIe siècle.—Mais, enfin, quel souvenir allez-vous garder
de Versailles?

JUSTIN: Je me rappellerai toujours d'abord la chapelle, si
gracieuse, si somptueuse et en même temps si mondaine; la
Galerie des Glaces, naturellement, parce qu'il n'y a pas de salle
plus impressionnante au monde; la chambre à coucher du roi;
les appartements privés de Marie-
Antoinette.[36] Et puis les jardins qui
sont aussi l'expression du classicisme
français.

FRANÇOISE: Est-ce que le jardin classique vous plaît en somme?

JUSTIN: Énormément. C'est vrai que
la nature y est subordonnée à l'art. Tous
ces bassins et parterres, ces fontaines et
statues, disposés dans un ordre absolu-
ment géométrique, peuvent très bien sembler artificiels, mais
c'est qu'il[37] y a beaucoup d'artificiel dans l'art. Je peux très
bien me figurer une représentation de Racine ou de Molière au
Quinconce du Midi.[38] Leur art a le même côté factice que le
décor du quinconce. C'est-à-dire, si vous voulez, que l'art est

---

of Mirrors in the Castle of Versailles. 32. Louis de Rouvroy, duc de Saint-Simon
(1675-1755), author of famous *Mémoires* of the court of Louis XIV. 33. *With
your "de."* The *de* in a French name generally indicates nobility. 34. Past participle of *devoir.* Translate: *must have been. Must have* translates by the *passé
composé* of *devoir* plus the infinitive of the main verb of the English. Do not
attempt to use a compound infinitive in this sense; all notion of tense must be
conveyed by *devoir.* 35. *Magisterial Nobility.* Bourgeois who became magis-
trates acquired a minor sort of nobility. 36. Marie-Antoinette, queen of Louis
XVI, had part of the castle rebuilt to suit her more delicate Eighteenth Century
taste. 37. *The fact is,* or *it is because.* 38. *Southern Quincunx.* A quincunx
is an area where trees are planted in parallel rows. 39. There are two Trianons
in the park of Versailles. The Grand Trianon is a pink marble palace erected for
Madame de Maintenon by Louis XIV. The Petit Trianon, erected by Louis XV, was

supérieur à la nature.

FRANÇOISE: Autrement dit, vous n'aimez pas le Petit Trianon[39] et le hameau de Marie-Antoinette?

JUSTIN: Pas tout à fait. Le temps a imprégné ces endroits de son charme aussi. Le seul fait de voir[40] ces endroits m'aide à mieux comprendre le XVIIIᵉ siècle qui, en réagissant contre le formalisme de l'époque classique, a cru retrouver[41] la nature et la vie simple dans un décor rustique. Mais examinez de près ce rustique. Les grottes sont en ciment; les maisons sont des joujoux; même les ruines sont fausses.

FRANÇOISE: C'est une époque qui a tellement cherché à être naturelle, par réaction peut-être contre l'acidité de gens comme Voltaire,[42] qu'elle a fini par[43] devenir complètement artificielle. Le bonhomme Jean-Jacques Rousseau[44] y est pour quelque chose.[45]

JUSTIN: On trouve la même simplicité artificielle dans la *Nouvelle Héloïse*[46] ou dans *l'Émile.*[46] Je crois qu'on ne lit plus guère que[47] *les Confessions.*[46]

FRANÇOISE: C'est lui en somme qui a mis notre littérature sur la pente du romantisme.

JUSTIN: Oui, mais je trouve que certains romantiques du

---

a favorite resort of Marie-Antoinette.   *40. Just seeing.*   41. Observe the meaning of the basic construction: *Il a cru voir:* He thought he saw. In almost all cases the French will replace a noun clause (a noun clause begins with *que:* that), which has the same subject as the main clause, with an infinitive construction. This is done even with a change of tense from one clause to the other. Example: *Il croit avoir vu:* He thinks he saw. This is not possible, however, with a future in the noun clause. Example: *Je crois que j'irai:* I think I will go.   42. A prolific writer of the Eighteenth Century (1694-1778), best known today for his ironical philosophical stories like *Candide.* In his day he was known as a dramatist and a poet. He is a rationalist and the antithesis of Rousseau.   43. Idiom: *finir par devenir:* to finally become.   44. Author (1712-1778) of novels and philosophical treatises which, in contrast to the rationalism of Voltaire, emphasized emotion and preached a return to nature.   45. *Has (had) something to do with it.*   46. Works of Rousseau.   47. *No one hardly ever reads anything but.*   48. Victor Hugo (1802-1885), the most prolific of the Romantics. Although he wrote many plays and novels, his real greatness is as a poet.   49. Alfred de Vigny (1797-1863):

XIXe siècle sont infiniment plus artistes. Prenez Hugo,[48] Vigny,[49] même Lamartine. ...[50]

FRANÇOISE: Ils sont rasants, ces vieilles barbes ...

O temps! suspends ton vol; et vous, heures propices!
Suspendez votre cours:
Laissez-nous savourer les rapides délices
Des plus beaux de nos jours.[51]

Toute cette poésie amoureuse ne nous dit rien,[52] à nous autres[53] modernes.

JUSTIN: Vous êtes dure. Mais ces vieilles barbes étaient imberbes, à l'exception de Victor Hugo qui a laissé pousser la sienne pour se mettre à la page[54] pendant sa vieillesse. La mode était alors aux barbes.[55] Vous n'allez pas me dire que vous n'aimez pas ...

VICTOR HUGO

Waterloo! Waterloo! Waterloo! morne plaine!
Comme une onde qui bout dans une urne trop pleine,
Dans ton cirque de bois, de coteaux, de vallons,
La pâle mort mêlait les sombres bataillons.[56]

Cette évocation poétique de la grande bataille peut très bien sembler artificielle en comparaison de la même scène traitée en prose et d'une façon réaliste dans *la Chartreuse de Parme*[57]— vous vous rappelez comment le jeune[58] Fabrice participe à la

more subtle but less gifted than Hugo, is known principally for his poetry although he also wrote novels and plays. *50.* Alphonse de Lamartine (1790-1869), the first French Romantic poet, wrote very sincere verse but less artistic than that of the other Romantics. *51. Oh time! Suspend thy flight; and you, propitious hours!/ Suspend your course:/ Let us taste the fleeting pleasures/ Of the most beautiful of our days. 52.* Idiom: *Cela ne me dit rien:* That means nothing to me, that leaves me cold. *53.* When a noun is used in apposition to *nous* or *vous* the adjective *autres* is required. Example: *We Americans: Nous autres Américains. 54.* Idiom: *Se mettre à la page* (slang): To get up to date. *55.* Idiom: *Beards were then in style. 56. Waterloo! Waterloo! Waterloo! dreary plain!/ Like water boiling in an urn too full,/ In thy circus of woods, of hillocks, of vales,/ Pale death mingled the somber battalions.* (From *Expiation* by Victor Hugo). *57. The Charterhouse Monastery of Parma* by Stendhal whose real name was Henri Beyle (1783-1842). Stendhal is perhaps better known for his *Le Rouge et le Noir* which, although written in the heyday of Romanticism, is one of the most profound

bataille sans y[59] rien comprendre—le poème de Victor Hugo n'en continue pas moins[60] à vous donner une émotion épique digne de *la Chanson de Roland*[61] ou même de Homère.[62]

FRANÇOISE: Chacun son goût.[63] Moi[64] je préfère quelque chose dans le genre de . . .[65]
J'ai plus de souvenirs que si j'avais mille ans.
Un gros meuble à tiroirs encombré de bilans,
De vers, de billets doux, de procès, de romances,
Avec de lourds cheveux roulés dans des quittances . . .[66]

JUSTIN: C'est du[67] Baudelaire,[68] n'est-ce pas? Malgré les dates, vous avouerez que c'est encore du romantisme. Vous êtes une romantique qui s'ignore. Aimez-vous aussi l'obscurité du symbolisme?[69]

FRANÇOISE: Oui, beaucoup. C'est notre plus belle poésie.

JUSTIN: Je vous défie de réciter *la Jeune Parque*[70] de Valéry[71] et, encore plus, de me l'expliquer.

FRANÇOISE:
Mystérieuse Moi, pourtant, tu vis encore!

---

of psychological novels.   58. An adjective with a proper noun requires an article. See lesson XVII, note *50*.   59. *About it.* The word *about* with the word *under-stand* translates as *à*. Example: *Je ne comprends rien à cette histoire.* Since one function of the pronoun *y* is to replace a prepositional phrase with *à* if the object of the preposition is a thing, we get: *Je n'y comprends rien*, when we substitute a pronoun for the phrase *à cette histoire*.   60. Idiom: *n'en + verb + pas moins:* none the less. *Il n'en continue pas moins:* He continues none the less.   61. The *Song of Roland,* the oldest and the greatest French epic written by an unknown author in about 1100.   62. Homer.   63. Idiom: *Everyone to his own taste.* 64. The disjunctive pronoun (see lesson II, note *15*, and lesson V, note *17*) is used when a pronoun is repeated for emphasis. This same emphasis may occur with a pronoun object. *He saw me:* Il m'a vu moi.   65. *Dans le genre de:* like. 66. *I have more keepsakes than if I were a thousand years old./ A large chest of drawers littered with balance sheets,/ With verses, love-notes, lawsuits, romances,/ With heavy hair rolled up in receipts . . .* (From *Spleen* by Baudelaire).

Tu vas te reconnaître au lever de l'aurore
Amèrement la même . . .[72]

J'avoue que c'est rudement difficile à retenir. Quant à l'expliquer, ce n'est pas trop difficile. Ici il s'agit de la Jeune Parque qui se réveille et qui regarde son corps en éprouvant les sensations que son corps lui communiquent. . . . Mais que dites-vous du roman? Vous aimez sans doute *Notre-Dame de Paris*,[73] les *Misérables*[74] ou peut-être même *Mauprat?*[75]

JUSTIN: Je suis plus difficile que cela. Donnez-moi du Flaubert,[76] du Stendhal, du Maupassant.[77] J'aime la clarté que ces grands romanciers apportent à l'étude de la conscience humaine. Je goûte difficilement l'obscurité de certains romanciers modernes. Prenez Proust, par exemple.

FRANÇOISE: Si vous allez me démolir Proust maintenant, gare à vous! Mais prenez plutôt votre bière et dépensissons, car l'heure avance. Nous devons sauter dans ce petit tramway qui nous conduira à la gare Versailles-Chantiers où il y a un beau train électrique en aluminium pour nous ramener à Paris-Montparnasse.

67. When the author's name is used to stand for his work, the French requires a partitive. *C'est du Baudelaire:* It is Baudelaire.   68. Charles Baudelaire (1821-1867), the father of modern French poetry. His life of misfortune resembles that of Edgar Allan Poe whom he translated.   69. Symbolism was the dominant school in French poetry at the end of the Nineteenth Century.   70. *The Young Parca* (Fate).   71. Paul Valéry (1871-1945), the greatest French poet of the Twentieth Century. He continued symbolism.   72. *Mysterious me, yet, thou livest still!/ Thou art going to recognize thyself at the break of dawn/ Bitterly the same . . .*   73. Romantic novel of Victor Hugo known in English as the *Hunchback of Notre-Dame.*   74. Also by Victor Hugo.   75. Romantic novel by George Sand whose real name was Aurore Dupin, baronne Dudevant (1804-1876).   76. Gustave Flaubert (1821-1880), realistic novelist, author of *Madame Bovary.*   77. Guy de Maupassant (1850-1893), realistic novelist, better known for his short stories.   78. An adjective derived from Versailles.   79. Navarre, an old kingdom in the region of the Pyrenees, was annexed to France when its king ascended the French throne under the name of Henri IV.

JUSTIN: Cela dit "Compagnie des Tramways Versaillais."[78] Comme votre tramway n'est pas plus grand qu'une litière, je comptais y lire "Tramway Officiel de Sa Majesté Louis XIV, Roi de France et de Navarre."[79]

FRANÇOISE: Mettez donc votre perruque et préparez-vous à sauter.

VOCABULAIRE POUR CETTE LEÇON

A

abandonner (abân̄donay) to abandon
absolument (apsolümân̄) adv. absolutely
acidité (aseedeetay) f. acidity
affranchir (afrân̄sheer) to free
aider (èday) to aid, help
aluminium (alümeenyom) m. aluminum
amoureux (amooreo), **amoureuse** (amooreoz) adj. amorous
ancêtre (ân̄sètr) m. ancestor
antiquité (ân̄teekeetay) f. antiquity
appartement (apartemân̄) m. apartment

apporter (aportay) to bring
artificiel, -le (arteefeesyèl) adj. artificial
artistique (arteesteek) adj. artistic
assis (asee) past part. of asseoir
autrement (ôtremân̄) adv. otherwise, differently. ... dit in other words

B

bachot (bashô) m. slang for baccalauréat (bachelor's examination)
bain (bèn̄) m. bath. ... de pieds footbath. ... de soleil sun-bath
baliverne (baleevèrn) f. twaddle
barbe (barb) f. beard, graybeard (in slang)
bassin (basèn̄) m. basin

bataille (batay) *f.* battle
bière (byèr) *f.* beer
blague (blag) *f.* kidding (slang)
bock (bok) *m.* glass of beer
bonhomme (bonom) *m.* old fellow
brave (brav) *adj.* worthy
bredouiller (br^edooyay) to mumble
broder (broday) to embroider

C

calé (kalay) *adj.* learned (slang)
caractéristique (karakt*ay*reesteek) *adj.*
  characteristic
cas (kâ) *m.* case
causer (kôzay) to converse, converse
  about
chance (shâⁿs) *f.* luck
chanter (shâⁿtay) to sing
chapelle (shapèl) *f.* chapel
charme (sharm) *m.* charm
chèvre (shèvr) *f.* goat
ciment (seemäⁿ) *m.* cement
clarté (klartay) *f.* clarity
compagnie (kôⁿpa*n*yee) *f.* company
comparaison (kôⁿparèzôⁿ) *f.* comparison
complètement (kôⁿplètmâⁿ) *adv.* completely
conscience (kôⁿsyâⁿs) *f.* conscience,
  mind
contenter (kôⁿtâⁿtay) to satisfy. se ...
  to be satisfied
courtisan (koorteezâⁿ) *m.* courtier
critique (kreeteek) *adj.* critical
cuistre (küeestr) *m.* pedant

D

dame (dam) *f.* lady
décor (daykor) *m.* setting
défier (dayfyay) to challenge
déguerpir (daygèrpeer) to decamp
demoiselle (d^emwazèl) *f.* damsel,
  young lady
dérober (dayrobay) to steal. à la

dérobée on the sly
deux (de^o) *adj.* tous les ... both
devenir (d^evneer) to become
difficile (deefeeseel) *adj.* difficult, hard
  to please
difficilement (deefeeseelmâⁿ) *adv.*
  with difficulty
digne (deeny) *adj.* worthy
dignité (deenyeetay) *f.* dignity
disposer (deespôzay) to arrange
duc (dük) *m.* duke
dur (dür) *adj.* hard, harsh

E

échelle (ayshèl) *f.* ladder, scale
électrique (aylèktreek) *adj.* electric
embrouiller (âⁿbrooyay) to mix up
enchanté (âⁿshâⁿtay) *adj.* delighted
énormément (aynormaymâⁿ) *adv.*
  enormously
envers (âⁿvèr) *prep.* towards
épique (aypeek) *adj.* epic
époque (aypok) *f.* period
éprouver (ayproovay) to experience
étude (aytüd) *f.* study
exception (èksèpsyôⁿ) *f.* à l'... de with
  the exception of

F • G

façon (fasôⁿ) *f.* way. de cette ... in
  this way
factice (faktees) *adj.* artificial
faute (fôt) *f.* fault, error, transgression
faux (fô), fausse (fôs) *adj.* false
figurer (feegüray) se ... to imagine
fort (for) *adj.* strong, good (in a subject)
gai (gay) *adj.* gay
gare (gar) *interj.* ... à vous watch out
gens (zhâⁿ) *m. pl.* people
gentil, -le (zhâⁿtee, -eey) *adj.* nice
géométrique (zhayomaytreek) *adj.*
  geometric
gloire (glwar) *f.* glory

goûter (*gootay*) to taste, enjoy, appreciate
gracieux (*grasye*o), **gracieuse** (*grasye*oz) *adj.* graceful
grec, grecque (grèk) *adj.* Greek
grotte (grot) *f.* grotto

H • I • J

habit (*abee*) *m.* suit
hameau (*amô*) *m.* hamlet
harmonieux (*armonye*o), **harmonieuse** (*armonye*oz) *adj.* harmonious
histoire (*eestwar*) *f.* history
historiographe (*eestoryograf*) *m.* historiographer (official historian)
humain (*ümèn*) *adj.* human
ignorer (*eenyoray*) to be unaware of
illustre (*eelüstr*) *adj.* illustrious
imberbe (*ènbèrb*) *adj.* beardless
imprégner (*ènpraynyay*) to impregnate
infiniment (*ènfeeneemân*) *adv.* infinitely
intrus (*èntrü*) *m.* intruder
ironique (*eeroneek*) *adj.* ironical
joujou (*zhoozhoo*) *m.* (m. pl.: -x) toy

L • M • N

limonade (*leemonad*) *f.* lemonade
litière (*leetyèr*) *f.* litter
littéraire (*leetayrèr*) *adj.* literary
littérature (*leetayratür*) *f.* literature
majesté (*mazhèstay*) *f.* majesty
malgré (*malgray*) *prep.* in spite of
méchant (*mayshân*) *adj.* naughty, nasty
médisance (*maydeezâns*) *f.* slander
mémoire (*maymwar*) *f.* memory. **avoir bonne ...** to have a good memory
moindre (*mwèndr*) *adj.* least
moiteur (*mwatèor*) *f.* moistness

mondain (*môndèn*) *adj.* worldly
mort (mor) *f.* death
naturel, -le (*natürèl*) *adj.* natural
nuance (*nüâns*) *f.* shade of meaning, subtle difference

O • P

officiel, -le (*ofeesyèl*) *adj.* official
ombre (*ônbr*) *f.* shadow, shade
ordre (ordr) *m.* order
originalité (*oreezheenaleetay*) *f.* originality
pair (pèr) *m.* peer
parole (parol) *f.* word
part (par) *f.* share. **à ...** except for
participer (*parteeseepay*) to participate
paume (pôm) *f.* palm (of the hand)
pavillon (*paveeyôn*) *m.* pavilion
pédantisme (*paydânteesm*) *m.* pedantry
pente (pânt) *f.* slope, downward path
perruque (pèrük) *f.* wig
pétrole (paytrol) *m.* petroleum. **roi du ...** oil baron
pis (pee) *adv.* worse
plaire (plèr) to please
plaisanterie (plèzântree) *f.* joke, joking
poème (poèm) *m.* poem
poésie (poayzee) *f.* poetry
poétique (poayteek) *adj.* poetic
postérité (postayreetay) *f.* posterity
préférer (prayfayray) to prefer
privé (preevay) *adj.* private
professeur (profèsèor) *m.* professor
propre (propr) *adj.* own
prouver (proovay) to prove

Q • R

quant (kân) *adv.* **... à** as for
ramener (ramnay) to bring back
rasant (râzân) *adj.* boring (slang)
réagir (rayazheer) to react

réaliste (r*a*yaleest) *adj.* realistic
recaler (r*e*kal*a*y) to "pluck" (reject in an examination)
réciter (r*a*yseetay) to recite
règne (rè*n*y) *m.* reign
remonter (r*e*mô*n*tay) to go back
rendre (râ*n*dr) to yield, to give up.
se ... dans un lieu to betake oneself
réparer (r*a*ypar*a*y) to repair, atone for
représentation (r*e*prayzâ*n*tasyô*n*) *f.* performance
représenter (r*e*prayzâ*n*tay) to represent, present (a play)
ressemblance (r*e*sâ*n*blâ*n*s) *f.* resemblance
retenir (r*e*tneer) to retain. ... une leçon to remember a lesson
réveiller (r*a*yvèyay) to awaken. se ... to awaken
romancier (româ*n*sy*a*y) *m.* novelist
romantique (româ*n*teek) *m.* Romanticist
romantisme (româ*n*teesm) *m.* Romanticism
rudement (rüdmâ*n*) *adv.* deucedly
rustique (rüsteek) *adj.* rustic

S • T

saisir (sèz*ee*r) to seize, grasp
sauter (sôt*a*y) to jump
sentir (sâ*n*teer) to feel, smell
sérieusement (sayrye*o*zmâ*n*) *adv.* seriously

simplicité (sè*n*pl*ee*seetay) *f.* simplicity
somme (som) *f.* sum. en ... in short
somptueux (sô*n*pt*üe*o), somptueuse (sô*n*pt*üe*oz) *adj.* sumptuous
souci (soosee) *m.* concern
subordonner (sübordon*a*y) to subordinate
supérieur (süp*a*yryè*o*r) *adj.* superior
surhumain (surümè*n*) *adj.* superhuman
tellement (telmâ*n*) *adv.* so much
temps (tâ*n*) *m.* time, weather. en même ... at the same time. de ... en ... from time to time
trac (trak) *m.* stagefright
traire (trèr) to milk. trayant, *pres. part.*
traiter (trèt*a*y) to treat
tramway (tramwè) *m.* tramway, tram
travers (travèr) *m.* n ... across, through
trêve (trèv) *f.* truce ... de enough
tutelle (tütèl) *f.* tutelage

U • V

uniformité (ün*ee*formeetay) *f.* uniformity
uniquement (üneekmâ*n*) *adv.* exclusively
venger (vâ*n*zhay) to avenge
vers (vèr) *m.* line (of poetry)
vieillesse (vyèyès) *f.* old age

VINGTIÈME LEÇON

Une Conversation à la Table

(Les quatre personnages, Françoise, Justin, et Madame et Monsieur de Nédélec, sont assis à table dans la salle à manger de l'appartement des Nédélec. De temps en temps Yvonne, la bonne, apporte les différents plats.)

Madame de N., *à Justin:* J'espère que vous aimez les écrevisses. Nous les mangeons souvent comme hors-d'œuvre.

Justin: C'est la première fois que j'en mange. Comment faut-il s'y prendre?[1]

Françoise: Il faut casser la carapace comme ceci; puis vous sucez.

Justin, *après avoir goûté:* Mais c'est très bon.

Madame de N., *à Yvonne:* Vous avez oublié de mettre les cuillers à soupe.

Justin: Mais c'est tout un travail[2] pour manger des écrevisses!

Françoise: Vous pensez! La prochaine fois on vous donnera des artichauts et vous verrez ce que c'est que[3] de travailler.

Madame de N.: Il faut dire que Françoise n'aime pas les artichauts. Par paresse, je suppose.

Françoise: Maman, tu vas nuire à ma réputation auprès de notre visiteur d'outre-mer. Il croit que je suis une jeune fille très sérieuse.

MADAME DE N.: Alors il faudrait le détromper au plus vite.[4] Henri, veux-tu nous couper du pain? *(Monsieur de N. se lève, sort un grand pain d'une corbeille, et commence à le couper en le tenant contre sa veste.)* Attention, Henri, tu vas te salir! *(Il remplit une petite corbeille de tranches de pain et la passe à Justin.)*

MONSIEUR DE N.: Du pain, Justin?

JUSTIN: Oui, Monsieur. . . . Merci. *(Monsieur de N. se rassied.[5])* Le pain français est ma plus grande joie. Les miches sont parfois longues comme des bâtons, parfois grosses comme celle que vous avez là. Et il y a autant de goûts différents qu'il y a de formes différentes.

MONSIEUR DE N.: Cela vient de ce[6] qu'il a été cuit par le boulanger du coin et non dans une grande usine comme chez vous. Je me rappelle que ce qu'on a voulu me servir comme pain à New-York était détestable. Faire le pain est un art en

FOOTNOTES: *1.* Idiom: *to go about it.   2. It's quite a job.   3.* In an indirect question *qu'est-ce que c'est que* (see lesson XVIII, note 25) becomes *ce que c'est que.* If either one of these expressions is followed by an infinitive, the infinitive is introduced by *de.   4. As quickly as possible.   5.* Present tense of *se rasseoir: to sit down again.   6. The fact that.   7. Not to say.   8.* Causal use of *faire.*

France, tout comme la fabrication du vin ou des fromages—de même que la gastronomie en général est très développée chez nous.

JUSTIN: En gastronomie les Français ont des habitudes enracinées, pour ne pas dire[7] des préjugés. Je me rappelle les protestations d'un Français à New-York à qui on voulait faire[8] manger des gaufres pour le petit déjeuner.

FRANÇOISE: Manger des gaufres pour le petit déjeuner! Je savais bien que vous mangiez des œufs sur le plat et du petit lard pour le petit déjeuner, mais manger des gaufres, ça me dépasse.[9]

JUSTIN: Je suis sûr que vous n'aimeriez pas non plus la salade pour dames comme on la prépare en Amérique, c'est-à-dire la laitue nature avec un petit édifice de fruits, de fromage à la crème, de noix, etc., le tout inondé de mayonnaise.

FRANÇOISE: J'avoue que la seule[10] idée de ce mélange me fait mal au cœur. Il n'y a rien à dire,[11] les Français n'aiment pas mélanger le salé et le sucré.

MONSIEUR DE N.: Justin, voulez-vous encore un peu de Bordeaux?[12]

JUSTIN: S'il vous plaît, Monsieur. . . . Mais ce poulet froid est délicieux!

In the construction *faire + an infinitive,* the infinitive must follow *faire* and is always in the active form although it may occasionally be translated in the passive. In such a construction the *agent* (the "do-er" of the action) will be expressed with *à* except where there might be a confusion with an indirect object, in which case *par* is used. Example: *Je fais lire un livre à (par) Jean:* I have (make, cause) John read a book, I have a book read by John. But the agent, as a pronoun, is always an indirect object. Example: *Je lui fais lire le livre:* I have the book read

MADAME DE N.: C'est le cas de le dire,[13] c'est la sauce qui fait le poulet. Savez-vous le nom de cette sauce?

JUSTIN: Non, Madame.

MADAME DE N.: Cela s'appelle *ail au lit*. J'espère que ce n'est pas trop fort pour votre palais si habitué au sucre.

JUSTIN: J'ai fait renouveler mon palais depuis mon arrivée à Paris. J'ai maintenant une marque française.

MONSIEUR DE N.: Vous avez lu[14] les journaux ce soir? Que pensez-vous de ce coup communiste?

JUSTIN: Je ne sais pas ce que je dois en penser, car tous les journaux parisiens se contredisent et se lancent des injures. *L'Humanité*[15] dit que le peuple vient d'empêcher un coup fasciste; *Le Figaro*[16] prétend qu'encore une fois la démocratie a été trahie. On ne trouve guère,[17] dans les journaux français, de renseignements objectifs . . . rien que des articles tendancieux.

MONSIEUR DE N.: J'avoue que je suis de votre avis. C'est pour cela que j'achète souvent *le New York Herald* qui est le seul journal bien renseigné à Paris.

JUSTIN: Pourquoi la presse est-elle si mal organisée?

MONSIEUR DE N.: Je crois que c'est d'abord à cause de la formule même[18] du journalisme français. On a tellement insisté sur la liberté de la presse, c'est-à-dire[19] sur le droit d'exprimer les opinions, que nous avons fini par avoir presque uniquement des journaux d'o-

---

by him. In such constructions all pronoun objects precede *faire*. Example: *Je le lui fais lire:* I make him read it. *9. That beats me. 10. Mere. 11. There is no denying it. 12.* In the sense of *vin de Bordeaux. 13.* Idiom: *no mistake. 14.* Past participle of *lire. 15.* The Communist daily newspaper. *16.* The leading Rightist daily paper for which François Mauriac writes. *17.* A negative which works the same as *ne . . . pas. 18.* Adverbial use of *même.* When *very* functions as an adjective, the equivalent French is an adverb following the noun.

pinion. Le journalisme objectif a sombré sous les opinions diverses, ou peut-être n'a-t-il jamais existé.

JUSTIN: Ce qui m'a frappé, c'est le format réduit de vos journaux.

MONSIEUR DE N.: La crise du papier[20] explique en ce moment le format réduit, mais vous savez que le journal parisien d'avant-guerre ne dépassait pas six ou huit pages.

JUSTIN: Pourquoi n'a-t-on pas eu l'idée de fonder un grand journal d'information[21] comme nous en avons chez nous en Amérique?

MONSIEUR DE N.: Je crois d'abord que c'est une question d'habitude. Comme le Français moyen a l'habitude des journaux à six pages, l'idée de lire un journal de quarante à cent pages lui répugnerait—même s'il y avait le papier nécessaire à la publication d'un tel journal. De plus le Français tient beaucoup à ce qu'on lui donne des opinions; il aime raisonner. L'idéal serait d'avoir pour chaque Français un journal personnel. D'ailleurs, c'est un peu ce qui s'est produit, car on n'a pas besoin de capitaux énormes, comme chez vous, pour fonder un journal.

JUSTIN: Avec un tel système avez-vous réellement la liberté de la presse?

MONSIEUR DE N.: Dans une très large mesure. Plus que chez vous où il y a, par exemple, beaucoup de grandes villes ayant[22] un seul journal. Comment voulez-vous qu'il y ait la liberté de la presse dans[23] ces conditions? Avant la guerre beaucoup de journaux français, il est vrai, vivaient de fonds secrets;

---

19. *That is to say.*   20. *The paper shortage.*   21. The French expressions *journal d'opinion* and *journal d'information* have little meaning in English. The discussion on this subject should readily bring out the difference.   22. Present participle of *avoir*.   23. English says *under*.   24. *I have allowed my knife to be carried off.* Compare this idiom with the discussion of *faire* in note 8.   25. This is used in the sense of *vous devriez:* you ought. *Il faut* is the strongest expression of necessity (see lesson XV, note 4). It may be followed by an infinitive without a subject or by a noun clause. Examples: *Il faut partir; Il faut que Jean parte.* If the subject of the noun clause is a pronoun, an infinitive construction is also

quelques-uns même de ces fonds étaient de source allemande. Mais avec la nouvelle loi de la presse, c'est devenu impossible maintenant.

JUSTIN: Pardon, je crois que j'ai laissé emporter[24] mon couteau encore une fois.

FRANÇOISE, *à Yvonne qui est encore occupée à desservir:* Voulez-vous apporter un autre couteau pour Monsieur Lambert? *(A Justin.)* Il faudrait[25] vous exercer pendant cinq minutes par jour à mettre votre couteau sur le porte-couteau[26] à côté de votre assiette; Yvonne prétend qu'elle n'y peut rien[27] et qu'elle vous offenserait en[28] y touchant.

JUSTIN: J'apprendrai peut-être un jour. Mais vous changez si souvent les assiettes et les fourchettes et cuillers que je me demande pourquoi le couteau fait exception.

MADAME DE N.: C'est peut-être qu'au moyen âge on avait besoin du couteau comme arme de défense. Il y a de ces habitudes[29] qui s'expliquent difficilement.

FRANÇOISE, *à Madame de N.:* Est-ce qu'on ne pourrait pas apporter le dessert tout de suite? Nous allons être en retard pour le théâtre. *(Yvonne sort.[30])*

MADAME DE N.: Bien sûr.[31] *(A Justin.)* Quelle pièce allez-vous voir ce soir?

possible. Example: *Il lui faut partir:* It is necessary for him to leave, *or* He must leave. If a pronoun occurs elsewhere in the sentence, so that the person involved is clearly understood, no indirect object pronoun is used before *il faut.* Thus one says: *Il faut vous rappeler que:* You must remember that.   26. The knife rest supports the tip of the knife to keep it from touching the tablecloth. It is improper to rest the knife on the plate.   27. Idiom: *she can do nothing about it.* 28. *En* with the present participle occasionally has the force of *by* or *while.* See lesson XVII, note 35.   29. *There are habits like this.*   30. *Exit Yvonne.*   31. *Of course.*   32. The English version was called *No Exit,* but actually the title is a

JUSTIN: Françoise m'emmène voir *Huis Clos*[32] au Vieux Colombier.[33]

MADAME DE N.: J'espère que vous pourrez me dire en revenant[34] ce que c'est que l'existentialisme.[35] Ce n'est pas la peine de lire les articles sur l'existentialisme; on n'y comprend rien, et les écrivains non plus.[36]

JUSTIN: Je me suis attaqué à *l'Etre et le Néant*[37] de Sartre, mais l'ouvrage m'a opposé une si forte résistance[38] que j'ai dû l'abandonner au milieu du premier chapitre.

MONSIEUR DE N.: Vous verrez[39] que *Huis Clos* n'est pas une pièce très gaie. Il y a trois personnages enfermés pour l'éternité dans un appartement meublé. Ce sont[40] des âmes damnées qui finissent par se torturer et se dévorer les unes les autres. Il y a un personnage qui dit: "L'Enfer, c'est les autres,"[40] ce qui[41] résume la partie existentialiste[42] de la pièce.

FRANÇOISE: Ne pourrait-on pas résumer l'existentialisme en disant que c'est le problème de l'existence ramené à l'échelle individuelle?

MADAME DE N.: Il me semble que Gide disait la même chose dans un style plus classique.

---

legal term meaning *In Camera*.   33. The famous experimental theatre in the street of the same name.   34. *When you come back*.   35. A philosophical and literary doctrine which rose to prominence during the occupation.   36. *And the writers neither*, i.e., *and the writers don't either*.   37. *Being and Non-Being*, a philosophical treatise.   38. *Put up much resistance*.   39. Future of *voir*.   40. *Ce* with the verb *être* requires a third plural verb if there is a third plural form in the predicate. In the statement, "L'Enfer, c'est les autres," the repetition of *ce* is colloquial, and, since *ce* here has an antecedent in the singular, a singular verb is required.   41. Another function of *ce qui, ce que* is as a relative pronoun without a precise antecedent. In the translation of the example in the text, the relative *which* would refer to the whole previous clause and not to a single word. See lesson XV, note 5.   42. The main idea of the play is that, in life, we allow our *existence* to be interfered with and dominated by others.   43. If the word *most* is an adjective, it translates *la plupart des*.   44. *Take a roguish pleasure*.

Monsieur de N.: Oui, on dirait que la plupart[43] des écrivains existentialistes se font un malin plaisir[44] à estropier la langue française. Mais quant à Sartre, l'auteur de *Huis Clos,* c'est différent.

Madame de N.: Et vous verrez le Vieux Colombier, ce petit théâtre sans prétentions de la Rive Gauche où Jacques Copeau,[45] avec ses brillants collaborateurs de *la Nouvelle Revue Française,*[46] a pour ainsi dire[47] créé le théâtre français contemporain.

Françoise: N'oublie pas, maman, qu'il y a aussi Lugné-Poe[48] et Jouvet[49]—mais cela nous entraînerait trop loin.[50] Justin, il va falloir nous mettre en route tout de suite, car nous devons changer au Châtelet,[51] ce qui allonge le trajet.

Madame de N.: Alors, au revoir. Amusez-vous bien!

(Par une transposition proscrite par les règles d'Aristote,[52] mais que le cinéma moderne utilise sans vergogne, nous retrouvons nos deux jeunes gens qui attendent sur le quai de Saint-Germain-des-Prés[53] sous l'écriteau "Direction Porte[54] de Clignancourt.")

Françoise: Alors c'est sûr que vous partez demain?

Justin: Comme je vous l'ai dit, je suis censé suivre les cours

45. Famous actor, born in 1879. Now co-director of the Comédie Française. *46.* The most famous French literary review founded by André Gide in 1909. The title is now banned because the last editor collaborated with the Germans. The successor of the *NRF* is known as *Les Temps Modernes* of which Sartre is the principal editor.   *47. So to speak.*   *48.* Aurélien-François Lugné-Poe (1869-1940), director of the famous experimental Théâtre de l'Œuvre.   *49.* Louis Jouvet, born in 1885, famous actor and director who has appeared more recently in motion pictures.   *50. That would get us too involved.*   *51.* An important square and subway junction taking its name from a medieval fortress which stood on the site.   *52.* The so-called unities of Aristotle, the unities of time, place, and action, governed the French classical theatre.   *53.* A subway stop taking its name from a church built in 1163. This is the nearest stop to the Vieux Colombier. *54.* The fact that they are under this sign indicates that they are returning home.

de vacances à Tours.[55] Ce n'est qu'à ce prix-là que j'ai pu persuader mes parents de me laisser passer l'été en France.

FRANÇOISE: Avec votre connaissance du français il vaudrait[56] mieux faire carrément une licence[57] à la Sorbonne.

JUSTIN: D'accord, mais cela n'est pas possible pendant l'été. Il faudra que je revienne une autre fois dès que[58] j'aurai fini mon bachot américain. J'ai encore une année de collège devant moi.

FRANÇOISE: Quoi! vous êtes encore au collège?

JUSTIN: Cela n'a rien d'étonnant.[59] Les termes collège et université sont synonymes, ou presque, aux États-Unis; le collège n'est pas une institution secondaire comme en France. Après l'école secondaire, l'étudiant américain passe quatre ans au collège. Si un étudiant français ayant déjà son baccalauréat entre au collège chez nous, il passe en troisième année.

FRANÇOISE: Alors le bachot américain est l'équivalent de la licence française qui prend généralement deux ans.

JUSTIN: Au contraire, les études en France sont plus avancées et on considère que la licence est l'équivalent du grade américain suivant, la maîtrise.[60]

FRANÇOISE: Que d'histoires![61] Mais ce n'est pas avec tous ces diplômes-là qu'on apprend le langage courant.

JUSTIN: Cela est vrai. C'est pourquoi je vous suis très reconnaissant de m'avoir reçu[62] si cordialement. Je ne me rendais pas compte quand je me suis inscrit à cette organisation pour la correspondance internationale que je serais reçu à bras ouverts[63] dès mon arrivée[64] à Paris.

FRANÇOISE: Une jeune fille qui se respecte[65] aurait hésité à courir au-devant[66] d'un jeune homme qu'elle connaît seulement par correspondance. Une pareille considération ne m'aurait pas arrêtée, vous devez vous en douter, mais j'avoue que j'ai été tout de même rassurée en constatant pendant notre première course en taxi que vous étiez tel que je vous avais imaginé.

JUSTIN: Je voudrais bien connaître ce portrait moral que vous aviez fait de moi.

FRANÇOISE: Vous êtes bien indiscret. Je vous dirai seulement que vous êtes plus sympathique que certains Américains qui froissent toutes nos habitudes françaises. Vous nous comprenez. Je suis sûre que nous serons toujours de très bons amis.

JUSTIN: J'ai si peu fréquenté la jeunesse française *(il hésite, puis se résout)* que je ne sais pas s'il serait présomptueux de vous demander la permission de vous tutoyer.

FRANÇOISE: Comme les Américains vont vite![67] Mais je veux bien. Cela vous donnera—cela te donnera l'occasion de mieux apprendre tes verbes. Mais voilà notre train. En tant que Français assimilé, tu n'oublieras pas cette fois que la fermeture de la porte est automatique.

VOCABULAIRE POUR CETTE LEÇON

A

accord (akor) *m.* agreement. **d'...**
agreed, in agreement
âge (âzh) *m.* **moyen** ... Middle Ages
ail (ay) *m.* garlic
allonger (alônzhay) to lengthen
âme (âm) *f.* soul
amuser (amüzay) **s'...** to have a good
time
arme (arm) *f.* arm
artichaut (arteeshô) *m.* artichoke
assimilé (aseemeelay) *adj.* assimilated
attaquer (atakay) to attack. **s'...** à to
attack
attention (atânsyôn) *interj.* watch out
auprès (ôprè) *adv.* ... **de** near, with
avis (avee) *m.* opinion

B • C

boulanger (boolânzhay) *m.* baker
brillant (breeyân) *adj.* brilliant
capital (kapeetal), (*pl.:* **capitaux**)
m. capital
carapace (karapas) *f.* shell
carrément (karaymân) *adv.* squarely,
without beating around the bush
censé (sânsay) *adj.* supposed to
changer (shânzhay) to change
chapitre (shapeetr) *m.* chapter
cœur (kèor) *m.* **avoir mal au** ... to
feel sick
collaborateur (kolaboratèor) *m.* collaborator
compte (kônt) *m.* account. **se rendre**
... to realize
constater (kônstatay) to observe, note
contemporain (kôntânporèn) *adj.*
contemporary
contredire (kôntredeer) to contradict
corbeille (korbèy) *f.* basket

cordialement (kordyalmân) *adv.* cordially
courant (koorân) *adj.* current, every-
day
course (koors) *f.* race, errand, trip
créer (krayay) to create

D

damner (dânay) to damn
délicieux (dayleesyeo), **délicieuse**
(dayleesyeoz) *adj.* delicious
démocratie (daymokrasee) *f.* democracy
dépasser (daypâsay) to surpass
desservir (daysèrveer) to clear away
the dishes
détromper (daytrônpay) to undeceive
développer (dayvlopay) to develop
dévorer (dayvoray) to devour
diplôme (deeplôm) *m.* diploma
divers, -e (deevèr) *adj.* diverse, different
douter (dootay) to doubt. **se** ... **de** to
suspect
droit (drwa) *m.* right

E

écrevisse (aykrevees) *f.* crayfish
emmener (ânmnay) to take, take away
empêcher (ânpèshay) to prevent
emporter (ânportay) to carry off
enfer (ânfèr) *m.* hell
enfermer (ânfèrmay) to shut up
énorme (aynorm) *adj.* enormous
enraciné (ânraseenay) *adj.* deep-rooted
estropier (èstropyay) to cripple
éternité (aytèrneetay) *f.* eternity
étudiant (aytüdyân) *m.* student
exercer (aygzèrsay). **s'...** to practice
exprimer (èkspreemay) to express

F • G

fabrication (fabreekasyôn) *f.* making, manufacture
fonds (fôn) *m. pl.* funds
fréquenter (fraykântay) to frequent
froisser (frwasay) to crumple, offend
gastronomie (gastronomee) *f.* gastronomy
gaufre (gôfr) *f.* waffle
grade (grad) *m.* degree
gras (grâ), **grasse** (grâs) *adj.* fat
gros (grô), **grosse** (grôs) *adj.* big
guère (gèr) *adv.* ne ... guère hardly, scarcely
guerre (gèr) *f.* war. d'avant-guerre pre-war

H • I

habitude (abeetüd) *f.* habit
hésiter (ayzeetay) to hesitate
hors-d'œuvre (ordèºvr) *m.* relish
idée (eeday) *f.* idea
individuel, -le (èndeeveedüèl) *adj.* individual
information (ènformasyôn) *f.* information
injure (ènzhür) *f.* insult
inonder (eenônday) to inundate
inscrire (ènskreer) s'... à to enroll in

J • L

jeunesse (zhèºnès) *f.* youth, young people
joie (zhwa) *f.* joy
journal (zhoornal), (*pl.:* **journaux**) *m.* newspaper
journalisme (zhoornaleesm) *m.* journalism
lancer (lânsay) to throw, hurl
liberté (leebèrtay) *f.* liberty
licence (leesâns) *f.* master's degree
loi (lwa) *f.* law

M • N

maman (mamân) *f.* mama
marque (mark) *f.* mark, brand
mélange (maylânzh) *m.* mixture
mélanger (maylânzhay) to mix
mener (mºnay) to lead
mettre (mètr) se ... en route to set out
miche (meesh) *f.* loaf
moyen, -ne (mwayèn, -èn) *adj.* average
nature (natür) *adj.* plain
nécessaire (naysèsèr) *adj.* necessary
noix (nwâ) *f.* nut
nuire (nüeer) ... à (quelque chose) to be harmful to, injure (something)

O • P

objectif (obzhèkteef), **objective** (obzhèkteev) *adj.* objective
œuf (èºf) *m.* egg. ... sur le plat fried egg
offenser (ofânsay) to offend
organiser (organeezay) to organize
oublier (oobleeay) to forget
outre-mer (ootrºmèr) *adv.* phrase beyond the sea
ouvrage (oovrazh) *m.* work
pain (pèn) *m.* bread, loaf of bread
palais (palè) *m.* palace, palate
par (par) *prep.* by, per
pareil, -le (parèy) *adj.* same, similar, such a
paresse (parès) *f.* laziness
peine (pèn) *f.* pain, trouble. ce n'est pas la ... it is not worth the trouble
personnage (pèrsonazh) *m.* character
plupart (plüpar) *f.* most
plus (plü) *adv.* de ... furthermore
porte-couteau (portkootô) *m.* knife rest
préjugé (prayzhüzhay) *m.* prejudice

présomptueux (prayzôⁿptüeᵒ), présomptueuse (prayzôⁿptüeᵒz) *adj.* presumptuous

presse (près) *f.* press

prétendre (praytâⁿdr) to pretend, claim

problème (problèm) *m.* problem

prochain (proshèⁿ) *adj.* next

produire (prodüeer) to produce. se ... to happen

proscrire (proskreer) to proscribe

protestation (protèstasyôⁿ) *f.* protest

R

raisonner (rèzonay) to reason

ramener (ramnay) to bring back, reduce

rassurer (rasüray) to reassure

reconnaissant (rᵉkonèsâⁿ) *adj.* grateful

réduire (raydüeer) to reduce

réellement (rayèlmâⁿ) *adv.* really

renseignement (râⁿsènymâⁿ) *m.* information

renseigner (râⁿsènyay) to inform

répugner (raypünyay) to be distasteful

résoudre (rayzoodr) se ... to make up one's mind

résumer (rayzümay) to sum up

retard (rᵉtar) *m.* delay. en ... late

revoir (rᵉvwar) to see again. au ... good-bye

rive (reev) *f.* bank

S

salé (salay) *adj.* salted, salty

salir (saleer) to dirty

secondaire (sᵉgôⁿdèr) *adj.* secondary

sérieux (sayryeᵒ), sérieuse (sayryeᵒz) *adj.* serious

seul (sèᵒl) *adj.* alone, single, only

sembler (sâⁿblay) to seem

sombrer (sôⁿbray) to founder

sortir (sorteer) to go out, take out

suivant (süeevâⁿ) *adj.* following

suivre (süeevr) to follow. ... un cours to attend a course

sympathique (sèⁿpateek) *adj.* likable

synonyme (seenoneem) *adj.* synonymous

T

tant (tâⁿ), *adv.* en ... que as

tendancieux (tâⁿdâⁿsyeᵒ), tendancieuse (tâⁿdâⁿsyeᵒz) *adj.* tendentious

torturer (tortüray) to torture

trahir (traeer) to betray

trajet (trazhè) *m.* trip

tranche (trâⁿsh) *f.* slice

travail (travay) *m.* work

travailler (travayay) to work

tutoyer (tütwayay) to address as *tu*

U • V

usine (üzeen) *f.* factory

utiliser (üteeleezay) to utilize

vacances (vakâⁿs) *f. pl.* vacation. cours de ... summer session

vergogne (vèrgony) *f.* shame

veste (vèst) *f.* suit coat

visiteur (veezeetèᵒr) *m.* visitor

vouloir (voolwar) ... bien to be willing

Reference Grammar

Although all the necessary grammatical explanations for each of the 20 Lessons have been provided in the footnotes of the lessons, a complete Reference Grammar is provided here for the convenience of the student. Each part of speech (the article, the noun, the verb, etc.) is explained thoroughly in all its uses. Therefore, should the student wish complete information about any point of grammar he can easily find it in the handy Reference Grammar.

PLAN FOR STUDY

Since the material of the *Reference Grammar* is not arranged in order of difficulty or frequency of occurrence but is *classified by subjects* (the Article, Noun, Adjective, etc.), it is suggested that the student refer to and study the following paragraphs along with each lesson. The easiest way of locating any paragraph (§) is to flip through the pages watching for the § number which is in **bold face** along side of the page number.

Lesson I   The definite article §1. The indefinite article §6. Genders of nouns §8. Agreement of the adjective §10 (a). Personal pronoun subjects §24. Nature of French verb §45. Present indicative §50 (a). Simple negation §23 (a). Inversion of the verb §60 (a) and (d).

Lesson II   The partitive article §6. Contractions with definite article §2 (a) to (f). Special uses of definite article §3. Imperative §56 (a) and (b). Future tense §52 (a) and (b). Demonstrative adjective §15.

Lesson III   Imperfect indicative §51 (a), §51 (b) 1 to 4. Past participle §49 (a). Compound tenses §55 (a). The compound past §55 (c). Conditional tense §53 (a) to (c). The indefinite adjective *tout* §12 (e).

Lesson IV   Personal pronoun objects §25. The verb *devoir* §62. Reflexive verbs §58. Demonstrative pronoun §28.

Lesson V   Adverb of quantity §22 (a) to (d). Disjunctive pronoun §26. Omission of definite article §4. Omission of indefinite article §7.

Lesson VI   The verb *faire* §63 (d). The pronoun *ce* §28 (f). Plural of nouns §9. Interrogative adjective §17.

Lesson VII   The preposition *chez* §36. Agreement of past participle §55 (b). Orthographical changing verbs §65 (d).

Lesson VIII   The preposition *de* §38. The relative pronoun §30 (a) and (b). The interrogative pronoun §31.

Lesson IX   Passive voice §59 (a) and (b). Irregular adjectives §10. The verb *avoir* §61 (e). Adjective as substantive §13. Present sub-junctive §57 (a), (b) and (e). Inversion of the verb §60.

Lesson X   Transitive and intransitive verbs §46. Reflexive pronoun §27 (a), (b) and (d). The infinitive §47.

Lesson XI   Agreement of the adjective §10. Subjunctive in noun clauses §57 (c). The demonstrative pronoun §28. The impersonal pronoun §29.

Lesson XII   Possessive relative *dont* §30 (f). Verbs in -*yer* §65 (c). Possessive adjective §16. Relative *ce qui* §30 (c).

Lesson XIII   The adverb §19, §20, §21. Special uses of future §52 (c) and (d). Infinitive in place of noun clause §57 (k). Possessive pronoun §32.

Lesson XIV   Negation §23. Present with *depuis* §50 (b). Article with parts of body §3 (g). Avoidance of passive §59 (c) and (d). Pronoun *on* §34.

Lesson XV   Position of the adjective §11. Pronoun *tout* §33. In-definite adjective §12. The preposition *à* §35. The preposition *dans* §37. The preposition *en* §39. Repetition of preposition §40. Com-pound prepositions §41. Position of preposition §42.

Lesson XVI   The relative pronoun §30. Coördinating conjunctions §43. Subordinating conjunctions §44. The present participle §48. The past participle §49.

Lesson XVII   The pluperfect indicative §55 (d). Future perfect §55 (e). Conditional perfect §55 (f). Irregular verbs §66. *Begin thorough study of irregular verbs.*

Lesson XVIII   The preterit §54. Past anterior §55 (g). The verb *faire* §63. The verb *pouvoir* §64.

Lesson XIX   Verbs in -*cer* and -*ger* §65 (a) and (b). Prefect sub-junctive §57 (h). Imperfect subjunctive §57 (i). Pluperfect sub-junctive §57 (j).

Lesson XX   Translation of *whoever* §57 (f). Review verbs.

REFERENCE GRAMMAR

THE ARTICLE

THE ADVERB

THE PRONOUN

THE PREPOSITION

participle: (1) with *avoir*; (2) with *être*; (3) reflexive verbs.
(c) The COMPOUND PAST: (1) definition; (2) formation.
(d) The PLUPERFECT INDICATIVE: (1) formation; (2) uses.
(e) The FUTURE PERFECT: (1) formation; (2) use; (3) implied futurity; (4) probability. (f) The CONDITIONAL PERFECT: (1) formation and normal use; (2) in conditional sentence; (3) after *quand même*.. (g) The PAST ANTERIOR: (1) use of; (2) formation.

REFERENCE GRAMMAR

The Article (L'Article)

§ 1 The Definite Article

(a) The definite article (*the* in English) is an adjective in French and changes its form to correspond to the gender and number of the noun modified.

le bateau	*the* boat (*masculine singular*)
la mère	*the* mother (*feminine singular*)
les bateaux	*the* boats (*masculine plural*)
les mères	*the* mothers (*feminine plural*)

(b) Before a word beginning with a vowel or mute *h* (see page 316), the vowels of *le* and *la* elide.

le + avion = l'avion	*the* airplane
la + eau = l'eau	*the* water
la + heure = l'heure	*the* hour
les avions	*the* airplanes
les heures	*the* hours

§ 2 Contractions of the Definite Article

(a) When *de* occurs before the article, the following contractions result:

de + le verre = du verre	*of the* glass
de + les verres = des verres	*of the* glasses

No contraction occurs with *de* + *la* and *de* + *l'*.

de la montre	*of the* watch
de l'heure	*of the* hour

Elision takes precedence over contraction (note above example). In speaking or writing, it is therefore necessary to anticipate a possible elision before deciding whether to contract.

(b) In a similar manner, *à* will contract with the following article.

à + le verre = au verre	*to the* glass
à + les verres = aux verres	*to the* glasses
à la montre	*to the* watch
à l'heure	*to the* hour

§ 3 Some Special Uses of the Definite Article

(a) A noun used in an abstract or in a general sense requires a

197

definite article in French, whereas the equivalent English usually omits the article.

Le pain est bon.	Bread is good.
Marie aime *la* musique.	Mary likes music.

Compare this with § 6.

(b)   The definite article is required before the name of a language.

Le français est une langue romane.   French is a Romance language.

This article is omitted if the name of the language directly follows the verb *parler*.

Nous parlons anglais.   We speak English.

(c)   The definite article is required before the name of a country.

Je visite *la* France.   I am visiting France.

For omission of this article with prepositions, see § 4(a) and § 4(b)

(d)   The definite article is required before a title preceding a person's name.

le docteur Bellanger	Doctor Bellanger
le capitaine Duchâtel	Captain Duchâtel

This article is not used, however, when *Monsieur, Madame, Mademoiselle* and their plurals precede names. It is also omitted in direct address.

Bonjour, Docteur Bellanger.   How do you do, Dr. Bellanger.

More normally, however, proper names are not used with titles in direct address. One should say more correctly:

Bonjour, Monsieur le Docteur.

(e)   The definite article is used before a day of the week taken in a general sense.

Il voit toujours son ami *le* lundi (or: *les* lundis).
He always sees his friend Monday (Mondays *or* on Monday).

When the day of the week is used in a specific sense, there is no article.

Il verra son ami lundi.   He will see his friend Monday (or: on Monday).

(f)   The definite article translates the English *per* or an indefinite article in expressions involving price and quantity.

Ces poires coûtent cinquante francs *la douzaine*.
These pears cost fifty francs *per* dozen (or: *a* dozen).

(g)   The definite article is used in place of the expected possessive adjective with parts of the body when there is no ambiguity as to the possessor.

Il lève *la* main.   He raises *his* hand.

BUT: *Sa* main saignait.   *His* hand was bleeding.

When an action is performed on a part of the body, an additional reflexive pronoun [see § 27] becomes necessary.

Elle *se* lave *les* mains.   She washes *her* hands.

When the action is performed on another person's body, an additional indirect pronoun object is needed.

Elle *lui* lave *les* mains.   She washes *his* hands.

§ 4 Omission of the Definite Article

(a)   After the preposition *en* [see § 3(b) and § 3(c)] the definite article is omitted.

en **France**	*in* France
en **anglais**	*in* English

There are a few idioms using *en* which do not omit the article.

en *l'*honneur de	in honor of
en *l'*air	in the air

(b)   After the preposition *de* there is no definite article in the following types of expressions.

(1)   After the idiom *avoir besoin de* when the following noun is used in a general sense.

J'ai besoin d'argent.   I need money.

(2)   After nouns expressing quantity.

Un kilo de beurre.   A kilogram of butter.

(3)   After *de* used in sense of *by* or *with* in a passive construction [see § 59].

La table était couverte *de* fleurs.   The table was covered *with* flowers.

(4)   After *de* in the sense of *from* [see § 38(e)] when the following word is an unmodified feminine country.

Il arrive *de* France.   He is arriving *from* France.

If the feminine country is modified by an adjective, a prepositional phrase or a relative clause, the article which normally occurs with the name of a country [see § 3(c)] will remain.

Il arrive *de la* Nouvelle Angleterre.   He is arriving from New England.

§ 5 The Indefinite Article

(a)   In the singular the indefinite article has a masculine and a feminine form agreeing with the noun modified.

un **parapluie**	an umbrella
une **couleur**	a color

§ 6   The Partitive Article

(a)   The partitive article consists of *de* + *the definite article* (agreeing with the noun modified). It contracts according to the rules set forth in § 2(a).

(b)   The partitive article is the plural of the indefinite article (which is omitted in English or expressed by the word *some*).

Voici *un* **homme.**	Here is *a* man.
Voici *des* **hommes.**	Here are men.
Voici *des* **hommes.**	Here are *some* men.

When a noun is unmodified, as in the second illustration above, try reducing the expression to a singular or try inserting the word *some* to complete the meaning. If the first method proves that an indefinite article would be used in the singular, the plural expression in French will require the partitive article. Or, if the word *some* clarifies the meaning of the English sentence, this is again proof that the French will use the partitive article.

(c)   The partitive article also translates *some* or *any* used in the singular.

Jean a *de la* **marmelade.**	John has *some* marmelade.
Voulez-vous *du* **pain?**	Do you want *any* bread?

Frequently [see § 6(b)] the words *some* or *any* are omitted in English. Test an unmodified noun by inserting *some* or *any* to complete the meaning. If this does not work, test for a *noun in a general sense* [see § 3(a)] by inserting the phrases "in general" or "generally speaking" to clarify the meaning.

Voulez-vous *du* *sucre?*	Do you want (*some*) sugar?

BUT: *Le pétrole* est la première industrie de la région.
Oil "generally speaking" is the principal industry of the region.

Refer to § 12(d) for the uses of *quelque* which also means *some*.

(d)   The partitive article shortens to *de* alone in the following cases:

(1)   After a negative verb.

Je n'ai pas *d'***amis.** I haven't *any* friends (I have *no* friends).

(2)   With a preceding adjective in the plural.

de **belles robes**   *some* beautiful dresses

(3)   After nouns and adverbs expressing a quantity.

Combien de lait? *how much* milk?   Un *carnet* de chèques a check *book*
Une *centaine* de pommes a *hundred* apples

The principal adverbs of quantity are *assez, autant, beaucoup, com-bien, moins, peu, trop, tant, plus*. Exceptions: *bien* and *la plupart*, which are *always* followed by *de* plus the article: *bien des gens; la plupart des livres; bien du pain; bien de la bière*.

(e)   The partitive article is omitted altogether in listings *(voici plusieurs choses: papier, plumes, encre, livres)*, as well as after *ni . . . ni (vous avez ni crayons, ni livres), sans (je suis sans argent)* and *avec (je le ferai avec plaisir)*.

§ 7   Omission of the Indefinite Article

(a)   After the verb *être* the indefinite article is not used with a noun designating nationality or profession if it is otherwise un-modified. See also § 28(f).

Jean est *docteur*.   John is *a doctor*.
Jean est *Français*.   John is *French, a Frenchman*.

(b)   A noun in apposition to another noun does not take an article if complete equality between the nouns is intended.

Monsieur Blanc, auteur de plusieurs romans, a signé le manifeste.
Mr. Blank, (*the* or *an*) author of several novels, signed the manifesto.

BUT: **Madame Villier, la sœur de Monsieur Blanc, a signé aussi.**
Mrs. Villier, the sister of Mr. Blank, signed also.

In the second example the phrase *la sœur de* is not intended in a sense of equality but *as a further explanation*.

The Noun (Le Nom)

§ 8   The Gender of Nouns

(a)   In French there are only two genders, *masculine* and *feminine*. Already the *neuter* had begun to merge with the other two genders in Vulgar Latin, from which French and the other Romance lan-guages are descended, and disappeared altogether in the early Middle Ages when French began to emerge as a distinctly separate group of dialects. As applied to *persons*, gender in French follows English usage, but *things* will be either masculine or feminine de-pending on the noun in question. Only a specialist in the history of the French language can explain why one noun designating a thing is masculine and another feminine, and his explanations would be useless to a beginner. Practically speaking, then, the beginner must memorize with each noun an article showing the gender so that he may associate the correct notion of gender with each noun.

There are no rules which permit one to recognize the gender of a noun at a glance, but it is useful to note that nouns ending in *-ié, -ion, -ée, -ice, -esse* are generally feminine and that nouns ending in *-age, -eau, -isme, -ment* are generally masculine.

Names of countries ending in *-e* are feminine with the notable exception of *le Mexique.*

la **France**	France
la **Belgique**	Belgium

BUT:	*le* **Mexique**	Mexico
	le **Canada**	Canada

The same rule applies to continents, provinces, states and regions.

la **Normandie**	Normandy
la **Virginie**	Virginia
le **Vermont**	Vermont

§ 9 The Plural of Nouns

(a)   Most nouns form their plural by adding *s* to the singular. This *s* is never pronounced except in linking.

le livre	the book		***les* livres**	the books

(b)   Nouns ending in *-s*, *-x*, and *-z* do not change to form the plural.

le **fils**	the son		***les* fils**	the sons
le **nez**	the nose		***les* nez**	the noses

(c)   Nouns ending in *-eau* or *-eu* take an *x* in the plural.

le **bateau**	the boat		***les* bateau*x***	the boats
le **neveu**	the nephew		***les* neveu*x***	the nephews

(d)   Some, but not all, nouns ending in *-ou* form their plural by adding *x*. The outstanding cases are:

bijou	jewel		**bijoux**	jewels
caillou	stone		**cailloux**	stones
chou	cabbage		**choux**	cabbages
genou	knee		**genoux**	knees
hibou	owl		**hiboux**	owls
joujou	toy		**joujoux**	toys
pou	louse		**poux**	lice

(e)   All nouns ending in *-al* and seven nouns ending in *-ail* form their plural in *-aux.*

journal	newspaper		**journaux**	newspapers
bail	lease		**baux**	leases
corail	corral		**coraux**	corrals
émail	enamel		**émaux**	enamels
soupirail	vent		**soupiraux**	vents
travail	work		**travaux**	works
vantail	folding door		**vantaux**	folding doors
vitrail	pane		**vitraux**	panes

(f) Some nouns have two plurals.

    (1) **ciel** heaven   **cieux, ciels** heavens

The first of the above plurals is used in a figurative sense. Compare the following:

> **Notre père qui êtes *aux cieux*.**   Our Father who art *in heaven*.
> **Cet artiste fait bien *les ciels*.**   This artist paints *skies* well.

    (2) **œil** eye   **yeux** eyes

But, in a compound noun, the plural of *œil* is *œils*.

> **un œil-de-bœuf** a bull's eye (round window)
> **des œils-de-bœuf** bull's eyes (round windows)

    (3) **aïeul, aïeule*** grandfather, grandmother
        aïeuls, aïeules grandfathers, grandmothers
        aïeux ancestors

(g) Family names do not add an *s* in the plural.

> **J'ai vu *les Maritain* ce matin.**   I saw *the Maritains* this morning.

When used for other purposes, family names take an *s*.

> **Il n'y a pas beaucoup de *Fords* dans cette ville.**
> There are not many Fords in this city.

(h) Compound nouns form their plural in various ways depending on the nature of the component parts:

    (1) If the compound noun is formed from an adjective and a noun or two nouns, each element of the compound is made plural.

> **gentilhomme** gentleman   **gentilshommes** gentlemen
> **bonhomme** old fellow   **bonshommes** old fellows
> **porte-fenêtre** French window   **portes-fenêtres** French windows

    (2) If the compound noun is formed with a verb, an adverb, a preposition or a conjunction, only the noun part is made plural.

> **portemanteau** coatrack   **portemanteaux** coatracks
> **contre-amiral** rear-admiral   **contre-amiraux** rear-admirals

    (3) If there is a preposition expressed or implied between two nouns in a compound word, only the first noun is made plural.

> **chef-d'œuvre** masterpiece   **chefs-d'œuvre** masterpieces
> **Hôtel-Dieu** city hospital   **Hôtels-Dieu** city hospitals

    (4) Many compound nouns, particularly most of those using hyphens (note some exceptions above), have invariable plurals.

> *le* **gratte-ciel** the skyscraper   *les* **gratte-ciel** the skyscrapers
> *le* **porte-monnaie** the purse   *les* **porte-monnaie** the purses

---

FOOTNOTE The common words are *grand-père* and *grand'mère*.

The Adjective (L'Adjectif)

§ 10 Agreement of the Adjective

(a) The adjective agrees in gender and number with the noun or pronoun which it modifies. To form the feminine of the adjective, add -e to the masculine singular. The plural of the adjective is formed by adding -s to the masculine or feminine singular.

Le livre est petit.	The book is little.
La chaise est petite.	The chair is little.
Les livres sont petits.	The books are little.
Les chaises sont petites.	The chairs are little.

(b) When used as adjectives, past participles [see § 49] ending in -é add another unpronounced -e to form the feminine.

la symphonie inachevée	the unfinished symphony

(c) Adjectives already ending in -e in the masculine cannot take an additional e in the feminine.

Le livre est difficile.	The book is difficult.
La leçon est difficile.	The lesson is difficult.

(d) Adjectives ending in -el, -eil, -en, -et, -on, -as, -os double the consonant before adding the feminine e.

MASCULINE		FEMININE
cruel	(cruel)	cruelle
pareil	(like)	pareille
ancien	(ancient)	ancienne
muet	(mute)	muette
bon	(good)	bonne
gras	(fat)	grasse
gros	(large)	grosse

(e) Adjectives ending in -er do not double the consonant but write a grave accent instead.

cher	(dear)	chère
étranger	(foreign)	étrangère

Many adjectives ending in -et [see § 10(d)] write a grave accent instead of doubling the consonant.

MASCULINE		FEMININE
complet	(complete)	complète
concret	(concrete)	concrète
discret	(discreet)	discrète

inquiet	(uneasy)	inquiète
replet	(corpulent)	replète
secret	(secret)	secrète

(f) Adjectives ending in *-f* change the *-f* to *-ve* for the feminine, and those ending in *-x* change to *-se.*

neuf	(new)	neuve
vif	(lively)	vive
heureux	(happy)	heureuse

(g) Most adjectives ending in *-eur* form their feminine normally.

| supérieur | superior | supérieure |
| meilleur | better | meilleure |

But those derived from a present participle [see § 48] by changing *-ant* to *-eur,* take *-euse* in the feminine.

| menteur | lying | menteuse |
| liseur | book-loving | liseuse |

Those ending in *-teur,* not deriving from a present participle, have the feminine form in *-trice.*

| protecteur* | protecting | protectrice |

(The present participle of this verb is *protégeant;* hence the adjective is not derived from the present participle).

(h) Adjectives ending in *-eau* or *-al* in the masculine singular form their masculine plurals like nouns with similar endings [see § 9(c) and § 9(e)].

| beau | beautiful | beaux |
| égal | equal | égaux |

There are two notable exceptions to the above rule.

| final | final | finals |
| fatal | fatal | fatals |

(i) The following adjectives have a second masculine form to be used before a noun beginning with a vowel or mute *h.*

beau	un *bel* homme	a handsome man
nouveau	un *nouvel* ami	a new friend
vieux	un *vieil* ami	an old friend

---

* Many nouns designating persons have similar endings to indicate the gender of the person. Examples: *acteur, actrice*: actor, actress; *lecteur, lectrice*: reader; *bienfaiteur, bienfaitrice*: benefactor.

(j) Table of common irregular adjectives:

	SINGULAR		PLURAL	
	Masculine	Feminine	Masculine	Feminine
(beautiful)	beau (bel)	belle	beaux	belles
(white)	blanc	blanche	blancs	blanches
(blue)	bleu	bleue	bleus	bleues
(good)	bon	bonne	bons	bonnes
(sweet)	doux	douce	doux	douces
(thick)	épais	épaisse	épais	épaisses
(false)	faux	fausse	faux	fausses
(crazy)	fou	folle	fous	folles
(cool)	frais	fraîche	frais	fraîches
(frank)	franc	franche	francs	franches
(nice)	gentil	gentille	gentils	gentilles
(Greek)	grec	grecque	grecs	grecques
(long)	long	longue	longs	longues
(shrewd)	malin	maligne	malins	malignes
(new)	nouveau (nouvel)	nouvelle	nouveaux	nouvelles
(public)	public	publique	publics	publiques
(red-headed)	roux	rousse	roux	rousses
(dry)	sec	sèche	secs	sèches
(Turkish)	turc	turque	turcs	turques
(old)	vieux (vieil)	vieille	vieux	vieilles

§ 11 Position of the Adjective

(a) When the adjective is adjacent to the noun which it modifies, it usually follows the noun. This is particularly true of *descriptive* adjectives, adjectives of *nationality, color* adjectives, and *past participles* or *present participles* used as adjectives.

> une fenêtre ronde   a round window (*description*)
> une ville française   a French city (*nationality*)
> une maison blanche   a white house (*color*)
> une chose résolue   a settled thing (*past participle*)
> une leçon intéressante   an interesting lesson (*present participle*)

(b) Certain short adjectives normally precede the noun.

autre	other	joli	pretty
beau	beautiful	long	long
bon	good	mauvais	bad
grand	great, tall	méchant	naughty, wicked
	large	meilleur	better, best
gros	big	nouveau	new
haut	high	petit	small, short, little
jeune	young	vieux	old

(c) Adjectives expressing an abstract quality frequently precede the noun although they may also follow.

une énorme difficulté	an enormous difficulty
un intrépide voyageur	an intrepid traveler

(d) Some adjectives change their meaning according to their position in relation to the noun modified.

une *ancienne* église	a *former* church
une église *ancienne*	an *ancient* church
le *brave* homme	the *good* man
l'homme *brave*	the *brave* man
une *certaine* chose	a *certain* thing
une chose *certaine*	a *sure* thing
cher ami	*dear* friend
un costume *cher*	an *expensive* suit
un *grand* homme	a *great* man
un homme *grand*	a *tall* man
la *même* faute	the *same* mistake
la faute *même*	the *very* mistake
ma *propre* chambre	my *own* room
une chambre *propre*	a *clean* room
le *pauvre* homme	the *unfortunate* man
l'homme *pauvre*	the *poor* man (without money)

(e) *Prochain* and *dernier* precede when used in the sense of a series and follow when used in a time expression involving the day, week, month or year.

la *prochaine* rue	the *next* street
le mois *prochain*	*next* month
le *dernier* obstacle	the last obstacle
le mois *dernier*	last month

(Note use of article in second and fourth examples.)

§ 12 Indefinite Adjectives

(a) The following indefinite adjectives require *ne* before the verb [see § 23(h)].

aucun, aucune	none, not any
nul, nulle	none, not any
pas un, pas une	none, not any

(b) The following indefinite adjectives follow English usage by taking no article.

Certains invités sont venus.	Certain guests have come.
Chaque invité est venu.	Each (every) guest came.

(c)   The plural indefinite adjective *plusieurs* is invariable, having the same form in the feminine as in the masculine.

> **plusieurs hommes**   several men
> **plusieurs femmes**   several women

(d)   The indefinite adjective *quelque* in the singular means *some* or *any* indefinite; in the plural is means *a few* or *some* in the sense of *a few* (compare with the use of the partitive article, § 6).

> **Il cherche *quelque* explication.**
> He is looking for *some* (any kind of) explanation.
> **Voulez-vous *quelques* livres?**
> Do you want *some* (i.e. *a few*) books?

(e)   The indefinite adjective *all* has the following forms:

> ***tout* le livre**   all the book, the whole book
> ***toute* la leçon**   all the lesson, the whole lesson
> ***tous* les livres**   all the books
> ***toutes* les leçons**   all the lessons

As in English, the definite article follows the adjective. To translate *the whole*, transpose to *all the* before translating.

Tout and *toute* are used without an article in the sense of *chaque* [see § 12(b)], particularly in adages.

> **A *tout* homme qui sait lire ...**   To every man who can read ...

(f)   An indefinite article precedes the indefinite adjective *tel*. It does not follow as in English.

> ***un* tel homme**   such *a* man
> ***de* tels hommes**   such men
> ***une* telle femme**   such *a* woman
> ***de* telles femmes**   such women

(g)   The indefinite adjective *quelconque* follows the noun modified. Note that an indefinite article precedes the noun in the singular, not a partitive article.

> **un livre quelconque**   any book whatever
> **des leçons quelconques**   any lessons whatever

§ 13   Use of the Adjective as a Substantive

Many adjectives can be used as substantives (that is to say, in the function of a noun) by placing an article before them and by giving them the gender of the noun referred to.

> **Voici trois cravates.**   Here are three neckties.
> **Voulez-vous *la rouge*?**   Do you want *the red one*?

Note that the English uses the pronoun *one* whereas the French has no equivalent.

§ 14 Comparison of Adjectives

(a) English has two systems for the comparison of adjectives. Some adjectives add the endings *-er, -est* (example: bigg*er*, bigg*est*) ; others use the adverbs *more* or *most* (example: *more beautiful, most beautiful*). The French has only the second of these systems. In a diminishing sense, both French and English use the adverbs *less* and *least*.

(b) The adverb *plus* or *moins* is placed before the adjective to form the comparative.

> **Cet homme est *plus (moins)* intéressant que cette femme.**
> This man is *more (less)* interesting than that woman.
> **Cette maison-ci est *plus (moins)* grande que celle-là.**
> This house is *bigger (less big)* than that one.

(c) The definite article and the adverb *plus* are placed before the adjective to form the superlative.

> **Cette leçon est *la plus* intéressante.**
> This lesson is *the most* interesting.

Sometimes the superlative may be mistaken for the comparative, in which case the comparative can be distinguished in this manner:

> **Cette leçon est la plus intéressante *des deux*.**
> This lesson is the more interesting (of the two).

Generally, however, the context will indicate clearly enough whether comparative or superlative is meant.

(d) In the case of an adjective normally following its noun, the entire superlative, including the definite article, will follow.

> **la leçon *la plus intéressante***   the most interesting lesson

Note in the above example that there are two definite articles, both agreeing with the noun. The following example will indicate more clearly which article is the sign of the superlative:

> **mes livres *les plus intéressants***   my most interesting books

In the case of an adjective normally preceding its noun, the superlative may either precede or follow.

> **la plus grande maison** ⎫
>   or   ⎬   the biggest house
> **la maison la plus grande** ⎭

Note in the first example above that the specific definite article found in the equivalent English absorbs the article sign of the superlative. This article would also be absorbed by a possessive adjective.

mon plus grand ami   my best (literally: biggest) friend

§ 15   The Demonstrative Adjective

(a)   The demonstrative adjective has the following forms: *ce* (masculine singular before word beginning with a consonant); *cet* (masculine singular before word beginning with a vowel or mute *h*); *cette* (feminine singular); *ces* (masculine and feminine plural).

SINGULAR

ce garçon	*this* (*that*) boy
cet homme	*this* (*that*) man
cette jeune fille	*this* (*that*) girl

PLURAL

ces garçons	*these* (*those*) boys
ces hommes	*these* (*those*) men
ces jeunes filles	*these* (*those*) girls

(b)   Unless a distinction among two or more things is being made, or unless special emphasis is desired, there is no need to distinguish in French between *this* or *that*, *these* or *those*. If it is necessary to distinguish or emphasize, *-ci* and *-là* are affixed to the noun.

ce livre-*ci*	*this* book	ces livres-*ci*	*these* books
ce livre-*là*	*that* book	ces livres-*là*	*those* books

§ 16   The Possessive Adjective

(a)   The possessive adjectives can best be learned in the following chart:

As to Noun Modified

		Masculine Singular	Feminine Singular	Plural (M. & F.)
As to Antecedent	SING.	mon (my)	ma (mon)	mes
		ton (thy)	ta (ton)	tes
		son (his, her, its)	sa (son)	ses
	PLUR.	notre (our)	notre	nos
		votre (your)	votre	vos
		leur (their)	leur	leurs

(b)   The choice of the form in terms of the antecedent presents no problem since the English equivalent serves as a guide. Once the form of the possessive adjective is chosen, however, it becomes necessary to make it agree in gender and number *with the noun which it modifies.* Thus one says:

mon chapeau	my hat	*mes* chapeaux	my hats
ma cravate	my necktie	*mes* cravates	my neckties

(c)   In the third person singular, note that the French is unable to distinguish the gender of the possessor. English says *his, her, its,* but French says:

son chapeau	*his* hat, *her* hat, *its* hat
sa cravate	*his* necktie, *her* necktie, *its* necktie

In order to make the distinction, should it be necessary, the French will use an additional prepositional phrase [see § 26(c) 10]. Unless this phrase is used, the third person singular possessive adjective will refer to the nearest possible antecedent.

Jean a perdu *sa cravate.*   John lost *his* (*not her*) necktie.

Do not confuse:

ses chapeaux	*his, her, its* hats
leurs chapeaux	*their* hats

(d)   If a feminine singular word, beginning with a vowel or mute *h*, is modified by a possessive adjective, the forms *mon, ton, son* must be used.

mon amie	(feminine)	*my* friend
ton amie	(feminine)	*thy* friend
son amie	(feminine)	*his, her, its* friend

(f)   Note that *leur* is both masculine and feminine singular and that *leurs* is both masculine and feminine plural.

leur ami	*their* friend (masculine)
leur amie	*their* friend (feminine)
leurs amis	*their* friends (masculine)
leurs amies	*their* friends (feminine)

§ 17   The Interrogative Adjective

(a)   The interrogative adjective has the following forms:

quel livre	(masculine)	*what, which* book
quelle cravate	(feminine)	*what, which* necktie
quels livres	(masculine plural)	*what, which* books
quelles cravates	(feminine plural)	*what, which* neckties

(b)   In the formula *what* + *verb* to be + *noun*, in what might be described as a "balanced equation," the interrogative adjective rather than the interrogative pronoun [see § 31] must be used.

The interrogative adjective will then agree with the noun in the predicate.

Quelle est la leçon?   *What* is the lesson? (The lesson is what?)

If a definition is expected as an answer, however, the expression *qu'est-ce que* (literary) or *qu'est-ce que c'est que* (conversational) must be used.

Qu'est-ce que c'est qu'une leçon?
(kèske sèkün lesôn)   What is a lesson?
Qu'est-ce qu'une leçon?
(kèskün lesôn)   What is a lesson?

(c)   The interrogative adjective is used with persons in this type of expression:

Quel est cet homme?   Who is this man?

The use of *quel*, instead of the expected *qui*, signifies: *What kind of man is he?*

§ 18   Cardinal and Ordinal Numbers

See Lesson 5.

The Adverb (L'Adverbe)

§ 19   Formation of the Adverb

(a)   The adverb is formed by adding -*ment* to the feminine singular of the adjective or to the masculine singular if it ends in a vowel.

heureuse happy (feminine)   heureusement happily, luckily
facile   easy (masculine)   facilement   easily
vrai   true (masculine)   vraiment   truly

(b)   Adjectives ending in -*ant* form the adverb in -*amment* and those ending in -*ent* form the adverb in -*emment*. The adverbial endings -*amment* and -*emment* are both pronounced -amân.

incessant   incessamment   incessantly
prudent   prudemment   prudently

(c)   Certain adjectives are irregular in that they take an acute accent on the e of the feminine adjective. These must be noted separately.

énorme   (masculine) enormous   énormément   enormously
précise   (feminine) precise   précisément   precisely

§ 20   Comparison of Adverbs

(a)   The adverb is compared like the adjective (see § 14) except that the article, sign of the superlative, is invariable since adverbs do not have gender.

Positive	Comparative
lentement (slowly)	**plus lentement** (more slowly)
	moins lentement (less slowly)

Superlative
le plus lentement   (the most slowly)
le moins lentement   (the least slowly)

(b)   Certain common adverbs are compared irregularly.

mal badly	**plus mal** worse	**le plus mal** the worst
	pis worse	**le pis** the worst
bien well	**mieux** better	**le mieux** (the) best
peu little	**moins** less	**le moins** (the) least

NOTE. As a modifier of the verb, the adverb *plus* can be used only when the comparison is completed. If the comparison is not complete, *more* will translate by the adverb *davantage*.

Je l'aime *plus* que Marie.   I like her *more* than Mary.
BUT: **Je l'aime *davantage* chaque jour.**
I like her *more* each day (comparison incomplete).

On the other hand, *more and more* translates as *de plus en plus*.

Je l'aime *de plus en plus*.   I like her *more and more*.

The idioms *less and less* and *better and better* have a similar construction: *de moins en moins, de mieux en mieux*.

§ 21   Position of the Adverb

(a)   If the adverb modifies a verb, its normal position is directly after the verb.

Il parle *très bien* le français.   He speaks French *very well*.
Je le vois *souvent* à Paris.   I *often* see him at Paris.

For emphasis, the adverb may go at the beginning of the sentence.

***Exceptionnellement*, il n'y aura pas de courrier demain.**
By exception there will be no mail tomorrow.

The adverb can never go between the pronoun subject and the verb, as is often the practice in English.

(b) In a compound tense, short adverbs normally go between the two parts of the verb.

Il a *toujours* compris.   He has *always* understood.

But certain common adverbs, principally adverbs of time, follow the past participle in compound tenses. They are:

aujourd'hui	today	**ici**	here
demain	tomorrow	**hier**	yesterday
autrefois	formerly	**tard**	late
		tôt	soon

Long adverbs, especially those ending in -*ment*, will tend rather to follow the past participle in a compound tense.

Il a parlé *lentement*.   He spoke slowly.

(c) Adverbs which are commonly used between the parts of a compound tense will precede the verb form when used with the infinitive.

pour *toujours* parler *correctement* in order *always* to speak *correctly*
pour *bien* comprendre to understand *well*

(d) The following adverbs or adverbial phrases, when placed at the beginning of the sentence, bring about an inversion of the verb [see § 60(a) (c)].

Peut-être a-t-il raison. *Perhaps* he is right.
Aussi* croyait-il à cette doctrine. *So* he believed in this doctrine.
Sans doute l'a-t-il vue. *Doubtless* he saw her.

Similar inversions exist in English but rarely do they correspond to an inversion in French.

Souvent je l'ai vu. *Often* have I seen him.
Surtout je voulais le voir. *Particularly* did I wish to see him.
Jamais je ne l'ai vu. *Never* did I see him.

(e) Adverbs modifying adjectives or other adverbs precede these forms as in English. This means that, if the adverb modifies an adjective following a noun, the adverb will occur between the noun and the adjective.

une *très belle* maison a *very beautiful* house
une leçon *très difficile* a *very difficult* lesson
Il le fait *trop* bien. He makes it *too* well.

---

* In any other position *aussi* means *also* or *too*. Example: Il y va *aussi*: He is going *too*.

THE ADVERB [§22] 215

§ 22 Adverbs of Quantity

(a) Adverbs of quantity translate certain English adjectives for which there is no adjectival equivalent in French. In this sense, they require the preposition *de* to introduce the noun.

J'ai *beaucoup de* livres.	I have *many* books.
J'ai *beaucoup de* difficulté.	I have *much* difficulty.
J'ai *trop de* livres.	I have *too many* books.
J'ai *trop de* difficulté.	I have *too much* difficulty.
J'ai *assez de* livres.	I have *enough* books.
J'ai *plus de* livres.	I have *more*[1] books.
J'ai *moins de* livres.	I have *fewer* books.
J'ai *moins de* difficulté.	I have *less*[1] difficulty.
J'ai *tant de* livres.	I have *so many* books.
J'ai *tant de* difficulté.	I have *so much* difficulty.
J'ai *autant de* livres que Jean.	I have *as many* books as John.
J'ai *autant de* difficulté que Jean.	I have *as much* difficulty as John.
J'ai *peu de* livres.	I have *few*[2] books.
J'ai *peu de* difficulté.	I have *little*[3] difficulty.
J'ai *un peu de* difficulté.	I have *a little* difficulty.
Combien de livres avez-vous?	*How many* books do you have?
Combien de difficulté avez-vous?	*How much* difficulty do you have?

(b) When used alone in the predicate of the sentence, adverbs of quantity require automatically the partitive pronoun *en* [see § 25 (f)] before the verb.

J'*en* ai *beaucoup*.	I have *many*.
J'*en* ai *trop*.	I have *too much*.
Combien en avez-vous?	*How many* do you have?

(c) If the adverb of quantity stands without a noun in a defective sentence (lacking a verb), it will have neither *de* nor *en*.

En avez-vous *beaucoup?* Oui, *beaucoup*.
Do you have *many?* Yes, *many*.

(d) It must not be forgotten that these adverbs of quantity were originally simple adverbs, in which sense there is no preposition *de*.

Je l'aime *beaucoup*.	I like it *very much*.
Je l'aime *autant*.	I like it *as much*.
Je l'aime *très peu*.	I like it *very little*.

---

[1] When *more* modifies a noun, it is an *adverb of quantity* with *de*. When it modifies an adjective or an adverb, it is the adverb *plus* without *de*. Example: La leçon est *plus difficile*: The lesson is *more difficult*. The same is true of *moins*, meaning *less*.

[2] Compare with *a few* which translates as *quelque* [see § 12(d)].

[3] Distinguish between *little* as an adjective, which is *petit*, and *little* in a quantitative sense. Une *petite* maison: A *little* house. Un *peu de* beurre: A *little* (quantity of) butter.

The adverb *beaucoup* can never be modified by another adverb. It means both *much* and *very much*.

The adverb *trop* means *too* when it modifies an adjective or an adverb.

   C'est *trop* difficile.   It is *too* difficult.

(e) In literary style, the adverb *bien* is used in the sense of *beaucoup* in a partitive construction, but it requires the definite article after it as well as the preposition *de*.

     bien des fois   *many* times

In this respect, *la plupart*, although not an adverb, is similar in construction.

    la plupart des hommes   *most* men

In the above example, *most* modifies a noun. When it modifies an adjective or an adverb, it is, of course, *le plus* (see § 14 and § 20).

(f) Expressions containing adverbs of quantity, *la plupart* with nouns, or adverbs of quantity or *la plupart* standing alone have a plural meaning. Any verb, past participle or adjective agreeing with them will therefore be in the plural.

Beaucoup d'hommes *sont* ici.	Many men *are* here.
Il y en a beaucoup qui *sont* ici.	Many *are* here.
La plupart *sont* ici.	Most *are* here.
Combien de livres avez-vous lus?	How many books have you read?

In the last example above note that the past participle agrees with the entire phrase *combien de livres* [see § 55(b)1].

§ 23   Negation

(a) Simple negation is made by placing *ne* before the verb and *pas* after it.* The *ne* will elide before any word beginning with a vowel.

Je *ne* comprends *pas*.	I do *not* understand.
Je *n'aime pas*.	I do *not* love.

If the verb has a pronoun object, the *ne* will go between the subject and the pronoun object.

   Je *ne* le comprends *pas*.   I do not understand it.

---

* Historically this is a double negative or, if you wish, a reenforced negative. The users of Vulgar Latin came to feel that *Non amo* was not sufficiently negative to mean *I do not love* and they reenforced it in this manner: *Non amo passum* (or *punctum*, etc.) : I do not love *a step's worth, a point's worth*, etc.

If the verb is inverted, the *pas* will follow the pronoun subject.

Ne comprenez-vous *pas?*	Don't you understand?
Ne le comprenez-vous *pas?*	Don't you understand it?

(b)   In a compound tense, the auxiliary is the verb and therefore all changes performed in terms of the verb are now performed in terms of the auxiliary, after which comes the past participle.

Je *n'ai pas* compris.	I have not understood.
Ne les avez-vous *pas* aimés?	Didn't you like them?

(c)   An infinitive is made negative by placing both *ne* and *pas* before it. If there is also a pronoun object, the *pas* will precede it.

pour *ne pas* les voir   in order *not* to see them

On the other hand, *avoir* and *être* are frequently made negative by placing *ne* and *pas* around them.

pour *ne pas* être malade	in order *not* to be sick
pour *n'être pas* malade	in order *not* to be sick

(d)   Present or perfect participles [see § 48] are made negative according to the rules given in § 23(a) and § 23(b).

n'étant pas malade   *not* being sick

(e)   Other negatives working the same as *ne pas* are as follows:

Je ne le vois *guère.*	I *hardly (scarcely)* see it.
Je ne le vois *jamais.*	I *never* see it.
Je ne le vois *plus.*	I *no longer* see it.
Je ne le vois *point.*	I see it *not at all.*

For emphasis, *jamais* may be placed at the beginning of the sentence, in which case it will still require *ne* before the verb but will not take an inversion as in English [see § 21(d)].

Jamais je ne l'ai vu.   *Never* have I seen him.

The adverb *jamais*, when used without a verb (and hence without a *ne*, since *ne* can never be used without a verb), means *never.*

L'avez-vous *jamais* vu? Non, *jamais.*
Have you *ever* seen him? No, *never.*

It is obvious from the above illustration also that *jamais* with a verb and no *ne* means *ever* instead of *never.*

(f)   The negatives *ne . . . personne* (no one) and *ne . . . rien* (nothing) work the same as *ne . . pas* in simple tenses.

Je *ne* vois *personne.*	I see *no one.*
Il *n'aime rien.*	He likes *nothing.*

In a compound tense, *ne . . . rien* continues to work like *ne . . . pas*, whereas with *ne . . personne* the second element of the negative comes after the past participle.

Je *n*'ai *rien* vu.	I have seen *nothing.*
Je *n*'ai vu *personne*.	I have seen *no one.*
	I have *not* seen *anyone.*

Rien and *personne*, being a type of pronoun, may also be the subject of the sentence. As such, they still require *ne* before the verb.

Rien *n*'est difficile.	*Nothing* is difficult.
Personne* *n*'est venu.	*No one* came.

Standing completely alone, *rien* and *personne* have a negative force like *jamais* [see § 23(e)].

Vous *n*'avez vu *personne*? Non, *personne*.
You have seen *no one*? No, *no one*.

Vous *n*'avez *rien* vu? Non, *rien*.
You have seen *nothing*? No, *nothing*.

(g) The negative *ne . . . que*, meaning *only*, can be used only to introduce the predicate of the verb. The *que* does not necessarily follow the verb directly. It will occupy the same position as the word *only* if the English sentence is carefully organized (which is frequently not the case).

Je *ne* le verrai *que* demain.	I will see him *only* tomorrow.
Je *n*'ai vu dans cette maison *que* Marie.	I saw in this house *only* Mary.

The adverb *seulement* may always be used instead of *ne . . . que*, although the latter may be stylistically preferable since French tends to shun the use of adverbs in *-ment*.

Je *n*'ai vu *que* Marie.	I have seen *only* Mary.
J'ai vu Marie *seulement*.	I saw Mary *only*.

If *only* modifies the verb, the simplest method is to use *seulement*.

Je regarde *seulement* . . .   I am *only* looking . . .

A special construction with *faire* is necessary to make *ne . . . que* refer to the verb.

Je *ne* fais *que* regarder.   I am *only* looking.

If *only* modifies the subject, use the adjective *seul* instead of an ad-

---

* Observe the masculine agreement when *personne* is used as a negative. Do not confuse this with the noun *la personne* (the person) which is always feminine, even when it obviously refers to a masculine individual.

verb. If the subject is a pronoun, the disjunctive form [see § 26(c)4] will therefore have to be used.

Jean *seul* vient.	*Only* John is coming.
Moi *seul* je viens.	*Only* I am coming.

(h)   The adjectives *aucun* (no, not any) and *nul* (no, not any) require *ne* before the verb, except in a defective sentence.

Aucune **femme *ne* viendra.**	*No* woman will come.
Nulle **raison *ne* suffira.**	*No* reason will suffice.

These adjectives also exist as substantives.

Aucun ne **conviendra.**	*None* will be fitting.
Nul **ne viendra.**	No one will come.

Aucun is more common than *nul*, but *aucun* should not be used except for special emphasis. Normally one says:

Je *n'ai pas* d'ami.	I have *no* friend.

It is preferable to put the negation with the verb, reserving *aucun* for special stress.

Je *n'ai aucun* ami.	I have *no* friend *at all*.

Aucun does not exist in modern French in a plural sense. In such a case, negation must be expressed with the verb.

Je *n'ai pas* d'amis.	I have *no* friends.

(i)   The negative *ni . . . ni (neither . . . nor)* requires a *ne* in any sentence having a verb.

Ni **Jean *ni* Marie *n'est* ici.**	*Neither* John *nor* Mary is here.
Je *ne* vois ni Jean ni Marie.	I see *neither* John *nor* Mary.

After *ni . . . ni*, all partitives [see § 6] and all articles used before a noun in a general sense [see § 3(a)] are omitted.

Je n'aime ni *eau* ni *vin*.	I like neither *water* nor *wine*.

BUT: **Je n'aime ni *le* pain ni *le* vin que le domestique a apportés.**
I like neither *the* bread nor *the* wine which the servant brought.

In the second example above, the nouns are specific, not general.

(j)   Certain negatives may be combined according to an intrinsic (that is, natural, not reducible to rules) word order. In such cases one *ne* serves for both negatives. Observe the following examples:

Je *n'ai jamais rien* vu.	I have *never* seen *anything*.
Je *n'ai jamais* vu *personne*.	I have *never* seen *anyone*.
Je *ne* veux *plus rien* voir.	I *no longer* want to see *anything*.
Il *n'a guère rien*.	He has *scarcely anything*.

(k) Certain verbs may be made negative without *pas*.

Je n'ose *(pas)* le dire.	I dare not say it.
Je ne sais *(pas)* ce qu'il veut dire.	I don't know what he means.
Il ne cesse de crier.	He does not stop shouting.
Il ne peut *(pas)* le faire.	He cannot do it.

(l) *Pas*, without *ne*, also occurs as an adverb modifying an adjective or an adverb.

C'est une leçon *pas* trop difficile.	It is a *not* too difficult lesson.
Il le fait rapidement, *pas* lentement.	He does it rapidly, *not* slowly.

(m) In a defective sentence (that is, lacking a verb) or in a fragment of a sentence set apart by a comma and having the same grammatical structure as a defective sentence, only *pas* can be used in the sense of *not*.

Pas moi.	*Not* I.
Marie viendra, mais *pas* Jean.	Mary will come, but *not* John.

In more literary French the tendency is to use *non pas* in the same situation.

Charles V devint roi à cette époque, *non pas* son frère.
Charles V became king at that period, *not* his brother.

(n) The negative *ne* occurs alone in certain expressions without having any meaning whatever in modern French. This type of *ne* is called a "pleonastic" *ne*. The "pleonastic" *ne* is required when an entire clause follows the conjunction *que* (*than* in a comparison).

Elle était plus grande que je *ne* croyais.   She was taller than I thought.

After *avant que* (before) and *à moins que* (unless) a pleonastic *ne* is found in literary style as well as a subjunctive [see § 57(e)].

Il fallait cesser avant qu'il *ne* tombât malade.
He had to stop before he fell sick.
Il viendra à moins que vous *ne* soyez malade.
He will come unless you are sick.

After an expression of *fear* a noun clause in literary style will have a pleonastic *ne* as well as a subjunctive [see § 57(c)1].

Il craignait que le gouvernement *ne* tombât.
He was afraid the government might fall.

The Pronoun (Le Pronom)

§ 24 Personal Subject Pronouns

(a) The personal pronoun subjects of the verb are:

SINGULAR		PLURAL	
je	I	nous	we
tu	thou (you)	vous	you
il	he, it (masc.)	ils	they (masc.)
elle	she, it (fem.)	elles	they (fem.)

In modern French, *vous* has come to have both a singular and a plural meaning, although it always requires a plural verb. This usage parallels English where *you*, although historically plural, is now used in both a singular and plural sense and yet it takes a plural verb in both cases. The English form *thou*, however, has practically disappeared. Corresponding to *thou*, there is in French the singular *tu* which is still used in speaking to close friends, relatives, children and animals. In the army, among enlisted men, and in many schools among students, it is also customary to use *tu*. In any case, *tu* exists only in a singular, meaning; speaking to a group of intimate friends, etc., *vous* must be used. In so-called sacred language, *vous* and not *tu* is the proper form of address [note the illustration in § 9(f)].

In the third person, since French has no neuter gender [see discussion in § 8(a)], the same pronouns are used for persons and for things.* Thus the pronoun *il* means *he* but also *it* when the antecedent is masculine. Study the following examples:

Voici un livre. *Il est bleu.*	Voici des livres. *Ils sont bleus.*
Here is a book. *It* is blue.	Here are some books. *They* are blue.
Voilà une cravate. *Elle est verte.*	Voilà des cravates. *Elles sont vertes.*
There is a necktie. *It* is green.	There are some neckties. *They* are green.

§ 25 Personal Pronoun Objects

(a) The following chart of personal pronoun objects should be memorized at the outset. All forms on this chart precede the verb in

---

* The rules governing the use of *ce* as the subject of the verb *être* [see § 28(f)] still apply even when there is a precise antecedent having gender. One says: Voilà Jean. *C'est mon ami. There is John. He is my friend.* Occasionally one hears: *Il est mon ami.* But the former expression is more correct. Compare also with § 7(a). One says: Voilà Jean Leblanc. *Il est docteur maintenant. There is John Leblanc. He is a doctor now.* But one also says: Voilà Jean Leblanc. *C'est un bon docteur. There is John Leblanc. He is a good doctor.* In the second case, the rules for the use of *ce* apply, and there is a change from the expected *il* to *ce*.

every case except the affirmative imperative [see § 25 (g)].

me			
te	le	lui	
se BEFORE	la BEFORE	leur BEFORE y BEFORE en	
nous	les		
vous			

In the above chart the pronoun objects follow an intrinsic (natural, not reducible to rule) word order which is the order in which they occur when there are two pronoun objects coming before the verb.* From the chart, for example, it is clear that *me* will precede *les* if they both are to come before the verb, that *leur* will precede *en,* etc.

Il *me les* donne.   He gives *them to me.*
Elle *les leur* donne.   She gives *them to them.*

(b)   Pronoun objects in the first column are direct, indirect and reflexive (for a discussion of the reflexive pronoun, see § 27). In other words, they have the following meanings:

DIRECT	INDIRECT	REFLEXIVE
me me	to me	myself, to myself
te thee	to thee	thyself, to thyself
se		himself, to himself
		herself, to herself
		itself, to itself
		oneself, to oneself
nous us	to us	ourselves, to ourselves
vous you	to you	yourself, to yourself
		yourselves, to yourselves

Before a vowel *me, te,* and *se* elide.

Elle *m'aime.*   She loves *me.*
Il *t'*en donnera.   He will give *thee* some.

(c)   Pronoun objects in the second column are third person **direct** objects.

le   him, it (masculine)
la   her, it (feminine)
les   them (masculine and feminine for persons or things)

Before a vowel, *le* and *la* will elide.

Elle *l'aime.*   She likes *it.*

---

* There never can be three pronoun objects, except in a sequence containing the conjunction *and.* In such a case all pronoun objects will follow the verb and will consequently be in the disjunctive form (see § 26(c)1).

But no contraction will occur with *à* or *de* if *le* is the object of an infinitive which they introduce [see § 47(c)].

J'ai oublié *de le* prévenir.	I forgot to warn him.
J'ai cherché *à le* voir.	I sought to see him.

(d)   Pronoun objects in the third column are third person indirect objects.

lui   to him, to her
leur   to them (masculine and feminine)

These pronouns apply only to persons and not to things. See further discussion in next paragraph.

(e)   The adverbial pronoun *y* means *there*, if the place has already been mentioned.

Je connais bien Paris. J'*y* vais cet été.
I know Paris well. I am going *there* this summer.

This adverbial pronoun also replaces a prepositional phrase consisting of *à* plus a pronoun object referring to a thing (such a construction with a pronoun object referring to a person would be the normal indirect pronoun object described in § 25(d) above).

Je n'*y* fais pas attention.   I pay no attention *to it.*
Marie m'a écrit une gentille lettre. J'*y* réponds en ce moment.
Mary wrote me a nice letter. I am answering *it* (literally *to it*) right now.

If the place has not been mentioned or if the speaker desires more emphasis than would be possible with the atonic form *y*, one uses *là.*

Je l'ai vu *là.*	I saw him *there* (place not previously mentioned).
***Là* je l'ai vu.**	*There* I saw him (place may have been previously mentioned but *there* is emphasized).

(f)   The partitive pronoun *en* translates as *some* or *any* when these forms stand alone. (For partitive article, see § 6).

J'*en* ai.	I have *some.*
***En* avez-vous?**	Have you any?

It is also equivalent to a prepositional phrase consisting of *de* followed by a pronoun referring to a thing.

J'*en* parle.	I am speaking *of it.*
J'*en* parle.	I am speaking *of them* (things).
BUT: **Je parle *d'eux.***	I am speaking *of them* (persons, masculine).

It translates *de* in the sense of *from* followed by a pronoun standing for a place (more commonly in English, we use *there* in that sense).*

Il *en* vient.	He is coming *from there*.

The pronoun *en* must be used automatically before the verb whenever an adverb of quantity [see § 22] or a number stand alone in the predicate.

J'*en* ai beaucoup.	I have many.
J'*en* ai six.	I have six.

(g) With the affirmative imperative, pronoun objects do not follow the rule given in § 25(a). Instead they come after the verb form, to which they are attached by hyphens, and they occur in the following order:

AFFIRMATIVE IMPERATIVE—DIRECT OBJECT—INDIRECT OBJECT—Y—EN.

Y and *en* always occur last, whether they seem to be direct or indirect objects. As noted previously [§ 25(a), footnote], a verb will never have more than one direct and one indirect pronoun object, and this remark applies as well to the affirmative imperative.

The forms of the pronouns and their meanings remain the same as in the basic chart § 25(a), except that *me* becomes *moi* (disjunctive) and *te* becomes *toi* (disjunctive). On the other hand, when *me* and *te* are to occur before *y* or *en* they elide instead of changing to *moi* and *toi*.

Donnez-*les*-*lui*.	Give *them to him*.
Donnez-*le*-*moi*.	Give *it to me*.
Donnez-*lui*-*en*.	Give *to him some*.
Donnez-*m'en*.	Give *to me some*.
Assieds-*toi*.	Sit down (seat *thyself*).

(h) In compound tenses the pronoun objects go before the auxiliary verb by virtue of the rule [see § 23(b)] that, in a compound tense, the auxiliary is the verb and all changes or additions normally made in terms of the verb are now made in terms of the auxiliary.

Je *les leur* ai donnés.	I gave *them to them*.
Elle *m'en* a donné.	She gave *me some*.

(i) If the verb is made negative, pronoun objects follow the *ne*.

Il ne *les lui* donne pas.	He does not give *them to him*.
Il ne *les lui* a pas donnés.	He did not give *them to him*.
Ne *les lui* avez-vous pas donnés.	Didn't you give them to him?

---

* In this connection, we call attention to the common idiom *en venir à* (to come to a point). *J'en viens maintenant à mon explication*: Now I come to my explanation.

This remark also applies to the negative imperative which is not an exception like the affirmative imperative [see § 25(g)].

Ne *m'en* donnez pas.   Don't give *me any.*

For the position of the pronoun object with a negative infinitive, see § 23(c).

§ 26 The Disjunctive Personal Pronoun

(a) The pronoun forms ending in mute "e" [such as those enumerated in § 25(a)] have a longer form which must be used in stressed positions in the sentence. In such stressed positions *me*, for example, becomes *moi*, *te* becomes *toi*, etc. These longer forms are called disjunctive pronouns.

(b) The disjunctive personal pronouns are as follows:

	SINGULAR		PLURAL	
1st Pers.	**moi**	me	**nous**	us
2nd Pers.	**toi**	thee, thyself	**vous**	you, yourself
3rd Pers.	**lui**	him	**eux**	them (masc.)
	elle	her	**elles**	them (fem.)
	soi	oneself		

(c) The disjunctive personal pronouns have the following functions:

(1) A pronoun in a compound subject or a compound object will be in the disjunctive.

Jean et *moi* (nous) sommes ici.   John and *I* are here.
Toi et *elle* (vous) êtes ici.   *Thou* and *she* are here.
J'ai vu Jean et *elle*.   I saw John and *her.*

In the first two examples above, note that a conjunctive (simple) pronoun subject may be, and frequently is, inserted. Whether the conjunctive pronoun subject is present or not, the verb will have the same form as though it were there.

(2) Any pronoun governed by a preposition or introduced by the conjunction *que* in the sense of *than* will be disjunctive.

avec *moi*   with *me*
sans *eux*   without *them*
Il est plus grand que *moi*.   He is bigger than *I.*

In an expression of quantity, the preposition *entre* (among) must be used before a disjunctive pronoun introduced by *de*.

beaucoup d'*entre* eux   many of them
trois d'*entre* nous   three of us

(3)   Any pronoun set apart by punctuation will be in the disjunctive form.

> **Qui est là? *Moi.***   Who is there? *I.*
> ***Lui,* malgré son âge, ne s'est jamais marié.**
> *He,* in spite of his age, never married.

(4)   If the pronoun subject is modified by an adjective, a prepositional phrase or a relative clause, the disjunctive pronoun must be used. The normal tendency in such a case is to repeat the subject with a conjunctive pronoun before the verb.

> ***Moi* seul, j'ai raison.**   *I* alone am right.
> ***Elle* seule a raison.**   *She* alone is right.
> ***Moi* qui le connais*, *je* crois ce qu'il dit.**
> *I* who know him believe what he says.

(5)   When a pronoun is repeated for emphasis, both a disjunctive and a conjunctive form are used. Repetition for emphasis is a common device in French and is particularly necessary in the case of atonic (unstressed) forms which cannot be pronounced with emphasis. Atonic forms like *je, tu, il, ils, me, te, se* can be emphasized only by a system of repetition.

> ***Moi, je* suis son ami.**   *I* am his friend.
> **Je l'ai vue *elle*.**   I saw *her.*

(6)   Any pronoun after the verb *être* will be disjunctive.

> **C'est *moi*.**   It is *I.*

(7)   After the affirmative imperative, disjunctive is required for object pronouns in the first and second person singular. For a full discussion of this point see § 25(g).

(8)   If the direct object of the verb, including the affirmative imperative, is first person, second person or reflexive (that is to say *me* [*moi*], *te* [*toi*], *se, nous, vous*), and there is also an indirect object pronoun, this indirect object pronoun will be expressed by *à* with the disjunctive.

> **Il s'explique *à elle*.**   He explains himself *to her.*
> **Ne me vendez pas *à eux*.**   Do not sell me *to them.*

(9)   If the pronouns *we, us,* or *you* have nouns in apposition to them, it is necessary to insert the adjective *autres*.

> **Nous *autres* Américains, nous croyons cela.**   We Americans believe this.
> **Je vous le dis, à vous *autres* Français.**   I say it to you Frenchmen.

---

* Note the form of the verb. In any relative clause, in English as well as in French, it is necessary to know the antecedent of the relative pronoun in order to select the proper form of the verb. In English one does not say *I who is his friend* but rather *I who am his friend*. Precisely the same thing is true of French.

Sometimes the *autres* is omitted, in which case the English translation requires *as* to complete the meaning.

Je vous le dis, à vous Français.   I say it to you as Frenchmen.

This last expression also exists in a singular:

Moi, professeur, je l'accepte.   As a professor, I accept it.

(10)   To clarify the meaning of a possessive adjective when it is ambiguous as to the gender of the possessor or to emphasize possession with a possessive adjective, the disjunctive pronoun may be used with the preposition *à*.

son livre *à lui*	*his* book
son livre *à elle*	*her* book
leur livre *à eux*	*their* (*masculine*) book
leur livre *à elles*	*their* (*feminine*) book
mon livre *à moi*	*my* (*emphasized*) book

§ 27   The Reflexive Pronoun

(a)   The reflexive pronoun reflects or refers back to the subject of the sentence.

> *She* does it *herself.*
> *She* does it to *herself.*
> She, *herself,* does it.

(b)   As an object pronoun, the reflexive has already been mentioned. See § 25(b) for the forms and positions of this type of pronoun.

When a reflexive pronoun object is placed before a verb, the verb then becomes a reflexive verb, which means in a compound tense [55(a)?] that it is conjugated with *être*.

Je *me le suis* fait.   I did it *to myself.*

(c)   The reflexive pronoun of the French may also have a *reciprocal* force, in which case it translates in English as *each other, to each other.*

Nous *nous* regardons.	We look at *ourselves.*	We look at *each other.*
Ils *se* regardent.	They look at *themselves.*	They look at *each other.*

Generally the context is sufficiently clear to indicate whether the pronoun is a simple reflexive or a reciprocal reflexive. If the context is not clear, it is necessary to add *l'un l'autre,* etc., as follows:

Nous nous aimons *l'un l'autre.*   We love *each other.*
(Two masculine or one masculine and one feminine)

228 [§27] THE PRONOUN

Nous nous aimons *l'une l'autre*.	We love *each other*. (Two feminine).
Nous nous aimons *les uns les autres*.	We love *each other*. (More than two masculine or more than two mixed genders).
Vous vous parlez *l'un* à *l'autre*.	You speak *to each other*.
Vous vous parlez *l'une* à *l'autre*.	You speak *to each other*.
Vous vous parlez *les uns aux autres*.	You speak *to each other*.
Vous vous parlez *les unes aux autres*.	You speak *to each other*.

In the above examples, the phrase *l'un l'autre* stands in apposition to (that is to say, it repeats) the object pronouns. In English *each other* is a direct or indirect object with no apposition.

They love *each other*.

But *each other* may also be the object of some preposition other than *to* in English, in which case the French preposition goes between the parts of the phrase *l'un l'autre*.* Study carefully the following examples:

Je les ai mis *l'un* sur *l'autre*.
I put them *on top of each other* (the one on the other).

Je les ai mis *les uns* sur *les autres*.
I put them *on top of each other* (more than two).

Il les trouve *les uns* sous *les autres*.
He finds them *under each other*.

(d)   If the reflexive pronoun is in apposition to the subject or the object, or if the reflexive pronoun object is repeated for emphasis (such repetition being characteristic of French), the disjunctive pronoun is used with the adverb *même* attached to it by a hyphen. Note carefully the position of this type of reflexive pronoun in the following examples:

Je le fais *moi-même*.	I do it *myself*.
J'ai vu Robert *lui-même*.	I saw Robert *himself*.
J'ai parlé à Anne *elle-même*.	I spoke to Anna *herself*.
On le fait *soi-même*.	One does it *oneself*.
Il se parle à *lui-même*.	He speaks *to himself*.
Elles se regardent *elles-mêmes*.	They look at *themselves* (emphasized or to distinguish from reciprocal when context requires).

---

* Never translate *the one* as *l'un*, *l'une* except in the phrase *l'un l'autre*. Sometimes, when a contrast is made, *les uns ... les autres* is split into two parts and then has the meaning *some ... others*. *Some do this; (the) others do that*. *Les uns font ceci; les autres font cela*. In all other cases, use the demonstrative pronoun [see § 28(b)].

§ 28 The Demonstrative Pronoun

(a) When the pronouns *this* or *that* have no precise antecedent giving number and gender, they translate as *ceci* and *cela*.

Cela n'est pas difficile.   *That* is not difficult.
Ceci n'est pas difficile.   *This* is not difficult.

French usage differs from English in the choice of *ceci* and *cela* to refer to a previously mentioned idea. In such a case, English can say either *this* or *that*, whereas French can say only *cela* (that).

Je ferai de mon mieux. *Cela* était toujours son dernier mot.
I will do my best. *This* was always his last word.

(b) If the English reads *this one, that one, these* or *those*, the equivalent French forms indicate the gender of the antecedent. The forms of this pronoun are as follows:

Singular		Plural	
celui-ci	this one (masculine)	**ceux-ci**	these (masculine)
celle-ci	this one (feminine)	**celles-ci**	these (feminine)
celui-là	that one (masculine)	**ceux-là**	those (masculine)
celle-là	that one (feminine)	**celles-là**	those (feminine)

Examples:

Il y a trois livres sur la table. *Celui-ci* est le mien.
There are three books on the table. *This one* is mine.

Voici trois cravates. *Celle-ci* est rouge.
Here are three neckties. *This one* is red.

(c) The adverbial suffixes *-ci* and *-là* must be omitted after the demonstrative pronoun when a relative clause or a prepositional phrase follow.

Ceux de mes amis qui viennent...   *Those* of my friends who come...
Ceux qui viennent...   *Those* who come...

In English the singular of *those who (which) come* is *the one who (which) comes*. In French *the one* is likewise a demonstrative pronoun [see § 27(c), footnote].

Celui qui vient...   *The one* who (which) comes...

If *the one* is a person, English may also say *he who, she who*, but in French this is still a demonstrative pronoun. *He who* and *she who* have a plural *they who*, which is likewise a demonstrative pronoun.

Celui qui gagne reçoit un prix.   *The one who* / *He who* } wins receives a prize.

Ceux qui le font auront une prime.

> The ones who ⎫
> They who ⎬ do it will get a bonus.
> Those who ⎭

From the above illustrations the following rule may be deduced: As subject of the sentence, never use a third person disjunctive pronoun followed by a relative clause, but always use a demonstrative pronoun instead.

However, the reverse is true if the same kind of grammatical construction follows a pronoun subject plus the verb *to be*.* In such a case, the disjunctive pronoun rather than the demonstrative pronoun must be used before the relative clause, and the sentence must be reorganized according to the following pattern:

> Never say: *I am the one who will do it.*
> But say: *It is I who will do it.*
> **C'est *moi* qui le ferai.**

(d)   If, in English, a noun in the possessive modifies an unexpressed noun, the French will supply a demonstrative pronoun for the unexpressed noun.

> **Il y a trois cravates dans cette boîte. *Celle de Jean* est verte.**
> There are three neckties in this box. *John's* is green.

(e)   The demonstrative pronoun is used to translate *the latter* and *the former*. *The latter*, being the nearer of the two, is *celui-ci, celle-ci, ceux-ci, celles-ci*. *The former*, being more remote, is *celui-là, ceux-là, ceux-là, celles-là*.

> **J'ai vu Jean et Marie. *Celle-ci* est mon amie.**
> I saw John and Mary. *The latter* is my friend.
> **J'ai vu Jean et Marie. *Celui-là* est mon ami.**
> I saw John and Mary. *The former* is my friend.

The latter† may also be translated as *ce dernier*, in the masculine only.

> **J'ai vu Marie et Jean. *Ce dernier* est mon ami.**
> I saw Mary and John. *The latter* is my friend.

(f)   The demonstrative pronoun *ce* is used only as the subject of

---

* The same kind of grammatical pattern can occur after a noun subject as well. In that case, neither the demonstrative nor the disjunctive pronoun will be used but instead the noun subject will move into the predicate of the verb *to be*. Do not say: *John is the one who will do it.* Say instead: *It is John who will do it*: C'est Jean qui le fera.

† *The latter*, as an adjective, is *dernier* with any type of agreement. In that sense, a demonstrative adjective always precedes. *Ce dernier individu*: The latter individual.

the verb *être* or the verb *devoir* compounded with *être*. It has the following functions:

(1) If the word *it*, as subject of the verb *to be*, refers to a previous idea but to no precise antecedent having number and gender, use *ce*.

> **Il aime peindre. *C*'est un métier intéressant.**
> He likes to paint. *It* is an interesting trade.

(2) If a modified noun (even modified by a simple article), a pronoun, a superlative. or a proper noun follows the verb *to be*, the pronoun *ce* is used in the sense of *it, he, she, they*. If the form in the predicate of the verb is third person plural, the subject will still be *ce* but the verb will be third plural.

C'est une longue leçon.	*It* is a long lesson.
C'est une amie de Marie.	*She* is a friend of Mary.
C'est moi.	*It* is I.
C'est Jean Lambert.	*He* is Jean Lambert.
Ce sont Jean et Marie qui viennent.	It is John and Mary who are coming.

(3) If a clause is the subject of the verb *être*, the pronoun *ce* serves as the functional subject of *être*.

> **Tout ce que je sais, c'est qu'il a raison.** All I know is that he is right.

There is also a natural tendency in French to repeat with a pronoun subject *ce* if a phrase or a clause intervenes between the subject and the verb *être*.

> **L'ami sur lequel j'ai toujours pu compter, c'est Jean.**
> The friend on whom I have always been able to count is John.

(4) In situations where the pronoun *ce* would be expected according to the rules set forth in paragraphs 1, 2, and 3 above but where the verb is something other than *être*, the pronoun *cela* will replace the pronoun *ce*.

> **Il aime peindre. *Cela* l'intéresse beaucoup.**
> He likes to paint. *It* interests him very much.

§ 29 The Impersonal Pronoun *il* (*it*)

(a) Certain verbs in both English and French are defective in that they can take only the impersonal pronoun *it* (in French *il*) as subject. This pronoun is called impersonal because it refers to no antecedent whatever and merely serves as the functional subject of the verb.

> **Il neige.** *It* is snowing.
> **Il pleut.** *It* is raining.

(b)   When *it* is followed by the verb *to be*, then by an adjective, then by a preposition, and finally by an infinitive having an object, *it* will be the functional subject *il* (since it is also a functional subject in English).

Il est facile de faire la leçon.   *It* is easy to do the lesson.

(c)   In literary style, to add variety to the expression, *il* impersonal may serve as the functional subject of the verb with the real subject following.* In the corresponding English *il* is replaced by the adverb *there*. With *il* as the subject, the French verb can be nothing but third singular. Note that English uses a third plural verb if the real subject is plural.

> **Il vient un homme.**   *There* comes a man.
> **Il vient des hommes.**   *There* come some men.

§ 30   The Relative Pronoun

(a)   The relative pronoun in English has the forms *who* (subject) or *whom* (object) for persons, and *which* (subject or object) or *that* for things. In French the forms are *qui* subject, *que* object for persons or things.

> **L'homme *qui* est ici ...**   The man *who* is here ...
> **Le livre *qui* est sur la table ...**   The book *which* is on the table ..
> **L'homme *que* j'ai vu ...**   The man *whom* I saw ...
> **Le livre *que* j'ai trouvé ...**   The book *that* I found ...
> **Le livre *qu'*on a trouvé ...**   The book *that* was found ...

Note in the last example above that *que* elides before a vowel.

(b)   If the relative pronoun is the object of a preposition, the forms are *qui* for persons, *lequel, laquelle, lesquels, lesquelles* for things. The longer relative indicates in its form the gender of the antecedent. It may also be used for persons after a preposition, but *qui* is more common.

> **L'homme avec** $\begin{cases} qui \\ lequel \end{cases}$ **je travaille ...**   The man with *whom* I work ...

> **Le crayon avec *lequel* j'écris ...**
> The pencil with *which* I am writing ...

---

* Another construction frequently found in literary style is the signpost *que*. For emphasis or for variety, the real subject may be replaced by *ce* before the verb *être*. In that case, the real subject, pointed out by the signpost *que, will follow* the normal predicate. *C'*est un grand écrivain *que* Molière: Molière is a great writer (Literally: He is a great writer *namely* Molière). This same signpost *que* occurs at the end of the phrase *qu'est-ce que c'est que* [see § 17(b)].*Qu'est-ce que c'est qu'un pronom?* (Literally: What is it that it is *namely* a pronoun? Meaning: What is a pronoun?).

La cravate sur *laquelle* il y a une tache . . .
The tie on *which* there is a spot . . .

(c) If the relative pronoun *which* refers not to a precise antecedent but to a whole phrase or clause, use *ce qui* (subject) or *ce que* (object).

Je chante tous les matins sous la douche, *ce qui* ennuie ma femme.
I sing every morning in the shower, *which* annoys my wife.

Je chante tous les matins sous la douche, *ce que* ma femme n'aime pas.
I sing every morning in the shower, *which* my wife does not like.

(d) By using the relative pronouns, *lequel, laquelle, lesquels, lesquelles* which indicate gender and number, the French language can sometimes construct with greater grammatical clarity a more complicated sentence than English.

Ce territoire est une province, gouverné par un préfet, *laquelle* a comme capitale une ville importante.

This region is a province, governed by a prefect, *which* (the province) has as its capital an important city.

(e) When *lequel, lesquels* or *lesquelles* follow the prepositions *de* or *à*, the normal rules of contraction apply [see § 2].

de + lequel = duquel   **à + lequel = auquel**
de + lesquels = desquels   **à + lesquels = auxquels**
de + lesquelles = desquelles   **à + lesquelles = auxquelles**

(f) The possessive relative pronoun *whose*, or *of whom* or *of which* translates as *dont*, but only if the relative clause can be organized in such a manner that *dont* is the first word.

In order to organize properly the French sentence replace *whose* with *of whom* or *of which* and rearrange the sentence so that *of whom* or *of which* comes first in the relative clause.

C'est l'homme *dont* je parlais.
He is the man *of whom* I was speaking.
(No change in word order necessary).

Voici la femme *dont* le mari est parti.
Here is the woman *whose* husband left.
(Changed to: *of whom* the husband left.
Note additional article "the").

Voici la femme *dont* j'ai vu le mari.
Here is the woman *whose* husband I saw.
(Changed to: *of whom* I saw the husband.
Note that English is inverted whereas French is not).

Il y avait une vieille maison *dont* la porte était ouverte.
There was an old house the door *of which* was open.
(Rearranged to: *of which* the door was open).

Il y avait deux maisons, *dont* une était la mienne.
There were two houses, one *of which* was mine.
(Changed to: *of which* one was mine).

In other words, there are two guiding principles in this rearrangement: 1) *Dont* will always come at the end of the clause except when the possessive relative modifies a noun introduced by a preposition (discussed immediately hereafter). 2) After *dont* there will always be normal declarative order, that is to say: subject, verb, object.

If *whose* or *of which* modify a noun governed by a preposition, *dont* must be replaced by *de qui* or *duquel*, etc. The French sentence must then be reorganized so that the possessive relative follows the noun introduced by the preposition.

Voici l'homme avec le fils *de qui (duquel)* j'ai voyagé.
Here is the man with *whose* son I traveled.
(Rearranged as: with the son *of whom*).

C'est un problème avec les détails *duquel* vous aurez beaucoup de difficultés.
It is a problem with the details *of which* you will have many difficulties.
(No rearrangement necessary).

(g) The adverb *où* (where) is substituted for the phrase *dans lequel* when the relative refers to a thing.

C'est la ville *où* je suis né.
It is the city *in which* (*où* substituted for *dans laquelle*) I was born.

(h) After the relative pronoun *que*, particularly in literary style, inversion is frequent, especially if the subject is longer than the verb or even more so if the subject is modified by some additional phrase or clause.

La difficulté *qu'*ont les hommes à comprendre...
The difficulty men have in understanding...
Les complications *qu'*avaient prévues tous les hommes clairvoyants..
The complications which all clear-sighted men had foreseen...

Note in the second illustration above that the noun subject follows the verb, even a compound verb. In other words, this inversion after the relative does not follow the normal rules of inversion in interrogative sentences [see § 60].

§ 31 The Interrogative Pronoun

(a) Interrogative pronouns are used in questions. Since they frequently resemble relative pronouns, it is easy to confuse the two types. Review especially § 30(a) and then study carefully the following chart:

	PERSONS		THINGS	
SUBJECT	qui*	who	qu'est-ce qui	what
OBJECT	qui	whom	que	what
OBJECT OF PREPOSITION	qui	whom	quoi	what

Examples:

Avec *qui* travaillez-vous?	With *whom* do you work
Qui est là?	*Who* is there?
Qu'est-ce qui est sur la table?	*What* is on the table?
Avec *quoi* travaillez-vous?	*What* are you working with?

(b) In an indirect question (a question within a declarative sentence) the interrogative pronoun for persons is still *qui* in all cases but for things it is *ce qui* (subject), *ce que* (object), *ce [preposition] quoi* (object of a preposition).

Je ne sais pas *qui* l'a fait.	I do not know *who* did it.
J'ignore *qui* il a consulté.	I do not know *whom* he consulted.
Je ne sais pas *ce qui* est sur la table.	I do not know *what* is on the table.
Je ne sais pas *ce qu'il* a fait.	I do not know *what* he did.

J'ignore *ce à quoi* il fait allusion.
I do not know *what* he is alluding to.

J'ignore *à quoi* il fait allusion.
(*A quoi* may be used without *ce*)
I do not know *what* he is alluding to.

J'ignore *ce dont* vous parlez.
I do not know *what* you are talking about.
(Literally: *that of which* you are speaking).

J'ignore *de quoi* vous parlez.
(*De quoi* may replace *ce dont*).
I don't know what you are talking about.

(c) *Which* as a pronoun, *which one* or *which ones* translate as *lequel* (masculine singular), *laquelle* (feminine singular), *lesquels* (masculine plural), *lesquelles* (feminine plural). This type of in-

---

* For emphasis there is an alternate form *qui est-ce qui.* Who is there? *Qui est-ce qui est ici?*

terrogative pronoun indicates the gender of the noun to which the pronoun refers.

Il y a trois cravates sur la table. *Laquelle* **est la vôtre?**
There are three neckties on the table. *Which one* is yours?

Lequel de ces livres voulez-vous?
Which one of these books do you want?

§ 32   The Possessive Pronoun

(a)   The possessive pronoun has the following forms:

PERSON	SINGULAR		PLURAL	
	MASCULINE	FEMININE	MASCULINE	FEMININE
1ST	le mien mine	la mienne	les miens	les miennes
2ND	le tien thine	la tienne	les tiens	les tiennes
3RD	le sien his, hers, its	la sienne	les siens	les siennes
1ST	le nôtre ours	la nôtre	les nôtres	les nôtres
2ND	le vôtre yours	la vôtre	les vôtres	les vôtres
3RD	le leur theirs	la leur	les leurs	les leurs

The gender of the possessive pronoun is determined by the gender of the antecedent. Its number, of course, is determined by the sentence in which it is used. In the third person singular the same confusion is likely to arise as in the case of the possessive adjective (see § 16) since the English by the use of *his, hers, its* distinguishes the gender of the possessor whereas the French indicates only the gender of the thing possessed. Thus *le sien* means, according to the context, either *his, hers* or *its.*

The article which precedes the possessive pronoun is part of the pronoun. Nevertheless the usual rules of contraction with *à* and *de* apply [see § 2].

Study the following examples:

Voici trois cravates. Celle-ci est *la mienne.*
Here are three neckties. This one is *mine.*

Voici trois cravates. Celle-ci est *la tienne*   (*thine*).
Voici trois cravates. Celle-ci est *la sienne*   (*his, hers*).
Voici trois cravates. Celle-ci est *la nôtre*   (*ours*).
Voici trois cravates. Celle-ci est *la vôtre*   (*yours*).
Voici trois cravates. Celle-ci est *la leur*   (*theirs*).

Les pères des deux jeunes filles attendent au salon. La première jeune fille parle *au sien.*
The fathers of the two girls are waiting in the living room. The first girl is speaking *to hers.*

(b)   After the verb *être*, if a distinction is being made between or among the various objects, the possessive adjective will be used. On the other hand, for simple possession after the verb *to be* (no distinction among objects), *à* is used with the possessor expressed as a disjunctive pronoun rather than as a possessive pronoun.

> **Voici trois livres. Celui-ci est *le mien*.**
> Here are three books. This one is *mine*.
>
> **Il n'y a qu'un seul livre et il est *à moi*.**
> There is only one book and it is *mine*.

§ 33   The Pronoun *tout* (*all*)

(a)   The adjective *all* [see § 12(e)] may also function as a pronoun, in which case it takes the gender of the word to which it refers.

> ***Tous* sont ici.**   *All are here.*

More commonly the English says: *They are all here.* The French can also say the same thing.

> **Ils sont *tous* ici.**
> **Elles sont *toutes* ici.** }   They are *all* here.

In a compound tense, the pronoun object *all* tends to take the position of an adverb, which is to say that it goes between the auxiliary verb and the past participle.

> **Je les ai *tous* vus.**   I saw them *all*.
> **Pour *tout* dire en un mot ...**   To put *everything* into a nutshell.

Frequently the English uses more complicated constructions which should be transposed as follows:

> *All of them* are here = They are *all* here.
> I saw *all of them* = I saw them *all*.

(b)   When a relative pronoun follows the pronoun *all*, it will be the compound relative [see § 30(c)].

> **Tout *ce que* je sais, c'est qu'il n'est pas malade.**
> All I know is that he is not sick.
>
> **Tout *ce qui* est sur la table est à moi.**
> All that is on the table is mine.

§ 34   The Pronoun *on* (*one*)

(a)   "One" as an indefinite pronoun translates as *on* which is never anything but third singular grammatically in spite of its many connotations. In English we frequently give the pronoun *you*, and even the pronoun *we*, an indefinite sense, in which case it should be replaced by the pronoun *one* before translation. In the same sense in English, we frequently say *people*.*

A Paris on parle français.
$\left\{\begin{array}{l}\text{In Paris } one \text{ speaks French.} \\ \text{In Paris } people \text{ speak French.} \\ \text{In Paris } you \text{ speak French.} \\ \text{In Paris } we \text{ speak French.}\end{array}\right.$

(b) *On* is commonly used to avoid a passive. See § 59(c).

The Preposition (La Préposition)

NOTE: Only a few important generalizations about the preposition will be mentioned here since prepositional usage is largely idiomatic. The student should form the habit of observing and learning separately every prepositional usage which differs from English. He should note that one gets *on* a train in English but *in* (dans) a train in French; that, in French, one walks *in* a street but *on* a boulevard; that, in French, one returns not five dollars *out of* ten but five dollars *on* ten *(trois dollars sur dix)*; etc.

§ 35 The Preposition à *(to, in, at, with)*

(a) This preposition is used to introduce an indirect noun object.

Jean parle à Paul. John is speaking *to* Paul.

Frequently the preposition *to* is omitted in English. In French the preposition à cannot be omitted before an indirect noun object.

Il donne le livre à Robert.
$\left\{\begin{array}{l}\text{He gives Robert the book.} \\ \text{He gives the book } to \text{ Robert.}\end{array}\right.$

(b) The preposition à serves in the sense of *in*, *to* or *at* with the name of a city.

Je vais à Paris. I am going *to* Paris.
Il n'a jamais été à Paris. He has never been *in* Paris.

(c) With masculine countries [for feminine countries see § 39(b)],

---

* In a sense of nationality or social class, *the people* is *le peuple* which takes a singular verb. *Le peuple français est de cet avis:* the French people are of this opinion. On the other hand, *the people* in a collective sense with no reference to nationality or social class is *les gens* which takes a plural verb. *Les gens vraiment compétents sont rares:* Truly competent people are rare (obviously *on* will not fit here since *one* cannot be inserted with meaning in the English sentence). Sometimes *les personnes* will have the meaning *people* when the speaker is thinking in terms of a series of individuals and not a group. *Les personnes qui paient leurs impôts à temps n'auront pas d'amende:* People (acting as individuals, not collectively) who pay their taxes on time will have no fine.

the preposition *à* has the meaning of *in* or *to*. In this case the masculine country retains its usual definite article [see § 3(c)].

Il va au Canada.   He is going to Canada.

(d)   The preposition *à* is used in some idioms in the sense of *in* where *dans* might be expected [see § 37].

au jardin	in the garden
au salon	in the living room

(e)   As noted previously [see § 32(b)], *à* is used after the verb *to be* to indicate simple possession.

(f)   A prepositional phrase with *à* frequently indicates the purpose for which a thing serves.

une tasse à café	{ a coffee cup { a cup for coffee
une machine à écrire	a writing machine (typewriter)

(g)   A prepositional phrase with *à* frequently translates a descriptive phrase beginning with *with* in English.

la dame *au* chapeau	the lady *with* a hat
un chapeau *à* plumes	a feathered hat (with feathers)
un chasseur *à* réaction	a jet fighter (with a jet)

(h)   The preposition *à* may never be used with a person after a verb of motion. Another verb which is not a verb of motion must be found to replace the verb of motion.

I *shall go to* John for his opinion.

Say: **Je demanderai son avis à Jean.**   (I shall ask John for his opinion).

(i)   For *à* with an infinitive, see § 47(c)3.

§ 36   The Preposition *chez* (*to, at the home of*)

This preposition means *to* or *at a place belonging to someone*, the nature of the place not being specified (although it is frequently implied by the rest of the context).

Il est *chez* Jean.	He is *at* John's [place] (John's room, John's house, John's barber shop, etc.).
Il va *chez* Jean.	He is going *to* John's.
Il va *chez* le docteur.	He is going *to* the doctor.

NOTE: In the light of the principle noted in § 35(h), the last example really has the meaning: *He is going to the doctor's [place]*. A common error is to wish to introduce another preposition before *chez* in the second and third illustrations above because the English reads *going to.* It is contrary to the nature of both English and French to have two prepositions in a row.

§ 37   The Preposition *dans* (*in*)

(a)   *Dans* is the common preposition indicating physical location. It translates as either *in* or *into.*

Jean est *dans* la maison.	John is *in* the house.

Il plonge son épée *dans* le corps de la bête.
He plunges his sword *into* the body of the beast.

(b)   If the name of a country is modified by an adjective, a prepositional phrase or a relative clause, the preposition *dans,* instead of *en* (see § 39) or *à* [see § 35(c)], will be used in the sense of *in, into,* or *to.*

dans la **Nouvelle Angleterre**	*in* New England
dans la **vieille France**	*in* old France
dans la **France du moyen âge**	*in* France of the Middle Ages

In the above examples, observe that the article normally used with the name of the country [see § 3(c)] is present.

§ 38   The Preposition *de* (*of*)

(a)   The preposition *de* is used to indicate simple possession.

le livre *de Jean*	John's book

See also the remark on possession after the verb *to be* [see § 32(b)].

(b)   If, in the equivalent English, a noun modifies another noun, the tendency in French is to place the modifying noun in a prepositional phrase with *de.*

une leçon *de géographie*	a *geography* lesson
une devanture *de magasin*	a *store* window

(c)   If, in a comparison, a number follows the word *than, de* replaces *que.*

J'en ai plus *de trois.*	I have more *than* three.

(d)   When an adjective or a past participle modify *quelque chose* (something), *rien* (nothing), or a number, the adjective or past participle will be placed in a prepositional phrase with *de.*

rien *de bon*	nothing *good*
quelque chose *de bon*	something *good*
rien *de cassé*	nothing *broken*
J'en ai trois *de rouge* et un *de noir.*	I have three *red* and one *black.*
Il y en a eu *trois de tué.*	There were *three killed.*

(e)   In French, *de* also has its original Latin meaning of *from*.

Il vient *de* Paris.   He comes *from* Paris.

When *de* is used with a feminine country in the sense of *from* the article is omitted, as already noted in § 4(b)4.

(f)   In a sense of literary or artistic authorship, *de* has the meaning of *by*.

un roman *de* Balzac	a novel *by* Balzac
De qui est ce roman?	*By* whom is this novel?
une peinture *de* Greuze	a painting *by* Greuze
De qui est cette peinture?	*By* whom is this painting?
	(*Whose* painting is this?)

In the last example, *A qui est cette peinture?* would mean *Who owns this painting?* [See §32(b)].

(g)   The material of which a thing is made is generally expressed with the preposition *de*.

une maison *de* bois	a *wooden* house
une montre *d'or*	a *gold* watch

§ 39   The Preposition *en* (*in, into*)

(a)   This preposition translates *in* or *into* when these words are used in an intangible sense rather than in the sense of location [see § 37].

Il s'exprime *en* français.	He expresses himself *in* French.
Il le traduit *en* français.	He translates it *into* French.

(b)   With unmodified [see § 37(b)] feminine [see § 8(a)] countries, *to, in* or into will translate as *en*.

Je vais *en* France cet été.	I am going *to* France this summer.
Je l'ai vu *en* France.	I saw him *in* France.
Est-elle allée *en* Belgique?	Did she go *into* Belgium?

(c)   It is contrary to the nature of the preposition *en* to have an article following it, and yet there are a few expressions in which an article does follow that preposition. [See § 4(a)].

(d)   For *en* with the present participle, see § 48(b).

§ 40   Repetition of Prepositions

When, in English, one preposition governs two words connected by the conjunction *and*, it will be necessary in French to repeat the preposition.

Je parle *à* Jean et *à* Marie.
I am speaking *to* John and Mary.

Il a parlé *sur* la France et *sur* la Belgique.
He spoke *on* France and Belgium.

§ 41 Compound Prepositions

From the French point of view there are no compound prepositions but rather adverbs with prepositions or prepositional phrases. Since these expressions correspond to simple prepositions in English, we shall refer to them as compound prepositions.

The following compound prepositions* should be noted:

Il marche *autour de* la maison.	He walks *around* the house.
L'avion passe *au-dessus de* la maison.	The airplane passes *above* the house.
Je ne connais pas les locataires *au-dessous de* nous.	I do not know the tenants *beneath* us.
Le tunnel passe *à travers* la montagne.	The tunnel passes *through* the mountain.
L'église est *en face de* la mairie.	The church is *opposite* the town hall.
Il ne le fait pas *à cause du* règlement.	He does not do it *because of* the regulation.
C'est *près d'*ici.	It is *near* here.
J'ai vu Marie *au lieu de* Jean.	I saw Mary *instead of* John.

In some cases, the English has a compound preposition, whereas the French has a simple preposition.

Il le fait *malgré* la difficulté.	He does it *in spite of* the difficulty.
Il arrive *devant* la maison.	He arrives *in front of* the house.

In cases where it is necessary to repeat compound prepositions [see § 40], the final element only of the preposition will be repeated if the last element is a simple preposition; otherwise the entire compound preposition must be repeated.

Il marche *autour de* la maison et *de* l'église.
He walks *around* the house and church.

§ 42 Position of the Preposition

It is contrary to the nature of the French language to end a sentence or a clause in a preposition. The English sentence must be rearranged so that the preposition no longer comes at the end.

This is the man I was speaking of = This is the man *of whom* I was speaking.

Voici l'homme dont je parlais.

---

* Most of these forms exist also as simple adverbs or as adverbial phrases. *Il marche tout autour*: He walks all around. *Elle habite en face*: She lives opposite. *C'est tout près*: It is near. *Ils habitent en dessous*: They live below. *Ils habitent au-dessus*: They live above. In this connection, note that *above* and *below* can never be followed by a pronoun referring to a thing; instead the adverb must be used. *Je n'ai rien mis au-dessous*: I put nothing beneath (it).

It is not normal in French to place a coördinating conjunction between prepositions as is sometimes done in rather stilted English.

Do not say: It was done *by* and *for* John.

Say: It was done *by* John and *for* John.

Cela a été fait *par* Jean et *pour* Jean.

The Conjunction (La Conjonction)

§ 43   Coördinating Conjunctions

These are *and* (et), *or* (ou), *but* (mais). They present no problem in translation. When repeated, the first will have the meaning *both . . . and*; the second, *either . . . or*.

Et Jean *et* Marie viennent.   *Both* John *and* Mary are coming.

Ou Jean *ou* Marie viendra.   *Either* John *or* Mary will come.

Particular care should be taken with the French conjunctions *car* (for) and *or* (now). The first is frequently confused with the preposition *pour* (for) and the second with the adverb *maintenant* (now).

Il le fera certainement, *car* il réussit toujours.
He will certainly do it, *for* he always succeeds.

***Or*, il n'a jamais été question d'autre chose.**
Now it was never a matter of anything else. (In this sentence *now* is a conjunction since it does not mean *at the present time*).

The coördinating conjunction *ni** has already been discussed under the heading of negatives [see § 23(i)]. In addition, we must note here that a preceding negation in French will tend to change *ou* to *ni* (nor) in situations where English says *or*.

Il n'a pas compris *ni* même vu la difficulté.
He has not understood *or* even seen the difficulty.

§ 44   Subordinating Conjunctions

All other conjunctions are called subordinating conjunctions. We shall not seek to define this term further, but shall restrict the remarks to a few practical observations.

---

* When *either* or *neither* are not used as coördinating conjunctions but rather as simple adverbs, both of them will translate as *non plus*. *Jean ne l'aime pas non plus*: John does not like it either. *Ni moi non plus*: Nor I either. *Ni Jean non plus*: John *neither*.

(a) Many subordinating conjunctions are in two parts: *avant que* (before), *après que* (after), *depuis que* (since), *afin que* (so that), *parce que* (because), etc. A common error in translation is to fail to recognize the function of *before, after,* and *since* as conjunctions when they introduce a clause (a clause contains a verb of its own) and to translate them by the prepositions *avant, après,* and *depuis.*

> **Je suis ici *depuis* son arrivée.**
> I have been here *since* his arrival.

> BUT: **Je suis ici *depuis qu'il* est arrivé.**
> I have been here *since* he arrived.

(b) It is necessary to distinguish between *puisque (since* in the sense of *because)* and *depuis que (since* in a time sense); and between *tandis que (while* in the sense of *whereas)* and *pendant que (while* in time sense).

> **Il est ici *depuis qu'elle* est tombée malade.**
> He has been here *since* she fell ill.

> **Elle n'a pas pu venir *puisqu'elle* est tombée malade.**
> She was not able to come *since* she fell ill.

> **Il chantera *pendant que* j'écoute.**
> He will sing *while* I listen.

> **Marie viendra *tandis que* Jean ne viendra pas.**
> Mary will come *while* (*whereas*) John will not.

(c) *Quand* and *lorsque* both mean *when,* the latter conjunction being more or less restricted to literary style. In some cases in English we use the word *when* in somewhat the function of a relative pronoun, as in the following expressions: *the moment when ...; the time when ...; the period when ...;* etc. French will say in such a case: *the moment in which. ...* But this will become in reality *the moment where ... (le moment où ...)* by virtue of the rule mentioned in § 30(g).

(d) The conjunction *que* in the sense of *that* can never be omitted.

> **Je crois *que* Jean vient.**
> I think John is coming; I think *that* John is coming.

(e) If the same conjunction is repeated in English at the beginning of two subordinate clauses connected by *and,* the French will not repeat the conjunction but will use *que* the second time.

> ***Quand* Jeanne est venue et *que* Marie l'a vue, il y a eu de la bagarre.**
> *When* Jane came and *when* Mary saw her, there was a free for all.

If *si* is the conjunction to be replaced by *que,* the second clause will require a verb in the subjunctive [see § 57].

> **Si vous désobéissez et *que* je m'en *aperçoive,* je vous punirai.**
> *If* you disobey and *if* I notice it, I will punish you.

The Verb (Le Verbe)

§ 45 The Nature of the French Verb

In English the form of the verb changes according to the subject. We say: I *am*, he *is*, thou *art*, we *are*, etc. In many cases, however, the English verb differs very little. For example, we say: I *read;* thou *readest;* he *reads;* we *read;* you *read;* they *read.* Since four of the six possible forms are identical, we are not especially conscious of the problem of *verb endings.* On the other hand, the French verb has an infinite variety of endings which differ according to the subject and according to the tense. Never use a French verb without being sure what ending it should have to meet the requirements of the context. The only way to learn verbs properly in French is to memorize them with their endings. It will take a lifetime to learn verb endings by intuition.

§ 46 Transitive and Intransitive Verbs

(a) Verbs which take a direct object are said to be *transitive.* Those which take no object or an object introduced by a preposition are said to be *intransitive.*

> TRANSITIVE: I *see* the boy.
>
> INTRANSITIVE: The boy *goes.*
>
> INTRANSITIVE: I *look* for the boy.

In general transitive verbs in English correspond to transitive verbs in French, and similarly for intransitives.

(b) The following common verbs are intransitive in English but transitive in French:

Il *regarde* le livre.	He *looks at* the book.
Il *cherche* le livre.	He *looks for* the book.
Nous *attendons* le train.	We *wait for* the train.
Il *écoute* la musique.	He *listens to* the music.
Il *ôte* son chapeau.	He *takes off* his hat.

(c) The following verbs are transitive in English but intransitive in French:

Il *entre dans* la maison.	He *enters* the house.
Il *entre en* Belgique.	He *enters* Belgium.
Je *réponds à* votre lettre.	I *answer* your letter.
Marie *ressemble à* son frère.	Mary *resembles* her brother.
Il *obéit à* son père.	He *obeys* his father.
Cette remarque *plaît à* Jean.	This remark *pleases* John.
Cela *convient à* Jean.	That *suits* John.

Il *se sert de* cette enveloppe.	He *uses* this envelope.
Il *se souvient de* Jean.	He *remembers* John.
Il *s'aperçoit de* sa faute.	He *notices* his mistake.

§ 47   The Infinitive   (l'infinitif)

(a)   The infinitive is the basic form of the verb from which all other forms are derived in the case of all regular verbs. In English the infinitive is always accompanied by a preposition: *to go, to read, to look,* etc. In French there are three main types of infinitives by which we distinguish the three regular conjugations: those ending in -*er* (first conjugation), those ending in -*ir* (second conjugation), and those ending in -*re* (third conjugation).

donner   to give   **finir**   to finish   **vendre**   to sell

In all tenses we shall observe the forms which are derived from these three basic infinitives.

(b)   The infinitive without a preposition may be used in the function of a noun as the subject of a verb.

Parler n'a jamais été son fort.
Speaking (to speak) has never been his strong point.

(c)   The infinitive may depend directly on another verb. In that case there are three possible constructions: no preposition, the preposition *à*, or the preposition *de* before the infinitive. The presence or absence of the preposition will depend not on the infinitive but on the verb which introduces the infinitive. Verbs may be classified in three categories according to whether they take no preposition, the preposition *à* or the preposition *de* to introduce a dependent infinitive. The following tables list the most common verbs in these three categories. Since it is not practical to memorize these lists, the student should form the habit of noting, every time such a grammatical construction occurs, whether the preposition is absent **or** present with a given introductory verb.

(1)   The following verbs take no preposition to introduce a dependent infinitive:

aimer	to like	**falloir**	to be necessary
aimer mieux	to prefer	**laisser**	to leave, allow, let
aller	to go	**oser**	to dare
compter	to intend	**pouvoir**	to be able
croire	to believe	**préférer**	to prefer
désirer	to desire	**savoir**	to know (how)
devoir	to have to	**sembler**	to seem

entendre   to hear
espérer   to hope
faire   to do, make

venir   to come
voir   to see
vouloir   to want, wish

EXAMPLES: J'aime mieux le faire.   I prefer *to* do it.
Elle vient me voir.   She is coming *to* see me.

(2)   The following verbs take the preposition *de* to introduce
a dependent infinitive:

avoir peur de   to be afraid
cesser de   to cease
craindre de   to fear
défendre de   to forbid
demander de   to ask
se dépêcher de   to hurry
dire de   to tell, order
écrire de   to write (to do)
essayer de   to try

finir de   to finish
ordonner de   to order
oublier de   to forget
permettre de   to permit
prier de   to beg, ask
promettre de   to promise
refuser de   to refuse
regretter de   to regret
remercier de   to thank

EXAMPLES: Elle *essaie de travailler.*   She *tries to work.*
Il *oublie de faire* son travail.   He *forgets to do* his work.

After the verbs of ordering *(défendre, demander, dire écrire, ordonner, permettre, prier, promettre)* the person affected by the order,
etc., will be expressed as an indirect object.

Je *lui* dis de travailler.   I tell *him* to work.
Elle ordonne *à Jean* de travailler.   She orders *John* to work.

In this connection the special idiom *venir de* must be mentioned.
Venir de with the verb in the present tense means *to have just done
something.*

Elle *vient de partir.*   She *has just left.*

If the English uses a pluperfect tense in the same construction, the
French will use an imperfect tense.

Elle *venait de partir.*   She *had just left.*

(3)   The following verbs take the preposition *à* to introduce a
dependent infinitive:

aider à   to help
s'amuser à   to amuse oneself
apprendre à   to learn, teach
arriver à   to succeed
avoir à   to have (to)
chercher à   to see, try
commencer à   to begin
consentir à   to consent
continuer à   to ocntinue

enseigner à   to teach
s'habituer à   to accustom oneself
hésiter à   to hesitate
inviter à   to invite
se mettre à   to begin
recommencer à   to begin again
réussir à   to succeed
songer à   to think, dream
tarder à   to delay in

EXAMPLES: **Elle cherche à le trouver.**   She tries *to* find him.
             Elle réussit à le voir.   She succeeds *in* seeing him.

(d) The infinitive may also depend on an adjective or a noun, in which case it will be introduced by either *à* or *de*. If the infinitive has a direct object either following it or directly preceding it, the preposition *de* will generally introduce the infinitive.

Il est facile *de* préparer la leçon.	It is easy *to* prepare the lesson.
Il est facile *de* la préparer.	It is easy *to* prepare it.
J'ai envie *de* le faire.	I want very much *to* do it.

An exception to the rule may be noted in this idiom, for example:

J'ai du mal *à* faire cela.	I have trouble (*in*) doing that.

If the infinitive is obviously without an object of its own following it or directly preceding it as a pronoun, the infinitive will act upon the subject or the object of the main verb of the sentence, in which case it will be introduced by the preposition *à*.

J'ai beacoup de leçons *à* faire.	I have many lessons *to* do.
Cette leçon est facile *à* faire.	This lesson is easy *to* do.
C'est facile *à* faire.	It is easy *to* do.*

When a passive [see § 59] infinitive follows a noun in English it will generally translate as *à* plus an active infinitive.

        C'est un livre *à lire*.   It is a book *to be read.*

From this we may deduce the following rule: if an infinitive depending on a noun and having no object of its own can be *construed as a passive*, use *à* before it.

        Il y a des devoirs *à* préparer pour demain.
        There are exercises *to* prepare (*to be prepared*) for tomorrow.

On the other hand, if the passive infinitive is followed by an *agent* [see § 59], the introductory preposition will still be *à* but the infinitive will remain passive.

        C'est un livre *à être lu* par tout le monde.
        It is a book *to be read* by everyone.

(e) The infinitive, introduced by *to* in English, may stand alone in the sentence and not depend on a verb, noun or adjective. In that

---

*Compare this with *Il est facile de faire cela* mentioned a few lines above. In *It is easy to do that* the pronoun *it* is a functional subject [having no antecedent; see § 29] and is therefore *il*. Also the infinitive *faire* has an object following it; therefore it is introduced by *de*. In *C'est facile à faire*, the pronoun *it* (*ce*) must refer to something previously mentioned, although not a precise antecedent. On the other hand, the infinitive *faire* has no object of its own and really acts upon the subject of the main verb (*ce*); hence the infinitive is introduced by *à*.

case, the English can be paraphrased as *in order to*. If the English reads *in order to* or if *to* can be construed as *in order to*, the French will use the preposition *pour*.

Il vous faudra beaucoup de temps *pour* apprendre cette leçon.
You will need a lot of time *to* (*in order to*) learn this lesson.

With *venir* and *aller* the infinitive may be constructed without *pour* even though there are intervening words.

J'irai en ville demain matin *voir* mes amis.
I shall go in town tomorrow morning *to see* my friends.

(f)   All prepositions in French, with the exception of *en* [see §48(b)] govern the infinitive form of the verb and not the present participle as in English.

> **sans le *voir***   without *seeing* him
> **pour le *voir***   in order *to see* him
> **au lieu de le *voir***   instead of *seeing* him
> **afin de le *voir***   in order *to see* him

The following special problems should also be noted:

(1)   Before an infinitive, the preposition *before* translates as *avant de* instead of *avant*.

> **avant de le voir**   before seeing him
> BUT: **J'arriverai *avant* lui.**   I shall arrive *before* him.

(2)   The preposition *après* (after) requires after it, not the simple infinitive, but the past infinitive.

> **après l'*avoir vu***   { after *seeing* him
>   { after *having seen* him

§ 48   The Present Participle   (le participe présent)

(a)   The present participle in French ends in *-ant* and corresponds to the ending *-ing* in English. In the case of regular verbs of the first and second conjugations, this ending is added to the stem obtained by removing the infinitive ending. In the case of regular second conjugation verbs, the characteristic *-iss-*, found also in the present indicative plural, the imperfect indicative, the present subjunctive, and the plural imperative, is also included in the verb.

> **donn-er**   **donn-*ant***   giving
> **fin-*ir***   **fin-*iss-ant***   finishing
> **vend-*re***   **vend-*ant***   selling

(b)   The present participle is never used to form a tense in French.

It exists only as a *gerundive*, which is to say a participle standing alone with no auxiliary verb.

As a gerundive, the present participle *without a preposition* indicates that the action occurred previous to the action of the main verb.

Sortant sa main de sa poche, il lui a donné quelques sous.
Taking his hand out of his pocket, he gave him a few pennies.

In the above example the action indicated by the participle *sortant* precedes that of the main verb *a donné*.

If the action indicated by the present participle is simultaneous with the action of the main verb, the preposition *en* will introduce the participle. In the corresponding English, this *en* will be either untranslated or will translate as *while* or *on*.

En le voyant, il a éclaté de rire.   *Seeing* him, he burst out laughing.
On seeing him, he burst out laughing.

En visitant la malle, le douanier a découvert de la contrebande.
While inspecting the trunk, the customs agent discovered contraband.

En is the only preposition which may occur before the present participle. As noted previously [see § 47(f)], all other prepositions govern the infinitive form of the verb.

Constructed with *en*, the present participle will always refer to the subject of the sentence.

Jean a dit quelques mots à Robert en regardant le livre.
Looking at the book, John said a few words to Robert.

(c)   In both English and French there is a form called the *perfect* participle which consists of the present participle of *avoir* or *être* plus the past participle.

ayant regardé   having looked

(d)   As noted previously [see § 11(a)], the present participle is frequently used as an adjective. The adjectival function of the present participle can easily be recognized by the position of the word in English: it always precedes its noun.

une leçon *intéressante*   an *interesting* lesson

If the present participle follows the noun in English, it is no longer an adjective but a *gerundive* [see § 48(b) above] and, in that case, *it will not agree like an adjective* in French.

La cérémonie *finissant* à trois heures, Jean a décidé de partir.
The ceremony *finishing* at three o'clock, John decided to leave.

NOTE: There is a tendency in French to use a phrase containing a participle, as in the example above, in the sense of *since* or *because*.

The English translation given above is awkward and should be paraphrased.

In some cases the *gerundive* may modify the object of the verb.

J'ai vu Jean *descendant* la rue.   I saw John *coming down* the street.

In such a case, the more common tendency in French is to substitute a relative clause for the present participle.

J'ai vu Jean *qui descendait* la rue.   I saw John coming down the street.

After the verbs of sensual perception, *voir* (to see), *entendre* (to hear), *sentir* (to feel), an infinitive construction commonly replaces a present participle.

J'ai entendu Marie *chanter.*   I heard Mary *sing* (*singing*).

One may also say:

J'ai entendu Marie *qui chantait.*   I heard Mary *sing* (with the meaning: *and she was singing*).

§ 49   The Past Participle   (le participe passé)

(a)   The past participle is formed by adding *-é* (FIRST CONJUGATION); *-i* (SECOND CONJUGATION), *-u* (THIRD CONJUGATION) to the stem of the verb obtained by removing the infinitive ending.

donn-*er*	**donn-é**	given
fin-*ir*	**fin-*i***	finished
vend-*re*	**vend-*u***	sold

(b)   For the use of past participles in the formation of compound tenses, see § 55(a).

(c)   The past participle is also found in what might be called an *ablative absolute* construction, to borrow a term from Latin grammar. In such a construction, the auxiliary verb of the English is not translated.

La ville une fois *prise*, César continua sa campagne.
The city once *having been taken*, Cæsar continued his campaign.

In the above example, the past participle agrees like an adjective because the auxiliary verb *to be* is understood and this is in reality a passive construction [see § 59].

(d)   For the use of the past participle as an adjective, see § 11(a).

§ 50 The Present Indicative* (le présent de l'indicatif)

(a) The present indicative tense indicates an action going on at the present time. If we take the sample verb *to give* in English, we find that there are three ways to indicate an action going on in the present: *I give, I am giving, I do give*. The French can say only *I give (je donne)*. In other words, the present tense of a French verb is always expressed in one word. The present indicative of regular verbs in French will be formed by taking the *stem* of the verb [the part remaining after the infinitive endings *-er*, *-ir*, and *-re* are removed; see § 47(a)] and adding to it the endings *italicized* in the illustrations below.

FIRST CONJUGATION:

	Singular		Plural	
1st Pers.	*je* **donne**	I give, am giving, do give	*nous* **donnons**	we give, are giving, do give
2nd Pers.	*tu* **donnes**	thou givest, art giving, dost give	*vous* **donnez**	you give, are giving, do give
3rd Pers.	*il* **donne**	he gives, is giving, does give	*ils* **donnent**	they give, are giving, do give
	elle **donne**	she gives, is giving, does give	*elles* **donnent**	they give, are giving, do give

SECOND CONJUGATION:

	Singular		Plural
1st Pers.	*je* **finis**	I finish, am finishing, do finish	*nous* **finissons**
2nd Pers.	*tu* **finis**	(etc.)	*vous* **finissez**
3rd Pers.	*il (elle)* **finit**		*ils* **finissent**

THIRD CONJUGATION:

	Singular		Plural
1st Pers.	*je* **vends**	I sell, am selling, do sell	*nous* **vendons**
2nd Pers.	*tu* **vends**	(etc.)	*vous* **vendez**
3rd Pers.	*il* **vend**		*ils* **vendent**

In the above examples, note that an *-iss-* is added to the stem of a regular *-ir* verb in the present indicative plural before the endings are attached [see remark under § 48(a)]. Note also that the third singular of an *-re* verb has no ending. Theoretically, the ending

---

* Since there are also present, imperfect and pluperfect *subjunctives* we shall use each time the word *indicative* in the sense of "not subjunctive" without attempting to define the term further. The term *subjunctive* will be defined in due course.

should be -*t*, but, since the stem of all -*re* verbs except *rompre* (to break) ends in *d*, a *t* could not be added in the days when every letter was pronounced in French. The third singular of *rompre* is *rompt* (now pronounced rô^n).

(b) In addition to its normal functions, the present tense is used in French to indicate an action begun in the past but continuing in the present. English will express the same notion by various past tenses.

> **Jean *est* ici depuis l'arrivée de Marie.**
> John *has been* here since Mary's arrival (*but* he is still here).

When the amount of time is specified, English will tend to use the preposition *for** in such a construction, whereas the French continues to use the word *depuis* (since).

> **Je *suis* ici *depuis* trois jours.**
> I *have been* here *for* three days (*but* I am still here).

To make a question of the above sentence, the French will continue to use *depuis* (since). Note how the equivalent English has changed:

> **Depuis combien de jours êtes-vous ici?**
> *How many days* (for how many days) have you been here?

> **Depuis quand êtes-vous ici?**
> *How long* have you been here?

The same notion of time beginning in the past but continuing in the present is commonly expressed by the idiom *il y a* + *the amount of time* + *que* + *the present tense*. *Voici* and *voilà* are frequently substituted for *il y a* in this idiom.

> **Il y a trois ans que je suis ici.**
> I have been here for three years.

> **Voici (voilà, cela fait) trois ans que je suis ici.**
> I have been here for three years.

This idiom may also be made into a question.

> **Combien de temps y a-t-il que vous êtes ici?**
> How long have you been here?

---

* With a future verb, *for* in this situation translates as *pour*. *Je serai ici pour trois jours*: I shall be here (for) three days. If the verb is in a past tense of any type or a conditional tense, *for* will translate as *pendant* (during) or will be omitted altogether, as it frequently is in English. *J'y ai été (pendant) trois jours*: I was there (for) three days.

§ 51   The Imperfect Indicative   (l'imparfait de l'indicatif)

(a)   The imperfect indicative of the three model regular verbs is as follows:

FIRST CONJUGATION:

	Singular		Plural	
1st Pers.	*je* **donn***ais*	I was giving	*nous* **donn***ions*	we were giving
2nd Pers.	*tu* **donn***ais*	thou were giving	*vous* **donn***iez*	you were giving
3rd Pers.	*il* **donn***ait*	he was giving	*ils* **donn***aient*	they were giving

SECOND CONJUGATION:

	Singular		Plural
1st Pers.	*je* **fin***issais*	I was finishing	*nous* **fin***issions*
2nd Pers.	*tu* **fin***issais*	(etc.)	*vous* **fin***issiez*
3rd Pers.	*il* **fin***issait*		*ils* **fin***issaient*

THIRD CONJUGATION:

	Singular		Plural
1st Pers.	*je* **vend***ais*	I was selling	*nous* **vend***ions*
2nd Pers.	*tu* **vend***ais*	(etc.)	*vous* **vend***iez*
3rd Pers.	*il* **vend***ait*		*ils* **vend***aient*

Note that the imperfect indicative of the second conjugation regular verb adds an *-iss-* to the stem before attaching the endings [see § 48(a)].

(b)   The imperfect indicative has the following functions:

(1)   It indicates an incomplete action in the past. In English the imperfect tense employs the auxiliary verbs *was* or *were*. As can readily be seen from the illustrations above, the imperfect indicative in French is not a compound tense but rather a simple tense.

Je *finissais* ma leçon à ce moment-là.
I *was finishing* my lesson at that time.

Sometimes in English we use a simple past tense where an imperfect would be more precise. If the imperfect tense can replace the simple past tense in an English sentence and thereby clarify the meaning, it is obvious that the French, which is infinitely more accurate in tense usage, will require the imperfect. *Note carefully the following example:*

I FINISHED THE BOOK WHILE JOHN READ HIS NEWSPAPER. This means either *I was finishing the book while John was reading his newspaper* or *I finished (completed action) the book while John was reading his newspaper. In either case,* the second verb clearly means *was reading* and not *read*. Hence there are two possible translations in French:

Je finissais le livre pendant que Jean lisait son journal.
J'ai fini le livre pendant que Jean lisait son journal.

(2) Description is normally expressed by the imperfect tense no matter what the equivalent English says as a past tense.

La maison était bleue.	The house *was* blue.
Le château dominait le village.	The castle *overlooked* the village.

(3) Customary, habitual or continually recurring action is expressed by the imperfect. These notions are conveyed in English by the phrase *used to* or *kept* [*doing*]. Hence if the meaning of the English verb is uncertain and *used to* or *kept* [*doing*] can be inserted to clarify, it is certain that French requires an imperfect tense in this situation.

Tous les matins il se levait à six heures.
Every morning he *got up* at six o'clock.
Every morning he *used to get up* at six o'clock.
Every morning he *would*[1] *get up* at six o'clock.

Toutes les cinq minutes il regardait la pendule.[2]
Every five minutes he *looked* at the clock.
Every five minutes he *kept looking at* the clock.

(4) In short, it may be said that, unless the action is precise and occurring at a point of time (negation or interrogation will not make it imprecise), however, the imperfect will be preferred to a more precise past tense.

Le roi Jean régnait à cette époque.
King John *reigned* at that time.

BUT: **Le roi Jean mourut en 1600.**
King John *died* in 1600.

As an extension of this notion, verbs of mental state and the verbs *avoir*, *être*, *pouvoir* and *devoir* are commonly put in the imperfect tense unless the speaker or writer desires greater vividness, in which case he will use a preterit [see § 54] or a compound past [see § 55(b)].

Jean était roi à cette époque.
John *was* king at that period.

---

[1] *Would* is also the characteristic sign of the conditional tense [see § 53(b)]. If *would* means *used to*, however, the tense required is not conditional but imperfect.

[2] It is possible to say also *Toutes les cinq minutes il a regardé la pendule*, giving emphasis to each individual action.

Jean *a été* roi jusqu'à la défaite de son armée.
John *was* king until the defeat of his army. (Time more
precise because of exact statement which ends sentence;
also notion that action of verb was complete since he
ceased to be king).

Le petit garçon avait une pomme quand je l'ai vu.
The little boy *had* an apple when I saw him. (He had
the apple and continued to have it; no end indicated
for action).

Le garçon *a eu* une pomme mais quelqu'un l'a volee.
The boy *had* an apple but someone stole it. (He lost
his apple; hence the action of *having* was completed).

Je *croyais* qu'il *avait* raison.
I *thought* he *was* right. (Neither verb has any precise
limits in time; the mental action is continuous).

J'ai *cru* qu'il *avait* raison, mais je me *trompais*.
I *thought* he *was* right, but I *was* mistaken. (The action
of the first verb is given precise limits to convey the
idea that the thinking came to an end).

(5)   Action begun in the remote past (the zone usually limited
to the pluperfect tense) but continuing in the simple past (the
zone usually indicated by the imperfect or the compound past
tenses), is expressed by *depuis* and the imperfect tense. For a
detailed analysis of this construction, turn back to § 50(b).

Note in the following examples how the English translation
changes when the imperfect tense replaces the present in the examples already used in § 50(b):

Jean *était* ici depuis l'arrivée de Marie.
John *had been* here since Mary's arrival.

J'*étais* ici depuis trois jours.
I *had been* here for three days.

Il *y avait* trois jours que j'étais là.
Cela *faisait* trois jours que j'étais là.
I *had been* there for three days.

In the last example above, note that not only has the main verb
been put in the imperfect but also the *il y a* and *cela fait* part of the
idiom. *Voilà* may also be used with an imperfect tense but not
voici.

(6)   For the uses of the imperfect tense in an *if* clause, see
§ 53(c).

§ 52   The Future Tense   (le futur)

(a)   In the first two regular conjugations the future is formed by adding to the *entire infinitive* the endings[1] shown below. In the third conjugation, the final *e* of the infinitive is dropped before adding the future endings.

FIRST CONJUGATION:

	Singular		Plural	
1st Pers.	*je* donnerai	I shall[2] (will) give	*nous* donnerons	we shall (will) give
2nd Pers.	*tu* donneras	thou (shalt) wilt give	*vous* donnerez	you will give
3rd Pers.	*il* donnera	he will give	*ils* donneront	they will give

SECOND CONJUGATION:

	Singular		Plural
1st Pers.	*je* finirai	I shall (will) finish	*nous* finirons
2nd Pers.	*tu* finiras	(etc.)	*vous* finirez
3rd Pers.	*il* finira		*ils* finiront

THIRD CONJUGATION:

	Singular		Plural
1st Pers.	*je* vendrai	I shall, will sell	*nous* vendrons
2nd Pers.	*tu* vendras	(etc.)	*vous* vendrez
3rd Pers.	*il* vendra		*ils* vendront

(b)   The French future, like the English future, expresses an action which will go on at a future time. English uses the auxiliaries *shall* and *will*[3] to convey this idea, whereas French, as noted above, expresses future time by a simple rather than a compound tense.

(c)   When the main verb of the sentence is future and there is a clause beginning with *quand* (when), *lorsque* (when: literary style),

---

[1] In reality these endings are the present tense of *avoir*. In Vulgar Latin, the simple future *amabo* (I shall love), for example, was replaced by *amare habeo* (I shall have to love), which is the ancestor of the French form *aimerai*.

[2] *Shall* may also mean obligation, especially in a third person. Generally French will employ a simple future in this sense. although a notion of obligation may also be more clearly expressed with *devoir* [see § 62].

[3] *Will* sometimes means volition and not future. *He will not do it* means either *He will not do it at a future time* or *He is not willing to do it*. In the second case, *will* indicates volition and will translate as the verb *vouloir: Il ne veut pas le faire.*

aussitôt que (as soon as), or *dès que* (as soon as: literary style), the verb of the clause will also be in the future.

Je le *verrai* quand il *viendra.*   I *shall see* him when he *comes.*
Je le *verrai* aussitôt qu'il *viendra.*   I *shall see* him as soon as he *comes.*

(d)   If the main verb of a sentence is present or future, the verb of an *if (si)* clause *will be present.* This rule should be compared with that mentioned in § 53(c).

Je le *verrai* s'il *vient.*   I *shall see* him if he *comes.*

Note that the French usage is the same as the English. A common error is to wish to use future in the *if* clause in French.

§ 53   The Conditional Tense   (le conditionnel)

(a)   The conditional tense is formed by placing the endings of the imperfect indicative [see § 51(a)] onto the stem for the future [see § 52(a)]. This rule knows no exceptions; it applies to irregular verbs (which frequently have irregular futures) as well as to regular verbs.

FIRST CONJUGATION:

	Singular		Plural	
1st Pers.	*je* **donnerais**	I should, would give	*nous* **donnerions**	we should, would give
2nd Pers.	*tu* **donnerais**	thou wouldst give	*vous* **donneriez**	you would give
3rd Pers.	*il* **donnerait**	he would give	*ils* **donneraient**	they would give

SECOND CONJUGATION:

	Singular		Plural
1st Pers.	*je* **finirais**	I should, would finish	*nous* **finirions**
2nd Pers.	*tu* **finirais**	(etc.)	*vous* **finiriez**
3rd Pers.	*il* **finirait**		*ils* **finiraient**

THIRD CONJUGATION:

	Singular		Plural
1st Pers.	*je* **vendrais**	I should, would sell	*nous* **vendrions**
2nd Pers.	*tu* **vendrais**	(etc.)	*vous* **vendriez**
3rd Pers.	*il* **vendrait**		*ils* **vendraient**

(b)   The conditional tense in English uses the auxiliaries *should* and *would*, whereas the French conditional, as noted above, is in one piece. Before deciding that these auxiliaries are an indication of the conditional, they must be analyzed according to the following principles:

(1) If *would* means *used to,* the verb in question will be imperfect and not conditional [see § 51(b)3].

(2) If *would* means *wanted* it is either imperfect or conditional of *vouloir* [see also § 51(b) 3, footnote 1].

Il ne *voulait* pas le faire.	He *would* not do it. He *did* not *want* to do it.
Jean a dit que Marie ne *voudrait* pas le faire.	John said that Mary *would* not do it. John said that Mary *would* not *be willing* to do it.

(3) If *should* means *ought* the translation will be the conditional of *devoir* [see § 62].

Otherwise the presence of the auxiliaries *should* or *would* indicates that the verb in question will be conditional in French.

Il a dit qu'il le lui *donnerait*.   He said that he *would give* it to her.

(c) If the main verb is conditional because of the specifications set forth in § 53(b) above and there is a clause beginning with *si* in the sense of *if**, the verb of that clause will automatically be imperfect, *no matter what the English says.* [Compare with §52(d)].

J'*irais* aussi s'il y *allait*.	I would go too if he *went*. I would go too if he *should go*. I would go too if he *were to go*.

NOTE: In the second translation of the example above, English usage suggests that the French verb ought to be in the conditional, but the rule in § 53(c) above permits no exceptions. *Should go* will have to translate as the imperfect tense of *to go.*

(d) With the conditional, *quand même* has the meaning of *even if.*

Quand même il le *prouverait*, je le ne croirais pas.
Even if he proved it, I would not believe it.

Même si may also be used, however, with the rule in § 53(c) applying.

(e) A double conditional separated by the conjunction *que* will likewise have the meaning *even if.*

Vous *seriez* son ami que vous ne *diriez* pas cela.
Even if you were his friend, you would not say that.

---

* *Si* also means *whether* or *if* in the sense of *whether* in indirect questions. In such a case, there is no problem of tense sequence but the tense will be whatever tense correctly corresponds to that of the English verb. *Je lui ai demandé s'il viendrait:* I asked him whether he would come.

§ 54 The Preterit (le passé simple)

(a) The preterit has scarcely been used in this book because it is a literary tense rarely encountered in conversation, and this book emphasizes oral French. However, the student will deal with it incessantly in reading so that he would do well to study it thoroughly.

(b) The preterit is formed by adding to the stem of the verb, if the verb is regular, the endings shown in the following examples:

FIRST CONJUGATION:

	Singular		Plural	
1st Pers.	*je* donn*ai*	I gave	*nous* donn*âmes*	we gave
2nd Pers.	*tu* donn*as*	thou gavest	*vous* donn*âtes*	you gave
3rd Pers.	*il* donn*a*	he gave	*ils* donn*èrent*	they gave

SECOND CONJUGATION:

	Singular		Plural
1st Pers.	*je* fin*is*	I finished	*nous* fin*îmes*
2nd Pers.	*tu* fin*is*	(etc.)	*vous* fin*îtes*
3rd Pers.	*il* fin*it*		*ils* fin*irent*

THIRD CONJUGATION:

	Singular		Plural
1st Pers.	*je* vend*is*	I sold	*nous* vend*îmes*
2nd Pers.	*tu* vend*is*	(etc.)	*vous* vend*îtes*
3rd Pers.	*il* vend*it*		*ils* vend*irent*

(c) The preterit indicates, in literary style, a *completed precise action* in the simple past. In other words, French literary style makes a distinction which conversational French has lost. Refer at this point to § 55(b) to make the comparison. In English we distinguish between *she went* and *she has gone*. Literary French makes the same distinction.

elle alla   she went
elle est allée   she has gone

If, in literary style, the action is not precise or if the time is not limited, the French will still use *compound past*. Compare the two examples:

Montaigne publia ses *Essais* en 1580.
Montaigne published his *Essays* in 1580.

Montaigne a écrit les *Essais*.
Montaigne wrote the *Essays*.

In the second example above we have only a general statement that Montaigne wrote the *Essays* without any reference to any precise act of writing at a given time. Hence the English *wrote* translates as *a écrit* instead of *écrivit*, even in literary style.

§ 55 Compound Tenses of the Indicative

(a) All compound tenses of both the indicative and the subjunctive [see § 57] are formed by the proper tense of the auxiliary plus the past participle [see § 49]. The auxiliary will be either *avoir* or *être* according to the following rules:

(1) If the verb is any one of the following, it will be conjugated with *être:*

aller to go		**partir**[2] to leave	
arriver to arrive		**passer**[1] to pass	
descendre[1] to descend, go down		**rentrer**[1] to return (home)	
devenir to become		**rester** to remain	
entrer to enter		**retourner**[1] to return[3]	
monter[1] to go up		**revenir**[3] to return	
mourir to die		**sortir**[2] to go out, leave	
naître to be born		**tomber** to fall	
		venir to come	

Most of the verbs in the above list are so-called *verbs of motion,* but not all verbs of motion (example: *courir*) are in the list. The only way to be sure that a verb is conjugated with *être* is to memorize the preceding list or else to consult it frequently. At any rate, it is certain that no verb, except a reflexive verb (see next paragraph), will be conjugated with *être* if it has a direct object.

(2) If the verb is reflexive [see § 58], the auxiliary used in the compound tense will be *être*. A verb becomes reflexive whenever a reflexive pronoun occurs before it.

	Elle *a coupé* le pain.	She *cut* the bread.
But:	**Elle *s'est coupée.***	She *cut herself.*

---

[1] These verbs also exist as transitives. In their second meaning, they are conjugated with *avoir*. Note the transitive meanings: *descendre* (to carry down, to go down [a stair, etc.]); *monter* (to go up [a stair, etc.], to carry up); *passer* (to pass [a thing]); *rentrer* (to pull in, carry in); *retourner* (to turn [a thing] around).

[2] *Partir de* means *to leave* (*go out of*) (*a place*). *Sortir de* means *to leave* (*go out of*) (*a place*). French also has the transitive verb *quitter* which means *to leave* (*a place*). The transitive verb *laisser* means *to leave* in the sense of *to leave behind.*

[3] *Retourner* means *to return* in the following sense: The speaker is at Point A and is going to return to Point B. *Revenir* means *to return* in the following sense: The speaker starts at Point A, goes to Point B, and *returns* or *comes back* to Point A.

(3) All other verbs, both transitive and intransitive, will be conjugated with *avoir*.

(b) In all compound tenses the past participle will agree *like an adjective* with the object, the subject, or will not agree as specified hereafter.

(1) Verbs conjugated with *avoir* have the past participle agree-ing like an adjective with the *preceding direct object*. This rule must be taken most literally*; if the direct object as a pronoun, or even as a noun, precedes the verb, there will be an agreement of the past participle.

> **Je *les* ai vus.**
> I saw *them*.

> **Marie *l'*a donnée à Jean.**
> Mary gave it (feminine) to John.

> **Voici les livres *que* vous avez demandés.**
> Here the books *which* you asked for.

> ***Combien de livres* avez-vous lus?**
> *How many books* have you read? [See § 22(f)]

If there is no *preceding direct object*, there is no agreement of the past participle.

> **J'ai donné le livre à Jean.**   I gave the book to John.

(2) Verbs conjugated with *être* (with the exception of reflexive verbs) have the past participle agreeing like an adjective with the *subject*.

> ***Elle* est allée.**   She went.
> ***Nous* sommes allés.**   We went.

(3) All reflexive verbs have the past participle agreeing with the preceding direct object (exactly the same as for *avoir*).

> **Elle *s'*est coupée.**   She cut *herself*.
> **Elle *s'est* levée.**   She got up.

> BUT: **Elle *s'*est coupé le doigt.**   She cut her finger.

By virtue of the rule that no verb in French can have two direct objects, it is clear in the third example above that *le doigt* is the direct object and that therefore *se* is an indirect object. Hence there is no agreement of the past participle.

---

* There is never any agreement, however, with the pronoun *en*. *Avez-vous vu des roses? Oui, j'en ai vu.* Did you see any roses? Yes, I saw some.

(c) The Compound Past (Le passé composé)

(1) This tense indicates in conversation a *completed* action in the past. In English we say *I gave, I have given, I did give* in such a case. In conversation, French makes no such distinction. In all cases it says *I have given (j'ai donné)*.

The uses of this tense should be contrasted with those of the imperfect indicative [§ 51] and the preterit [§ 54]. For the compound past in literary style, see particularly § 54(c).

(2) The compound past is expressed by the *present indicative* of the auxiliary plus the past participle.

First Conjugation:

	Singular		Plural	
1st Pers.	j'ai donné	I gave, have given, did give	nous avons donné	we gave, have given, did give
2nd Pers.	tu as donné	thou gavest, hast given	vous avez donné	you gave, have given, did give
3rd Pers.	il a donné	he gave, has given, did give	ils ont donné	they gave, have given, did give

Second Conjugation:

	Singular		Plural
1st Pers.	j'ai fini	I finish, have finished, did finish	nous avons fini
2nd Pers.	tu as fini	(etc.)	vous avez fini
3rd Pers.	il a fini		ils ont fini

Third Conjugation:

	Singular		Plural
1st Pers.	j'ai vendu	I sell, have sold, did sell	nous avons vendu
2nd Pers.	tu as vendu	(etc.)	vous avez vendu
3rd Pers.	il a vendu		ils ont vendu

As noted above [§ 55(a)1], certain verbs are conjugated with *être* and have the past participle agreeing with the subject. Observe the various agreements of the past participle:

SINGULAR

je suis allé	I (*masc.*) went, have gone, did go
je suis allée	I (*fem.*) went, have gone, did go
tu es allé	thou (*masc.*) wentest, hast gone
tu es allée	thou (*fem.*) wentest, hast gone
il est allé	he went, has gone, did go
elle est allée	she went, has gone, did go

PLURAL

nous sommes allés	we (*masc.*) went, have gone, did go
nous sommes allées	we (*fem.*) went, have gone, did go
vous êtes allé	you (*masc. sing.*) went, have gone, did go
vous êtes allée	you (*fem. sing.*) went, have gone, did go
vous êtes allés	you (*masc. pl.*) went, have gone, did go
vous êtes allées	you (*fem. pl.*) went, have gone, did go
ils sont allés	they went (*masc.*) have gone, did go
elles sont allées	they went (*fem.*) have gone, did go

(d) The Pluperfect Indicative (Le plus-que-parfait)

(1) This tense is formed with the auxiliary *had* in English and with the *imperfect tense* of the auxiliaries *avoir* and *être* in French.

FIRST CONJUGATION:

	Singular		Plural	
1st Pers.	j'avais donné	I had given	nous avions donné	we had given
2nd Pers.	tu avais donné	thou hadst given	vous aviez donné	you had given
3rd Pers.	il avait donné	he had given	ils avaient donné	they had given

SECOND CONJUGATION:

	Singular		Plural
1st Pers.	j'avais fini	I had finished	nous avions fini
2nd Pers.	tu avais fini	(etc.)	vous aviez fini
3rd Pers.	il avait fini		ils avaient fini

THIRD CONJUGATION:

	Singular		Plural
1st Pers.	j'avais vendu	I had sold	nous avions vendu
2nd Pers.	tu avais vendu	(etc.)	vous aviez vendu
3rd Pers.	il avait vendu		ils avaient vendu

(2) The pluperfect in French has the same function as the pluperfect in English and presents no problem in translation.

(e) The Future Perfect (Le futur antérieur)

(1) This tense in English has a double auxiliary *shall have* or *will have*. In French it is composed of the *future tense* of the auxiliary *avoir* or *être* plus the past participle.

FIRST CONJUGATION:

	Singular		Plural	
1st Pers.	j'aurai donné	I shall have given, will have given	nous aurons donné	we shal. have given, we will have given
2nd Pers.	tu auras donné	thou wilt have given	vous aurez donné	you will have given
3rd Pers.	il aura donné	he will have given	ils auront donné	they will have given

SECOND CONJUGATION:

	Singular		Plural
1st Pers.	j'aurai fini	I shall have finished	nous aurons fini
2nd Pers.	tu auras fini	(etc.)	vous aurez fini
3rd Pers.	il aura fini		ils auront fini

THIRD CONJUGATION:

	Singular		Plural
1st Pers.	j'aurai vendu	I shall have sold	nous aurons vendu
2nd Pers.	tu auras vendu	(etc.)	vous aurez vendu
3rd Pers.	il aura vendu		ils auront vendu

(2) Ordinarily this tense presents no problem in translation. When the English is *future perfect* the corresponding French is likewise.

(3) The rule set forth in § 52(c) also applies to the future perfect. In a sentence requiring the future after *quand, lorsque, aussitôt que* or *dès que*, either part of the sentence may have the verb in the future perfect.

Quand il *viendra*, elle *sera déjà partie*.
When he *comes*, she *will* already *have left*.

Quand elle *aura compris*, il *sera* trop tard.
When she *has understood*, it *will be* too late.

Note particularly in the second illustration above that the English past tense translates as a future perfect.

(4) The future perfect is sometimes used to indicate probability.

Elle *sera déjà partie*.   She *has probably left* already.

(f) **The Conditional Perfect** (Le conditionnel passé).

(1) The conditional perfect is recognized by the compound auxiliaries *should have* and *would have* (with the exceptions noted

in § 53(b)3. In French it is formed by the *conditional* of the auxiliary plus the past participle.

FIRST CONJUGATION

	Singular		Plural	
1st Pers.	j'aurais donné	I should have given, I would have given	nous aurions donné	we should have given, we would have given
2nd Pers.	tu aurais donné	thou wouldst have given	vous auriez donné	you would have given
3rd Pers.	il aurait donné	he would have given	ils auraient donné	they would have given

SECOND CONJUGATION

	Singular		Plural
1st Pers.	j'aurais fini	I should have finished, I would have finished	nous aurions fini
2nd Pers.	tu aurais fini	(etc.)	vous auriez fini
3rd Pers.	il aurait fini		ils auraient fini

THIRD CONJUGATION

	Singular		Plural
1st Pers.	j'aurais vendu	I should have sold, I would have sold	nous aurions vendu
2nd Pers.	tu aurais vendu	(etc.)	vous auriez vendu
3rd Pers.	il aurait vendu		ils auraient vendu

(2) In a sentence containing an *if* clause, if the main verb is conditional perfect, the verb of the clause will be pluperfect [see § 55(d)].

> Si elle *était venue*, il l'*aurait vue*.
> If she *had come*, he *would have seen* her.

(3) After *quand même*, *quand* in the sense of *quand même* or *au cas où*, the conditional perfect will translate as English pluperfect [see § 53(d)].

> Quand même il *serait venu*, il n'*aurait* rien *vu*.
> Even if he *had come*, he *would have seen* nothing.

> Au cas où[1] il *serait venu*, je le lui *aurais dit*.
> In case he *had come*, I *would have told* him so.[2]

---

[1] *Au cas où* is always followed by a conditional tense. *Vous le lui direz au cas où il viendrait*: You will tell him so in case he should come.

[2] With *dire* (to say), *espérer* (to hope), *faire* (to do), *croire* (to believe), the English word *so* translates as the pronoun object *le*. *Je le crois*: I believe so. If the verb *être* has no predicate, this same pronoun object *le* must be supplied. *Etes-vous Américain? Oui, je le suis.* Are you an American? Yes, I am (so).

(g)   **The Past Anterior** (Le passé antérieur)

(1)   This tense has no equivalent in English. It is a literary tense used after *quand, lorsque, aussitôt que* and *dès que* in situations where English and conversational French would both use a pluperfect.

Quand le roi *eut été* informé du complot, il ordonna qu'on lui tranchât la tête.
When the king *had been* informed of the plot, he ordered that his head be chopped off.

(2)   This tense is formed by the *preterit* of *avoir* or *être* plus the past participle.

FIRST CONJUGATION

	Singular		Plural	
1st Pers.	j'eus donné	I had given	nous eûmes donné	we had given
2nd Pers.	tu eus donné	thou hadst given	vous eûtes donné	you had given
3rd Pers.	il eut donné	he had given	ils eurent donné	they had given

§ 56   The Imperative   (l'impératif)

(a)   The imperative is the form of the verb used in giving a direct command. In English there is but one imperative, and it corresponds only to the unexpressed pronoun *you*. In the case of the verb *to give*, for example, the imperative would be *give!* French has two imperatives, one corresponding to an unexpressed *vous* in formal address or in a plural sense in informal address, and one corresponding to *tu* for informal address in the singular. There is also in French a first personal plural imperative which, since it has no English equivalent, must be translated by the phrase *let us*.

In almost every case, including irregular verbs, the imperative is spelled the same as the present indicative form corresponding to the unexpressed pronoun.

SECOND CONJUGATION

	Singular		Plural	
1st Pers.	....		finissons	let us finish!
2nd Pers.	finis	finish!	finissez	finish!
3rd Pers.	....		....	

THIRD CONJUGATION

	Singular	Plural
1st Pers.	....	**vendons** let us sell
2nd Pers.	**vends** sell	**vendez** sell
3rd Pers.	....	....

In the first conjugation, however, the second singular imperative lacks the *s* found in the present indicative.

FIRST CONJUGATION

	Singular	Plural
1st Pers.	....	**donnons** let us give
2nd Pers.	**donne** give	**donnez** give
3rd Pers.	....	....

This remark applies also to the irregular verb *aller* whose second singular imperative is *va* and to irregular verbs like *ouvrir* whose present singular has the same endings as a first conjugation verb and whose second singular imperative is therefore *ouvre*.

If the pronoun object forms *y* or *en*, however, follow the second singular imperative in the first conjugation (or a second conjugation verb which resembles a first conjugation verb in its present tense), the *s* will reappear.

Donnes-en à Marie.	Give Mary some.
Vas-y!	Go ahead (literally: go there)!

(b) For the first person singular and third person singular and plural, there is no true imperative. Instead the present subjunctive [see § 57(b)] with *que* is used in the sense of *let*.

Singular		Plural	
que je donne*	let me give	....	....
....	....	....	....
qu'il donne	let him give	**qu'ils donnent**	let them give

(c) The imperative has a future connotation, and therefore future will occur after *quand, lorsque, aussitôt que* and *dès que* if the main verb is imperative [see § 52(c)].

Donnez-le-lui quand il *viendra*.   Give it to him when he *comes*.

§ 57 The Subjunctive (le subjonctif)

(a) The subjunctive mood exists in English but *rarely does it correspond to a subjunctive in French. In English, we say If I were*

---

* If *let* means *permit* or *allow*, as it generally does in modern French, the verb *laisser* (*to let* or *allow*) will be preferred, particularly in conversation. Say *Laissez-moi vous parler* (Let me speak to you) and not *Que je vous parle*.

king, which is subjunctive, but we already know [see § 53(c)] that the corresponding verb in French will be imperfect indicative. On the other hand, we say *I wish I were king*, which happens to correspond to a subjunctive in French.

In general, we may say that the French subjunctive conveys a notion that a thing is *not necessarily so*. In reality, this generalization is of little help. Practically speaking, we must learn to recognize a series of individual cases in French where *certain conditions in the main part of the sentence* bring about automatically a *not necessarily so* (subjunctive) situation in a following subordinate clause. These automatic situations will be enumerated in § 57(c) to § 57(f).

(b) **The Present Subjunctive** (Le présent du subjonctif)

The present subjunctive of regular verbs is formed, in the case of the first and third conjugations, by adding to the stem of the verb the endings given in the examples below. In the second conjugation the regular verb has between the stem and the ending the same *-iss-* which occurs also in the plural of the present indicative, the imperfect indicative, the plural imperative and the present participle. There being no one characteristic translation for the French subjunctive, as we shall note presently, it would be more misleading than helpful to translate the following examples:

	FIRST CONJUGATION	SECOND CONJUGATION	THIRD CONJUGATION
		SINGULAR	
1st Pers.	je donne	je finisse	je vende
2nd Pers.	tu donnes	tu finisses	tu vendes
3rd Pers.	il donne	il finisse	il vende
		PLURAL	
1st Pers.	nous donnions	nous finissions	nous vendions
2nd Pers.	vous donniez	vous finissiez	vous vendiez
3rd Pers.	ils donnent	ils finissent	ils vendent

(c) The subjunctive will be used in *noun clauses* (a noun clause begins with *que* [that] and serves as the object of the verb, occupying the place usually held by a noun) which are the objects of verbs or phrases expressing the following conditions:

(1) *Emotion.*

Je regrette qu'il *vienne*.	I am sorry that he *is coming*.
C'est dommage qu'il *vienne*.	It is a pity that he *is coming*.

J'ai peur qu'il *vienne* †.	I am afraid he *is coming*.
Il est bon qu'il *vienne*.	It is good he *is coming*.

(2) *Volition.*

Je veux qu'il le *fasse*.	I want him *to do it*.
Elle entend que Jean *soit* prêt.	She intends that John *be* ready.

In the first example above, observe that English uses an infinitive construction with the object pronoun *him* serving as the subject of the infinitive. In French, infinitives cannot have subjects. Instead a noun clause must replace the infinitive.*

I want John *to do it* = I want *that John do it*.
Je veux que Jean le *fasse*.

(3) *Doubt.*

Je doute que Jean *vienne*.	I doubt that (whether) John *is coming*.
Il n'est pas sûr que Jean *vienne*.	It is not certain that John *is coming*.
Je ne crois pas que Jean *vienne*.	I don't think John *is coming*.
Croyez-vous que Jean *vienne?*	Do you think John *is coming?*

In the last example above the speaker is exceedingly doubtful that John is coming and he conveys his doubt by a subjunctive in the noun clause. If it was certain that John was coming and he wanted only confirmation, he would say: *Croyez-vous que Jean viendra?* Do you think John will come?

(4) *Necessity.*

Il faut que Jean *vienne*.
It is absolutely necessary that John *come*.

Il n'est pas nécessaire que Jean *vienne*.
There is no need for John *to come*.

(d) The subjunctive will occur automatically in relative clauses depending on the following types of antecedents.

(1) *An indefinite antecedent.*

Je ne connais *personne* qui *puisse* faire cela.
I know *no one* who *can* do that.

---

† In literary style one says *J'ai peur qu'il ne vienne*. Verbs of fearing take not only a subjunctive but also a pleonastic *ne* [see § 23(n)] in a following noun clause.

The only time any French construction appears to approximate the English infinitive construction is in a sentence like this: *I ask John to do it*. But in this case, the French says: *Je demande à Jean de le faire* (I ask John to do it). *Je demande que Jean le fasse* means *I demand that John do it*.

Il cherche *quelqu'un* qui *puisse* faire cela.
He is looking for *someone* who *can* do that.

Je cherche *un homme* qui *puisse* faire cela.
I am looking for *a man* who *can* do that.

In the last example this man does not necessarily exist; he is therefore indefinite. If he exists, there is no subjunctive.

J'ai trouvé *un homme* qui *peut* faire cela.
I have found *a man* who *can* do that.

(2) *An antecedent modified by a superlative* or the words "first," "last," "only" (which have a superlative force).

C'est le livre *le plus intéressant* que j'*aie* jamais lu.
It is *the most interesting* book I *have* ever read.

C'est la *dernière* statue qu'il *ait* faite.
It is the *last* statue which he *made*.

(e) The subjunctive occurs *automatically* after the following conjunctions:

Bien qu'il *soit* malade, il viendra.
Although he *is* sick, he will come.

Il viendra *quoiqu'il soit* malade.
He will come *although* he *is* sick.

Il parlera lentement *afin que* vous *puissiez* comprendre.
He will speak slowly *so that* you *may* understand.

Il parlera lentement *pour que* vous *puissiez* comprendre.
He will speak slowly *so that* you *may* understand.

Il viendra *à moins qu'il soit* malade.
He will come *unless* he *is* sick.

Il vous le dira *pourvu que* vous ne le *disiez* à personne.
He will tell you *provided (that)* you *tell* no one.

Il viendra *avant que vous partiez*.
He will come *before* you *leave*.

Il l'a fait *sans que* vous le *sachiez*.
He did it *without* your *knowing* it.

Autant que je sache, c'est Marie qui l'a fait.
As far as I *know*, it is Mary who did it.

Avant que and *à moins que* take a pleonastic *ne* in literary style [see § 23(n)]. Note also in the above illustration the peculiar English construction which results as a translation of *sans que*. *Sans* alone normally translates the preposition *without*, and, like all prepositions in French except *en*, it governs the infinitive form of the verb: *sans le voir* (without seeing him). If, in English, the present participle following *without* has a subject expressed as a simple noun or as a possessive adjective, French will have a subordinate clause with *sans que* and a subjunctive.

sans que Jean le voie	*without* John *seeing* him
sans qu'il le voie	*without* his *seeing* him

(f)   The subjunctive is required in various more or less idiomatic expressions involving the words *whoever, whatever, however,* etc. In some cases no subjunctive occurs because, as will be seen from the illustrations below, French substitutes demonstratives and relatives for the more complicated constructions. Study carefully the following examples:

(1)   *Whoever, whomever, whomsoever.*

Celui qui le *fera* sera puni.
Whoever does it will be punished. (No subjunctive).

Qui *veut* le voir n'aura qu'à demander.
Whoever wishes to see him will have only to ask. (No subjunctive).

Quiconque le *trouvera,* pourra le regarder.
Whoever finds it will be able to look at it. (No subjunctive).

Qui que vous *soyez,* parlez.
Whoever you *are,* speak. (*Qui que* requires subjunctive).

Qui que ce *soit* qui *ait* écrit cela, c'est un imbécile.
Whoever it was who wrote that, he is an imbecile. (*Qui que* requires subjunctive).

Qui que ce *soit* qu'ils *choisissent,* ils auront un bon président.
Whomever they *choose,* they will have a good president. (*Qui que* requires subjunctive).

(2)   *Whatever, whatsoever.*

Quoi que vous *fassiez,* vous ne vous tromperez pas.
Whatever you *do,* you will not make a mistake. (*Quoi que* requires subjunctive).

Quoi que ce *soit* qui le *rende* malade, il se remettra bientôt.
Whatever is making him sick, he will recover soon. (*Quoi que* requires subjunctive).

Quelque désire qu'il *ait* de bien faire, il est incompétent.
Whatever desire he *may have* to do well, he is incompetent. (*Quelque* in sense of *whatever* requires subjunctive).

Quelle que *soit* la raison, il n'a pas compris.
Whatever the reason *is,* he did not understand. (*Quel que* in sense of *whatever* requires subjunctive).

Il n'a jamais dit *quoi que ce soit.*
He has never said *anything whatever.* (Idiom; *quoi que* requires subjunctive).

Il n'a pas *la moindre* raison de le faire.
He has not *the least** reason to do it (He has no reason whatever [whatsoever] to do it). (No subjunctive).

***N'importe qui* pourra le faire.**
Anyone (*whatever*) can do it. (Idiom; no subjunctive).

Il fera *n'importe quoi.*
He will do *anything* (*whatever*). (Idiom; no subjunctive).

(3) *However.*

***Quelque* grande *qu'elle soit,* elle fait l'enfant.**
However big she *is,* she acts like a child. (*Quelque* plus *que* requires subjunctive).

***Quelque* longtemps *qu'il ait travaillé,* il n'a rien produit.**
However long he worked, he produced nothing. (Subjunctive).

***Si* experte *qu'elle soit,* elle n'y comprend rien.**
However expert she *is,* she doesn't understand a thing about it. (*Si...que* is a synonym for *quelque...que*).

***Quelle que soit* votre méthode, vous y arriverez.**
However you do it, you will succeed. (No translation in French; expression must be paraphrased).

(4) *Wherever, whenever.*

***Où que* vous *soyez,* je vous trouverai.**
Wherever you *are,* I shall find you. (*Où que* takes subjunctive).

***Quand* vous *viendrez,* je vous le dirai.**
Whenever you *come,* I shall tell you. (No subjunctive; there is no word for *whenever*).

(g) Once it has been determined that conditions in the main part of the sentence require a subjunctive in the subordinate clause, the next two problems are to select the proper verb and to put it into the proper tense with little regard for what the English says. In the following examples, note how the English verb is expressed in the part of the sentence which requires a subjunctive in French.

I doubt that (if) he *will come.* (Come)
I preferred that he *should go.* (Go)

---

* Do not confuse *least* as an adjective, which is *moindre*, with *least* as an adverb. *Il n'a pas la moindre raison*: He hasn't the least reason. *Il l'aime le moins*: He likes it the least. See also § 14.

> I preferred to *have* him *go*. (Go)
> It is necessary that he *give* a reason. (Give)
> He is looking for someone who *may do* the work. (Do)

In the above sentences we are interested in knowing three things: 1) that the main part of the sentence sets up a condition requiring a subjunctive; 2) that the verb in the subjunctive will be Come, Go, Give, Do; 3) that the action of the subjunctive clause did not occur before the action of the main verb.

If the action in the subjunctive clause did not occur before the action of the main verb, the present tense will be used even though the English may have a future.

Je doute qu'il *vienne*.   I doubt whether he $\begin{cases} \textit{is coming.} \\ \textit{will come.} \end{cases}$

(h)   **The Perfect Subjunctive)** (Le passé du subjonctif).

This tense is formed by the present tense of *avoir* or *être* plus the past participle. It might be described as the compound past tense turned into the subjunctive.

	First Conjugation	Second Conjugation	Third Conjugation
	SINGULAR		
1st Pers.	j'aie donné	j'aie fini	j'aie vendu
2nd Pers.	tu aies donné	tu aies fini	tu aies vendu
3rd Pers.	il ait donné	il ait fini	il ait vendu
	PLURAL		
1st Pers.	nous ayons donné	nous ayons fini	nous ayons vendu
2nd Pers.	vous ayez donné	vous ayez fini	vous ayez vendu
3rd Pers.	ils aient donné	ils aient fini	ils aient vendu

If the main verb of the sentence is *present* or *future*, the *perfect subjunctive* is used in both conversational and literary style to indicate that the action in the subjunctive clause occurred *prior to the action of the main verb.*

> **Je suis content qu'il *soit venu*.**   I am glad that he *has come.*
> **Je doutais qu'il *soit venu*.**   I doubted whether he *had come.*

In conversational style [see § 57(j) for literary style in this regard], the perfect subjunctive is used *in every case* where the action of the subjunctive clause occurred before the action of the main verb, *no matter what the English says.*

(i) **The Imperfect Subjunctive** (L'imparfait du subjonctif)

In the case of regular verbs, this tense is formed by adding the following endings to the stem of the verb:

	First Conjugation	Second Conjugation	Third Conjugation
		SINGULAR	
1st Pers.	je donna*sse*	je fini*sse*	je vend*isse*
2nd Pers.	tu donna*sses*	tu fini*sses*	tu vend*isses*
3rd Pers.	il donn*ât*	il fin*ît*	il vend*ît*
		PLURAL	
1st Pers.	nous donna*ssions*	nous fini*ssions*	nous vend*issions*
2nd Pers.	vous donna*ssiez*	vous fini*ssiez*	vous vend*issiez*
3rd Pers.	ils donna*ssent*	ils fini*ssent*	ils vend*issent*

Note from the above examples that the endings are identical in the second and third conjugations and that the imperfect subjunctive of the second conjugation happens to be identical in spelling with the present subjunctive, except in the third person singular *(il finît)*. The imperfect subjunctive is used *in literary style only* when the main verb is any past or either conditional tense and when the action of the subjunctive clause *did not occur prior to the action of the main verb.*

> **Je *doutais* qu'il *vînt*.** I *doubted* that he *was coming.*

(j) **The Pluperfect Subjunctive** (Le plus-que-parfait du subjonctif)

(1) This tense consists of the imperfect subjunctive of the auxiliaries *être* or *avoir* plus the past participle.

	First Conjugation	Second Conjugation	Third Conjugation
		SINGULAR	
1st Pers.	j'eusse donné	j'eusse fini	j'eusse vendu
2nd Pers.	tu eusses donné	tu eusses fini	tu eusses vendu
3rd Pers.	il eût donné	il eût fini	il eût vendu
		PLURAL	
1st Pers.	nous eussions donné	nous eussions fini	nous eussions vendu
2nd Pers.	vous eussiez donné	vous eussiez fini	vous eussiez vendu
3rd Pers.	ils eussent donné	ils eussent fini	ils eussent vendu

(2) The pluperfect subjunctive is found only in literary style when the main verb is in a past or conditional tense and when the action in the subjunctive clause occurred *prior to the action of the main verb.*

> **Le roi était très fâché qu'il l'*eût fait*.**
> The king was very angry that he *had done* it.

(3) The pluperfect subjunctive is frequently used in literary style in place of a conditional perfect.

Le roi lui demanda s'il l'*eût fait*.
The king asked him whether he *would have done* it.
Le roi lui a demandé s'il l'*aurait fait*. (Conversational).

In a sentence involving an *if* clause, the pluperfect subjunctive will also be used in the *if* clause if it is used in place of a conditional perfect in the main clause.

S'il eût fait cela, il eût été puni.
If he had done that, he would have been punished.

A double pluperfect subjunctive may replace a double conditional perfect.

Eût-il fait cela, il eût été puni.
Had he done that, he would have been punished.

(k) If the subject of a noun clause is the same as the subject of the main verb, the tendency in French is to avoid a noun clause.

Il croit *avoir* raison.   He thinks he *is* right.

This frequently has the effect of avoiding a subjunctive, which is considered desirable in French.

Il a peur de le *manquer*.   He is afraid of *missing* it (to replace: *He* is afraid that *he* will miss it).

Il a peur de l'*avoir manqué*.   He is afraid that he *missed* it.

Similarly, French will avoid a clause beginning with a subordinating conjunction if the same person is the subject of the main clause and of the subordinate clause.

Il l'a fait avant de *partir*.   He did it before *leaving* (to replace: *He* did it before *he* left).

Après l'*avoir vu*, il lui a parlé.   After *having seen* him, he spoke to him (to replace: After *he* had seen him, *he* spoke to him).

§ 58   The Reflexive Verb   (le verbe pronominal)

(a) Any verb becomes reflexive when a reflexive pronoun object occurs before it. *I wash myself* is reflexive both in English and in French. The reflexive verb is much more common in French than in English. For example, French cannot say *I sit down*; it has to say *I seat myself*. In some cases, there is not even a reflexive equivalent in English for a reflexive verb in French. Thus French says *Je me sers de cela* (which can be translated in English only as *I use that*, which is obviously not reflexive). For the sake of simplification, we may say that some verbs are already reflexive as we look them up in a dictionary or vocabulary list while other verbs we accidentally make reflexive when we place a reflexive pronoun before them. From the French point of view there is, in reality, no difference between these two types of reflexive verbs.

(b)   For a discussion of the reflexive pronoun, turn to § 27. Since verbs are so frequently used in the reflexive in French, the student should learn to conjugate them rapidly in all tenses, beginning with the present.

SINGULAR

1st Pers.	je *me* lave	I wash *myself*
2nd Pers.	tu *te* laves	thou washest *thyself*
3rd Pers.	il *se* lave	he washes *himself*
	elle *se* lave	she washes *herself*

PLURAL

1st Pers.	nous *nous* lavons	we wash *ourselves*
2nd Pers.	vous *vous* lavez	you wash *yourself* (*yourselves*)
3rd Pers.	ils *se* lavent	they wash *themselves* (*masc.*)
	elles *se* lavent	they wash *themselves* (*fem.*)

For the construction of reflexive verbs in the compound tense, see § 55(a)2 and § 55(b)3. Study the following illustrations of *se laver* in the compound past, noting the agreement of the past participle:

SINGULAR

1st Pers.	je *me* suis lavé	I washed *myself* (*masc.*)
	je *me* suis lavée	I washed *myself* (*fem.*)
2nd Pers.	tu *t*'es lavé	thou didst wash *thyself* (*masc.*)
	tu *t*'es lavée	thou didst wash *thyself* (*fem.*)
3rd Pers.	il *s*'est lavé	he washed *himself*
	elle *s*'est lavée	she washed *herself*

PLURAL

1st Pers.	nous *nous* sommes lavés	we washed *ourselves* (*masc.*)
	nous *nous* sommes lavées	we washed *ourselves* (*fem.*)
2nd Pers.	vous *vous* êtes lavé	you washed *yourself* (*masc. sing.*)
	vous *vous* êtes lavée	you washed *yourself* (*fem. sing.*)
	vous *vous* êtes lavés	you washed *yourselves* (*masc.*)
	vous *vous* êtes lavées	you washed *yourselves* (*fem.*)
3rd Pers.	ils *se* sont lavés	they washed *themselves* (*masc.*)
	elles *se* sont lavées	they washed *themselves* (*fem.*)

(c)   For the use of the reflexive verb to avoid a passive, see § 59(c).

§ 59   The Passive Voice   (la voix passive)

(a)   A verb is said to be passive when the subject no longer acts but is acted upon.

ACTIVE: The dog bites the man.
PASSIVE: The man is bitten by the dog.

In a passive construction the person or thing performing the action (the *dog* in the illustration above) is called the *agent*. It is clear from the illustration above that the passive is formed in English by the proper tense of the auxiliary *to be* plus the past participle. The French passive is constructed in exactly the same manner: the proper tense of *être* plus *the past participle*. The first problem is to recognize a passive, and the second problem is to select the proper tense of the auxiliary.

The man *had been* bitten.

In the above illustration, the verb *to bite* is in the passive. Since its auxiliary is obviously pluperfect, we get as a result:

L'homme *avait été* mordu.

In a passive construction, the past participle of the verb (but not of the auxiliary) agrees like an adjective with the subject.

La femme **est mordue par un chien.**
The *woman* is bitten by a dog.*

La femme **a été mordue par un chien.**
The *woman* has been bitten by a dog.

(b)   Normally the agent of a passive construction is introduced by *par* (by). However, when there is no real action indicated by the passive (in other words, when the situation is completely static), the agent will be introduced by *de* which sometimes translates as *by* and sometimes as *with*.

La femme a été mordue *par* un chien.
The woman has been bitten *by* a dog.

La table est couverte *d'*une nappe.†
The table is covered *by* (*with*) a tablecloth.

(c)   When the *agent* is expressed with the passive there is no way to avoid the passive except by changing the meaning of the sen-

---

* Never attempt to translate literally *The woman is being bitten by a dog*. The idea is too vivid to be rendered by a passive in French. Say something such as: *Il y a un chien qui mord la femme.*

† If a pronoun were to replace the word *nappe*, it would be *en*. [See § 25(f)]. *La table en est couverte*: The table is covered by it.

tence. If the *agent* is not expressed, but would be introduced by *par* if expressed, French prefers to avoid the passive in the following manner:

(1) *If the subject is a thing,* use the impersonal pronoun subject *on* with an active verb or use a reflexive verb as follows:

On parle français ici. French *is spoken* here (literally: *One speaks* French here).
Le français se parle ici. French *is spoken* here.
Ces livres se publient à Paris. These books *are published* in Paris.

(2) *If the subject is a person,* the *on* construction, but not the reflexive, may be used, provided that the action is one which can logically be done by another person.

On m'a piqué plusieurs fois.
I have been given injections several times.

BUT: **J'ai été blessé.** I have been wounded (there is no indication that a person wounded me; it might have been a thing).

(d) A common error in constructing a passive is to forget that the subject of the English passive might logically be an indirect object if the verb were not passive, as in the following example:

John was given an apple — *To John* an apple was given.
On a donné une pomme à Jean.

The same problem arises when an English transitive verb translates as a French intransitive.

The letter was answered yesterday (But French says: The letter was answered *to* yesterday).

On a répondu à la lettre hier.

§ 60 Inversion of the Verb

(a) Any verb with a pronoun subject may be made interrogative by placing the pronoun subject after the verb if it is a simple verb form or after the auxiliary if it is a compound form. The pronoun subject is then attached to the verb by a hyphen. If the third singular verb form ends in a vowel, a *-t-* with hyphens on each side is inserted.

SINGULAR

	INTERROGATIVE PRESENT		INTERROGATIVE PAST	
1st Pers.	....	....	(ai-je donné)	have I given?
2nd Pers.	**donnes-tu?**	dost thou give?	**as-tu donné**	hast thou given?
3rd Pers.	**donne-t-il?**	does he give?	**a-t-il donné**	has he given?

PLURAL

1st Pers.	donnons-nous?	do we give?	avons-nous donné?	have we given?
2nd Pers.	donnez-vous?	do you give?	avez-vous donné?	have you given?
3rd Pers.	donnent-ils?	do they give?	ont-ils donné?	have they given?

(b) ' For negative interrogative, see § 23.

(c)   To invert with a noun subject, the word order is *noun subject + verb + pronoun subject* (referring back to noun subject)

| Jean est-il ici? | Is John here? |
| Marie est-elle partie? | Did Mary leave? |

(d)   In conversation, inversion is frequently avoided by the use of *est-ce que* (is it that) which is placed before any declarative sentence to make it interrogative.

| Est-ce que Jean vient? | Is John coming? |

Since the form *donné-je* is no longer used in modern French, it is almost always necessary to express interrogation in the first person with *est-ce que*. In conversation about the only forms now inverted are *dois-je, puis-je* and sometimes *ai-je* or *suis-je*.

Especial care must be exercised in placing *est-ce que* in a question beginning with an interrogative word. The English sentence should be paraphrased in terms of *is it that*.

> **Combien de dollars *est-ce* que cela coûte?**
> How many dollars *does* that cost? (Literally: How
> many dollars *is it that* that costs?)
>
> **Qu'*est-ce que* Jean va faire?**
> What *is* John going to do? (What *is it that* John
> is going to do?)

(e)   With *que, où, combien, comment,* and *quand* a simple verb form may precede a noun subject in spite of the rule in § 60(c).

Quand *partira* votre mère?	When *will* your mother *leave?*
Combien *coûte* ce livre?	How much *does* this book *cost?*
Comment *va* Jean?	How *is* John?
Que *répond* Robert?	What does Robert *answer?*

§ 61   Uses of the Verb *avoir*

(a)   For the conjugation of the verb *avoir*, see § 66, tables of irregular verbs.

(b)   In expressions involving a person's health, the verb *avoir* is found in the following idioms:

> **J'ai mal à la tête, aux yeux, etc.**
> My head, my eyes, etc., hurt me (literally: I have a
>   hurt in my head, my eyes, etc.)
>
> **J'ai la migraine, etc.**
> I have a headache, etc.
>
> **Qu'avez-vous?**
> What is the matter with you?

(c)   *Avoir* is used in expressions of age.

> **Quel âge avez-vous?**   How old are you? (Literally: What age
>   have you?)
>
> **J'ai trois ans.**   I am three years old. (Literally: I
>   have three years).

(d)   *Avoir à* is sometimes used in sense of *devoir* (see § 62).

> **J'ai à *travailler* ce soir.**   I have *to work* tonight.

(e)   The idiom *il y a* means *there is* or *there are* as a statement of fact.

> **Il y a un livre sur la table.**
> There is a book on the table. (The fact is true
>   that there is a book on the table).
>
> **Y a-t-il des livres sur la table?**
> Are there some books on the table?
>
> **Il doit y avoir des livres sur la table.**
> There must be some books on the table.

Il y a should be compared with *voilà*, which implies a gesture.

> **Voilà un livre.**
> There is a book (look at it).

Voici, similar in construction to *voilà*, means *here is* or *here are*. Never say *Ici est*.

> **Voici un livre.**   Here is a book.

Voilà and *voici* may have pronoun objects. Observe carefully the translation.

> **Le voilà.**   There he is (Literally: See him there).
> **Les voici.**   Here they are (Literally: See them here).

§ 62 The Verb *devoir*

(a) For the conjugation of *devoir* see tables of irregular verbs in § 66.

(b) *Devoir* is a main verb expressing a notion of necessity or obligation. When it has a direct object it means to *owe*.

Je *dois* **trois dollars.**   I *owe* three dollars.

When it is followed by a dependent infinitive it expresses obligation or necessity with relation to the time normally indicated by the tense or with relation to a time which would be considered future to the normal time of that tense. Study the following examples carefully:

	Normal Time	Future Time
je *dois* **partir**	I *must* leave, I *have* to leave, I *am obliged* to leave	I *was (supposed)* to leave
je *devais* **partir**	I *had* to leave, I *was obliged* to leave	I *was (supposed)* to leave
j'ai *dû* **partir**	I *must have* left, I *have had to* leave, I *had to* leave, I *have been obliged to* leave, I *was obliged* to leave	....
je *devrai* **partir**	I *shall have to* leave, I *shall be* obliged to leave	....
je *devrais* **partir**	I *should* leave, I *ought to* leave	....
j'avais *dû* **partir**	I *had had to* leave	....
j'aurais *dû* **partir**	I *would have had to* leave, I *ought to have* left	I *was (supposed)* to *have* left
je *dus* **partir**	I *had to* leave, I *was obliged* to leave	....

From the above illustrations, it is evident, for example, that the English auxiliary *must* becomes the main verb *devoir* in French and that the main verb of the English becomes a dependent infinitive. Another principle to observe is that all notion of tense should be conveyed by the verb *devoir* under normal circumstances.

J'ai *dû* **partir à onze heures.**   I *must have* left at eleven o'clock.

Devoir in the present tense is incorrect in the above sentence. On the other hand, if the force of the action continues through the present, it is possible to say:

Elle doit *être* partie.   She must *be* gone (she *is* still gone).

§ 63   The Verb *faire*

(a)   For the conjugation of *faire* see tables of irregular verbs in § 66.

(b)   *Faire* means *to make* or *to do* as main verbs. It does not exist as an auxiliary verb in French [review § 50(a) and § 55(c)1]. Never attempt to use *faire* when *do* or *did* stand alone in English with another verb understood.

> **Etes-vous allé en ville aujourd'hui? Oui, j'y *suis allé*.**
> Did you go to town today? Yes I *did*.

(c)   In a *causal* construction *faire* means *to have something done*. Note the difference in word order in French.

Je *fais lire* le livre.   I *have* the book *read*. (I *cause* the book *to be read*.)

The dependent infinitive must always follow *faire*.

If the object acted upon is a *normal pronoun object*, it will go before *faire* and not before the infinitive.

> **Je *le* fais lire.**   I have *it* read.
> **Je le fais lire *par* Jean.**   I have it read *by* John.

If the agent is a pronoun, it will normally be expressed as an indirect pronoun object before the verb *faire*.

> **Je le *lui* ai fait faire.**   I had it done by *him*.
> (I had him do it.)

(d)   The verb *faire* is used in the following expressions having to do with the weather:

Quel temps fait-il?	What kind of weather is it?
il fait beau (temps)	it is good weather
il fait mauvais (temps)	it is bad weather
il fait froid	it is cold
il fait chaud	it is hot
il fait frais	it is cool
il fait doux	it is mild
il fait du vent	it is windy
il fait sec	it is dry
il fait jour	it is day
il fait nuit	it is night

§ 64   The Verb *pouvoir*

(a)   For the conjugation of *pouvoir* see tables of irregular verbs in § 66.

(b)   *Pouvoir* conveys a notion of physical ability, expressed in

---

English as *to be able* or by the auxiliaries *can* or *could*. Note the translations of the following synopsis:

je *peux* le faire	I *can* do it	I *am able to* do it
je *pouvais* le faire	I *could* do it	I *was able to* do it
j'*ai pu* le faire	I *could* do it, I *could have* done it	I *have been able* to do it, I *was able to* do it.
je *pus* le faire	I *could do* it	I *was able to* do it
je *pourrai* le faire	....	I *shall be able to* do it
je *pourrais* le faire	I *could do* it	I *would be able to* do it
j'*avais pu* le faire	....	I *had been able to* do it
j'*aurais pu* le faire	....	I *would have been able to* do it

(c) Mental ability is frequently expressed with *savoir*.

Je sais le faire. I can do it (lit.: I know how to do it).

(d) As with *devoir* [see § 62(b)], all notion of tense must be expressed with *pouvoir* rather than the dependent infinitive.

§ 65 Orthographical Changing Verbs

In the first conjugation there are certain classes of verbs which are regular in every respect except that the spelling has to make certain compensations for the pronounciation which remains consistent and regular.

(a) Verbs ending in -*cer*. The pronunciation of this verb remains entirely consistent but a cedilla (ç) must be written under the letter *c* whenever it occurs before the vowels *a* or *o* to prevent it from having a *k* pronunciation. Note the following examples for the verb *effacer (to erase)*.

PRESENT PARTICIPLE	PRESENT INDICATIVE	IMPERFECT INDICATIVE	PRETERIT
effaçant	j'efface	j'*effaçais*	j'*effaçai*
	tu effaces	tu *effaçais*	tu *effaças*
	il efface	il *effaçait*	il *effaça*
	nous *effaçons*	nous effacions	nous *effaçâmes*
	vous effacez	vous effaciez	vous *effaçâtes*
	ils effacent	ils *effaçaient*	ils effacèrent

(b) Verbs ending in -*ger*. The pronunciation of this verb also remains entirely consistent but an *e* must be inserted after the letter *g* whenever it occurs before *a* or *o* so that the soft *zh* pronunciation may be retained. Note the following examples for the verb *changer* (*to change*).

Present Participle	Present Indicative	Imperfect Indicative	Preterit
changeant	je change	je *changeais*	je *changeai*
	tu changes	tu *changeais*	tu *changeas*
	il change	il *changeait*	il *changea*
	nous *changeons*	nous changions	nous *changeâmes*
	vous changez	vous changiez	vous *changeâtes*
	ils changent	ils *changaient*	ils changèrent

(c) Verbs in -*yer*. Such verbs alter both spelling and pronunciation. Whenever, in the conjugation, *y* occurs before a mute e verb ending, it changes to *i*. For the purposes of this rule, the *e* of the *er* infinitive ending when the infinitive is used as the stem for the future or conditional is considered to be a mute *e* and the pronunciation changes. Example: *nettoyer* (nètwayay) changes to *nettoierai* (nètwaray). Study the following illustrations of *nettoyer* (to clean):

Present Indicative	Present Subjunctive	Future	Conditional
je *nettoie*	que je *nettoie*	je *nettoierai*	je *nettoierais*
tu *nettoies*	que tu *nettoies*	tu *nettoieras*	tu *nettoierais*
il *nettoie*	qu'il *nettoie*	il *nettoiera*	il *nettoierait*
nous nettoyons	que nous nettoyions	nous *nettoierons*	nous *nettoierions*
vous nettoyez	que vous nettoyiez	vous *nettoierez*	vous *nettoieriez*
ils *nettoient*	qu'ils *nettoient*	ils *nettoieront*	ils *nettoieraient*

(d) Verbs ending in "*e* + *consonant* + *er*."

In such cases the rule that an "*e*" before a mute "*e*" takes a grave accent applies. For the purposes of the rule, the *e* of the *er* infinitive used as the stem for the future or conditional is a mute *e*. Note that the application of this rule means also a change in pronunciation; one says *vous menez* (voo m^enay) but *ils mènent* (eel mèn), *mener* (m^enay) but *mènerai* (mènray). Study carefully the following examples of *mener* (to lead).

Present Indicative	Present Subjunctive	Future	Conditional
je *mène*	que je *mène*	je *mènerai*	je *mènerais*
tu *mènes*	que tu *mènes*	tu *mèneras*	tu *mènerais*
il *mène*	qu'il *mène*	il *mènera*	il *mènerait*
nous menons	que nous menions	nous *mènerons*	nous *mènerions*
vous menez	que vous meniez	vous *mènerez*	vous *mèneriez*
ils *mènent*	qu'ils *mènent*	ils *mèneront*	ils *mèneraient*

If the stem of the infinitive already has an acute *é*, this will likewise change to grave *è* before a mute *e*, except in the future and conditional. Note following examples of verb *espérer* (to hope).

<table>
<tr><td colspan="2">PRESENT INDICATIVE</td><td colspan="2">PRESENT SUBJUNCTIVE</td></tr>
<tr><td>j'espère</td><td>nous espérons</td><td>que j'espère</td><td>que nous espérions</td></tr>
<tr><td>tu espères</td><td>vous espérez</td><td>que tu espères</td><td>que vous espériez</td></tr>
<tr><td>il espère</td><td>ils espèrent</td><td>qu'il espère</td><td>qu'ils espèrent</td></tr>
</table>

Verbs ending -*eler* and some verbs ending -*eter* double the consonant before a mute *e*, which phonetically has the same effect as writing a grave accent. Note *appeler* (to call).

PRESENT INDICATIVE	PRESENT SUBJUNCTIVE	FUTURE	CONDITIONAL
j'appelle	que j'appelle	j'appellerai	j'appellerais
tu appelles	que tu appelles	tu appelleras	tu appellerais
il appelle	qu'il appelle	il appellera	il appellerait
nous appelons	que nous appelions	nous appellerons	nous appellerions
vous appelez	que vous appeliez	vous appellerez	vous appelleriez
ils appellent	qu'ils appellent	ils appelleront	ils appelleraient

§ 66 Irregular Verbs

(a) Verbs are said to be irregular when they do not conform to the pattern of the three regular verbs *donner*, *finir* and *vendre* which have been used as illustrations for each tense. Even in irregular verbs, distinct patterns can be noted and studied.

(b) In the second conjugation there is a class of irregular verbs, of which *dormir* (turn to next page) is an example, which follow an almost regular pattern. Other such verbs are *partir, sentir, servir, sortir.* These verbs drop not only the infinitive ending to form the present singular but also the final consonant of the stem *(dor-, par-, sen-, ser-, sor-)*; they then add -*s*, -*s*, -*t*. All other forms of the verb are regular except that the characteristic -*iss*- of the second conjugation is missing in the present participle, plural of the present tense, imperfect indicative, present subjunctive, and plural imperative.

(c) Another characteristic feature of irregular verbs is that many of them have a change of vowel in the present tense, the first and second plural having the vowel of the infinitive and the entire singular and the third plural having another vowel. Such a verb is *pouvoir* (to be able; can):

<table>
<tr><td colspan="2">PRESENT INDICATIVE</td></tr>
<tr><td>je peux</td><td>nous pouvons</td></tr>
<tr><td>tu peux</td><td>vous pouvez</td></tr>
<tr><td>il peut</td><td>ils peuvent</td></tr>
</table>

(d) Generally speaking the following relationships should be carefully observed in the study of irregular verbs.

(1) *The present participle.* Note first its relation to the infinitive If it is not regularly derived from the infinitive, it will be italicized. If it is regular, it will be in bold face. From it, we get the following:

> Present Plural
> Imperfect Indicative
> Imperative Plural
> Present Subjunctive

If these forms are regularly derived from the present participle, they will be italicized. If not, they will bear an asterisk. If they derive regularly from a present participle which is itself regular, they will be in bold face (used for completely regular forms).

(2) *Infinitive.* The *future tense* is derived from the infinitive. If the future tense of the irregular verb is regular, it will be in bold face. If the future is irregular, it will bear an asterisk. Whether the future is irregular or not, the *conditional* will always have the same stem.

(3) *Past Participle.* If this is regularly derived from the infinitive, it will be in bold face. If it is irregular, it will be light face roman. Frequently there is a relationship between the *past participle* and the *preterit.* If there is such a relationship, it will be indicated by the symbol (§).

(4) *Preterit.* The *imperfect subjunctive* will always derive from the *preterit,* whether that form is regular or irregular. This relationship is denoted by the symbol (§), if the past participle is the basis for the derivation of the preterit. If the preterit is not related to the past participle, the connection between the preterit and the imperfect subjunctive is pointed out by the daggar symbol (†). To form the imperfect subjunctive, remove from the forms of the preterit the following letters -s, -s, -t, -ˆmes, -ˆtes, -rent; add to what remains the subjunctive endings -sse, -sses, -ˆt, -ssions, -ssiez, -ssent.

Model 2nd Conjugation Irregular Verbs

INFINITIVE AND PARTICIPLES	INDICATIVE			
	PRESENT	IMPERFECT	PRETERIT	FUTURE
2d Class -ir Verbs **Dormir** (to sleep) dormant dormi	dors dors dort dormons dormez dorment	dormais dormais dormait dormions dormiez dormaient	dormis dormis dormit dormîmes dormîtes dormirent	dormirai dormiras dormira dormirons dormirez dormiront
	COMPOUND PAST	PLUPERFECT	PAST ANTERIOR	FUTURE PERFECT
	ai dormi as dormi a dormi avons dormi avez dormi ont dormi	avais dormi avais dormi avait dormi avions dormi aviez dormi avaient dormi	eus dormi eus dormi eut dormi eûmes dormi eûtes dormi eûrent dormi	aurai dormi auras dormi aura dormi aurons dormi aurez dormi auront dormi

Auxiliary Verbs

	PRESENT	IMPERFECT	PRETERIT	FUTURE
Auxiliary Verb **Avoir** (to have) ayant eu	ai as a avons avez ont	avais avais avait avions aviez avaient	eus eus eut eûmes eûtes eurent	aurai auras aura aurons aurez auront
	COMPOUND PAST	PLUPERFECT	PAST ANTERIOR	FUTURE PERFECT
	ai eu as eu a eu avons eu avez eu ont eu	avais eu avais eu avait eu avions eu aviez vu avaient eu	eus eu eus eu eut eu eûmes eu eûtes eu eurent eu	aurai eu auras eu aura eu aurons eu aurez eu auront eu
	PRESENT	IMPERFECT	PRETERIT	FUTURE
Auxiliary Verb **Etre** (to be) étant été	suis es est sommes êtes sont	étais étais était étions étiez étaient	fus fus fut fûmes fûtes furent	serai seras sera serons serez seront
	COMPOUND PAST	PLUPERFECT	PAST ANTERIOR	FUTURE PERFECT
	ai été as été a été avons été avez été ont été	avais été avais été avait été avions été aviez été avaient été	eus été eus été eut été eûmes été eûtes été eurent été	aurai été auras été aura été aurons été aurez été auront été

MODEL 2ND CONJUGATION IRREGULAR VERBS

CONDITIONAL	IMPERATIVE	SUBJUNCTIVE	

PRESENT CONDITIONAL / **PRESENT** / **IMPERFECT**

PRESENT CONDITIONAL	IMPERATIVE	PRESENT	IMPERFECT
dormirais		dorme	dormisse
dormirais	dors	dormes	dormisses
dormirait		dorme	dormît
dormirions	dormons	dormions	dormissions
dormiriez	dormez	dormiez	dormissiez
dormiraient		dorment	dormissent

PAST CONDITIONAL / **PAST** / **PLUPERFECT**

PAST CONDITIONAL		PAST	PLUPERFECT
aurais dormi		aie dormi	eusse dormi
aurais dormi		aies dormi	eusses dormi
aurait dormi		ait dormi	eût dormi
aurions dormi		ayons dormi	eussions dormi
auriez dormi		ayez dormi	eussiez dormi
auraient dormi		aient dormi	eussent dormi

AUXILIARY VERBS

PRESENT CONDITIONAL	IMPERATIVE	PRESENT	IMPERFECT
aurais		aie	eusse
aurais	aie	aies	eusses
aurait		ait	eût
aurions	ayons	ayons	eussions
auriez	ayez	ayez	eussiez
auraient		aient	eussent

PAST CONDITIONAL		PAST	PLUPERFECT
aurais eu		aie eu	eusse eu
aurais eu		aies eu	eusses eu
aurait eu		ait eu	eût eu
aurions eu		ayons eu	eussions eu
auriez eu		ayez eu	eussiez eu
auraient eu		aient eu	eussent eu

PRESENT CONDITIONAL	IMPERATIVE	PRETERIT	IMPERFECT
serais		sois	fusse
serais	sois	sois	fusses
serait		soit	fût
serions	soyons	soyons	fussions
seriez	soyez	soyez	fussiez
seraient		soient	fussent

PAST CONDITIONAL		PAST	PLUPERFECT
aurais été		aie été	eusse été
aurais été		aies été	eusses été
aurait été		ait été	eût été
aurions été		ayons été	eussions été
auriez été		ayez été	eussiez été
auraient été		aient été	eussent été

Irregular Verbs

INFINITIVE AND PARTICIPLES	INDICATIVE			
	PRESENT	IMPERFECT	PRETERIT	COMPOUND PAST
1. Acquérir (to acquire) acquérant § acquis	*acquiers *acquiers *acquiert acquérons acquérez *acquièrent	acquérais acquérais acquérait acquérions acquériez acquéraient	§ acquis acquis acquit acquîmes acquîtes acquirent	ai § acquis as acquis a acquis avons acquis avez acquis ont acquis
2. Aller (to go) allant allé	*vais *vas *va allons allez *vont	allais allais allait allions alliez allaient	allai allas alla allâmes allâtes allèrent	suis allé(e) es allé(e) est allé(e) sommes allé(e)s êtes allé(e)(s) sont allé(e)s
3. S'asseoir (to seat) asseyant § assis	*assieds[1] *assieds *assied asseyons asseyez asseyent	asseyais[1] asseyais asseyait asseyions asseyiez asseyaient	§ assis assis assit assîmes assîtes assirent	me suis § assis(e) t'es assis(e) s'est assis(e) nous sommes assis(es) vous êtes assis(e)(s) se sont assis(es)
assoyant[2]	*assois *assois *assoit assoyons assoyez *assoient	assoyais assoyais assoyait assoyions assoyiez assoyaient		
4. Battre (to beat) battant § battu	*bats *bats *bat battons battez battent	battais battais battait battions battiez battaient	battis battis battit battîmes battîtes battirent	ai § battu as battu a battu avons battu avez battu ont battu
5. Boire (to drink) buvant § bu	*bois *bois *boit buvons buvez *boivent	buvais buvais buvait buvions buviez buvaient	§ bus bus but bûmes bûtes burent	ai § bu as bu a bu avons bu avez bu ont bu

[1] For lack of space, the reflexive pronoun objects are omitted. These should be understood to read: je m'assieds, je m'asseyais, etc.

[2] This verb has alternate forms.

IRREGULAR VERBS

FUTURE	CONDITIONAL	IMPERATIVE	SUBJUNCTIVE	
			PRESENT	IMPERFECT
*acquerrai	*acquerrais		*acquière	§ acquisse
acquerras	acquerrais	*acquiers	acquières	acquisses
acquerra	acquerrait		acquière	acquît
acquerrons	acquerrions	acquérons	acquérions	acquissions
acquerrez	acquerriez	acquérez	acquériez	acquissiez
acquerront	acquerraient		acquièrent	acquissent
*irai	*irais		*aille	allasse
iras	irais	*va	*ailles	allasses
ira	irait		*aille	allât
irons	irions	allons	allions	allassions
irez	iriez	allez	alliez	allassiez
iront	iraient		*aillent	allassent
*assiérai	*assiérais		asseye	§ assisse
assiéras	assiérais	*assieds-toi	asseyes	assisses
assiéra	assiérait		asseye	assît
assiérons	assiérions	asseyons-nous	asseyions	assissions
assiérez	assiériez	asseyez-vous	asseyiez	assissiez
assiéront	assiéraient		asseyent	assissent
*assoirai	*assoirais		*assoie	
assoiras	assoirais	*assois-toi	*assoies	
assoira	assoirait		*assoie	
assoirons	assoirions	assoyons-nous	assoyions	
assoirez	assoiriez	assoyez-vous	assoyiez	
assoiront	assoiraient		*assoient	
battrai	battrais		batte	battisse
battras	battrais	*bats	battes	battisses
battra	battrait		batte	battît
battrons	battrions	battons	battions	battissions
battrez	battriez	battez	battiez	battissiez
battront	battraient		battent	battissent
boirai	boirais		*boive	§ busse
boiras	boirais	*bois	*boives	busses
boira	boirait		*boive	bût
boirons	boirions	buvons	buvions	bussions
boirez	boiriez	buvez	buviez	bussiez
boiront	boiraient		*boivent	bussent

INFINITIVE AND PARTICIPLES	INDICATIVE			
	PRESENT	IMPERFECT	PRETERIT	COMPOUND PAST
6. **Conclure** (to conclude) *concluant* § conclu	*conclus *conclus *conclut concluons concluez concluent	concluais concluais concluait concluions concluiez concluaient	§ conclus conclus conclut conclûmes conclûtes conclurent	ai § conclu as conclu a conclu avons conclu avez conclu ont conclu
7. **Conduire** (to lead) *conduisant* § conduit	*conduis *conduis *conduit conduisons conduisez conduisent	conduisais conduisais conduisait conduisions conduisiez conduisaient	† conduisis conduisis conduisit conduisîmes conduisîtes conduisirent	ai § conduit as conduit a conduit avons conduit avez conduit ont conduit
8. **Connaître** (to be acquainted) *connaissant* § connu	*connais *connais *connaît connaissons connaissez connaissent	connaissais connaissais connaissait connaissions connaissiez connaissaient	§ connus connus connut connûmes connûtes connurent	ai § connu as connu a connu avons connu avez connu ont connu
9. **Coudre** (to sew) *cousant* § cousu	couds couds coud cousons cousez cousent	cousais cousais cousait cousions cousiez cousaient	† cousis cousis cousit cousîmes cousîtes cousirent	ai § cousu as cousu a cousu avons cousu avez cousu ont cousu
10. **Courir** (to run) *courant* § couru	*cours *cours *court courons courez courent	courais courais courait courions couriez couraient	§ courus courus courut courûmes courûtes coururent	ai § couru as couru a couru avons couru avez couru ont couru
11. **Craindre** (to fear) *craignant* § craint	*crains *crains *craint craignons craignez craignent	craignais craignais craignait craignions craigniez craignaient	† craignis craignis craignit craignîmes craignîtes craignirent	ai § craint as craint a craint avons craint avez craint ont craint

FUTURE	CONDITIONAL	IMPERATIVE	SUBJUNCTIVE PRESENT	IMPERFECT
conclurai	conclurais		*conclue*	§ conclusse
concluras	conclurais	*conclus	*conclues*	conclusses
conclura	conclurait		*conclue*	conclût
conclurons	conclurions	*concluons*	*concluions*	conclussions
conclurez	concluriez	*concluez*	*concluiez*	conclussiez
concluront	concluraient		*concluent*	conclussent
conduirai	conduirais		*conduise*	† conduisisse
conduiras	conduirais	*conduis	*conduises*	conduisisses
conduira	conduirait		*conduise*	conduisît
conduirons	conduirions	*conduisons*	*conduisions*	conduisissions
conduirez	conduiriez	*conduisez*	*conduisiez*	conduisissiez
conduiront	conduiraient		*conduisent*	conduisissent
connaîtrai	connaîtrais		*connaisse*	§ connusse
connaîtras	connaîtrais	*connais	*connaisses*	connusses
connaîtra	connaîtrait		*connaisse*	connût
connaîtrons	connaîtrions	*connaissons*	*connaissions*	connussions
connaîtrez	connaîtriez	*connaissez*	*connaissiez*	connussiez
connaîtront	connaîtraient		*connaissent*	connussent
coudrai	coudrais		*couse*	† cousisse
coudras	coudrais	couds	*couses*	cousisses
coudra	coudrait		*couse*	cousît
coudrons	coudrions	*cousons*	*cousions*	cousissions
coudrez	coudriez	*cousez*	*cousiez*	cousissiez
coudront	coudraient		*cousent*	cousissent
*courrai	*courrais		*coure*	§ courusse
courras	courrais	*cours	*coures*	courusses
courra	courrait		*coure*	courût
courrons	courrions	*courons*	*courions*	courussions
courrez	courriez	*courez*	*couriez*	courussiez
courront	courraient		*courent*	courussent
craindrai	craindrais		*craigne*	† craignisse
craindras	craindrais	*crains	*craignes*	craignisses
craindra	craindrait		*craigne*	craignît
craindrons	craindrions	*craignons*	*craignions*	craignissions
craindrez	craindriez	*craignez*	*craigniez*	craignissiez
craindront	craindraient		*craignent*	craignissent

INFINITIVE AND PARTICIPLES	INDICATIVE			
	PRESENT	IMPERFECT	PRETERIT	COMPOUND PAST
12. Croire (to believe) *croyant* § cru	*crois *crois *croit croyons croyez *croient	croyais croyais croyait croyions croyiez croyaient	§ crus crus crut crûmes crûtes crurent	ai § cru as cru a cru avons cru avez cru ont cru
13. Croître (to grow) *croissant* § crû	*croîs *croîs *croît croissons croissez croissent	croissais croissais croissait croissions croissiez croissaient	§ crûs crûs crût crûmes crûtes crûrent	ai §crû as crû a crû avons crû avez crû ont crû
14. Cueillir (to pick) *cueillant* **cueilli**	cueille cueilles cueille cueillons cueillez cueillent	cueillais cueillais cueillait cueillions cueilliez cueillaient	**cueillis cueillis cueillit cueillîmes cueillîtes cueillirent**	**ai cueilli as cueilli a cueilli avons cueilli avez cueilli ont cueilli**
15. Devoir (to owe, have to) *devant* § dû, due[1]	*dois *dois *doit devons devez *doivent	devais devais devait devions deviez devaient	§ dus dus dut dûmes dûtes durent	ai § dû as dû a dû avons dû avez dû ont dû
16. Dire (to say, tell) *disant* § dit	*dis *dis *dit disons *dites disent	disais disais disait disions disiez disaient	§ dis dis dit dîmes dîtes dirent	ai §dit as dit a dit avons dit avez dit ont dit
17. Ecrire (to write) *écrivant* § écrit	*écris *écris *écrit écrivons écrivez écrivent	écrivais écrivais écrivait écrivions écriviez écrivaient	† écrivis écrivis écrivit écrivîmes écrivîtes écrivirent	ai § écrit as écrit a écrit avons écrit avez écrit ont écrit

[1] The masculine singular form of the past participle takes a circumflex accent to distinguish it from the word *du*. The other forms have no accent (*dû, due, dus, dues*).

FUTURE	CONDITIONAL	IMPERATIVE	SUBJUNCTIVE PRESENT	IMPERFECT
croirai	croirais		*croie	§ crusse
croiras	croirais	*crois	*croies	crusses
croira	croirait		*croie	crût
croirons	croirions	croyons	croyions	crussions
croirez	croiriez	croyez	croyiez	crussiez
croiront	croiraient		*croient	crussent
croîtrai	croîtrais		croisse	§ crusse
croîtras	croîtrais	*croîs	croisses	crusses
croîtra	croîtrait		croisse	crût
croîtrons	croîtrions	croissons	croissions	crussions
croîtrez	croîtriez	croissez	croissiez	crussiez
croîtront	croîtraient		croissent	crussent
*cueillerai	*cueillerais		cueille	cueillisse
cueilleras	cueillerais	*cueille	cueilles	cueillisses
cueillera	cueillerait		cueille	cueillît
cueillerons	cueillerions	cueillons	cueillions	cueillissions
cueillerez	cueilleriez	cueillez	cueilliez	cueillissiez
cueilleront	cueilleraient		cueillent	cueillissent
*devrai	*devrais		*doive	§ dusse
devras	devrais	*dois	*doives	dusses
devra	devrait		*doive	dût
devrons	devrions	devons	devions	dussions
devrez	devriez	devez	deviez	dussiez
devront	devraient		*doivent	dussent
dirai	dirais		dise	§ disse
diras	dirais	*dis	dises	disses
dira	dirait		dise	dît
dirons	dirions	disons	disions	dissions
direz	diriez	*dites	disiez	dissiez
diront	diraient		disent	dissent
écrirai	écrirais		écrive	† écrivisse
écriras	écrirais	*écris	écrives	écrivisses
écrira	écrirait		écrive	écrivît
écrirons	écririons	écrivons	écrivions	écrivissions
écrirez	écririez	écrivez	écriviez	écrivissiez
écriront	écriraient		écrivent	écrivissent

296 [§66] IRREGULAR VERBS

INFINITIVE AND PARTICIPLES	INDICATIVE			
	PRESENT	IMPERFECT	PRETERIT	COMPOUND PAST
18. Envoyer (to send) *envoyant* envoyé	*envoie *envoies *envoie envoyons envoyez *envoient	envoyais envoyais envoyait envoyions envoyiez envoyaient	envoyai envoyas envoya envoyâmes envoyâtes envoyèrent	ai envoyé as envoyé a envoyé avons envoyé avez envoyé ont envoyé
19. Faire (to do, make) *faisant*[1] § fait	*fais *fais *fait faisons *faites *font	faisais[1] faisais faisait faisions faisiez faisaient	† fis fis fit fîmes fîtes firent	ai § fait as fait a fait avons fait avez fait ont fait
20. Falloir[2] (to be necessary) § fallu	*il faut	**il fallait**	§ il fallut	il a § fallu
21. Fuir (to flee) *fuyant* § fui	*fuis *fuis *fuit fuyons fuyez *fuient	fuyais fuyais fuyait fuyions fuyiez fuyaient	§ fuis fuis fuit fuîmes fuîtes fuirent	ai § fui as fui a fui avons fui avez fui ont fui
22. Haïr (to hate) *haïssant* haï	*hais *hais *hait haïssons haïssez haïssent	haïssais haïssais haïssait haïssions haïssiez haïssaient	haïs haïs haït haïmes haïtes haïrent	ai haï as haï a haï avons haï avez haï ont haï
23. Lire (to read) *lisant* § lu	*lis *lis *lit lisons lisez lisent	lisais lisais lisait lisions lisiez lisaient	§ lus lus lut lûmes lûtes lurent	ai § lu as lu a lu avons lu avez lu ont lu

[1] The *ai* of the stem of these forms is pronounced like mute *e*. (*zh*e f*e*zè).
[2] Used in third person singular only.

FUTURE	CONDITIONAL	IMPERATIVE	SUBJUNCTIVE PRESENT	IMPERFECT
*enverrai	*enverrais		*envoie	envoyasse
enverras	enverrais	*envoie	*envoies	envoyasses
enverra	enverrait		*envoie	envoyât
enverrons	enverrions	envoyons	envoyions	envoyassions
enverrez	enverriez	envoyez	envoyiez	envoyassiez
enverront	enverraient		*envoient	envoyassent
*ferai	*ferais		*fasse	† fisse
feras	ferais	*fais	fasses	fisses
fera	ferait		fasse	fît
ferons	ferions	faisons	fassions	fissions
ferez	feriez	*faites	fassiez	fissiez
feront	feraient		fassent	fissent
*il faudra	*il faudrait		*il faille	§ il fallût
fuirai	fuirais		*fuie	§ fuisse
fuiras	fuirais	*fuis	*fuies	fuisses
fuira	fuirait		*fuie	fuît
fuirons	fuirions	fuyons	fuyions	fuissions
fuirez	fuiriez	fuyez	fuyiez	fuissiez,
fuiront	fuiraient		*fuient	fuissent
haïrai	haïrais		haïsse	haïsse
haïras	haïrais	*hais	haïsses	haïsses
haïra	haïrait		haïsse	haït
haïrons	haïrions	haïssons	haïssions	haïssions
haïrez	haïriez	haïssez	haïssiez	haïssiez
haïront	haïraient		haïssent	haïssent
lirai	lirais		lise	§ lusse
liras	lirais	*lis	lises	lusses
lira	lirait		lise	lût
lirons	lirions	lisons	lisions	lussions
lirez	liriez	lisez	lisiez	lussiez
liront	liraient		lisent	lussent

INFINITIVE AND PARTICIPLES	INDICATIVE			
	PRESENT	IMPERFECT	PRETERIT	COMPOUND PAST
24. Mettre (to put) *mettant* § mis	*mets *mets *met mettons mettez mettent	*mettais* *mettais* *mettait* *mettions* *mettiez* *mettaient*	§ mis mis mit mîmes mîtes mirent	ai § mis as mis a mis avons mis avez mis ont mis
25. Mourir (to die) *mourant* § mort	*meurs *meurs *meurt mourons mourez *meurent	*mourais* *mourais* *mourait* *mourions* *mouriez* *mouraient*	† mourus mourus mourut mourûmes mourûtes moururent	suis § mort(e) es mort(e) est mort(e) sommes mort(e)s êtes mort(e)(s) sont mort(e)s
26. Naître (to be born) *naissant* § né	*nais *nais *naît naissons naissez naissent	*naissais* *naissais* *naissait* *naissions* *naissiez* *naissaient*	† naquis naquis naquit naquîmes naquîtes naquirent	suis § né(e) es né(e) est né(e) sommes né(e)s êtes né(e)(s) sont né(e)s
27. Ouvrir (to open) *ouvrant* § ouvert	*ouvre* *ouvres* *ouvre* *ouvrons* *ouvrez* *ouvrent*	*ouvrais* *ouvrais* *ouvrait* *ouvrions* *ouvriez* *ouvraient*	† ouvris ouvris ouvrit ouvrîmes ouvrîtes ouvrirent	ai § ouvert as ouvert a ouvert avons ouvert avez ouvert ont ouvert
28. Peindre (to paint) *peignant* § peint	peins peins peint peignons peignez peignent	*peignais* *peignais* *peignait* *peignions* *peigniez* *peignaient*	† peignis peignis peignit peignîmes peignîtes peignirent	ai § peint as peint a peint avons peint avez peint ont peint
29. Plaire (to please) *plaisant* § plu	*plais *plais *plaît plaisons plaisez plaisent	*plaisais* *plaisais* *plaisait* *plaisions* *plaisiez* *plaisaient*	§ plus plus plut plûmes plûtes plurent	ai § plu as plu a plu avons plu avez plu ont plu

FUTURE	CONDITIONAL	IMPERATIVE	SUBJUNCTIVE PRESENT	IMPERFECT
mettrai	mettrais		*mette*	§ misse
mettras	mettrais	*mets	*mettes*	misses
mettra	mettrait		*mette*	mît
mettrons	mettrions	*mettons*	*mettions*	missions
mettrez	mettriez	*mettez*	*mettiez*	missiez
mettront	mettraient		*mettent*	missent
*mourrai	*mourrais		*meure	† mourusse
mourras	mourrais	*meurs	*meures	mourusses
mourra	mourrait		*meure	mourût
mourrons	mourrions	*mourons*	*mourions*	mourussions
mourrez	mourriez	*mourez*	*mouriez*	mourussiez
mourront	mourraient		*meurent	mourussent
naîtrai	naîtrais		*naisse*	† naquisse
naîtras	naîtrais	*nais	*naisses*	naquisses
naîtra	naîtrait		*naisse*	naquît
naîtrons	naîtrions	*naissons*	*naissions*	naquissions
naîtrez	naîtriez	*naissez*	*naissiez*	naquissiez
naîtront	naîtraient		*naissent*	naquissent
ouvrirai	ouvrirais		*ouvre*	† ouvrisse
ouvriras	ouvrirais	*ouvre*	*ouvres*	ouvrisses
ouvrira	ouvrirait		*ouvre*	ouvrît
ouvrirons	ouvririons	*ouvrons*	*ouvrions*	ouvrissions
ouvrirez	ouvririez	*ouvrez*	*ouvriez*	ouvrissiez
ouvriront	ouvriraient		*ouvrent*	ouvrissent
peindrai	peindrais		*peigne*	† peignisse
peindras	peindrais	*peins	*peignes*	peignisses
peindra	peindrait		*peigne*	peignît
peindrons	peindrions	*peignons*	*peignions*	peignissions
peindrez	peindriez	*peignez*	*peigniez*	peignissiez
peindront	peindraient		*peignent*	peignissent
plairai	plairais		*plaise*	§ plusse
plairas	plairais	*plais	*plaises*	plusses
plaira	plairait		*plaise*	plût
plairons	plairions	*plaisons*	*plaisions*	plussions
plairez	plairiez	*plaisez*	*plaisiez*	plussiez
plairont	plairaient		*plaisent*	plussent

INFINITIVE AND PARTICIPLES	INDICATIVE			
	PRESENT	IMPERFECT	PRETERIT	COMPOUND PAST
30. **Pleuvoir**[1] (to rain) *pleuvant* § plu	*il pleut	*il pleuvait*	il § plut	il a §plu
31. **Pouvoir** (to be able) *pouvant* § pu	*peux, puis *peux *peut pouvons pouvez *peuvent	*pouvais* *pouvais* *pouvait* *pouvions* *pouviez* *pouvaient*	§ pus pus put pûmes pûtes purent	ai § pu as pu a pu avons pu avez pu ont pu
32. **Prendre** (to take) *prenant* § pris	**prends** **prends** **prend** prenons prenez *prennent	*prenais* *prenais* *prenait* *prenions* *preniez* *prenaient*	§ pris pris prit prîmes prîtes prirent	ai § pris as pris a pris avons pris avez pris ont pris
33. **Recevoir** (to receive) *recevant* § reçu	*reçois *reçois *reçoit recevons recevez *reçoivent	*recevais* *recevais* *recevait* *recevions* *receviez* *recevaient*	§ reçus reçus reçut reçûmes reçûtes reçurent	ai § reçu as reçu a reçu avons reçu avez reçu ont reçu
34. **Résoudre** (to resolve, to solve) *résolvant* § résolu	*résous *résous *résout résolvons résolvez résolvent	*résolvais* *résolvais* *résolvait* *résolvions* *résolviez* *résolvaient*	§ résolus résolus résolut résolûmes résolûtes résolurent	ai § résolu as résolu a résolu avons résolu avez résolu ont résolu
35. **Rire** (to laugh) *riant* § ri	*ris *ris *rit rions riez rient	*riais* *riais* *riait* *riions* *riiez* *riaient*	§ ris ris rit rîmes rîtes rirent	ai § ri as ri a ri avons ri avez ri ont ri

[1] Used only in third person singular.

		IMPERATIVE	SUBJUNCTIVE	
FUTURE	CONDITIONAL		PRESENT	IMPERFECT

*il pleuvra	*il pleuvrait		*il pleuve*	il § plut
*pourrai	*pourrais		*puisse	§ pusse
pourras	pourrais		puisses	pusses
pourra	pourrait		puisse	pût
pourrons	pourrions		puissions	pussions
pourrez	pourriez		puissiez	pussiez
pourront	pourraient		puissent	pussent
prendrai	prendrais		*prenne	§ prisse
prendras	prendrais	prends	*prennes	prisses
prendra	prendrait		*prenne	prît
prendrons	prendrions	prenons	prenions	prissions
prendrez	prendriez	prenez	preniez	prissiez
prendront	prendraient		*prennent	prissent
*recevrai	*recevrais		*reçoive	§ reçusse
recevras	recevrais	*reçois	*reçoives	reçusses
recevra	recevrait		*reçoive	reçût
recevrons	recevrions	recevons	recevions	reçussions
recevrez	recevriez	recevez	receviez	reçussiez
recevront	recevraient		*reçoivent	reçussent
*résoudrai	*résoudrais		*résolve*	§ résolusse
résoudras	résoudrais	*résous	*résolves*	résolusses
résoudra	résoudrait		*résolve*	résolût
résoudrons	résoudrions	résolvons	*résolvions*	résolussions
résoudrez	résoudriez	résolvez	*résolviez*	résolussiez
résoudront	résoudraient		*résolvent*	résolussent
rirai	rirais		*rie*	§ risse
riras	rirais	*ris	*ries*	risses
rira	rirait		*rie*	rît
rirons	ririons	rions	*riions*	rissions
rirez	ririez	riez	*riiez*	rissiez
riront	riraient		*rient*	rissent

INFINITIVE AND PARTICIPLES	INDICATIVE			
	PRESENT	IMPERFECT	PRETERIT	COMPOUND PAST
36. **Savoir** (to know) *sachant* § su	sais sais sait savons savez savent	savais savais savait savions saviez savaient	§ sus sus sut sûmes sûtes surent	ai § su as su a su avons su avez su ont su
37. **Suffire** (to be sufficient) *suffisant* **suffi**	*suffis *suffis *suffit suffisons suffisez suffisent	*suffisais* *suffisais* *suffisait* *suffisions* *suffisiez* *suffisaient*	**suffis** **suffis** **suffit** **suffîmes** **suffîtes** **suffirent**	ai suffi as suffi a suffi avons suffi avez suffi ont suffi
38. **Suivre** (to follow) *suivant* § suivi	*suis *suis *suit suivons suivez suivent	*suivais* *suivais* *suivait* *suivions* *suiviez* *suivaient*	§ suivis suivis suivit suivîmes suivîtes suivirent	ai § suivi as suivi a suivi avons suivi avez suivi ont suivi
39. **Tenir** (to hold, keep) *tenant* § tenu	*tiens *tiens *tient tenons tenez *tiennent	*tenais* *tenais* *tenait* *tenions* *teniez* *tenaient*	† tins tins tint tînmes tîntes tinrent	ai § tenu as tenu a tenu avons tenu avez tenu ont tenu
40. **Vaincre** (to conquer) *vainquant* § vaincu	*vaincs *vaincs *vainc vainquons vainquez vainquent	*vainquais* *vainquais* *vainquait* *vainquions* *vainquiez* *vainquaient*	† vainquis vainquis vainquit vainquîmes vainquîtes vainquirent	ai § vaincu as vaincu a vaincu avons vaincu avez vaincu ont vaincu
41. **Valoir** (to be worth) *valant* § valu	*vaux *vaux *vaut valons valez valent	*valais* *valais* *valait* *valions* *valiez* *valaient*	§ valus valus valut valûmes valûtes valurent	ai § valu as valu a valu avons valu avez valu ont valu

| | | IMPERATIVE | SUBJUNCTIVE | |
FUTURE	CONDITIONAL		PRESENT	IMPERFECT
*saurai	*saurais		sache	§ susse
sauras	saurais	sache	saches	susses
saura	saurait		sache	sût
saurons	saurions	sachons	sachions	sussions
saurez	sauriez	sachez	sachiez	sussiez
sauront	sauraient		sachent	sussent
suffirai	suffirais		suffise	suffisse
suffiras	suffirais	*suffis	suffises	suffisses
suffira	suffirait		suffise	suffît
suffirons	suffirions	suffisons	suffisions	suffissions
suffirez	suffiriez	suffisez	suffisiez	suffissiez
suffiront	suffiraient		suffisent	suffissent
suivrai	suivrais		suive	§ suivisse
suivras	suivrais	*suis	suives	suivisses
suivra	suivrait		suive	suivît
suivrons	suivrions	suivons	suivions	suivissions
suivrez	suivriez	suivez	suiviez	suivissiez
suivront	suivraient		suivent	suivissent
*tiendrai	*tiendrais		*tienne	† tinsse
tiendras	tiendrais	*tiens	*tiennes	tinsses
tiendra	tiendrait		*tienne	tînt
tiendrons	tiendrions	tenons	tenions	tinssions
tiendrez	tiendriez	tenez	teniez	tinssiez
tiendront	tiendraient		*tiennent	tinssent
vaincrai	vaincrais		vainque	† vainquisse
vaincras	vaincrais	*vaincs	vainques	vainquisses
vaincra	vaincrait		vainque	vainquît
vaincrons	vaincrions	vainquons	vainquions	vainquissions
vaincrez	vaincriez	vainquez	vainquiez	vainquissiez
vaincront	vaincraient		vainquent	vainquissent
*vaudrai	*vaudrais		*vaille	§ valusse
vaudras	vaudrais	*vaux	*vailles	valusses
vaudra	vaudrait		*vaille	valût
vaudrons	vaudrions	valons	valions	valussions
vaudrez	vaudriez	valez	valiez	valussiez
vaudront	vaudraient		*vaillent	valussent

INFINITIVE AND PARTICIPLES	INDICATIVE			
	PRESENT	IMPERFECT	PRETERIT	COMPOUND PAST
42. **Venir** (to come) *venant* § venu	*viens *viens *vient venons venez *viennent	venais venais venait venions veniez venaient	† vins vins vint vînmes vîntes vinrent	suis § venu(e) es venu(e) est venu(e) sommes venu(e)s êtes venu(e)(s) sont venu(e)s
43. **Vêtir** (to dress) *vêtant* § vêtu	*vêts *vêts *vêt vêtons vêtez vêtent	vêtais vêtais vêtait vêtions vêtiez vêtaient	vêtis vêtis vêtit vêtîmes vêtîtes vêtirent	ai § vêtu as vêtu a vêtu avons vêtu avez vêtu ont vêtu
44. **Vivre** (to live) *vivant* § vécu	*vis *vis *vit vivons vivez vivent	vivais vivais vivait vivions viviez vivaient	§ vécus vécus vécut vécûmes vécûtes vécurent	ai § vécu as vécu a vécu avons vécu avez vécu ont vécu
45. **Voir** (to see) *voyant* § vu	*vois *vois *voit voyons voyez *voient	voyais voyais voyait voyions voyiez voyaient	† vis vis vit vîmes vîtes virent	ai § vu as vu a vu avons vu avez vu ont vu
46. **Vouloir** (to wish, want) *voulant* § voulu	*veux *veux *veut voulons voulez *veulent	voulais voulais voulait voulions vouliez voulaient	§ voulus voulus voulut voulûmes voulûtes voulurent	ai § voulu as voulu a voulu avons voulu avez voulu ont voulu

¶ *Veuille, veuillons* and *veuillez* are used to express a less strong and less personal desire, or to render a request in a polite form: *Veuillez me suivre,* please be kind enough to follow me. This form of the imperative therefore does *not* express a real command to wish or desire something.

A literal order to wish or make a person wish to do something is expressed by

		IMPERATIVE	SUBJUNCTIVE	
FUTURE	CONDITIONAL		PRESENT	IMPERFECT
*viendrai	*viendrais		*vienne	† vinsse
viendras	viendrais	*viens	*viennes	vinsses
viendra	viendrait		*vienne	vînt
viendrons	viendrions	*venons*	*venions*	vinssions
viendrez	viendriez	*venez*	*veniez*	vinssiez
viendront	viendraient		*viennent	vinssent
vêtirai	vêtirais		*vête*	vêtisse
vêtiras	vêtirais	*vêts	*vêtes*	vêtisses
vêtira	vêtirait		*vête*	vêtît
vêtirons	vêtirions	*vêtons*	*vêtions*	vêtissions
vêtirez	vêtiriez	*vêtez*	*vêtiez*	vêtissiez
vêtiront	vêtiraient		*vêtent*	vêtissent
vivrai	vivrais		*vive*	§ vécusse
vivras	vivrais	*vis	*vives*	vécusses
vivra	vivrait		*vive*	vécût
vivrons	vivrions	*vivons*	*vivions*	vécussions
vivrez	vivriez	*vivez*	*viviez*	vécussiez
vivront	vivraient		*vivent*	vécussent
*verrai	*verrais		*voie	† visse
verras	verrais	vois	*voies	visses
verra	verrait		*voie	vît
verrons	verrions	*voyons*	*voyions*	vissions
verrez	verriez	*voyez*	*voyiez*	vissiez
verront	verraient		*voient	vissent
*voudrai	*voudrais	*veux ⎫	*veuille	§ voulusse
voudras	voudrais	*veuille ⎭	*veuilles	voulusses
voudra	voudrait	*voulons* ⎫	*veuille	voulût
voudrons	voudrions	*veuillons ⎭	*voulions*	voulussions
voudrez	voudriez	*voulez* ⎫	*vouliez*	voulussiez
voudront	voudraient	*veuillez ⎭	*veuillent	voulussent

the forms *veux, voulons, voulez*. Examples: *Voulons finir le travail,* let us make ourselves want to finish the job; *Voulez guérir,* have the will to get well again. These forms, in practice, are used mainly in a negative sense: *Ne m'en veux pas,* an idiomatic usage meaning 'Don't be angry with me.'

GUIDE TO FRENCH PRONUNCIATION
Part II

This section continues the explanation of French pronunciation offered on pages 19 through 23. While Part I describes the articulation of the French language in terms of similar English sounds (through a simplified phonetic spelling), Part II describes French sounds in relation to French spelling. After the student has progressed through some of the lessons, he should study Part II from time to time as he continues. He will then be able to pronounce any French word without needing a phonetic guide since he will know how each of the French vowels and consonants is pronounced.

Les Voyelles

THE VOWELS   (lay vwayèl)

A - a

This vowel has two pronunciations in French:

First Pronunciation[1]: **a**

Except for the cases enumerated in the next paragraph, the vowel "a" is pronounced **a**:

flamme (flam) flame   **là** (la) there
canne (kan) cane   **parla** (parla) spoke
balle (bal) ball   **cela** (s^ela) that
bal (bál) ball, dance   **mêla** (mèla) mixed

Second Pronunciation: **â**

1. The vowel always has this long pronunciation when it is spelled with a circumflex accent:

mât (mâ) mast   **mâle** (mâl) male
pâte (pât) paste   **château** (*sh*âtô) castle

---

1. For the method of articulating these sounds indicated by diacritical markings, the reader should turn back to the section entitled *Guide to French Pronunciation, Part I*, Pg. 19.

306

2. Most Frenchmen pronounce a long "a" when the vowel is followed by a z sound:

phrase (frâz) sentence   **base** (bâz) base

3. In the speech of many, but not all, Frenchmen, the vowel "a" is long when followed by -*tion* or by -*ss*:

nation (nâsyôⁿ) nation   **passion** (pâsyôⁿ) passion
consolation (kôⁿsolâsyôⁿ)   **passer** pâs*ay*) to pass
  consolation

4. The letter "a" in "as" or "az" final is generally pronounced **â**:

pas (pâ) step   **as** (âs) ace
cas (kâ) case   **hélas!** (*ay*lâs) alas!
repas (rᵉpâ) meal   **gaz** (gâz) gas

E - e

This vowel has three pronunciations and, in a fourth case, it is altogether mute:

First Pronunciation: *ay*

1. When there is an acute accent over the vowel:
défilé (*dayfeelay*) parade   **été** (*aytay*) summer

2. When the vowel occurs in the infinitive ending of the -*er* conjugation:

parler (parl*ay*) to speak   **chanter** (shâⁿt*ay*) to sing

3. When it is followed by a mute "z":
allez (al*ay*) go   **chanterez** (shâⁿtᵉr*ay*) (you)
assez* (as*ay*) enough   will sing
                                     nez (n*ay*) nose

4. When it is followed by a mute "d" in words ending "ied":

pied (py*ay*) foot   **sied** (sy*ay*) suit

5. In monosyllables, when it is followed by "s":

mes (m*ay*)ᐟ my   **des** (d*ay*) of the   **ces** (s*ay*) these

---

* Note that this word is pronounced with a short **a**.
ᐟ Some Frenchmen pronounce **mè**, particularly in combinations like **mèzâⁿfâɴ**

Second Pronunciation: è

1. When there is a grave accent over the vowel:

près (prè) near   **procès** (prosè) lawsuit
problème (problèm) problem   **zèle** (zèl) zeal

2. When there is a circumflex accent over the vowel:
même (mèm) same   **tête** (tèt) head

3. When written without an accent mark in a closed syllable (a closed syllable is one in which the last pronounced sound is a consonant):

cesser (sès*ay*) to cease   **pelle** (pèl) shovel
appel (apèl) call   **mer** (mèr) sea

4. When it precedes final mute "t" or "ct":
effet (*ay*fè) effect   **respect** (rèspè) respect

Third Pronunciation: e

1. When written without an accent mark and when it is the last letter of a syllable in the middle of a word (i.e., when it is in an *open syllable,* which is one ending in a vowel):

leçon (l^{e}sô^n) lesson   **reçu** (r^{e}sü) received

2. When in monosyllables such as:

me (m^e) me   **le** (l^e) the
te (t^e) thee   **de** (d^e) of

3. When the *rule of the three consonants applies* (according to the rule of the three consonants, the vowel "e" without an accent mark will be pronounced if it is preceded by *more than one* consonant and followed by *one*):

chargerai (sharzh^{e}ray) (I) shall load
département (daypart^{e}mâ^n) department
votre chapeau (votr^e shapô) your hat

Fourth Pronunciation: Completely mute

1. The vowel "e" is completely mute at the end of words, unless it is the only vowel or unless the *rule of the three consonants* causes it to be pronounced in a word group (as, for example, in the phrase "votre chapeau" noted just above):

table (tabl) table   **farce** (fars) farce

2. When, in the interior of a word, the vowel "e" is preceded by *only one* consonant and followed by one:

rêverie (rèvr*ee*) reverie   **seulement** (sè^{o}lmâ^n) only
maintenant (mè^{n}tnâ^n) now (the *rule of the three consonants* does not apply in this word because the first "n" is unpronounced)

3. When "s" is added in order to form the plural of words which end in "e" and in the termination "es" in the second singular of verbs:

salles (sal) halls
fables (fabl) fables
tu parles (tü parl) thou speakest
tu regardes (tü r^{e}gard) thou lookest

4. Also, in the third person plural of verbs, the termination "ent" is silent:

ils parlent (*ee*l parl) they speak
ils flattent (*ee*l flat) they flatter

5. The "e" is also silent when put after "g", in order that this letter may take, before "a", "o", "u", the sound which it has before "e", "i", viz., that which we represent diacritically as *zh*, as in:

il mangea (*ee*l mâ^n*zha*) he ate
changeons (*shâ^{n}zhô^n*) let us change

I - i

This vowel has two pronunciations. (See also *compound vowels.*)

First Pronunciation: ee

Whether written with or without a circumflex accent, the vowel "i" has this pronunciation unless it is followed by another vowel in the same syllable:

finir (f*ee*neer) to finish   **abîme** (abeem) abyss

Second Pronunciation: y

When followed by another vowel in the same syllable*:

pied (py*ay*) foot
miel (myèl) honey
vision (veezyô^n) vision
diable (dyabl) devil

---

* Some consonant combinations make it impossible to pronounce **y**. For example: crier (kr*ee*ay), oublier (oobl*ee*ay).

O - o

This vowel has two pronunciations:

First Pronunciation: ô

1. When it has a circumflex accent:

trône (trôn) throne   hotel (ôtèl) hotel

2. At end of word when it is the last pronounced element:

bravo (bravô) bravo   pot (pô) pot
numéro (nümayrô) number   dos (dô) back

3. Before a z sound:

rose (rôz) rose   poser (pôzay) to place

Second Pronunciation: o

In all other cases, the vowel "o" is short:

bosse (bos) hump   votre (votr) your
botte (bot) boot   potage (potazh) soup

U - u

This vowel has two pronunciations and is silent in a third case:

First Pronunciation: ü

Except when followed by another vowel in the same syllable, or except in the *compound vowels* mentioned later, the vowel "u" has this pronunciation with or without a circumflex accent:

lune (lün) moon   tribu (treebü) tribe
bu (bü) have drunk   mûr (mür) ripe

Second Pronunciation: ü

The vowel "u" has this pronunciation when followed by another vowel in the same syllable:

lui (lüee) to him   écuelle (ayküèl) bowl

Third Pronunciation: Silent

Except in a few rare words, "u" is mute if it is preceded by "g" or "q":

guide (geed) guide   quitter (keetay) to leave

Y - y

This vowel has the same pronunciation as "i" and is governed by the same rules. (See also the *compound vowel* "oy".)

type (t*ee*p) type   **y** (*ee*) there

NOTE: In the common word *pays*, observe the unusual pronunciation: *payee*.

Voyelles Composées

COMPOUND VOWELS   (vwayèl kô^{n}pôz*ay*)

Eu and Oẽu

This compound vowel with two spellings is, phonetically speaking, a simple (pure) vowel and has two pronunciations:

First Pronunciation: e^o

1. In an open syllable (a syllable of which the last pronounced element is a vowel), "eu" and "œu" have this pronunciation:

peu (p*e*^{o}) little   **vœu** (v*e*^{o}) vow

2. In a syllable closed by a z sound:

        douloureuse (dooloor*e*^{o}z), painful

Second Pronunciation: è^o

1. In a closed syllable (a syllable ending in a consonant):

neuf (n*è*^{o}f) nine   **leur** (l*è*^{o}r) their

2. In an open syllable followed by "r" at the beginning of the next syllable:

heureux (*è*^{o}r*e*^{o}) happy   **peureux** (p*è*^{o}r*e*^{o}) fearful

Ai and Ay

This compound vowel with two spellings is, phonetically speaking, a pure vowel and has two pronunciations:

First Pronunciation: è

In any position except final position in word:

semaine (s^{e}mèn) week   **donnais** (donè) (I) was giving

Second Pronunciation: ay
In final position in word:
j'ai (*zhay*) I have   mai (m*ay* or mè) May

Special Pronunciation for -ayer:
In pronouncing this common type of verb or any of the forms derived from it, the letter "y" is actually pronounced twice; for example, the verb *payer* is pronounced as though it were spelled *pai-yay*. Additional examples:

essayer (*ay*sèy*ay*) to try   payons (pèyô^n) (we) pay

Ei
Pronounced è. Example: Seine (sèn) Seine

Au and Eau
Both are the simple vowel sound ô:
chaud (*shô*) hot   beau (bô) beautiful
autorité (ôtor*eetay*) authority   manteau (mâ^{n}tô) cloak

Oi and Oy
This spelling combination produces two sounds, a semi-vowel plus a vowel: wa or occasionally wâ.*

noir (nwar) black   gloire (glwar) glory
Troyes (trwa) Troyes

If "oy" is followed by another vowel, "y" is pronounced twice, first in the combination "oi" and then as a semi-vowel "y":

royal (rway*a*l) royal   voyons (vwayô^n) (we) see
ployer (plway*ay*) to bend   employé (â^{n}plway*ay*) employee

Ou
This simple vowel has two pronunciations.

First Pronunciation: oo
Whether with or without a circumflex or grave accent, it is a pure vowel:
goût (g*oo*) taste   doux (d*oo*) sweet   où (*oo*) or

---

* With "oi" in final position in a word, many Frenchmen pronounce wâ. Sometimes the difference in length of the vowel is used to distinguish words as *soi* (swa) *oneself*, and *soie* (swâ) *silk.*

Second Pronunciation: w

When followed by another vowel in the same syllable, "ou" becomes a semi-vowel:

ouest (wèst) west   **oui** (wee) yes
Louis (lwee) Louis

Les Voyelles Nasales

THE NASAL VOWELS   (lay vwayèl nazal)

A vowel is nasalized whenever it is followed by "m" or "n" in the same syllable, in which case the "m" or "n" is absorbed by the vowel and is no longer pronounced.

Am - An - Em - En

These spelling combinations have two pronunciations.

First Pronunciation: $\hat{a}^n$

This is the usual pronunciation:

ambition ($\hat{a}^n$beesyô^n) ambition   **embraser** ($\hat{a}^n$brâzay) to kindle
manteau (mâ^{n}tô) cloak   **sentir** (sâ^{n}teer) to feel

Second Pronunciation: $\grave{e}^n$

Exceptionally, "en" at the end of a number of common words will be pronounced: $\grave{e}^n$.

bien (byè^n) well   **ancien** ($\hat{a}^n$syè^n) ancient

Im - In - Ym - Yn - Aim - Ain - Ein

These spelling combinations are pronounced: $\grave{e}^n$

imbécile (è^{n}bayseel) imbecile   **faim** (fè^n) hunger
fin (fè^n) end   **main** (mè^n) hand
thym (tè^n) thyme   **ceinture** (sè^{n}tür) belt

Om and On

These spelling combinations are pronounced: $\hat{o}^n$

ombre (ô^{n}br) shade   **plonger** (plô^{n}zhay) to dive

Um and Un

These spelling combinations are pronounced: e^n

parfum (parfe^n) perfume   **jeun** (zhe^n) fasting
un (e^n) a, one   **brun** (bre^n) brown

THE CONSONANTS

Les Consonnes

The Consonants   (*lay* kô^{n}son)

B - b

This consonant has two pronunciations.

1. Normally this consonant is pronounced: **b**

balle (bal) ball   **boulet** (*bool*è) bullet

2. Followed by "s," it is generally pronounced: **p**

absent (apsâ^n) absent   **absolu** (apsolü) absolute

C - c

This consonant has two pronunciations.

First Pronunciation: **s**

1. Followed by "e" or "i":

ceci (s^{e}s*ee*) this   **facile** (fas*ee*l) easy

2. When spelled with a cedilla "ç":

garçon (garsô^n) boy   **effaçons** (èfasô^n) (we) erase

Second Pronunciation: **k**

Followed by "a" or "o":

carton (kartô^n) cardboard   **contrôle** (kô^{n}trôl) inspection

Ch - ch

This spelling combination, which is in reality a single consonant, has two pronunciations:

First Pronunciation: **sh**

This is the normal pronunciation for "ch":

charité (*sha*ree*tay*) charity   **chercher** (*shè*r*shay*) to seek

Second Pronunciation: **k**

In some exceptional words "ch" has this pronunciation:

écho (*a*ykô) echo   **Christ** (kr*ee*st) Christ
chronologie (kronolo*zhee*)   **chaos** (kaô) chaos
  chronology   **orchestre** (orkèstr) orchestra
chœur (kè^{o}r) choir

D - d

Normally this consonant is pronounced **d**:

sud (süd) south   **douche** (*doosh*) shower

In linking (see section entitled *Liaison*), this consonant will become **t**:

un grand homme (e^n grâ^{n}tom) a great man

F - f

Normally this consonant is pronounced **f** as in English. The following exceptions should be noted:

1. In linking (see section entitled *Liaison*), it is pronounced **v**:

neuf ans (nè^{o}vâ^n) nine years

2. In these unusual words the "f" is unpronounced:

clef (kl*ay*) key   **nerf** (nòr) nerve
            chef-d'œuvre (*shay*dè^{o}vr) masterpiece

3. In these unusual words, the "f" is pronounced in the singular but not in the plural:

un œuf (e^nnè^{o}f) an egg   **des œufs** (*day*ze^o) some eggs
un bœuf (e^n bè^{o}f) an ox   **des bœufs** (*day* be^o) some oxen

G - g

This consonant has three pronunciations:

First Pronunciation: g

When followed by "a", "o", or "u":

garder (gard*ay*) to guard   **gond** (gô^n) hinge

NOTE: As indicated when discussing the vowel "u", the "u" is generally unpronounced when placed after "g" to keep the "g" hard:

guide (geed) guide   **longue** (lô^{n}g) long

The following words may be noted as exceptions to this rule:

aiguille (*aygüeey*) needle   **linguiste** (lè^{n}güeest) linguist

Second Pronunciation: zh

When followed by "e", "i", or "y":

génie (*zhaynee*) genius   **gymnase** (*zhee*mnâz) gymnasium

NOTE: In the conjugation of -*ger* verbs, it is necessary to keep the "g" soft by inserting an "e" whenever the verb ending begins with "a" or "o":

mangea (mâⁿ*zh*a) (he) ate   **mangeons** (mâⁿ*zh*ôⁿ) (we) eat

NOTE: If there is a second "g" before an "e", the first "g" is hard: **suggéré** (süg*zh*ayray) suggested

Third Pronunciation: k

In linking (see section on *Liaison*), "g" becomes **k**:

   de rang en rang (dᵉ râⁿkâⁿ râⁿ) from rank to rank

Gn - gn

This spelling combination is one consonant sound and is pronounced: *ny*

   compagne (kôⁿpa*ny*) country
   compagnon (kôⁿpa*ny*ôⁿ) companion

NOTE: Some unusual words have the "g" and "n" pronounced separately:

   diagnostic (dyagnost*ee*k) diagnostic

H · h

In no case is "h" pronounced in French, but there are two types of "h" which have a different effect on the adjacent sounds:

1. Mute "h":

When the "h" is what is called "mute," linking and elision (see sections on these subjects) will take place as though the word in question began with a vowel:

   un homme (eⁿnom) a man   **l'homme** (lom) the man

2. Aspirate "h":

Although the so-called "aspirate h" is no longer pronounced in French, its presence at the beginning of the word will prevent linking and elision:

   le héros (lᵉ ayrô) the hero   **une hache** (ün a*sh*) an ax

The only way to be sure that an "h" is aspirate is to consult a French dictionary which will distinguish a "mute h" from an "aspirate h."

NOTE: In the spelling combinations "rh" and "th", the "h" is mute:

rhétorique (r*a*ytor*ee*k) rhetoric   **cathédrale** (kat*a*ydral) cathedral

J - j

Always pronounced: *zh*
jeudi (*zh*e°dee) Thursday   **joli** (*zh*olee) pretty

K - k

Found only in words foreign to French, and pronounced the same as in English:

kangourou (kân*goo*roo) kangaroo

L - l

This consonant has two pronunciations:

First Pronunciation: l

This is the usual pronunciation for single or double "l" (exceptions are noted in the next paragraph).

long (lôn) long   **salle** (sal) hall   **allée** (al*a*y) path

Second Pronunciation: y

In the following combinations, "l" or "ll" has the **y** pronunciation:

1. "il" in combination "eil" or "ail" at end of word:

soleil (sol*è*y) sun   **pareil** (par*è*y) like
travail (travay) work   **émail** (*a*ymay) enamel

2. "ll" in combination "ill":

pastille (past*ee*y) drop   **vieillard** (vy*a*yyar) old man
NOTE: Observe the following exceptions:

1. "Ill" in the initial syllable produces a double "l":

illusion (eellüzyôn) illusion   **illimité** (eelleemeetay) unlimited

2. In certain words "ill" is pronounced: *eel.*

mille (m*ee*l) thousand   **ville** (v*ee*l) city
tranquille (trân*keel*) quiet
3. In most words the "l" in "il" final is pronounced:

civil (seev*ee*l)   **vil** (v*ee*l) vile   **fil** (f*ee*l) thread

But in some words the "l" in "il" final is mute:

baril (bar*ee*) barrel   fusil (füz*ee*) gun
gentil (*zh*â*n*tee) nice   gril (gr*ee*) grating
persil (pèrs*ee*) parsley   sourcil (soors*ee*) eyebrow

M - m   N - n

Normally these are pronounced m and n. As noted above in the section on nasal vowels, these consonants will nasalize the vowel and will not therefore be pronounced separately whenever they occur after the vowel and are in the same syllable. This is the case except when another vowel occurs directly after them, in which case they belong to the next syllable and cannot nasalize the preceding vowel. Compare:

ampleur (â^{n}plè^{o}r) amplitude   ami (am*ee*) friend
Note the following exceptional cases:

1. Normally the doubling of a nasal consonant prevents nasalization:

flamme (flam) flame   ancienne (â^{n}syèn) ancient

2. In some exceptional words, doubling of the nasal consonant does not prevent nasalization:

ennoblir (â^{n}nobl*ee*r) to ennoble   ennui (â^{n}n*üee*) boredom

3. In some unusual words such as *damner* (dân*ay*) and its derivatives and *automne* (ôton), but not *automnal* (ôtomnal), the "m" is altogether mute.

4. The presence of a final mute "e" after a nasal consonant will prevent nasalization:

une (ün) a, one   fortune (fortün) fortune

P - p

Normally this consonant is pronounced p as in English. The following exceptions should be noted:

1. "P" is unpronounced when preceded by "m" or followed by "t":

temps (tâ^n) time   sept (sèt) seven
compter (kô^{n}t*ay*) to count   baptiste (bat*ee*st) Baptist

2. In the word *corps.* "p" is unpronounced: (kor).

3. "Ph", as in English, is pronounced **f**.

    philosophie (*feelosofee*) philosophy

4. In the combination "ps", "p" is pronounced, contrary to the English:

    psychologie (pseekolo*zhee*) psychology

Q - q

This consonant usually occurs in the combination "qu" which is pronounced **k**:

qualité (kal*eetay*) quality   **quotidien** (koteedyè^n) daily

In a few words "qu" is pronounced **kw**:

équestre (*ay*kwèstr) equestrian   **aquatique** (akwat*eek*) aquatic
aquarelle (akwarèl) watercolor   **équation** (*ay*kwâsyô^n) equation
équateur (*ay*kwatè^{o}r) equator   **quadrupède** (kwadrüpèd) quadruped

R - r

This consonant is pronounced **r**:

It is unpronounced in final position when preceded by "e":

    parler (parl*ay*) to speak   **dernier** (dèrny*ay*) last

Note the following exceptions to this rule:

    mer (mèr) sea   **hiver** (*eev*èr) winter
    fer (fèr) iron   **cancer** (kâ^{n}sèr) cancer
    amer (amèr) bitter   **enfer** (â^{n}fèr) hell
    cuiller (küeeyèr) spoon   **Lucifer** (lüseefèr) Lucifer

The pronunciation of the double "rr" does not differ materially from that of the single letter, except perhaps in the case of words beginning "arr", "err", "irr", "orr", and in the future of verbs where the "r" is doubled in the final syllable, when the rolling sound is slightly emphasized:

    irrégulier (*eer*raygüly*ay*) irregular
    je verrai (zh^e vèrr*ay*) I will see
    il courra (*eel* koorra) he will run

S - s

This consonant has two pronunciations:

First Pronunciation: s

This is the pronunciation in all cases except those noted hereafter:

seul (sè°l) alone   poisson (pwasô^n) fish

Second Pronunciation: z

When one "s" occurs between two vowels:

oser (ôzay) to dare   vision (veezyô^n) vision

In prefix *trans* followed by a vowel:

transatlantique (trâ^{n}zatlâ^{n}teek) transatlantic

The following exceptions should also be noted:

1. Final "s" is silent except in the following words:

as (âs) ace	jadis (zhadees) formerly
autobus (ôtobüs) bus	lis (lees) lily
bis (bees) encore!	mars (mars) March
gratis (gratees) gratis	ours (oors) bear
fils (fees) son	maïs (maees) maize, corn
atlas (atlâs) atlas	rébus (raybüs) conundrum
hélas! (aylas) alas!	vis (vees) screw

tous (toos) all (as a pronoun only)

2. "Sc" is pronounced s:

scène (sèn) scene   science (syâ^{n}s) science

T - t

This consonant has two pronunciations:

First Pronunciation: t

This is the normal pronunciation.

tous (toos) all (as a pronoun only)

As the final letter of a word it is unpronounced except in the following words:

abrupt (abrüpt)	Christ (kreest)
dot (dot) dowry	déficit (dayfeeseet) deficit
chut (shüt) silence!	est (èst) east
lest (lèst) ballast	granit (graneet or granee) granite

net (nèt) clean
rapt (rapt) theft
transit (trân̄zeet) transit
brut (brüt) raw (material)
but (büt or bü) object
correct (korèkt) correct

indult (èⁿdült) privilege
mat (mat) unpolished
ouest (wèst) west
tost (tost) toast
tact (takt) tact

Second Pronunciation: s

1. In endings -*tion*, -*tial*, -*tiel* and -*tieux*:

situation (seetüasyôⁿ) situation   essentiel (èsâⁿsyèl) essential
facétieux (fasaysyeᵒ) facetious

2. In verbs ending -*tier* and occasionally in the noun ending -*tie*:

balbutier (balbüsyay) to stammer
initier (eeneesyay) to initiate
prophétie (profaysee) prophesy
démocratie (daymokrasee) democracy

V - v

This letter is always pronounced: v

W - w

This consonant has two pronunciations:

First Pronunciation: v

In some words borrowed from English it will have this pronunciation:
wagon (vagôⁿ) goods wagon
wagon-lit (vagôⁿ lee) sleeping car

Second Pronunciation: w

In other words borrowed from English it will have this pronunciation:
wattman (watman) motorman
tramway (tramwè) tram, tramway

X - x

This letter has four pronunciations.

First Pronunciation: ks

The letter "x" will have this pronunciation in all cases except as noted in the following paragraphs:

sexe (sèks) sex   index (èⁿdèks) index

fixer (*feeksay*) to fix   **préfix** (pr*ayfeeks*) prefix
exception (èksèpsyô^n) exception

Second Pronunciation: **gz**

"X" will have the pronunciation **gz** when it occurs in the initial syllable "ex" followed by a vowel or by an "h":

examen (ègzamè^n) examination   **exact** (ègza) exact
exhorter (ègzort*ay*) to exhort   **exalté** (ègzalt*ay*) exalted

Third Pronunciation: **s**

In some exceptional words "x" is pronounced **s**:

soixante (swasâ^{n}t) sixty   **dix** (d*ees*) ten
six (s*ees*) six   **Bruxelles** (brüsèl) Brussels*

Fourth Pronunciation: **z**

1. In ordinals derived from *deux, six* and *dix:*

deuxième (de^{o}zyèm) second   **dixième** (d*ee*zyèm) tenth
sixième (s*ee*zyèm) sixth

2. In linking (see section on *Liaison*), "x" becomes **z:**

deux enfants (de^{o}zâ^{n}fâ^n)

"X" will be mute as the sign of the plural (in irregular plurals) or in *deux, six,* and *dix* when used before a word beginning with a vowel or mute "h":

chapeaux (*sh*apô) hats   **dix livres** (d*ee* l*ee*vr) ten books

Z - z

Normally this consonant is pronounced **z**. In final position, except in linking (see *Liaison*), it is mute.

CONSONNES DOUBLES

The following are the consonants which are often found doubled in French but pronounced as if they were single: **b, c, d, f, g, l, m, n, p, s, t;** the double **c** (cc) and double **g** (gg) form exceptions to this rule when followed by **e** or **i;** also the double **l** (ll) when preceded by **i,** and the **r** and **s;** e. g.:

accent (ak sâ^n) accent   **famille** (fam*eey*) family

* Natives of that city pronounce it (brüksèl), however.

DIPHTONGUES

When two vowels together form part of, or in themselves constitute a syllable, they are given the name of diphthong; these diphthongs, like the vowels, are divided into the *simple*, the *compound* and the *nasal*. The simple diphthongs are: **ia, iè, io, oe, ua, ue, ui;** e. g.:

ia in diable (dyabl) devil
iè in pièce (pyès) piece
io in violer (vyol*ay*) to violate
oe in moelle (mwal) marrow
ua in suave (s*üa*v) suave
ue in continue (kô^{n}teen*ü*) (he) continues
ui in cuivre (k*üe*evr) copper

DIPHTONGUES COMPOSÉES

Are those in which a simple vowel is pronounced in connection with a compound one which follows it immediately, as in:

iai (yè) in **niais** (nyè) silly
iau (yô) in **miauler** (myôl*ay*) to miaow
oue (wè) in **fouet** (fwè) a whip
oui (w*ee*) in **Louis** (*loo*cc) Louis
icu (yc^o) in **monsieur** (m^{e}sye^o) sir

DIPHTONGUES NASALES

Are those formed by the simple or the compound diphthongs followed by **m** or **n**:

ien in **orient** (orya^u) orient   **oin** in **loin** (lw*è*n′) fai
ion in **lion** (lyô^n) lion   **ouen** in **Rouen** (rwâ^n′) Rouen

SIGNES ORTHOGRAPHIQUES

The orthographical signs are: The apostrophe (*l'apostrophe*) (’), the cedilla (*la cédille*) (ç), the diæresis (*le tréma*) (··) and the hyphen, which is used to unite words as in English (*le trait d'union*) (-).

DE L'APOSTROPHE (’)

This accent is used as a substitute for the vowels **a, e** or **i,** and to prevent their union when any one of them is followed by the other.

A, for instance, is subject to elision in the article *la* preceding a vowel or silent *h:*

l'âme (lâm) the soul, and not **la âme**

E is subject to the same rule:

1. When preceding a vowel or silent *h* in the words **le, je, me, te, se, de, ce, ne** and **que**, *provided, however*, that in the case of **je, ce, le, la**, *these words do not occur immediately after a verb*; e. g.:

c'est (sè) it is, and not **ce est**
j'aime (*zh*èm) I love, and not **je aime**
l'homme (lom) man, and not **le homme**
est-ce encore vous? (ès â^{n}kor v*oo*) is that you again?

2. Whenever the words **lorsque** (lorsk^e), *when*, **puisque** (püeesk^e), *since*, or **quoique** (kwak^e), *although*, are immediately followed by **il, elle, on, un, une;** e. g.:

lorsqu'il parle (lorsk*eel* parl) when he speaks
quoiqu'on dise (kwakô^n d*eez*) although it may be said

3. Also in the words **entre** (â^{n}tr), *between*, and **presque** (prèsk^e) *almost*, whenever they enter into the formation of a compound word; e. g.:

entr'acte (â^{n}trakt) between acts
presqu'île (prèsk*eel*) peninsula

4. In the word **quelque** when used in connection with **un, une** or **autre:**

quelqu'un (kèlke^n) somebody
quelqu'autre (kèlkôtr) some other person

5. Also in the word **grande** when combined with various feminine words in their compounds; e. g.:

grand'mère (grâ^{n}mèr) grandmother
grand'peur (grâ^{n}per) great fear
grand'faim (grâ^{n}fè^n) great appetite

I is suppressed in the conjunction **si** followed by the pronouns **il** and **ils**, an apostrophe being substituted:

s'il vient (s*eel* vyè^n) if he comes
s'ils partent (s*eel* part) if they go

LA CÉDILLE (ç)

Is always used under the letter **c** when required to give it the sound of *s* before the vowels **a, o** and **u:**

façade (fasad) face (of a building) **leçon** (l^{e}sô^n) lesson

LE TRÉMA (¨)

Is used, as in English, to give a distinct sound to a letter which would not have it according to ordinary rules; e. g.:

naïf (na*eef*) innocent, instead of **naif** (n*ayf*)
Saül (saül) Saul, instead of **Saul** (sôl)

LE TRAIT D'UNION (-)

1. Is placed between the verb and the pronoun when used in the interrogative or imperative forms:

parlerons-nous? (parleiô^n n*oo*) shall we speak
donnez-moi (don*ay* mwa) give me

NOTE.—If there are two pronouns after the verb, a hyphen is used between each of them, as in:

laissez-le-moi (lès*ay* l^e mwa) leave it to me
passez-la-lui (pas*ay* la l*üee*) pass it (fem.) to him

2. It is used in collective compound words; e. g .:

c'est-à-dire (sè ta d*eer*) that is to say
tête-à-tete (tè ta tèt) tete-a-tete

3. Also before and after a euphonic *t;* e. g.:

parle-t-il? (parl^e t*eel*) does he speak?
va-t-elle? (va tel) does she go?

4. It is always used before the word **même** (mèm), *self,* preceded by a personal pronoun, as in:

moi-même (mwa mèm) myself   **lui-même** (l*üee* mèm) himself

5. With the words **ci** (s*ee*) *here,* and **là** (la) *there,* whenever they are placed after a noun or a pronoun or before a participle; e. g.:

celui-ci (sel*üee* s*ee*) this one   **celui-là** (scl*üee* la) that one

6. And lastly with the cardinal numbers in their compound forms:

dix-sept (d*ee* sèt) 17   **trente-cinq** (trâ^{n}t sè^{n}k) 35

LIAISON DES MOTS

LINKING OF WORDS   (lèzô^n day mô)

Final mute consonants, when followed by a word beginning with a *vowel* or *silent h,* are carried forward and pronounced at the beginning of this word when its meaning is intimately connected with that of the preceding one of the sentence. This is known as *liaison* in French. When carried forward according to this rule, the *s* and *x* are pronounced **z,** *d* becomes **t,** *f* becomes **v,** and *c* and *g* become **k:**

 mes amis (mayzamee) my friends
 aux armes (ôzarm) to arms
 grand homme (grâ^{n}tom) great man
 avec elle (avèkèl) with her

For the purposes of linking, words are considered to be intimately connected in the following sequences:

1. A noun and its modifiers:

les hommes importants (layzomzè^{n}portâ^n) the important men
Note these two exceptions:
First: No linking is possible between a masculine noun in the singular and a following adjective:

le port important (l^e por è^{n}portâ^n) the important port

Second: In other cases linking with a following adjective is optional:

des leçons intéressantes (day l^{e}sô^{n}zè^{n}tayrèsâ^{n}t OR
day l^{e}sô^n è^{n}tayrèsâ^{n}t) some interesting lessons

2. An adjective and a modifying adverb:

très important (trèzè^{n}portâ^n) very important

3. A pronoun subject and verb:

 nous avons (noozavô^n) we have

4. A verbal sequence:

nous comptions employer (noo kô^{n}tyô^{n}zâ^{n}plwayay) we expected to use
il n'a jamais été (eel na zhamèzaytay) he has never been
vous avez eu (voozavayzü) you have had
EXCEPTION: There is usually no linking in an inverted compound tense:
 avez-vous aimé (avay voo èmay) have you loved

5. A preposition and the word which it introduces:

sans autre explication (sân̄zôtr èkspleekasyôn̄) without any other explanation

6. Forms of *avoir* and *être* with whatever follows:

il est ici (*eelèteesee*) he is here

DIVISION DES SYLLABES

Words are divided into syllables according to the following rules:

1. Syllables should, as much as possible, begin with a consonant, as in:

Mo-ra-li-té   A-ma-bi-li-té

2. If there are two consonants together they should be divided between the syllables, as in:

hom-mo (om)   **Vil-le** (veel)   **En-ten-du** (ân̄ tân̄ dü)

3. When l or r are the second of two consonants combined, or if the combination be *gn*, both are carried forward to the beginning of the next syllable:

E-gli-se (*aygleez'*)   **Nô-tre** (nôtr)   **Vi-gne** (veeny)

4. H preceded by another consonant is always pronounced in connection with the vowel immediately following it. This occurs in:

Dé-shon-neur (day zo nèʳr)   **I-nhu-main** (eenümè)

5. The consonant *x* is always pronounced in connection with the vowel which precedes it, as in:

Ex-il (èg-zeel) exile

FRENCH-ENGLISH DICTIONARY

A

a (avoir) has
à at, to
abandonner to abandon
abeille *f.* bee
abonner, s' to subscribe
abord, d' at first
aboutir à to end in, to lead to
abréger to cut short, be brief
absent,-e absent
absenter, s' to absent oneself
abside *f.* apse
absolument absolutely
accélérateur *m.* accelerator
accent *m.* accent, stress
accepter to accept
accès interdit no trespassing
accident *m.* accident
accompagner to accompany
accord *m.* agreement
    d'... OK, agreed
    être d'... to agree
accuser to accuse
achat *m.* purchase
    faire des achats to shop
acheter to buy
acide borique *m.* boric acid
acidité *f.* acidity
acier *m.* steel
acte *m.* act
activité *f.* activity
actuel,-le present, now
actuellement at present,
    nowadays
addition *f.* bill
admiration *f.* admiration
admirer to admire
adresse *f.* address
adresser to address, to send
    s'...à to speak to someone

adulte grown up
aérien,-ne aerial, air
aérodrome *m.* airport
affaire *f.* affair, business
    ...s *f. pl.* business, things
affiche *f.* bill (of a theater)
affluence *f.* flow
    heure d'... rush hour
affranchir to free
affranchissement *m.* postage
âge *m.* age
    moyen ... Middle Ages
âgé,-e old
agence *f.* agency
    ...de voyages travel agency
agenda *m.* journal
agent (de police) *m.*
    policeman
agir to act
    s'...de to be a question of
agneau *m.* lamb
agréable agreeable, nice,
    pleasant
aider to aid, help
aiguille *f.* needle
ail *m.* garlic
aile *f.* wing
ailleurs elsewhere
    d'... moreover
aimable kind, pleasant
aimer to like, to love
    ...mieux to prefer
ainsi thus
    ...que as well as
air *m.* air, appearance
    courant d'... draft
    avoir l'...de to look like
ajouter to add
ajusté,-e adjusted, close fitting
ajuster to adjust

alentours neighborhood
aux ... de in the
neighborhood of
allemand,-e German
aller to go
...bien to be well
s'en ... to go away
...et retour round trip
ça va that's OK
allô! hello!
allonger to lengthen
s' ... to lie down
allumage m. ignition
allumer to light, to turn the
light on
allumette f. match
allure f. speed, clip
à bonne ... at a good clip
alors then, well!
altitude f. altitude
aluminium m. aluminum
amabilité f. kindness
âme f. soul
amener to bring
amer, amère bitter
américain,-e m., f. American
ami,-e m., f. friend
amidon m. starch
amoureux,-euse amorous
ample wide
ampoule f. electric light bulb
amusant,-e amusing
amuser to amuse
s' ... to have a good time
an m. year
ananas m. pineapple
ancêtre m. ancestor
ancien,-ne old, ancient, former
anglais,-e m., f. Englishman,
Englishwoman, English
(language)
Angleterre f. England
année f. year
anniversaire m. anniversary,
birthday
annoncer to announce
annuaire m. telephone book
annuler to cancel
antiquité f. antiquity
août m. August
apercevoir to perceive

s' ... de to realize
à peu près about
appareil m. device; camera
appartement m. apartment
appartenir to belong
appeler to call
s' ... to be called, named
je m'appelle my name is
appétit m. appetite
apporter to bring
apprendre to learn, to teach
appris,-e learned
(s') approcher to approach, to
come near
approfondir to go into
deeply
appuyer to support, lean, press
après after
...que after
d' ... according to
après-demain day after
tomorrow
après-midi m., f. afternoon
arbre m. tree
architecte m. architect
argent m. money, silver
argenterie f. silverware
argot m. slang
aristocratique aristocratic
arme f. weapon
armée f. army
armoire f. wardrobe
arranger to arrange
s' ... to manage to
arrêt m. stop
(s') arrêter to stop
arrière f. back, rear
à l' ... in the rear
arrivée f. arrival
arriver to arrive, happen
art m. art
artichaut m. artichoke
article m. article
artificiel,-le artificial
artiste m. artist; adj. artistic
ascenseur m. elevator
asperge f. asparagus
aspirine f. aspirin
assaisonnement m. seasoning
assemblée f. assembly

asseoir, s' to sit down
assez enough, rather
assiette f. plate
assimilé assimilated
assis,-e seated
assister à to be present at, attend
assortir to sort, to match
assurance f. assurance, insurance
assurément assuredly, surely
atelier m. workshop
attacher to attach
... du prix à to set a value on something
(s') attaquer (à) to attack
attaque f. attack
attendre to wait, to wait for
s'... à to expect
attention! watch out!
attentivement attentively
atterrir to land (an airplane)
attirer to attract, to draw
attraper to catch
au (à+le) at the, to the
... contraire on the contrary
aube f. dawn
aucun,-e any
ne ... not any, no, none
au-dessous under, underneath
au-dessus above, on top
augmenter to increase
aujourd'hui today
... même this very day
auparavant previously
auprès close to
... de f. near
au revoir good bye
aussi also, too
aussitôt immediately, soon
... que as soon as
autant as much, so much
auteur m. author
authentique authentic
autobus m. bus
automatique automatic
automne f. autumn
automobile f. automobile, car
autour around

autre other
autrefois formerly
autrement otherwise, differently
... dit in other words
auxquelles to which
avance f. advance
à l'... in advance
en ... fast, ahead of time
avancer to advance, to be fast
avant before
avant-hier day before yesterday
avec with
aventure f. adventure
avion m. airplane
avis m. opinion, notice
aviser to warn, inform
avoir to have
... l'air de to appear
... besoin to need
... faim to be hungry
... soif to be thirsty
... tort to be wrong
... chaud to be warm
avouer to confess
avril m. April

B

bachot m. slang for baccalauréat, bachelor's examination
bagage m. baggage
bague f. ring (on finger)
baguette f. wand
baigner, se to take a bath
baignoire f. bathtub
bail m. lease
bain m. bath
... de pieds foot bath
... de soleil sun bath
baisse f. subsidence, fall
en ... dropping
bal m. ball (dance)
baliverne f. twaddle
ballon m. balloon
banane f. banana
bandage m. bandage
banlieue f. outskirts, suburbs
banque f. bank
bar m. bar

barbe *f.* beard
baromètre *m.* barometer
barrer to block
barrière *f.* barrier, gate
bas,-se low
bas *m.* stocking
bassin *m.* basin
bataille *f.* battle
bateau,-x *m.* ship, boat
bâtiment *m.* building
bâton *m.* stick
beau, bel, belle beautiful, fine
beaucoup much, very much
 many
 ...de much, a great deal,
 a lot of, many
beau-frère *m.* brother-in-law
beauté *f.* beauty
bécane *f.* bicycle
belge Belgian
belle-soeur *f.* sister-in-law
bénéfice *m.* profit
béret *m.* cap
besoin *m.* need
 avoir ...de to need
beurre *m.* butter
bibliothèque *f.* library
bicyclette *f.* bicycle
bien all right, comfortable,
 very well
 ...entendu of course
 ...que although
bientôt soon
 à ... see you soon, so long
bienveillance *f.* kindness
bière *f.* beer
bijou,-x *m.* jewel
bijoutier *m.* jeweler
bijouterie *f.* jewelry
billet *m.* bill, paper money,
 ticket
 ...de passage passage, boat
 ticket
bisque *f.* shellfish soup
blague *f.* kidding (slang)
blaireau *m.* shaving brush
blanc, blanche white
blanchisserie *f.* laundry
blé *m.* wheat
bleu,-e blue
blouse *f.* blouse

bock *m.* glass of beer
boeuf *m.* beef
boire to drink
bois *m.* wood
boisson *f.* drink
boîte *f.* box
 ...de nuit *f.* night club
bon, bonne good, fine
bonhomme *m.* old fellow
bonjour good day, hello,
 good morning
bon marché cheap
bonne *f.* maid
bonsoir good evening
bonté *f.* goodness, kindness
bord *m.* edge
 ...de la mer seashore
border to border
Bottin *m.* Bottin (Paris
 telephone directory)
bouche *f.* mouth
boucher *m.* butcher
boucle *f.* curl
 ...s d'oreille earrings
boue *f.* mud
boulanger *m.* baker
boulevard *m.* boulevard
bouquet *m.* bouquet
bourse *f.* stock exchange
bout *m.* end
 tout au ...at the very end
bouteille *f.* bottle
boutique *f.* shop
bouton *m.* button
 ...de manchette cuff link
boxe *f.* boxing
bracelet *m.* bracelet
bracelet-montre *m.* wrist
 watch
bras *m.* arm
brave good, brave
bredouiller to mumble
bretelles *f.* suspenders
brillant brilliant
brique *f.* brick
briquet *m.* lighter
broder to embroider
broderie *f.* embroidery
brosse *f.* brush
 ...à dents *f.* toothbrush
bruit *m.* noise

brûler to burn
brumeux,-euse foggy
brun,-e brown
bulletin *m.* bulletin, report,
bureau,-x *m.* desk, office
... de poste post office
... de tabac cigar store
but *m.* goal
buvard *m.* blotter

C

ça that, this
c'est ... that's it, O.K.
cabaret *m.* cabaret
cabine *f.* cabine
... téléphonique telephone
booth
cabinet *m.* toilet
cable *m.* cablegram
cacahuète *f.* peanut
cadeau *m.* gift
café *m.* coffee, café
cahier *m.* notebook
caisse *f.* case, cash-box
caissier, caissière cashier
calé learned (slang)
caleçon *m.* underdrawers,
shorts
calendrier *m.* calendar
camion *m.* truck
campagne *f.* country,
campaign
à la ... in the country
faire la ... de to go through
the campaign of
canapé *m.* sofa
canard *m.* duck
caoutchouc *m.* rubber
... s *m.* rubbers
capitale *f.* capital (city)
capitonner to pad
capotage *m.* overturn, upset
capter les ondes to tune in
(a radio)
car for
caractére *m.* character
caractéristique characteristic
carafe *f.* decanter
carapace *f.* shell
carbone *m.* carbon
carotte *f.* carrot

carré square
carreau *m.* check, square
carrément plainly
carte *f.* card
... d'identité identification
card
donner les ... s to deal the
cards
... des vins wine list
carte postale illustrée *f.*
picture postcard
cas *m.* case, circumstance
casquette *f.* cap
casser to break
cathédrale *f.* cathedral
cause *f.* cause
a ... de because
causer to converse, to converse
about
cave *f.* cellar, cellar club
caviar *m.* caviar
ce it, they
ce, cet, cette this, that
ceinture *f.* belt
cela that
célèbre famous
celle *f.* the one, she, it
... -ci *f.* this one
... -là that one
celui *m.* the one
... -ci *m.* this one
... -là *m.* that one
censé supposed to
cent *m.* a hundred
pour ... per cent
centaine *f.* about a hundred
centime *m.* centime (100th
part of a franc)
centre *m.* center
au ... in the center
cependant however
céréale *f.* cereal
certainement certainly
cerveau *m.* brain, mind
ceux the ones, they
... -ci these
... -là those
chacun,-e each
chaise *f.* chair
chaise-longue *f.* deck-chair
chaleur *f.* heat

chambre *f.* room
...à coucher bedroom
chambre meublée *f.* furnished
room
chance *f.* luck
bonne... good luck
change *m.* exchange
changer to change
chanson *f.* song
chanter to sing
chapeau,-x *m.* hat
...de paille straw hat
chapelle *f.* chapel
chapitre *m.* chapter
chaque each, every
charmant,-e charming
charme *m.* charm
charpentier *m.* carpenter
chasse *f.* hunt, chase
chasser to hunt, to drive away,
to dismiss
chat *m.* cat
château *m.* castle
...fort fortress
chaud,-e hot, warm
avoir... to be hot, warm
(said of a person)
faire... to be hot, warm
(said of the weather)
chauffage *m.* heating
chauffer to heat, to warm
chauffeur *m.* driver, chauffeur
chaussette *f.* sock
chaussure *f.* shoe
chef *m.* chief, chef
chemin *m.* roadway
...de traverse crossroad,
sideroad
...de fer railroad
chemise *f.* shirt
...de nuit *f.* nightgown
chèque *m.* check
...de tourisme *m.*
travelers check
cher, chère dear, expensive
chercher to look for
envoyer... to send for
chéri,-e *m., f.* darling
cheval *m.* horse
cheveu,-eux a hair, hair
cheville *f.* ankle

chèvre *f.* goat
chevreau *m.* kid
chez at, at the house of
...Jean at John's place
...lui at his place
chic fine, elegant, grand
chichi *m.* frill
chien *m.* dog
chocolat *m.* chocolate
choisir to choose
choix *m.* choice
chose *f.* thing
chou *m.* cabbage
choux-fleur *m.* cauliflower
ciel *m.* sky
cigare *m.* cigar
cigarette *f.* cigarette
ciment *m.* cement
cinéma *m.* motion picture
house
cinq five
cinquante fifty
cinquième fifth
circulation *f.* traffic
circuler to spread, to circulate
cirer to shine (shoes)
ciseaux *m. pl* scissors
cité *f.* city
citer to quote, to cite
citoyen,-ne citizen
citron *m.* lemon
citronnade *f.* lemonade
clair,-e clear, light
clarté *f.* clarity, light
classe *f.* class
classique classical
clavier *m.* keyboard
clef *f.* key, wrench
client *m.* customer
climat *m.* climate
clinique *f.* clinic
clou *m.* nail
coeur *m.* heart
avoir mal au... to feel sick
cognac *m.* brandy
cogner to knock
coiffer to fix the hair of
se... to fix one's hair
coiffeur *m.* barber,
hairdresser
coin *m.* corner

col *m.* collar
colère *f.* anger
en ... angry
colis *m.* parcel
... postal parcel post
collaborateur *m.* collaborator
collège *m.* college, school
colonne *f.* column
combien de how many, how
  much
combinaison *f.* slip
comble *m.* top, zenith
... de malheur to top it all
comédie *f.* comedy
commander to order
comme as, like, since
... ci, ... ça so so
... il faut proper, refined
commencement *m.* beginning
au ... in the beginning
commencer to begin, to start
comment how
... va? how is ...?
commerce *m.* commerce, trade
commercial,-e business
commissariat *m.* police
  station
commode practical
commode *f.* dresser
communément commonly
communication *f.*
  communication
communiquer to communicate
compagnie *f.* company
comparaison *f.* comparison
comparer compare
compartement *m.*
  compartment
complet *m.* suit of clothes
complet, complète complete,
  full
complètement completely
complicité *f.* agir de ...
  to act in collusion
compliment *m.* compliment
compliqué,-e complicated
composer to compose
comprendre to understand
comptabilité *f.* accounting
comptant ready, in cash
payer au ... to pay cash

compte *m.* account; bill
se rendre ... to realize
compter to expect, to count
compteur *m.* meter
concert *m.* concert
concierge *m.,f.* building
  superintendent
conclure to conclude
conducteur *m.* driver
conduire to conduct, drive,
  take, lead
conduite *f.* conduct
conférence *f.* lecture
confiture *f.* jam
confort *m.* comfort
... moderne modern
  conveniences
confortable comfortable
connaissance *f.* acquaintance,
  knowledge
connaissement *m.* bill of
  lading
connaître to be acquainted
  with, to know
consacrer to devote
conscience *f.* conscience,
  mind
conseil *m.* advice, counsel
conservatoire *m.* conservatory
considération *f.* regard,
  esteem
considérer to consider
consigne *f.* checkroom (in a
  railroad station)
mettre à la ... to check
  (a parcel)
consister to consist
constamment constantly
constater to ascertain, observe
  the fact that
construire to construct, to
  build
construit constructed
consulat *m.* consulate
consultation *f.* consultation,
  visit
consulter to consult
conte *m.* story
contemporain,-e
  contemporary
content,-e happy

contenter to satisfy
se ... to be satisfied
conter to relate, to tell
continental,-aux m.
 continental
continuer to continue
contraire contrary
 au ... on the contrary
contrarié,-e upset
contraste m. contrast
 faire ... to contrast
contrat m. contract
contre against
 par ... on the other hand
contredire to contradict
 sans contredit without
 question
contrôler to check
controlleur m. ticket collector
convenable convenient
convenir to agree, to suit
convenu,-e agreed
conversation f. conversation
copie f. copy
coque f. shell (of egg)
coquet,-te dainty, trim
corbeille f. basket
cordialement cordially
cordonnier m. shoemaker
corps m. body
correspondence f. mail,
 correspondence
corridor m. corridor
corriger to correct
corsage m. blouse
costume m. suit
 ... de bain m. bathing
 suit
côte f. hill, incline, shore,
 coast
côté m. side
 du ... de in the direction of
 de l'autre ... on the other
 side
 à ... de beside
côtelette f. cutlet, chops
coton m. cotton
 ... hydrophile m.
 absorbent cotton
cou m. neck
coucher to sleep

se ... to go to sleep
chambre à ... f. bedroom
couché,-e lying down
couchette f. berth
coudre to sew
couleur f. color
coup m. stroke, blow
 tout à ... suddenly
 tout d'un ... suddenly
 ... de soleil m. sunburn
coupe f. haircut
couper to cut
 se ... to cut oneself
cour f. courtyard
couramment commonly,
 ordinarily
 parler ... to speak with
 ease, rapidly
courant current, everyday
courant m. current
 dans le ... de la semaine
 during the week
 être au ... de to be
 informed of
coureur m. runner
courir to run
couronne f. crown
courrier m. mail
cours m. course
course f. errand, race
 ... de chevaux horse race
 ... à pied foot race, track
 meet
 faire les courses to shop
court,-e short
courtisan m. courtier
cousin,-e m.,f. cousin
coussin m. pillow
coût m. cost
couteau,-x m. knife
coûter to cost
coutume f. custom, habit
couture f. sewing, tailoring
couturier dressmaker
couvert m. cover, shelter
 le temps est ... the weather
 is cloudy
couverture f. cover, blanket
couvrir to cover
craindre to fear
cravate f. tie, necktie

crayon *m.* pencil
crédit *m.* credit
  à ... on credit
créer to create
crème *f.* cream, cold cream
  ...à barbe *f.* shaving
  cream
crêpe *m.* crepe
crevaison *f.* puncture
crever to blow out (said of a
  tire)
crier to shout
crise *f.* crisis
critique critical
croire to believe, to think
cru,-e believed, thought
cuillère *f.* spoon
cuir *m.* leather
cuire to cook
cuisine *f.* kitchen
cuisinière *f.* cook
cuisse *f.* leg (of meat)
cuit,-e cooked
  bien ... well cooked
culotte *f.* panties
cure dent *m.* toothpick
curieux, -euse curious, funny,
  strange
cuvette *f.* wash basin
cylindre *m.* cylinder

D

dactylographe *m. f.* typist
dame *f.* lady
damner to damn
danger *m.* danger
dangereux,-euse dangerous
dans in, into
danser dance, to
date *f.* date
davantage more
de of, from, by, with
déballage *m.* unpacking
débarquer to disembark, to
  land
de bonne heure early
debout standing, up
débrouiller,-se to manage
décembre *m.* December
déclaration *f.* statement
déclarer to declare, to bid

décoller to take off (aviation)
décolorer to bleach
décor *m.* setting
décorer to decorate
dedans inside
défaire to undo
défendre to defend, to forbid
défense d'entrer no
  admittance
défier to challenge
degré *m.* degree
déguerpir to decamp
dehors outside
déja already
déjeuner *m.* lunch
  petit ... breakfast
déjeuner to lunch, to have
  lunch
délabré,-e dilapidated
délicat,-e delicate
délicatesse *f.* delicacy
délicieux,-euse delicious
demain tomorrow
  à ... see you tomorrow
demander to ask
  se ... to wonder
déménager to move away
demeurer to live, to reside
demi,-e half
demi-tour *m.* right about face
démocratie *f.* democracy
demoiselle *f.* young lady
démolir to demolish
dent *f.* tooth
dentelle *f.* lace
dentiste *m.* dentist
dépanneur *m.* service man,
  garage man
départ *m.* departure
dépasser to surpass
dépêche *f.* telegram
(se) dépêcher to hurry
dépendre to depend
déplacer to move
  se ... to move
déposer to set down,
  to deposit
depuis since, for
  ... que since
déranger to disturb, to
  inconvenience

dernier,-ère last
dérober to steal
  à la dérobée on the sly
derrière behind
des some, of the, from the
dès from
  ... que as early as, as soon as
désagréable unpleasant
descendre to go down, get off
désespéré,-e desperate
déshabiller, se to undress
désirer to desire, to wish
désolé sorry, dejected
dessert *m.* dessert
desservir to clear away the dishes
dessous beneath, under
dessus above, on, over
détester to dislike, to detest
destination *f.* destination
détaillé,-e detailed
détraqué,-e out of order
détromper to undeceive
dette *f.* debt
deux two
deuxième second
devant in front of, before
développer to develop
devenir to become
devoir *m.* duty, lesson
devoir to have to, to owe,
dévorer to devour
diamant *m.* diamond
différence *f.* difference
différent-e different
difficile difficult
difficulté *f.* difficulty
digestion *f.* digestion
digne worthy
dignité *m.* dignity
dimanche *m.* Sunday
dîner *m.* dinner
dîner to dine
diplôme *m.* diploma
dire to say, to tell
  à vrai ... to tell the truth
  vouloir ... to mean
direct,-e direct
directement directly
direction *f.* direction, management

discuter to argue, to discuss, to dispute
disparaître to disappear
disposer to dispose, to arrange
distance *f.* distance
distingué,-e distinguished
dit,-e said, told
divers,-e diverse, different
diviser divide
dix ten
dix-sept seventeen
docteur *m.* doctor
doigt *m.* finger
domestique *m., f.* servant
domicile *m.* home
  à ... at home
dommage *m.* damage, pity,
  c'est ... it's a pity;
  that's too bad
donc therefore
donner to give
  ... sur la rue to face the
  street
dont whose, of whom, of
  which
dormir to sleep
douane *f.* customs
  custom-house
douanier *m.* customs officer
double double
doubler to double
douche *f.* shower
douleur *f.* pain, sorrow
doute *m.* doubt
  sans ... doubtless
douter to doubt
  se ... de to suspect
doux, douce sweet
douzaine *f.* dozen
douze twelve
dramaturge *m.* dramatist
drap *m.* sheet
(se) dresser to rise up
droit,-e right
  à ... on the right
drôle funny
du (de+le) some
duc *m.* duke
dur,-e tough, hard
durer to last

E

eau *f.* water
...courrante running water
...gazeuse *f.* soda water
...minérale *f.* mineral
water
éblouir to dazzle
échange *m.* exchange
échelle *f.* ladder
éclair *m.* lightning
éclairer to light up
éclatant,-e brilliant
école *f.* school
écouter to listen (to)
écrevisse *f.* crayfish
écrire to write
écrit,-e written
écriteau *m.* sign
écrivain *m.* writer
édifice *m.* building
édition *f.* edition, publication
effet *m.* effect
en ... that's true
effets *m.* clothes, personal
effects
égal,-e equal
être ... to make no difference
égarer to mislay
s' ... to lose one's way
église *f.* church
égratignure *f.* scratch
eh bien! well!
électricité *f.* electricity
électrique electric
élégant,-e elegant
élève *m., f.* student, pupil
élevé,-e high
élever to lift, to raise
élire to elect
elle she, it, her
elles *f.* they, them
emballer to pack
embêtant,-e annoying
embarquer to embark, to sail
embouteillage *m.* traffic jam
embrasser to kiss
embrouiller to mix up
s' ... to get mixed up
emmener to take along

empaqueter to pack up
empêcher to prevent
empeser to starch
emplacement *m.* site
employé,-e *m., f.* employee
emporter to carry off
empresser, s' to hurry
en in, into, of it, of them,
some, by, on, upon, while
enchanté,-e charmed, delighted
encore yet, still
pas ... not yet
encre *f.* ink
encrier *m.* inkstand
endormir, s' go to sleep
endroit *m.* place, spot
enfance *f.* childhood
enfant *m., f.* child
enfer *m.* hell
enfermer to shut up
enfin finally
engrais *m.* fertilizer
ennuyer to annoy, to bother
s' ... to be bored
énorme enormous
énormément enormously
enraciné deeply rooted
enregistrer to check (baggage);
to register (a letter)
en retard late
ensemble together
enseigner to teach
ensuite then, afterwards
entendre to hear
...dire to hear (say)
entendu,-e heard, agreed
bien ... of course
enthousiasme *m.* enthusiasm
entier,-ère entire
entourer to surround
entre among, between
entr'acte *m.* intermission
entrée *f.* entrance
entrer to enter
...dans to enter
...en relation to get in
touch
enveloppe *f.* envelope
envelopper to wrap up
envers towards
envie *f.* fancy, desire

environs *m.pl.* surroundings, vicinity
en voiture! all aboard!
envoyer to send
... chercher to send for
épatant,-e swell, fine
épaule *f.* shoulder
épicerie *f.* grocery store
épicier, épicière *m., f.* grocer
épingle *f.* pin
épique *adj.* epic
éponge *f.* sponge
époque *f.* epoch
épreuve *f.* print
éprouver to experience, to feel, to test
erreur *f.* error, mistake
escalier *m.* stairway
(s') esclaffer to burst out laughing
espagnol,-e Spanish
espèce *f.* kind
espérer to hope
essayer to try, try on
essence *f.* gasoline
est *m.* east
estimer to value
estomac *m.* stomach
estropier to cripple
et and
établir to establish
étage *m.* floor, story
étain *m.* tin
état *m.* state, condition
Etats-Unis *m.pl.* United States
été *m.* summer
éteindre to extinguish, turn light off
éternité *f.* eternity
étoffe *f.* cloth
étoile *f.* star
étouffer to suffocate
étrange strange
étranger, étrangère foreign
etranger,-ère foreigner
être to be
... à la page to be up to date
... au courant de to be informed, to be aware of

... en train de to be in the act of, to be engaged in
étroit,-e narrow, tight
étude *f.* study
étudiant,-e student
étudier to study
européen,-ne European
eux they, them
évanouir, s' to faint
évènement *m.* event
évidemment obviously
évier *m.* sink
éviter to avoid
exact,-e exact
examen *m.* examination
examiner to examine
excepté except
exception *f.* exception
à l'... de with the exception of
exercer to exercise, train
excercice *m.* exercise, drill
excursion *f.* excursion
excuser to excuse
exemplaire *m.* duplicate, copy
exemplaire *adj.* exemplary
exemple *m.* example
par ... for example
exercer, s' to practice
expérience *f.* experience
experimenté,-e experienced
explication *f.* explanation
expliquer to explain
exportation *f.* export
exporter to export
exprès on purpose
express *m.* express train
exprimer to express
extraordinaire extraordinary
extrême extreme

F

fabrication *f.* manufacturing
fabriquer to manufacture
face *f.* face
en ... across the street
fâché,-e angry
fâcher to make angry
se ... to become angry
facile easy

façon *f.* manner, way
 de cette ... in this way
 de ... que so that
 d'une ... générale in a
  general way
facteur *m.* postman
factice artificial
facture *f.* bill (to be paid)
faible weak
faim *f.* hunger
 avoir ... to be hungry
faire to do, to make
 ... attention to pay
  attention, to be careful
 ... beau to be fine weather
 ... chaud to be hot, warm
 ... froid to be cold
 ... mal à to hurt
 ... peur à to frighten
 ... plaisir to please
 ... du soleil to be sunny
 ... du vent to be windy
 ... la toilette to get ready
  (dressed)
 ... le compte to draw up a
  bill
 ... les bagages to pack for a
  trip
 ... une promenade to take a
  walk
 ... un tour to take a walk
 se ... to become
 s'en ... to worry
 s'y ... to become used to
fait *m.* deed, fact
 au ... to the point
 en .. de as regards
falloir to be necessary, to have
 to, must
fameux,-euse famous
famille *f.* family
fatigué,-e tired
fatiguer to tire
 se ... to get tired
faute *f.* fault, mistake
fauteuil *m.* armchair
faux, fausse false, wrong
favori, favorite favorite
fée *f.* fairy
félicitation *f.* congratulation
femme *f.* wife, woman

... de chambre *f.*
 chambermaid
... de journée charwoman
fenêtre *f.* window
fer *m.* iron
 chemin de ... railroad
 ... à cheval horseshoe
fermer to close, to shut
fermeture *f.* closing, closing
 time, fastening
 ... éclair *f.* zipper
fête *f.* festival
feu *m.* fire
feuille *f.* leaf
 ... de papier sheet of paper
feutre *m.* felt, felt hat
février *m.* February
fiancé,-e betrothed
fièvre *f.* fever, temperature
figurer, se to imagine
fil *m.* thread
filer to ride (fast)
filet *m.* fillet
fille *f.* daughter
 petite ... little girl
film *m.* film, moving picture
fils *m.* son
filtre *m.* filter
fin *f.* end
finir to finish
flanelle *f.* flannel
flatter to flatter
flèche *f.* arrow, spire
fleur *f.* flower
fleuriste *m.,f.* florist
flottant,-e floating
flotter to float
foie *m.* liver
foire *f.* fair, market
fois *f.* time (in the sense of
 occurrence)
 à la at once, at the same
  time
 une ... once
 deux ... twice
foncé,-e dark
fonctionner to function,
 to work
fond *m.* bottom
fonds *m.pl.* funds
fontaine *f.* fountain

football *m.* football
forcer to force
formalité *f.* formality
forme *f.* form
en .. de in the form of
former to form
se . . . to be made up
(said of a train)
formule *f.* formula
fort,-e strong, much, very
much, hard
fou, fol, folle crazy
foule *f.* crowd
fourchette *f.* fork
fourneau *m.* stove
. . . à gaz gas stove
fourrure *f.* fur
foyer *m.* lounge, lobby,
hearth
frais, fraîche fresh, cool
fraise *f.* strawberry
franc, franche frank, sincere
franc *m.* franc (French
monetary unit)
France *f.* France
français,-e *m.,f.* Frenchman,
Frenchwoman, French
frapper to hit, strike, knock
frein *m.* brake
fréquenter to frequent
frère *m.* brother
frire to fry
froid,-e cold
froisser to wrinkle, to
crumple, to offend
fromage *m.* cheese
frontière *f.* border
fruit *m.* fruit
fumée *f.* smoke
fumer to smoke
fumeur *m.* smoking
compartment
fuselage *m.* fuselage
fur *m.* rate
au . . . et à mesure
progressively
future *m.* future

G

gaffe *f.* social, error, blunder
gagner to earn, to win

gai,-e gay
gaine *f.* girdle
galerie *f.* gallery, department
store
gallo-romain Gallo-Roman
gant *m.* glove
garage *m.* garage
garantir to guarantee
garçon *m.* boy, waiter
garder to keep
gardien *m.* guardian
gare *f.* railroad station
gare *interj.* beware!
. . . à vous watch out
garniture *f.* trimming
gastronomie *f.* gastronomy
gâteau,-x *m.* cake
gâter to spoil
gauche *f.* left
à . . . to the left
gaufre *f.* waffle
gaz *m.* gas
gelée *f.* frost
geler to freeze
gendarme *m.* policeman
général general
genou *m.* knee
gens *m.* people
gentil,-le nice, kind
géométrique geometric
gérant *m.* manager
gilet *m.* vest
glace *f.* mirror, ice cream,
ice, pane
glacé,-e iced
glacer to ice, freeze
glacière *f.* refrigerator
gloire *f.* glory
golf *m.* golf
gomme *f.* eraser
gorge *f.* throat
avoir mal à la . . . to have a
sore throat
gothique Gothic
goût *m.* taste
goûter to taste, enjoy
gouvernement *m.* government
gracieux,-euse graceful
grade *m.* degree
grand,-e big, great, large
grandement greatly

grandeur *f.* size, bigness
gras,-se fat
gratte-ciel *m.* skyscraper
gratter to scratch, scrape
grec,-que Greek
grève *f.* strike (of labor)
groom *m.* bell-boy
gros, grosse big, fat
grotte *f.* cave
guère not much
ne . . . hardly, scarcely
guérir to cure
guerre *f.* war
guichet *m.* box office
guide *m.* guide
guider to guide

H

habillement *m.* clothing
habiller, s' to dress (oneself)
habit *m.* clothes, garb
habitant *m.* inhabitant
habiter to live, dwell
habitude *f.* custom, habit
d' . . . usually
habituer, s' to get
accustomed to
*halte *f.* halt
*hameau *m.* hamlet
*haricot *m.* bean
harmonieux,-euse harmonious
*hausse *f.* rise (in prices)
*haut,-e high
en . . . upstairs, above
*haut *m.* top
*hauteur *f.* height
hélas! alas!
*héler to hail
hélices *f. pl.* propellers
herbe *f.* grass
hésiter to hestitate
heure *f.* hour, o'clock
à l' . . . on time
c'est l' . . . it's time
de bonne . . . early
tout à l' . . . shortly
heureusement fortunately
heureux, heureuse happy,
fortunate

hier yesterday
histoire *f.* history
historiographe *m.*
historiographer
historique historical
hiver *m.* winter
*homard *m.* lobster
homme *m.* man
honneur *m.* honor
honoraires *m.* fee
honorer to honor
hôpital *m.* hospital
horaire *m.* timetable
horloge *f.* public clock
horloger *m.* watchmaker
horlogerie *f.* watchmaker's
shop
*hors d'oeuvre *m.* relish
hôtel *m.* hotel
. . . de ville city hall
huile *f.* oil
humain,-c human
humidité *f.* humidity

I

ici here
par . . . this way
idée *f.* idea
ignorer to be unaware of
il he, it
. . . y a there is, there are
île *f.* island
illustre illustrious
ils they
image *f.* picture
imaginer to imagine
imberbe beardless
immédiat,-c immediate
immédiatement immediately
impatient-e impatient
impériale *f.* top deck
(of bus, etc.)
voiture à . . . double-decker
car
imperméable *m.* raincoat
importance *f.* importance
importe, n' anything; it
does not matter; I don't care
importer import, to

* An asterisk before the following words indicates that the *h* is
aspirate, allowing no elision or liaison.

impôt *m.* tax
...sur le revenu income tax
imprégner to impregnate
impressionant,-e impression
impressioner to impress
imprévu,-e unforeseen
inconnu,-e unknown
indicateur *m.* timetable
indiquer to indicate, to tell
indirect,-e indirect
individuel,-le individual
inférieur,-e inferior, lower
infini infinite
infiniment infinitely
infirmière *f.* nurse
information *f.* information
informer to inform
ingénieur *m.* engineer
injure *f.* insult
innombrable countless,
  innumerable
inonder to inundate
inquiéter, s' to become
  worried
inscrire to inscribe, write
  down
  se faire... to register
  s'...à to enroll in
insecticide *m.* insect repellent
insister to insist
installer to install, to settle
  s'... to move in
instant *m.* instant, moment
  à l'...just now
instantané *m.* snapshot
institut *m.* institute
intellectuel,-le intellectual
intelligence *f.* intelligence
intention *f.* intention,
  purpose
interdit forbidden
intéressant,-e interesting
intérêt *m.* interest
intérieur,-e interior
interprète *m.* interpreter
intersection *f.* crossing
interurbain,-e long distance
intrépide intrepid
introduction *f.* introduction
intrus *m.* intruder
inutile useless

invitation *f.* invitation
invité *m.* guest
invité invited
inviter to invite
ironique ironical
irréel,-le unreal
italien Italian
itinéraire *m.* itinerary

J

jamais never
jambe *f.* leg
jambon *m.* ham
janvier *m.* January
jaquette *f.* jacket
jardin *m.* garden
jaune yellow
je I
jeu *m.* game
  vieux... old fashioned
jeudi *m.* Thursday
jeune young
jeunesse *f.* youth, young
  people
joie *f.* joy
joli,-e pretty
jouer to play
  ...de to play (an
  instrument)
  ...à to play (a game)
joueur *m.* player
jouir de to enjoy
jouet *m.* toy
joujou,-x *m.* toy
jour *m.* day
  ...de congé holiday
journal,-aux *m.* newspaper
journalisme *m.* journalism
journée *f.* day
juillet *m.* July
juin *m.* June
jupe *f.* skirt
jupon *m.* petticoat
jusque until
jusqu'à till, until
jusqu'à ce que until
jusque-là up to then
juste just, exactly
  au... exactly
justement just, precisely
justice *f.* justice

K

kilo *m.* kilogram
kilogramme *m.* kilogram
kilomètre *m.* kilometer
kiosque *m.* newsstand, pavillion

L

la *f.* the, her, it
là there
... bas over there
... haut up there
lac *m.* lake
lacet *m.* lace
laid,-e ugly
laideur *f.* ugliness
laine *f.* wool
laisser to leave, to let
lait *m.* milk
laitue *f.* lettuce
lame *f.* blade
... à rasoir *f.* razor blade
lampe *f.* lamp
lancer to throw, to hurl
langouste *f.* crayfish
langue *f.* language, tongue
lapin *m.* rabbit
lard *m.* fat
le petit ... bacon
large broad, wide
lavabo *m.* wash basin
laver to wash
se ... to wash oneself
le *m.* the, him, it
leçon *f.* lesson
lecture *f.* reading
léger, légère *adj.* light
légume *m.* vegetable
lendemain *m.* next day
lentement slowly
lequel, laquelle, lesquels, lesquelles who, which one
les *pl.* the, them
lettre *f.* letter
... recommandée registered letter
... de crédit *f.* letter of credit
leur their, them
le ... theirs

lever to raise
se ... to get up
lèvre *f.* lip
liaison liaison, connection
liberté *f.* freedom, liberty
librairie *f.* bookstore
libre free, vacancy
licence *f.* master's degree
liège *m.* cork
lieu *m.* place
au ... de in place of
ligne *f.* line
limonade *f.* lemonade
linge de corps *m.* underwear
lire to read
lit *m.* bed
... à deux places *m.* double bed
... jumeaux *m.* twin beds
litière *f.* litter
littéraire *f.* literary
littérature *f.* literature
livraison *f.* delivery, shipment
livre *m.* book
... des recettes cash book
livre *f.* pound
livrer to deliver
loger to lodge
loi *f.* law
loin far
lointain,-e distant
long,-ue long
longtemps longtime
lorsque when
louer to rent, to praise
loup *m.* wolf
avoir une faim de ... to be dying of hunger
lourd heavy
loyer *m.* rent
lui he, her, him, to her, to him, to it
lumière *f.* light
lundi *m.* Monday
lune *f.* moon
... de miel honeymoon
lunettes *f.* eye glasses

M

M. Mr.
ma my

machine *f.* machine
...à coudre sewing machine
...à écrire typewriter
Madame, Mme Madam, Mrs.
mademoiselle Miss
magasin *m.* store
magique *adj.* magic
magnifique magnificent
mai *m.* May
main *f.* hand
maintenant now
dès... beginning now
mairie *f.* town hall
mais but
maison *f.* house
...de commerce business
firm
majesté *f.* majesty
majestueusement majestically
mal badly
pas... enough, rather well
mal *m.* harm, evil
...à la gorge *m.* sore throat
...à la tête *m.* headache
...aux dents *m.* toothache
...au ventre *m.* stomach-
ache
malade *m.,f.* sick person, sick
...imaginaire
hypochondriac
maladie *f.* sickness
malentendu *m.*
misunderstanding
malgré in spite of
malheur *m.* unhappiness
malheureusement
unfortunately
malheureux, malheureuse
m.,f. unfortunate
malle *f.* trunk
malsain,-e unhealthy
maman *f.* mother
manche *f.* sleeve
manchette *f.* cuff
mandat-poste *m.* money order
manger to eat
manicure *m.* manicurist
manque *m.* lack
manquer to miss
...de to lack, to be out of
manteau *m.* coat

marchand *m.* merchant
marchander bargain, to
marchandise *f.* merchandise
marche *f.* walking
marché *m.* market
bon... cheap
marcher to go, to walk
le faire... make it work
mardi *m.* Tuesday
mari *m.* husband
mariage *m.* marriage,
marque *f.* mark, brand
mars *m.* March
massage facial face massage
matelas *m.* mattress
matériel *m.* equipment
matin *m.* morning
matinée *f.* morning,
mauvais,-e bad
me me, to me, myself
méchant,-e bad, unimportant
médecin *m.* physician
médecine *f.* medicine
(profession)
médicament *m.* medicine (as
prescribed by a physician)
médisance *f.* slander
mélange *m.* mixture
mélanger to mix
melon *m.* melon
membre *m.* member
même same, even, self
de... likewise
de...que just as
mémoire *f.* memory
avoir bonne... to have a
good memory
mener to lead
mensonge *m.* lie
menton *m.* chin
menu *m.* menu
mer *f.* sea
merci thanks
mercredi *m.* Wednesday
mère *f.* mother
merveilleux, merveilleuse
marvellous, wonderful
mes my
mesdames *f.* ladies
message *m.* message
messieurs gentlemen

mesure *f.* measure
metal *m.* metal
métro subway
mettre to place, to put, to put on
se ... à to start
se ... au courant de to become familiar with
se ... en to dress in
meuble *m.* piece of furniture
meubler to furhish
miche *f.* loaf
midi *m.* noon
miel *m.* honey
mien, mienne mine
mieux better
le ... the best
milieu *m.* middle
au beau ... in the very middle
mille a thousand
mine *f.* appearance
avoir mauvaise ... to look bad
minuit *m.* midnight
minute *f.* minute
miroir *m.* mirror
misère *f.* misery, poverty
mode *f.* fashion, style
moderne modern
modiste *f.* milliner
moi I, me, to me
moindre least
moins less
à ... que unless
au ... at least
du ... at least
... cher cheaper
mois *m.* month
moiteur *f.* moistness
moitié *f.* half
molle soft
moment *m.* moment
en ce ... now
mon, ma, mes my
mondain wordly
monde *m.* people, world
tout le ... everybody
monnaie *f.* currency, small change
monsieur mister, sir

monter to go up, climb
montre *f.* watch
... en or goldwatch
montrer to show
monument *m.* public or historic building
moquer to mock
se ... de to make fun of
morceau *m.* bit, piece
mordre to bite
mort *f.* death
mort,-e dead
mot *m.* word
moteur *m.* engine
mouche *f.* fly
mouchoir *m.* handkerchief
mouillé,-e wet
mourir to die
moustache *f.* moustache
moustique *m.* mosquito
moutarde *f.* mustard
mouvement *m.* movement
mouton *m.* sheep
moyen average
munir to furnish, supply
mur *m.* wall
musée *m.* museum
musicien, musicienne *m., f.* musician
musique *f.* music
mystérieux, mystérieuse mysterious

N

nage *f.* swimming
nager to swim
naissance *f.* birth
nappe *f.* tablecloth
nature *f.* nature
nature *adj.* plain
naturel,-le natural
naturellement naturally
néanmoins nevertheless
nécéssaire necessary
ne ... pas not
ne ... que only
ne ... rien not anything, nothing
nef *f.* nave
neige *f.* snow
neiger to snow

n'est-ce pas? isn't it so?
net,-te clear, net
nettoyer to clean
    ...à sec to dry clean
neuf,-ve new
neuf nine
neveu *m.* nephew
ni neither
noblesse *f.* nobility
noir,-e black
noix *f.* nut
    ...de coco cocoanut
nom *m.* name
nombre *m.* number
non no, not
non plus neither
nord *m.* north
nos our
notaire *m.* notary
notamment notably
notre our
nous we, us, to us, ourselves
nous-mêmes ourselves
nouveau, nouvel, nouvelle
    new (different)
de nouveau again, anew
nouvelle *f.* news, short story
novembre *m.* November
nuance *f.* shade of meaning,
    subtle difference
nuire to be hurtful, injurious
nuit *f.* night
numéro *m.* number
    ...d'appel phone number

O

obélisque *m.* obelisk
objectif,-ive objective
objet *m.* object, thing
obliger to oblige
obscurité *f.* obscurity,
    darkness
observation *f.* observation
obtenir to obtain, to get
occupant *m.* occupant
occupation *f.* business,
    occupation
occupé,-e busy
occuper to occupy
    s'...de to take care of,

to be busy with
octobre *m.* October
octogonal octagonal
oeil *m.* eye
odeur *f.* odor, smell
oeuf *m.* egg
    ...à la coque soft-boiled
    egg
    ...sur le plat fried egg
oeuvre *f.* work
offenser to offend
officiel,-le official
offre *f.* offer
offrir to offer
oignon *m.* onion
oiseau *m.* bird
ombre *f.* shadow
ombrelle *f.* beach umbrella
omelette *f.* omelet
omettre to omit
on one, they, we, you
oncle *m.* uncle
onde *f.* wave
onduler (les cheveux) wave
    (the hair)
ongle *m.* fingernail
    faire les ...s manicure the
    nails
onze eleven
opéra *m.* opera
opinion *f.* opinion
opposer to oppose
or *m.* gold
orage *m.* storm
orange *f.* orange
ordonnance *f.* prescription
    (of a doctor)
ordre *m.* order
oreille *f.* ear
    boucle d' ...s earrings
oreiller *m.* pillow
organiser to organize
orienter to incline; to tend
    s'... to move towards,
    to direct oneself
originalité *f.* originality
os *m.* bone
oser to dare
ou or
où where

oublier to forget
ouest *m.* west
oui yes
outre-mer beyond the sea
ouvert,-e open
ouvrage *m.* work
ouvrir to open

P

paiement *m.* payment
pain *m.* bread
  petit ... roll
pair *m.* peer
paire *f.* pair
paix *f.* peace
palais *m.* palace, palate
  ... de justice court house
pâle pale
pamplemousse *m.* grapefruit
panne *f.* breakdown (of an
  automobile)
pansement *m.* dressing (*med.*)
pantalon *m.* trousers
pantoufles *f.* bedroom
  slippers
papeterie *f.* stationery store
papier *m.* paper
  ... à lettres writing paper
  ... carbone *m.*
  carbon paper
paquet *m.* package
par by, per
  ... an a year, per year
  ... jour a day, per day
  ... semaine a week, per
  week
  ... avion by air mail
paraître to appear
parapluie *m.* umbrella
parc *m.* park
parce que because
pardessus *m.* overcoat
pardon *m.* pardon
pardonner to pardon
pareil,-le same, similar, such a
parent *m.* parent
parent,-e relative
paresse *f.* laziness
paresseux,-euse lazy
parfait,-e perfect
parfaitement perfectly

parfois sometimes
parfum *m.* perfume
parisien,-ne Parisian
parler to speak
parmi among, between
parole *f.* word
part *f.* part, share
  à ... except for
  d'autre ... on the other
  hand
  quelque ... somewhere
participer to participate
particulier,-ère private
partie *f.* part
  faire ... de to be part of
partir to depart, to go away,
  to leave
  à ... de beginning with
partout everywhere
parvenir to reach
pas *m.* step, pace
  au ... de course at a run
pas not
  ... du tout not at all
passeport *m.* passport
passer to pass, to spend (time)
  se ... to take place
  se ... de to do without
passerelle *f.* gangplank
passionant,-e exciting
pâte *f.* paste
  ... dentifrice tooth paste
pâté meat paste
  ... de foie gras goose-liver
  paste
patiner to skate
pâtisserie *f.* pastry
pâtissier,-ère *m., f.* pastrymaker
patriote *m.* patriot
patron *m.* pattern, boss
paume *f.* palm (of the hand)
pauvre poor
pavillon *m.* pavilion
payer to pay
pays *m.* country
paysage *m.* scenery (in the
  countryside)
peau *f.* skin
  y laisser sa ... not to come
  out alive

pêche *f.* peach
peigne *m.* comb
peindre to paint
peine *f.* pain, trouble
 à ... hardly, scarcely
 avoir de la ... to have
 trouble, difficulty
peinture *f.* painting
pellicule *f.* film negative
pendant during
pendule *f.* wall clock
pénétrer to penetrate
pensée *f.* thought
penser to think
 ...à to think of (about)
 ...de to think of (have an
 opinion of)
pension *f.* boarding-house
 ...complète board and
 room
pente *f.* slope
percevoir to perceive
perdre to lose
père *m.* father
perfectionner, se to improve
périr to perish
permanente *f.* permanent
 wave
permettre to permit
perruque *f.* wig
personnage *m.* character
personne *f.* person
personnel,-e personal
perspective *f.* vista
persuader to persuade
peser to weigh
petit,-e little, small
pétrole *m.* petroleum
 roi du ... oil baron
peu little
 à ... près about, almost
 un tout petit ... very little
peur *f.* fear
 avoir ... to be afraid
peut-être perhaps
pharmacie *f.* pharmacy,
 drugstore
pharmacien *m.* pharmacist,
 druggist
photo *f.* photograph
phrase *f.* sentence

piano *m.* piano
pièce *f.* play, room
 ...d'identité identification
 paper
pied *m.* foot
piéton *m.* pedestrian
pilote *m.* pilot
pilule *f.* pill
pipe *f.* pipe
pire worse
 le ... the worst
pis worse
 le ... the worst
pittoresque picturesque
placard *m.* poster
place *f.* seat, square
placer to place, to put, to
 invest
plafond *m.* ceiling
plage *f.* beach
plaindre to pity
plaire to please
plaisanter to joke
plaisanterie *f.* joke
plaisir *m.* pleasure
plan *m.* map (of a city)
planche *f.* board
plancher *m.* floor
plante *f.* plant
plat *m.* dish, course
plat,-e flat
plateau *m.* tray
plate-forme *f.* platform
plein,-e full
pleuvoir to rain
pli *m.* fold
plonger to dive
pluie *f.* rain
plume *f.* pen
plupart *f.* majority, most
plus more, most
 au ... at most
plusieurs several
plutôt rather
pneu *m.* tire
pneumatique *m.* special
 delivery letter (delivered by
 underground pneumatic
 tube in Paris)
poche *f.* pocket
poème *m.* poem

poésie *f.* poetry
poète *m.* poet
poétique poetic
poids *m.* weight
point *m.* point
... de vue point of view
pointure *f.* size
poire *f.* pear
poireaux *m. pl.* leeks
poisson *m.* fish
poivre *m.* pepper
poli,-e polite
police *f.* police
politique political
pomme *f.* apple
pomme de terre *f.* potato
... en purée mashed potato
pompe *f.* pump
pont *m.* bridge
porc *m.* pork
porche *f* porch (church
architecture)
port *m.* harbor, port
porte *f.* door
... cochère carriage gateway
porte-couteau *m.* knife rest
portefeuille *m.* bill-fold
porte-monnaie *m.* change
purse
porte-plume *m.* fountain pen
porter to carry, to wear
se ... bien to be well
porteur *m.* porter
portière *f.* car door
portillon *m.* wicket (gate)
portion *f.* share, helping
poser to place, to put,
... une question to ask a
question
position *f.* position
posséder to possess
possible possible
poste *m.* radio station
poste *f.* post office
poste aérienne *f.* airmail
poste restante *f.* general
delivery
postérité *f.* posterity
potage *m.* soup
poudre *f.* powder

poudrer to powder
se ... to powder one's face
poule au riz *f.*
chicken fricassee
poulet *m.* chicken
pouls *m.* pulse
poumon *m.* lung
pour for, in order to
pourboire *m.* tip
pourquoi why
poursuivre to pursue,
to continue
pourtant however,
nevertheless
pousser to push, to grow
pouvoir to be able
pratique practical
préalablement previously
préciser to specify
préfecture *f.* departmental
capital
préfecture de police police
headquarters
préférer to prefer
préjugé prejudice
premier,-ère first
prendre to take
... par to follow
se ... à to go about (doing
something)
préparer to prepare
près near
... de near
de ... close up
présent *m.* present
à ... now
présenter to present
présomptueux, -euse
presumptuous
presque almost,nearly
presser to hurry
prêt,-e ready
prétendre to pretend, to claim
prêter to lend
prévenir to give notice,
to warn
prier to beg, pray
primer to take precedence
principal,-e principal, main
printemps *m.* spring

privé,-e private
prix *m.* price, prize
  à des... raisonnables
  reasonably priced
problème *m.* problem
prochain,-e next
procuration *f.* power of
  attorney
procurer to procure
  se... to obtain
produire to produce
  ...se to come forward
produit *m.* product
professeur *m.* professor,
  teacher
professionel,-le professional
profiter to take advantage of
profond,-e profound
programme *m.* program
projet *m.* plan
promenade *f.* promenade
  ...en voiture ride
  faire une... to take a walk
promener to promenade,
  to take for a walk
  se...à cheval to go horse-
  back riding
  se...à pied to walk
  se...en auto to take a ride
promettre to promise
propos *m.* subject;
  à... by the way
propre clean, own
proprement properly
  ...dit properly so-called
propriété *f.* property
proscrire to proscribe
protestation *f.* protest
prouver to prove
prune *f.* plum
puis then, moreover
puisque since
pyjamas m. pyjamas

Q

quai *m.* pier, dock, platform
  (of a station)
qualité *f.* quality
quand when
  ...même just the same
quant à as to, as for

quart *m.* quarter
  ...d'heure quarter-hour
quartier *m.* section (of a city)
quatorze fourteen
quatre four
quatrième fourth
que that, what, which, whom
  ce... that, which what, than
  ne... only
quel, quelle, quels, quelles
  what, which
quelque any, some
quelquefois sometimes
quelques-uns,-unes a few,
  some
qu'est-ce que? what
  ...'il y a? what is it?
  what's the matter?
question *f.* question
qui who? whom? that, which
  ce... that, which, what
quinzaine *f.* fortnight
quinze fifteen
quitter to leave, to quit
quoi? what?
  il n'y a pas de... don't
  mention it

R

raccrocher to hang up
raconter to tell (about),
  relate
radiateur *m.* radiator
radio *f.* radio
rafraîchir to refresh, to cool
rafraîchissement refreshment
railleur *m.* scoffer
raisin *m.* grapes
raison *f.* reason, right
  avoir... to be right
raisonnable reasonable
raisonner to reason
ramener to bring back
rang *m.* row; rank
rapide fast
rappeler to recall
  se... to remember
rapporter to bring back
rapprocher, se to draw
  closer to
rasant (slang) boring

raser to shave
rasoir *m.* razor
rassurer to reassure
rayonne *f.* rayon
réagir to react
réaliste realistic
recaler to flunk (reject in an examination)
récemment recently
recevoir to receive
réciter to tell, recite
recommander to recommend
... **une lettre** register a letter
reconnaissant grateful
reconnaître to recognize
reçu receipt
récupérer to recover
réduire to reduce
réel,-le real
réellement really
refaire to remake
refuser to refuse
regarder to look at
regarde, ça ne vous ... pas it's none of your business
règle *f.* rule, ruler
régler to pay (a bill); to regulate
règne *m.* reign
regret *m.* regret
reine *f.* queen
rejoindre to joint, to meet
remarquer to notice
faire ... to call one's attention to
se faire ... to attract attention
remercier to thank
remettre to postpone, to put again
remonter to go back
remplacer to replace
remplir to fill
rencontre *f.* meeting, encounter
aller à la ... de to go to meet
rencontrer to meet
rendez-vous *m.* appointment, meeting-place, engagement

rendre to give back, to render
se ... to betake oneself, to go
se ... compte to realize
se ... dans un lieu to betake oneself
renseignement *m.* information
renseigner, se inquire, to
rentrer to go back, to return
répandre to spread
réparer to repair
repas *m.* meal
repasser to iron
répertoire repertory
répéter to repeat
répondre to answer
repos *m.* rest
reposer to replace, to put again, to rest
se ... to rest
représentant *m.* representative, agent
représenter to represent
représentation *f.* performance (of a play)
repriser to mend
répugner to be distasteful
réseau *m.* network
reservoir à essence *m.* gas tank
résidence *f.* residence
résoudre to resolve
s ... to make up one's mind
respect *m.* respect
respirer to breathe
ressemblance *f.* resemblance
ressembler to resemble
ressort *m.* spring
restaurant *m.* restaurant
reste *m.* rest, remainder
rester to stay, to remain
restriction *f.* restriction
résumer to sum up
rétablir to reestablish
se ... to regain one's health
retard *m.* delay
en ... late
retarder to be slow, to delay
retenir to retain
retourner to return
se ... to turn around

retrouver to find again,
   to meet
réussir to succeed
réveil m. alarm clock
réveiller to waken
   se ... to wake up
revenir to return, come back
revenu m. income
revoir to see again
   au ... good-bye, so long
rez-de-chaussée f. ground
   floor
rhume m. cold
   attraper un ... to catch cold
rideau,-x m. curtain
riche rich
rien nothing
rire to laugh
rive f. bank (of a river)
rivière f. river
robe f. dress
rognon m. kidney
roi m. king
rôle m. part (in a play)
roman m. novel
roman adj. romanesque
romancier m. novelist
romantique m. Romanticist
romantisme m. Romanticism
rompre to break
rond,-e round
rosbif m. roast beef
rose f. rose
rôti m. roast
rôti,-e roasted
rôtir to roast
roue f. wheel
rouge red
   ... à lèvres m. lipstick
rouler to roll, to run
route f. road, route
ruban m. ribbon
rubis m. ruby, jewel (watch)
rudement deucedly, harshly
rue f. street
ruine f. ruin
russe m., f. Russian
Russie f. Russia
rustique rustic

S

sable m. sand
sac m. bag
   ... à main handbag
saignant,-e raw
saigner to bleed
saisir to seize
saison f. season
salade f. salad
sale dirty
salé,-e salted
salir to dirty
salle f. hall, room
   ... à manger dining room
   ... de bain bathroom
   ... de théâtre playhouse,
   theater
   ... d'attente waiting room
   ... des bagages baggage
   room
salon m. living-room
salutation f. greeting
samedi m. Saturday
sandwich m. sandwich
sans without
   ... que without
santé f. constitution, health
satisfaire to satisfy
sauf except
sauter to jump
sauver to save
   se ... to go, to run along
savoir to know
savon m. soap
   ... à barbe m. shaving
   soap
sceau m. seal
scène f. stage, scene
second,-e second
seize sixteen
séjour m. sojourn, stay
sel m. salt
selon according to
semaine f. week
sembler to seem
semelle f. sole (of shoe)
sens unique m. one-way street
sentiment m. sentiment
sentir to feel, to smell
   se ... to feel

sept seven
septembre *m.* September
sérieux,-euse serious
serré,-e tight
serrure *f.* lock
serviette *f.* napkin, towel
  ... hygiénique sanitary
    napkin
  ... de bain bath towel
service *m.* favor, service
  à votre ... at your service
servir to serve
  se ... de to use, to make
    use of
ses his, her
seul,-e alone
seulement only, solely
short *m.* shorts
siècle *m.* century
si yes, so
siège *m.* seat
signe *m.* sign
signer to sign
s'il vous plaît if you please
simplicité *f.* simplicity
simplement simply
sincère sincere
sincèrement sincerely
six six
ski, faire du to ski
ski *m.* ski
smoking *m.* tuxedo
soeur *f.* sister
soie *f.* silk
  ... artificielle *f.* artificial
    silk
soif *f.* thirst
soir *m.* evening
soirée *f.* evening party
soixante-dix seventy
soixante-quinze seventy-five
soldat *m.* soldier
soleil *m.* sun
  le lever du ... sunrise
  le coucher du ... sunset
sombre dark
somme *f.* sum
  en ... in short
somptueux,-euse sumptuous
son his, her, its
sonder to feel out

sonner to sound, ring
sonnette *f.* bell, buzzer
sorte *f.* kind, type
  de ... que so that
sortie *f.* exit
sortir to go out
souci *m.* worry
soudain sudden
souffle *m.* breath
souffrir to suffer
souhaiter to wish
soulier *m.* shoe
soupe *f.* soup
souper *m.* supper
souper to have supper
sourd,-e deaf
sourire *m.* smile
sous under
souscrire to subscribe
soutien *m.* support
soutien-gorge *m.* brassiere
souvenir remembrance
  se ... de to remember
souvent often
spectacle *m.* spectacle, show
spectateur *m.* spectator
sport *m.* sport
sportif,-ve sporting
subordonner to subordinate
subventionner to subsidize
succursale *f.* branch
  (of a firm)
sucre *m.* sugar
sucré,-e sweet
sucrier *m.* sugar bowl
sud *m.* south
suffire to suffice
Suisse *f.* Switzerland
suisse *adj.* Swiss
suite *f.* continuation, suite
  tout de ... immediately,
suivant,-e following
suivre to follow
  ... un cours to attend a
    course
sujet *m.* subject
supérieur,-e superior
supprimer to suppress
sur on
sûr, sûre sure

surhumain,-e superhuman
sur-le-champ on the spot, right away; right there and then
sur mesure custom made
surprendre to surprise
surprise *f.* surprise
surtout above all, especially
surveiller to supervise, to watch
sympathie *f.* sympathy
sympathique likable
sympthôme *m.* symptom
syndicat *m.* syndicate, union (of workers)
synonyme *m.* synonym
système *m.* system

T

tabac *m.* tobacco
  bureau de ... tobacco store
table *f.* table
tableau *m.* picture, painting
tablier *m.* apron
tâcher to try
taille *f.* waist, stature
tailler to cut
tailleur *m.* tailor
  costume ... woman's suit
talent *m.* talent
talon *m.* heel
tandis que whereas
tant so many, so much
  ... de so many, so much
  ... que as long as
tante *f.* aunt
tapis *m.* rug
tard late (in the day)
tarder to delay, to defer
  ... à to be late in, to delay, to put off
  ... de to be anxious to
tarte *f.* pie
tas *m.* pile, lot
tasse *f.* cup
taux *m.* rate
  ... de change rate of exchange
taxe *f.* tax
taxi *m.* taxi
teindre to dye
tel,-le such a

téléphone *m.* telephone
  coup de ... telephone call
téléphoner to telephone
téléphoniste *m., f.* telephone operator
tellement so, so much
témoin *m.* witness
tempête *f.* storm
temps *m.* time, weather,
  à ... on time
  de ... en ... once in a while
  en même ... at the same time
tendance *f.* tendency
tendancieux,-euse tendentious
tendre tender
tenir to hold
  ... à to be anxious to, to be fond of
  ... compte to take into account, to heed
  ... de to resemble, to take after
tennis *m.* tennis
tenter to tempt
terminus *m.* terminal
terrasse *f.* terrace, sidewalk café
tête *f.* head
  avoir mal à la .... to have a headache
thé *m.* tea
théâtre *m.* theater
thermomètre *m.* thermometer
tiens well!, indeed!
tiers *m.* third
timbre *m.* stamp
tirer to pull
  se ... d'affaire to get along, to manage
  se bien ... de to come off well
  ... d'un mauvais pas to get out of a bad fix
tissu *m.* cloth
toile *f.* linen
toilette *f.* toilet
  faire sa ... to get dressed
toit *m.* roof
tomate *f.* tomato
tombeau *m.* tomb

tomber to fall
torrent *m.* torrent
à ... s pouring
tort *m.* wrong
avoir ... to be wrong
torturer to torture
tôt soon, early
toucher to cash, to touch
toujours always, still
tour *f.* tower
tour *m.* tour, trip, turn
tourelle *f.* turret
tourne-vis *m.* screw-driver
tourner to turn
tournoi *m.* tournament
tout-e, tous, toutes all, every
.... à coup suddenly
.... à fait entirely
... d'un coup suddenly
... de même anyhow, just
the same
toux *f.* cough
trac *m.* stage fright
trahir to betray
train *m.* train
en ... de in the act of
traire to milk
trait *m.* trait
traite *f.* draft (commercial)
traiter to treat
trajet *m.* trip
tramway *m.* trolley
tranche *f.* slice
transaction *f.* transaction
transatlantique transatlantic
un train ... a transatlantic
boat train
transpiration *f.* perspiration
transporter to transport, carry
travail *m.* work
travailler to work
travers *m.* breadth
à. .. across, through
traversée *f.* crossing
traverser *f.* cross
trempé,-e soaked
très very
trêve *f.* truce
... de enough
triste sad
tristesse *f.* sadness

tromper to deceive
se ... to be wrong
trop too, too much
trottoir *m.* sidewalk
trouver to find
se ... to be (in a place)
tu you
tutelle *f.* tutelage
tutoyer to address familiarly,
as tu

U

un,-e *m. f.,* a, an, one
uniformité *f.* uniformity
uniquement exclusively
université *f.* university
urgence *f.* urgency
us *m. pl.* usages
... et coutumes ways and
customs
usage *m.* use costum
usine *f.* factory, plant
utile useful
utiliser to use

V

vacances *f.pl.* vacation,
cours de ... summer session
vaisselle *f.* the dishes
vaguement vaguely
valable valuable
valeurs *f.* valuables, securities
valise *f.* suitcase, valise
vallée *f.* valley
valoir to be worth
... mieux to be better
(preferable)
... la peine to be worth
the trouble
vapeur *f.* steam
veau *m.* veal
véhicule *m.* vehicle
veine *f.* luck
avoir de la ... to be lucky
velours *m.* velvet
vendeuse *f.* saleslady
vendre to sell
vendredi *m.* Friday
venger to avenge
venir to come
... de to have just

vente *f.* sale
vergogne *f.* shame
vérité *f.* truth
verre *m.* glass
vers about, toward
vert,-e green
vertige *m.* dizziness
veste *f.* jacket
vestiaire *m.* checkroom,
cloakroom
veston *m.* sport coat
vêtement *m.* dress, garment,
clothes
veuillez please
viande *f.* meat
...**frigorifiée** frozen meat
vie *f.* life, living
vieillesse *f.* old age
vieux, vieil, vieille old
vieux jeu old-fashioned
vif, vive alive
ville *f.* city, town
en pleine... in the center
of the city
vin *m.* wine
vinaigre *m.* vinegar
vingt twenty
vingtaine *f.* about twenty
vis *f.* nut
visa *m.* visa
visage *m.* face
visière *f.* vizor
visite *f.* visit
...**douanière** *f.* customs
examination
visiter to visit
visiteur *m.* visitor
vite quickly, fast

vitrail,-aux *m.* stained glass
window
voici here is, here are
voie *f.* way, track
voilà there is; well!, there you
are!
voir to see
voisin,-e *m. f.*, neighbor,
neighboring
voiture *f.* automobile,
carriage, railway car
voix *f.* voice
volant *m.* steering wheel
voler to fly, to steal
volontiers willingly
vos your
votre your
vôtre yours
vouloir to want
...**bien** to be willing
vous you
voyage *m.* trip
voyager to travel
voyageur,-euse *m.* traveler
vrai,-e true
vraiment truly, really
vue *f.* sight, view, eyesight

W X Z

wagon *m.* railroad car
wagon-lit *m.* sleeping-car
wagon-restaurant *m.* dining
car
y there (place already
mentioned)
y a-t-il? is there? are there?
zéro *m.* zero

ENGLISH-FRENCH
DICTIONARY

A

a un, une
able, to be pouvoir
about à peu près
above au-dessus, dessus
absent absent,-e
absolutely absolument
absorbent cotton coton
 hydrophile m.
accelerator accélérateur m.
accept accepter
accent accent m.
accident accident m.
accompany accompagner
according to selon
account compte m.
accuse, to accuser
accustomed, to be habituer
acquaintance connaissance f.
across à travers
across the street en face
act, to agir
act acte m.
activity activité f.
address adresse f.
address, to adresser
address familiarly, to tutoyer
admire admirer
advice, conseil m.
afraid, to be avoir peur
after après
afternoon après-midi f.
afterwards ensuite
again de nouveau
against contre
age âge m.

agent représentant m.
agree, to être d'accord
agreeable agréable
airplane avion m.
air line route aérienne f.
airplane avion m.
airport aérodrome m.
air mail par avion
air sickness mal de l'air m.
air valve soupape d'air f.
alarm clock réveil m.
alcohol alcool m.
alive vif, vive
all tout, tous
all aboard! en voiture!
almost presque
alone seul,-e
already déjà
also aussi
always toujours
America Amérique f.
American américain,-e
amiable aimable
among parmi, entre
amusing amusant,-e
and et
angry fâché,-e
announce annoncer
annoying ennuyeux,-euse
answer réponse f.
answer, to répondre
any aucun,-e
anyhow tout de même
apartment appartement m.
appear paraître
appearance air m.
appetite appétit m.

apple pomme *f.*
appointment rendez-vous *m.*
approach, to approcher
approximately à peu près
April avril *m.*
argue discuter
armchair fauteuil *m.*
arrange arranger
arrival arrivée *f.*
arrive arriver
art art *m.*
artificial artificiel,-le
as comme
as for quant à
as much autant
as soon as aussitôt que,
   dès que
as to quant à
ask, to demander
ask a question, to
   poser une question
asparagus asperge *f.*
aspirin aspirine *f.*
at chez, à
attach attacher
attack, to attaquer
August août *m.*
aunt tante *f.*
authentic authentique
author auteur *m.*
automatic automatique
automobile voiture *f.*
avenue avenue *f.*
average moyen,-ne
avoid éviter

B

bacon petit lard *m.*
bad mauvais,-e
badly mal
bag sac *m.*
baggage bagage *m.*
   ...check bulletin de
   bagage
baker boulanger *m.*
ball *(dance)* bal *m.*
banana banane *f.*
band-aid pansement *m.*
bandage bandage *m.*
bank banque *f.*

bank *(of a river)* rive *f.*
bar bar *m.*
barber coiffeur *m.*
bargain, to marchander
barometer baromètre *m.*
barrel tonneau *m.*
basin bassin *m.*
basket corbeille *f.*
bath bain *m.*
bathe se baigner
bathing suit
   costume de bain *m.*
bathroom salle de bain *f.*
bathtub baignoire *f.*
be, to être
beach plage *f.*
beach umbrella ombrelle *f.*
bean haricot *m.*
beard barbe *f.*
beautiful beau, bel, belle
beauty beauté *f.*
because parce que, à cause de
become, to devenir
bed lit *m.*
bedroom chambre à coucher *f.*
bedroom slippers pantoufles *f.*
bee abeille *f.*
beef boeuf *m.*
beer bière *f.*
before avant
beg, to prier
begin commencer
beginning commencement *m.*
beginning with à partir de
behavior conduite *f.*
behind derrière
Belgian belge
believe croire
bell sonnette *f.*
bell-boy chasseur *m.*
belong appartenir
berth couchette *f.*
best, the le meilleur
better *adv.* mieux
better *adj.* meilleur,-e
between entre
beware *interj.* gare
bicycle bicyclette, bécane *f.*
big grand,-e
bill addition *f.* (restaurant);
   facture (all else)

bill (cash) billet *m.*
bill-fold portefeuille *m.*
bird oiseau *m.*
birth naissance *f.*
birthday anniversaire *m.*
bite, to mordre
bitter amer,-ère
black noir,-e
blade lame *f.*
blanket couverture *f.*
bleach, to faire décolorer
bleed saigner
blouse blouse *f.*
blow coup *m.*
blow out, to crever
blue bleu,-e
blunder gaffe *f.*
boarding-house pension *f.*
boat bateau *m.*
body corps *m.*
boiled bouilli,-e
bolt boulon *m.*
bone os *m.*
book livre *m.*
bookstore librairie *f.*
border frontière *f.*
border, to border
bored, to be s'ennuyer
boric acid acide borique *m.*
boring rasant (slang)
boss patron *m.*
bother, to ennuyer
bottle bouteille *f.*
bottom fond *m.*
box boîte *f.*
box office guichet *m.*
boy garçon *m.*
bracelet bracelet *m.*
brake frein *m.*
branch (of tree) branche *f.*
branch (of a firm) succursale *f.*
brand marque *f.*
brandy cognac *m.*
brassiere soutien-gorge *m.*
breakfast petit déjeuner *m.*
bread pain *m.*
breadth travers *m.*
break, to casser
breakdown (of an automobile)
   panne *f.*
breath souffle *m.*

breathe respirer
bridge pont *m.*
bring apporter
bring back ramener
   rapporter
broken (out of order)
   detraqué,-e
brother frère *m.*
brush brosse *f.*
build, to construire
building bâtiment, édifice *m.*
bus autobus *m.*
business affaires *f.pl.*
business commercial,-e
business firm
   maison de commerce *f.*
busy occupé,-e
but mais
butter beurre *m.*
button bouton *m.*
buy, to acheter
buzzer sonnette *f.*
by par

C

cabaret cabaret *m.*
cabbage chou *m.*
cabin cabine *f.*
cablegram cable *m.*
cake gâteau,-x *m.*
call appeler
campaign campagne *f.*
cancel, to annuler
cap casquette *f.*
capital capital *m.*
car auto *f.*
car door portière *f.*
carbon carbone *m.*
carburetor carburateur *m.*
card carte *f.*
carpenter charpentier *m.*
carrot carotte *f.*
carry porter
carry off emporter
case cas *m.*
cash a check encaisser un
   chèque
castle chateau,-x *m.*
cat chat *m.*

catch attraper
cathedral cathédrale *f.*
cauliflower choux-fleur *m.*
cause cause *f.*
cave grotte *f.*
caviar caviar *m.*
ceiling plafond *m.*
celebrate, to célébrer
cellar cave *f.*
cement ciment *m.*
center centre *m.*
central heating chauffage
  central *m.*
century siècle *m.*
cereals céréales *f. pl.*
certainly certainement
chair chaise *f.*
chalk craie *f.*
chambermaid femme de
  chambre *f.*
change monnaie *f.*
change, to changer
change purse porte-monnaie
  m.
chapel chapelle *f.*
chapter chapitre *m.*
character caractère,
  personnage *m.*
characteristic caractéristique
charm charme *m.*
charmed enchanté,-e
charming charmant,-e
cheap bon marché
cheaper moins cher
check chèque *m.*
check, to contrôler, voir
checkroom consigne *f.*
  vestiaire *m.*
cheese fromage *m.*
chef chef *m.*
chest caisse *f.*
chicken fricassee poule au riz
  f.
chief chef *m.*
child enfant *m. f.*
chin menton *m.*
chocolate chocolat *m.*
choice choix *m.*
choose choisir
chop côtelette *f.*
church église *f.*

cigar cigarre *m.*
cigarette cigarette *f.*
city ville *f.*
city hall hôtel de ville *m.*
claim, to prétendre
clarity clarté *f.*
class classe *f.*
classical classique
climate climat *m.*
clean, to nettoyer
clean propre
clear clair,-e, net,-te
clear the table desservir
climb monter
clinic clinique *f.*
cloakroom vestiaire *m.*
clock horloge *f.*
close, to fermer
close fitting ajusté,-e
closing fermeture *f.*
cloth étoffe, tissue, toile *f.*
clothes vêtements *f. pl.*
  toile *f.*
clothing habillement *m.*
cloud nuage *m.*
coat manteau *m.*
coffee café *m.*
cold froid,-e
cold (head) rhume *m.*
collar col *m.*
color couleur *f.*
column colonne *f.*
comb peigne *m.*
comb (hair) coiffer
  (les cheveux)
come venir
comedy comédie *f.*
comfort confort *m.*
comfortable confortable
commerce commerce *m.*
commonly communément
communicate, to
  communiquer
communication
  communication *f.*
company compagnie *f.*
compare, to comparer
comparison comparaison *f.*
compartment compartiment
  m.

complete complet,-ète
completely complètement
complicated compliqué,-e
compliment compliment m.
concert concert m.
conclude to conclure
condition état f.
congratulation félicitation f.
conservatory conservatoire m.
consider, to considérer
consist, to consister
constantly constamment
consulate consulat m.
consult, to consulter
consultation consultation f.
continental continental,-aux
continuation suite f.
continue, to continuer
contract contrat m.
contradict contredire
contrary contraire m.
contrast contraste m.
convenient convenable
conversation conversation f.
converse, to causer
cook cuisinier,-ère m.,f.
cook, to cuire
cooked cuit,-e
cool frais, fraîche
copy copie f.
copy (duplicate) exemplaire
m.
cordially cordiallement
cork liège m.
corner coin m.
correct, to corriger
corridor corridor, m.
cost prix m.
cost, to coûter
cotton coton m.
cough toux f.
count compter
countless innombrable
country campagne f.
pays m.
course (in school) cours m.
course plat m.
court house palais de justice
m.
courtier courtisan m.
courtyard cour f.

cousin cousin m., -e f.
cover couvert m.
cover, to couvrir
cow vache f.
cray-fish langouste f.
crazy fou, folle
cream crème f.
cream one's face, to
se pommader
create, to créer
credit crédit m.
crisis crise f.
critical critique
cross, to traverser
crossing traversée f.
crowd foule f.
cuff manchette f.
cuff link bouton de manchette
m.
cup tasse f.
cure, to guérir
curl boucle f
currency monnaie f.
current courant
curtain rideau m.
custom coutume f.
custom-house douane f.
custom made sur mesure
customer client m.
customs douane f.
customs examination
visite douanière f.
customs officer douanier m.
cut, to couper, tailler
cutlet côtelette f.
cylinder cylindre m.

D

dainty coquet,-te
damage dommage m.
damn, to damner
damp humide
dance, to danser
danger danger m.
dangerous dangereux,-euse
dare, to oser
dark sombre, foncé,-e
darkness obscurité f.
darling chéri,-e
date date f.
daughter fille f.

dawn aube *f.*
day jour *m.* journée *f.*
dead mort,-e
deaf sourd,-e
dear cher, chère
death mort *f.*
debt dette *f.*
decanter carafe *f.*
deceive, to tromper
December décembre *m.*
deck-chair chaise-longue *f.*
declare déclarer
decorate décorer
deed fait *f.*
defend défendre
degree degré, grade *m.*
delay retard *m.*
delay, to retarder
delicacy délicatesse *f.*
delicate délicat,-e
delicious délicieux,-euse
deliver livrer
delivery livraison *f.*
demolish, to démolir
dentist dentiste *m.*
depart, to partir
departmental capital
   préfecture *f.*
departure départ *m.*
depend, to dépendre
deposit, to déposer
desire, to désirer
desk bureau *m.*
dessert dessert *m.*
destination destination *f.*
detailed détaillé,-e
detective policier *m.*
detest, to détester
develop, to développer
devote, to consacrer
diamond diamant *m.*
dictionary dictionnaire *m.*
die, to mourir
difference différence *f.*
difference, make no être égal
different différent,-e, divers,-e
difficult difficile
difficulty difficulté *f.*
digestion digestion *f.*
dine, to dîner

dining-car wagon-restaurant
   m.
dining-room salle à manger
dinner dîner *m.*
diploma diplôme *m.*
direct direct,-e
directly directement
dirty, to salir
dirty sale
disappear, to disparaître
discover, to découvrir
discuss, to discuter
disembark débarquer
disgust repulsion *f.*
dish plat *m.*
dishes vaisselle *f.*
distance distance *f.*
distant lointain,-e
distinguished distingué,-e
disturb déranger
dive, to plonger
divide diviser
dizziness vertige *m.*
do, to faire
dock quai *m.*
doctor médecin *m.*
   docteur *m.*
door porte *f.*
double double
double to doubler
double bed lit à deux places
   m.
doubt doute *m.*
doubt, to douter
down à bas
dozen douzaine *f.*
draft courant d'air *m.*
draft (commercial) traite *f.*
dramatist dramaturge *m.*
draw closer, to se rapprocher
dress robe *f.*
dress, to habiller
dressmaker couturier *m.*
dressed, to get faire sa toilette,
   s'habiller
dresser commode *f.*
dressing gown robe de
   chambre *f.*
drink, to boire
drink boisson *f.*
drive, to conduire

driver chauffeur, conducteur *m.*
driver's license permis de conduire *m.*
drugstore pharmacie *f.*
druggist pharmacien *m.*
dry clean, to faire nettoyer à sec
duck canard *m.*
during pendant
duty devoir *m.*
dwell, to habiter
dye, to faire teindre

E

each chacun,-e, chaque
ear oreille *f.*
early tôt
earn gagner
earring boucle d'oreille *f.*
easily facilement
east est *m.*
easy facile
eat manger
edge bord *m.*
effect effet *m.*
egg oeuf *m.*
    soft-boiled . . .oeuf à la coque
    fried . . . oeuf sur le plat
eight huit
eighteen dix-huit
eighth huitième
elbow coude *m.*
elect élire
electric électrique
electricity électricité *f.*
elegant élégant,-e, chic
elevator ascenceur *m.*
eleven onze
elsewhere ailleurs
embark s'embarquer
embroider, to broder
employee employé,-e *m., f.*
empty vide
end bout *m.*, fin *f.*
engine moteur *m.*
engineer ingénieur *m.*
England Angleterre *f.*
English anglais,-e

enjoy jouir de
enormous énorme
enormously énormément
enough assez
enter, to entrer
enthusiasm enthousiasme *m.*
entire entier,-ère
entirely entièrement
entrance entrée *f.*
envelope enveloppe *f.*
epoch époque *f.*
equal égal,-e
equipment matériel *m.*
eraser gomme *f.*
error erreur *f.*
especially surtout
establish établir
evening soir *m.*
    soirée *f.*
event évènement *m.*
everybody tout le monde
everywhere partout
exact exact,-e, exactement
exactly au juste
examination examen *m.*
examine examiner
example exemple *m.*
    for . . . par exemple
excellent excellent,-e
except sauf,excepté
exception exception *f.*
excess luggage bagage en excédent *m.*
exchange échange *m.*
exchange, to échanger
exciting passionant,-e
exclusively uniquement
excursion excursion *f.*
excuse excuser
excuse me pardonnez-moi
exercise exercice *m.*
exit sortie *f.*
expensive cher, chère
experience expérience *f.*
experience, to éprouver
experienced expérimenté
explain expliquer
explanation explication *f.*
export, to exporter
express, to exprimer
expression expression *f.*

extinguish éteindre
extraordinary extraordinaire
extreme extrême
eye oeil m.
eye glasses lunettes f.
eyesight vue f.

F

face figure f., visage m.
face massage massage facial
factory usine f.
faint, to s'évanouir
fall, to tomber
Fall automne f.
false faux, fausse
family famille f.
famous célèbre, fameux,-euse,
  illustre
far loin
fare prix du billet m.
fashion mode f.
fast vite, rapide
fat gros,-se
fat gras m.
father père m.
favor service m.
favorable favorable
favorite favori,-ite
fear peur f.
fear, to craindre
February février m.
fee honoraires m., pl.
feel, to se sentir, sentir
feel out, to sonder
feel sick, to avoir mal au coeur
felt hat feutre m.
fertilizer engrais m.
festival fête f.
fever fièvre f.
fifteen quinze
fifth cinquième
fifty cinquante
fill, to remplir
fillet filet m.
film rouleau m.
film negative pellicule f.
filter filtre m.
finally enfin
find trouver
find again retrouver

find out (about) se renseigner
finger doigt m.
finger nail ongle m.
finish finir
fire feu m.
first premier,-ère
first (at) d'abord
fish poisson m.
fish, to pêcher
fishing pêche f.
five cinq
flannel flanelle f.
flat plat,-e
flatter, to flatter
flight vol m.
float, to flotter
floor étage m., plancher m.
floor, first rez-de-chaussée m.
florist fleuriste m., f.
flower fleur f.
fluently couramment
fly mouche f.
fly, to voler
foggy brumeux,-euse
fortress château fort m.
fold pli m.
follow suivre
following suivant,-e
fond of, to be tenir à
foot pied m.
football football m.
for car, pour
forbid défendre
forbidden interdit,-e
force, to forcer
foreign étranger,-ère
foreigner étranger,-ère m., f.
fork fourchette f.
forget oublier
form, to former
form forme f.
formality formalité f.
formerly autrefois
formula formule f.
fortress château fort m.
fortunately heureusement
fountain fontaine f.
fountain pen porte-plume m.
four quatre
fourteen quatorze

fourth quatrième
franc franc *m.* (money)
France France *f.*
free libre
freedom liberté *f.*
freeze, to geler
French français,-e
fresh frais, fraîche
Friday vendredi *m.*
friend ami,-e *m., f.*
frighten faire peur à
frill chichi *m.*
frost gelée *f.*
fruit fruit *m.*
fry, to frire
function, to fonctionner
funds fonds *m.pl.*
funny drôle
fur fourrure, *f.*
furnish fournir, meubler
furnished room chambre
   meublée *f.*
furniture (piece of) meuble *m.*

G

gallery galerie *f.*
game jeu *m.*
gang plank passerelle *f.*
garage garage *m.*
garage man dépanneur *m.*
garden jardin *m.*
garlic ail *m.*
garment vêtement *m.*
garters jarretières *f.*
gas gaz *m.*
gasoline essence *f.*
gas tank réservoir à essence
   m.
gastronomy gastronomie *f.*
gate barrière *f.*
gauze bandage
   gaze hydrophile *f.*
gay gai,-e
general général,-e
general delivery poste
   restante *f.*
generally généralement
gentlemen messieurs
geometric géométrique
get up, to se lever

gift cadeau m.
girdle gaine *f.*
girl jeune fille *f.*
give, to donner
give back rendre
glass verre *m.*
glory gloire *f.*
glove gant *m.*
go aller
go down, to descendre
go out, to sortir
go up, to monter
goat chèvre *f.*
God Dieu
gold or *m.*
golf golf *m.*
good bon,-ne
good-bye au revoir
good day bonjour
good evening bonsoir
good luck bonne chance
good morning bonjour
government gouvernement
   m.
graceful gracieux,-euse
grape raisin *m.*
grapefruit pamplemousse *m.*
grateful reconnaissant,-e
grass herbe *f.*
gravy jus *m.*
great grand,-e
Greek grec,-que
green vert,-e
greeting salutation *f.*
grocery store épicerie *f.*
grow, to croître, pousser,
   grandir
guarantee to garantir
guardian gardien *m.*
guest invité *m.* or *f.*
guide, to guider
guide guide *m.*

H

habit coutume *f.*
haircut coupe *f.*
hairdresser coiffeur *m.*
half demi,-e, moitié *f.*
hail, to héler
hall porter garçon *m.*

halt halte *f.*
ham jambon *m.*
hamlet hameau *m.*
hand main *f.*
handbag sac à main *m.*
handkerchief mouchoir *m.*
handlebar guidon *m.*
hang up raccrocher
happy content,-e, heureux,
  -euse
harbor port *m.*
hard dur,-e
harmful, to be nuire à
harmonious harmonieux,-euse
harshly rudement
hat chapeau,-x
have, to avoir
have to, to devoir, falloir
he il
head tête *f.*
headache mal à la tête *m.*
health santé *f.*
healthy sain,-e
hear entendre
heart coeur *m.*
hearth foyer *m.*
heat chaleur *f.*
heat, to chauffer
heating chauffage *m.*
heavy lourd
heel talon *m.*
height hauteur *f.*
hell enfer *m.*
hello bonjour
help, to aider
helping portion *f.*
her elle, son, sa
here ici
here is, are voici
hesitate, to hésiter
hide, to cacher
high haut,-e, élevé,-e
high school collège *m.*,
  lycée *m.*
hill côte *f.*
hire, to louer
historical historique
history histoire *f.*
hit, to frapper
hitchhike, to faire de l'auto-
  stop

hold, to tenir
holiday jour de congé *m.*
holidays vacances *f.*
home domicile *m.*
honey miel *m.*
honeymoon lune de miel *f.*
honor, to honorer
honor honneur *m.*
hope, to espérer
horse cheval,-aux *m.*
horse-cab fiacre *m.*
hospital hôpital *m.*
hot chaud,-e
hotel hôtel *m.*
hour heure *f.*
house maison *f.*
how comment
how many combien
how much combien
however cependant, **pourtant**
human humain,-e
humidity humidité *f.*
humor humour *m.*
hundred cent *m.*
hunger faim *f.*
hungry, to be avoir faim
hungry affamé,-e
hunting chasse *f.*
hurry, to se dépêcher
hurt, to faire mal
husband mari *m.*

I

I je
ice glace *f.*
ice-cream glace *f.*
idea idée *f.*
identification card carte
  d'identité *f.*
identification paper pièce
  d'identité *f.*
identify, to identifier
identity identité *f.*
if si
ignition allumage *m.*
imagine, to se figurer,
  imaginer
immediate immédiat,-e
immediately tout de suite
  immédiatement
impatient impatient,-e

import importation *f.*
import, to importer
importance importance *f.*
impress impressioner
impression impression *f.*
impressive impressionant,-e
improve, to se perfectionner
in dans, en
in front of devant
in order to pour
income revenu *m.*
income tax impôt sur le
revenu *m.*
inconvenience, to déranger
increase augmenter
indicate, to indiquer
indirect indirct,-e
indirectly indirectement
individual individuel,-le
inferior inférieur
infinite infini,-e
infinitely infiniment
inform aviser
information renseignement *m.*
information *f.*
informed, to be être au courant de
inhabitant habitant *m.*
ink encre *f.*
inquire, to se renseigner
inscribe inscrire
insect repellent insecticide *m.*
inside dedans
insist, to insister
institute institut *m.*
insult injure *f.*
insurance assurance *f.*
intellectual intellectuel,-le
intelligence intelligence *f.*
intention intention *f.*
interest intérêt *m.*
interesting intéressant,-e
interior intérieur,-e
intermission entr'acte *m.*
interpreter interprète *m.*
intrepid intrépide
introduction introduction *f.*
intruder intrus *m.*
invitation invitation *f.*
invite inviter
invited invité,-e

iodine iode *m.*
iron fer *m.*
iron, to repasser
ironical ironique
island île *f.*
it il, elle
Italian italien,-ne
itinerary itinéraire *m.*

J

jack cric *m.*
jacket veste, jaquette *f.*
jam confiture *f.*
janitor concierge *m.,f.*
January janvier *m.*
jewel bijou,-x *m.*
jeweler bijoutier *m.*
join rejoindre
joke plaisanterie *f.*
joke, to plaisanter
journal (personal) agenda *m.*
joy joie *f.*
July juillet *m.*
jump sauter
June juin *m.*
justice justice *f.*

K

keep garder
key clef *f.*
kidding (slang) blague,
plaisanterie *f.*
kidney rognon *m.*
kilogram kilo *m.*
kilometer kilomètre *m.*
kind gentil,-le
kind sorte, espèce *f.*,
genre *m.*
kindness bienveillance *f.*
king roi *m.*
kiss, to embrasser
kitchen cuisine *f.*
knee genou *m.*
knife couteau *m.*
knock cogner, frapper
know connaître, savoir
knowledge connaissance *f.*
known connu,-e

L

labor main d'oeuvre *f.*
lace dentelle *f.*
lace, shoe lacet *m.*
lack, to manquer de
ladder échelle *f.*
ladies mesdames *f.*
lady dame *f.*
lake lac *m.*
lamb agneau *m.*
lamp lampe *f.*
lamp bulb ampoule *f.*
land, to débarquer
land (an airplane) atterrir
language langue *f.*
large grand,-e
last, dernier,-ère
last, to durer
late tard,-e
laugh rire
laundry blanchisserie *f.*
law loi *f.*
laziness paresse *f.*
lazy paressuex,-euse
lead, to mener
leaf feuille *f.*
learn apprendre
lease bail *m.*
least moindre
leather cuir *m.*
leave quitter, laísser
lecture conférence *f.*
left gauche *f.*
leg (meat) cuisse *f.*
leg (limb) jambe *f.*
lemon citron *m.*
lemonade limonade *f.*
lend, to prêter
lengthen allonger
less moins
lesson leçon *f.*
let, to laisser
letter lettre *f.*
letter of credit lettre de
  crédit *f.*
lettuce laitue *f.*
liaison liaison *f.*
library bibliothèque *f.*
lie mensonge *m.*
life vie *f.*

light clair,-e
light lumière *f.*
light, to allumer
light up, to éclairer
lighter briquet *m.*
lightning éclairs *m.pl.*
likable sympathique
like, to aimer
like comme
line ligne *f.*
linen toile *f.*
lip lèvre *f.*
lipstick rouge à lèvres *m.*
liqueur liqueur *f.*
listen écouter
literary littéraire
literature littérature *f.*
little petit,-e, peu
live demeurer, habiter
liver foie *m.*
living room salon *m.*
loaf miche *f.*
lobster homard *m.*
lock serrure *f.*
lodge, to loger
long long,-ue
long distance call interurbain
long time longtemps
look at regarder
look for chercher
look like, to avoir l'air de . . .
lose, to perdre
lost perdu,-e
lot tas *m.*
lounge foyer *m.*
love, to aimer
low bas,-se
luck chance, veine *f.* (slang)
lucky, to be avoir de la veine
lunch, to déjeuner
lunch déjeuner *m.*
lung poumon *m.*

M

machine machine *f.*
magic magique *adj.*
magnificent magnifique
maid bonne *f.*
mail courrier *m.*
ma a principal,-e

majesty majesté *f.*
majority plupart *f.*
make faire
man homme *m.*
manage, to se tirer d'affaire
se débrouiller
management direction *f.*
manager directeur,-trice,
gérant,-e
manicurist manicure *m.*
manner façon *f.*
manufacture, to fabriquer
manufacturing fabrication *f.*
map plan *m.*
March mars *m.*
mark marque *f.*
market marché *m.*
marriage, wedding mariage *m.*
marvellous merveilleux-euse
mashed potato purée de
pomme de terre *f.*
match allumette *f.*
mattress matelas *m.*
May mai *m.*
me moi
meal repas *m.*
mean, to vouloir dire
measure mesure *f.*
meat viande *f.*
medicine médicament *m.*
meet rencontrer
meeting assemblée, rencontre
f.
melon melon *m.*
member membre *m.*
memory mémoire *f.*
mend, to repriser
menu menu *m.*
merchant marchand *m.*
merchandise marchandise *f.*
message message *m.*
metal métal *m.*
meter compteur *m.*
middle milieu *m.*
midnight minuit *m.*
milliner modiste *f.*
milk lait *m.*
milk, to traire
mind esprit *m.*
mine mien, mienne
mineral water eau minérale *f.*

minute minute *f.*
mirror glace *f.*, miroir *m.*
misfortune malheur *m.*
mislay égarer
Miss mademoiselle
miss, to manquer
mistake erreur *m.*, faute *f.*
mister monsieur *m.*
misunderstanding malentendu
m.
mix, to mélanger
mixture mélange *m.*
mob foule *f.*
mock moquer
modern moderne
moistness moiteur *f.*
moment moment, instant *m.*
Monday lundi *m.*
money argent *m.*
money order mandat-poste *m.*
monkey wrench clef anglaise *f.*
month mois *m.*
monument monument *m.*
moon lune *f.*
more plus, davantage
moreover puis, d'ailleurs
morning matin *m.*, matinée *f.*
mosquito moustique *m.*
most plupart
mother maman, mère *f.*
motor moteur *m.*
mountain montagne *f.*
moustache moustache *f.*
mouth bouche *f.*
move, to déplacer
move away, to déménager
move in s'installer
movement mouvement *m.*
movie camera apparcil ciné-
matographique *m.*
movie theatre cinéma *m.*
moving picture film *m.*
Mr. Monsieur, M.
Mrs. Madame, Mme
much beaucoup
museum musée *m.*
music musique *f.*
music hall music hall *m.*
musician musicien,-ne
mustard moutarde *f.*

my mon, ma, mes
mysterious mysterieux,-ieuse

N

nail clou, ongle (finger) *m.*
name nom *m.*
napkin serviette *f.*
narrow étroit,-e
natural naturel,-le
naturally naturellement
nature nature *f.*
nave nef *f.*
near près
nearly presque
necessary nécessaire
neck cou *m.*
necktie cravate *f.*
need, to avoir besoin de
needle aiguille *f.*
neighbor voisine,-e *m.*
neighborhood aientours *m. pl.*
neither ni, non plus
    . . . nor, ni . . . ni
nephew neveu *m.*
network réseau *m.*
never jamais
nevertheless pourtant,
    néanmoins
new neuf,-ve, nouveau,
    nouvel,-le
news nouvelles *f. pl.*
newspaper journal,-aux *m.*
newsstand kiosque *m.*
next prochain-e
next day lendemain *m.*
night nuit *f.*
night club boîte de nuit *f.*
nightgown chemise de nuit *f.*
nine neuf
nineteen dix-neuf
no admittance! défense
    d'entrer!
no trespassing accès interdit
noise bruit *m.*
no non
nobility noblesse *f.*
noise bruit *m.*
noon midi *m.*
north nord *m.*
not pas, ne . . . pas

not . . . anything ne . . . rien
notably notamment
notary notaire *m.*
notebook cahier *m.*
nothing rien
notice avis *m.*
notice, to remarquer
novel roman *m.*
November novembre *m.*
now maintenant
nowadays actuellement
number numéro *m.*
nurse infirmière *f.*
nut noix *f.*

O

obelisk obélisque *m.*
object objet *m.*
objective objectif,-ive
oblige obliger
observation observation *f.*
observe, to constater
obtain obtenir
obviously évidemment
occupant occupant *m.*
occupation occupation *f.*
occupy occuper
octagonal octogonal
October octobre *m.*
odor odeur *f.*
of de
of course bien entendu
offend, to offenser, froisser
offer, to offrir
offer offre *m.*
office bureau *m.*
official officiel,-le
often souvent
oil huile *f.*
ointment pommade *f.*
O.K. d'accord
old vieux, vieille, ancien,-ne
old age vieillesse *f.*
old-fashioned vieux jeu,
    suranné,-e
omelet omelette *f.*
on sur, dessus
once une fois
one un,-e
one way street sens unique *m.*

onion *m.* oignon
only seulement
open ouvert,-e
open, to ouvrir
opera opéra *m.*
opinion opinion *f.,* avis *m.*
oppose, to opposer
or ou
orange orange *f.*
order ordre *m.*
order, to commander
organize organiser
originality originalité *f.*
other autre
otherwise autrement
our notre, nos
ourselves nous-mêmes
outside dehors
over dessus, sur
over there là bas
overcoat pardessus *m.*
overseas outre-mer
overturn capotage *m.*
owe, to devoir
own propre
oysters huîtres *f.*

P

pack, to emballer
package paquet *m.*
page page *f.*
pain peine, douleur *f.,* mal *m.*
paint, to peindre
painting peinture *f.,*
   tableau *m.*
pair paire *f.*
palace palais *m.*
palate palais *m.*
pale pâle
palm (of hand) paume *f.*
panties culotte *f.*
paper papier *m.*
parcel colis *m.*
parcel post colis postal *m.*
pardon, to pardonner
pardon pardon *m.*
parent parent,-e *m., f.*
Parisian parisien,-ne
park the car garer la voiture
part part, partie *f.*

participate participer
pass, to passer
passport passeport *m.*
pastry pâtisserie *f.*
pastrymaker pâtissier,-ère
patriot patriote *m.*
pattern patron *m.*
pavillon kiosque *m.*
pay payer, régler
pay cash payer au comptant
payment paiement *m.*
peace paix *f.*
peach pêche *f.*
peanut cacahuète *f.*
pear poire *f.*
peas petits pois *m.*
pedal pédale *f.*
pedestrian piéton *m.*
peer pair *m.*
pen plume *f.*
pencil crayon *m.*
people monde, gens *m.*
pepper poivre *m.*
per par
perceive apercevoir
per cent pour cent
perfect parfait,-e
perfectly parfaitement
performance représentation *f*
perfume parfum *m.*
perhaps peut-être
perish, to périr
permanent wave permanente
   f.
permit, to permettre
person personne *f.*
personal personnel,-le
perspiration transpiration *f.*
persuade persuader
petroleum pétrole *m.*
petticoat jupon *m.*
pharmacy pharmacie *f.*
photograph photo *f.*
physician médecin *m.*
piano piano *m.*
picture tableau *m.*
picture postcard carte postale
   illustrée *f.*
picturesque pittoresque
pie tarte *f.*
piece morceau *m.*

pier quai *m.*
pile tas *m.*
pill pilule *f.*
pillow oreiller, coussin *m.*
pilot pilote *m.*
pin épingle *f.*
pineapple ananas *m.*
pipe pipe *f.*
pity, to plaindre, avoir
  pitié de
place endroit, lieu *m.*
place, to placer, mettre
plan projet *m.*
plant plante *f.*
plate assiette *f.*
platform plate-forme *f.*
  quai *m.*
play pièce *f.*
play, to jouer
player joueur *m.*
playhouse salle de théâtre *f.*
pleasant aimable
please veuillez, s'il vous plaît
please, to plaire à
pleasure plaisir *m.*
plum prune *f.*
pocket poche *f.*
poem poème *m.*
poet poète *m.*
poetic poétique
poetry poésie *f.*
point point *m.*
police headquarters préfecture
  de police *f.*
police station commissariat *m.*
policeman gendarme, agent
  (de police) *m.*
polite poli
political politique
politics politique *f.*
poor pauvre
pork porc *m.*
port port *m.*
porter porteur *m.*
position position *f.*
possess, to posséder
possible possible
postage affranchissement *m.*
postman facteur *m.*
post office poste *f.*
postpone remettre

potato pomme de terre *f.*
pound livre *f.*
poverty misère *f.*
powder poudre *f.*
powder, to poudrer
practical commode, pratique
practice, to s'exercer
praise, to louer
pray prier
precise précis,-e
precisely justement
prefer préférer
prejudice préjugé *m.*
prepare préparer
prescription ordonnance *f.*
present actuel,-le
present, to présenter
press,to appuyer
presumptuous presomptueux,
  -euse
pretend, to prétendre
pretty poli,-e
prevent empêcher
previously auparavant
price prix *m.*
principal principal
print épreuve *f.*
private particulier,-ère,
  privé,-e
prize prix *m.*
probably probablement
professional professionel,-le
procure procurer
produce, to produire
product produit *m.*
professional professionel,-le
profitable profitable
profound profond-e
program programme *m.*
promenade promenade *f.*
promise, to promettre
properly proprement
propose, to proposer
proscribe, to proscrire
protest protestation *f.*
prove prouver
pull, to tirer
pulse pouls *m.*
pump pompe *f.*
punctual ponctuel,-le
puncture crevaison *f.*

purchase, to acheter
purchase achat *m.*
pure pur,-e
purpose intention *f.*
purpose, on exprès
pursue, to poursuiure
push, to pousser
put placer, mettre
pyjamas pyjamas *m.*

Q

quality qualité *f.*
quarter quart *m.*
queen reine *f.*
question question *f.*
quickly vite
quit quitter
quote, to citer

R

rabbit lapin *m.*
race course *f.*
radiator radiateur *m.*
radio radio *f.*
radio station poste *m.*
railroad chemin de fer *m.*
railroad-car wagon *m.*
    voiture *f.*
railroad station gare *f.*
rain pluie *f.*
rain, to pleuvoir
raincoat imperméable *m.*
raise lever
rank rang *m.*
rate taux *m.*
rate of exchange taux de
    change
rather plutôt
raw saignant,-e
rayon rayonne *f.*
razor rasoir *m.*
razor blade lame à rasoir *f.*
reach, to parvenir
react réagir
read lire
reading lecture *f.*
ready prêt,-e
real réel,-le
realistic réaliste
really réellement, vraiment

rear arrière
reason, to raisonner
reason raison *f.*
reasonable raisonnable
reassure, to rassurer
recall, to rappeler
receipt reçu *m.*
receive recevoir
recently récemment
reception réception *f.*
recognize reconnaître
recommend recommander
recover récupérer
red rouge
reduce réduire
refresh, to rafraîchir
refreshment rafraîchissement
    m.
refrigerator glacière *f.*
refuse refuser
register se faire inscrire,
    enregistrer
register a letter faire recom-
    mander une lettre
registered letter lettre recom-
    mandée *f.*
regret regret *m.*
regret, to regretter
reign règne *m.*
relate raconter
relation relation *f.*
relative parent,-e
relish hors d'oeuvre *m.*
remake refaire
remain rester
remember se souvenir de
rent loyer *m.*
rent, to louer
repair réparer
repeat répéter
replace remplacer
represent représenter
resemblance ressemblance *f.*
resemble, to ressembler
reside demeurer
residence résidence *f.*
resolve résoudre
respect respect *m.*
rest (remainder) reste *m.*
rest repos *m.*
restaurant restaurant *m*

restriction restriction *f.*
retain retenir
return retourner, rentrer, revenir
ribbon ruban *m.*
rice riz *m.*
rich riche
ride promenade en voiture *f.*
right droit,-e
right away sur-le-champ
ring, to sonner
ring bague *f.* (on finger)
rise hausse *f.* (in prices)
river fleuve *m.*
road route *f.*, chemin *m.*
roast rôti *m.*
roast, to rôtir
roast beef rosbif *m.*
roasted rôti,-e
roll petit pain *m.*
roll, to rouler
roof toit *m.*
room chambre, pièce, salle *f.*
rose rose *f.*
rough rude
round rond,-e
row rang *m.*
rubber caoutchouc *m.*
ruby rubis *m.*
rug tapis *m.*
ruin ruine *f.*
ruler règle *f.*
run courir
run along, to se sauver
runner coureur *m.*
running water eau courante *f.*
rush hour heure d'affluence *f.*
Russia Russie *f.*
Russian russe
rustic rustique

S

sad triste
sadness tristesse *f.*
safe sauf, sauve
sail, to s'embarquer
salad salade *f.*
sale vente *f.*
saleslady vendeuse *f.*
salesman vendeur *m.*

salmon saumon *m.*
salt sel *m.*
salted salé,-e
same même
sand sable *m.*
sandwich sandwich *m.*
sanitary napkin, serviette hygiénique *f.*
satisfy, to contenter, satisfaire
Saturday samedi *m.*
save sauver
say, to dire
scarcely à peine
scene scène *f.*
scenery paysage *m.*
school école *f.*
scissors ciseaux *m.*
scrape, to gratter
scratch égratignure *f.*
scratch, to gratter
screw-driver tourne-vis *m.*
sea mer *f.*
seal sceau *m.*
season saison *f.*
seasickness mal de mer *m.*
seasoning assaisonnement *m.*
seat place *f.*, siège *m.*
second (time) seconde *f.*
second second,-e, deuxième
section of a city quartier *m.*
securities valeurs *f. pl.*
see voir
see again revoir
seem, to sembler
seize saisir
sell vendre
send envoyer
. . . for envoyer chercher
sentence phrase *f.*
sentiment sentiment *m.*
September septembre *m.*
serious sérieux,-euse
seriously pour de bon
servant domestique *m., f.*
serve servir
set décor *m.*
set, to mettre
setting décor *m.*
seven sept
seventeen dix-sept
seventy soixante-dix

several plusieurs
sew, to coudre
sewing couture *f.*
shadow ombre *f.*
shake, to secouer
share part *f.*
shave, to raser
shaving brush blaireau *m.*
shaving cream crème à
  barbe *f.*
shaving soap savon à barbe *m.*
she elle
sheep mouton *m.*
sheet drap *m.*
sheet of paper feuille de
  papier *f.*
shell, egg coque *f.*
shellfish soup bisque *f.*
shine, to (shoes) cirer
ship bateau, navire *m.*
shipment livraison *f.*
shirt chemise *f.*
shoe soulier *m.*, chaussure *f.*
shoemaker cordonnier *m.*
shop boutique *f.*
shop, to faire des achats,
  faire les courses
short court,-e
short caleçon *m.* (underwear)
short, in en somme
shoulder épaule *f.*
shout, to crier
show spectacle *m.*
show, to montrer
shower douche *f.*
shut, to fermer
shut up enfermer
sick malade
sickness maladie *f.*
side côté *m.*
sidewalk trottoir *m.*
sidewalk café terrasse *f.*
sign signe, pancarte, écriteau
  m.
sign, to signer
silent silencieux,-euse
silk soie *f.*
silverware argenterie *f.*
similar pareil,-le
simplicity simplicité *f.*
simply simplement

since depuis
  (because) puisque
sincere sincère, franc,-che
sincerely sincèrement
sing chanter
sir monsieur *m.*
sister soeur *f.*
sit down s'asseoir
six six
sixteen seize
size grandeur *f.*
  (clothing) taille
  numero . . .
skate, to patiner
skating patinage *m.*
skating rink patinoire *f.*
ski ski *m.*
ski, to faire du ski
skid, to déraper
skin peau *f.*
skirt jupe *f.*
sky ciel *m*
skyscraper gratte-ciel *m.*
slander médisance *f.*
sleep, to dormir
sleep, go to s'endormir
sleeping-car wagon-lit *m.*
sleeve manche *f.*
slice tranche *f.*
slip, to glisser
slip combinaison *f.*
slipper pantoufle *f.*
slope pente *f.*
slowly lentement
small petit,-e
smell, to sentir
smile sourire *m.*
smoke fumée *f.*
smoking compartment
  fumeur *m.*
snapshot instantané *m.*
snow neige *f.*
snow, to neiger
soaked trempé,-e
soap savon *m.*
sock chaussette *f.*
soda water eau gazeuse *f.*
sofa canapé *m.*
soft mou, molle
soldier soldat *m.*
sole semelle *f.*

some des, quelque, quelques-
   uns
sometimes parfois,
   quelquefois
somewhere quelque part
so much tant, tellement
son fils *m.*
song chanson *f.*
soon bientôt
sore throat mal à la gorge *m.*
sorrow peine, douleur *f.*
sorry désolé,-e
soul âme *f.*
sound, to soner
soup potage *m.*
south sud *m.*
Spanish espagnol,-e
speak parler
special delivery letter express,
   pneumatique *m.* (in Paris)
specify préciser
spectator spectateur *m.*
speed vitesse *f.*
spend, to dépenser
spite of, in malgré
splendid splendide
split, to fendre
spoil, to gâter
sport sport *m.*
sporting sportif,-ive
spot endroit *m.*
spread répandre
spring ressort *m.*
spring (season) printemps *m.*
spirits of ammonia
   ammoniaque
sponge éponge *f.*
spoon cuillère *f.*
sport coat veston *m.*
spring printemps *m.*
square carré,-e
square place *f.*
stage scène *f.*
stained glass window vitrail
stairway escalier *m.*
stamp timbre *m.*
standing debout
star étoile *f.*
starch amidon *m.*
starch, to empeser
start, to commencer

state état *m.*
statement déclaration *f.*
stationary store papeterie *f.*
stature taille *f.*
stay séjour *m.*
stay, to rester
steal voler
steam vapeur *f.*
steering wheel volant *m.*
stick bâton *m.*
still encore
stocking bas *m.*
stomach estomac *m.*
stomach ache mal au
   ventre *m.*
stop, to arrêter
stop arrêt *m.*
stopover escale *f.*
store magasin *m.*
storm tempête *f.*, orage *m.*
story (floor) étage *m.*
strange curieux, étrange
strawberry fraise *f.*
street rue *f.*
strike grève *f.*
string ficelle *f.*
strong fort,-e
student étudiant,-e
study, to étudier
study étude *f.*
subject propos, sujet *m.*
subordinate, to subordonner
subscribe s'abonner
subsidize, to subventionner
subtle difference nuance *f.*
suburb banlieue *f.*
subway métro *m.*
succeed réussir
such a tel,-le
sudden soudain,-e
suddenly tout à coup
suffer souffrir
suffice suffire
suffocate étouffer
sugar sucre *m.*
sugar-bowl sucrier *m.*
suit complet, costume *m.*
suit (woman's) costume
   tailleur *m.*
suitcase valise *f.*
sum somme *f.*

summer session cours de
vacances *f. pl.*
summer été *m.*
sumptuous somptueux,-euse
sun soleil *m.*
sun bath bain de soleil *m.*
sun-burn coup de soleil *m.*
sun glasses lunettes de soleil *f.*
Sunday dimanche *m.*
sunrise lever du soleil *m.*
sunset coucher de soleil *m.*
superb superbe
superior supérieur,-e
supervise surveiller
supper souper *m.*
supply, to munir
support soutien *m.*
supposed to censé,-e
sure sûr,-e
surely assurément
surprise surprise *f.*
surprise, to surprendre
surround entourer
suspect, to se douter de
suspenders bretelles *f.*
sweet sucré,-e, doux, douce
swell épatant,-e
swim, to nager
swimming nage *f.*
Switzerland Suisse *f.*
sympathy sympathie *f.*
symptom symptôme *m.*
syndicate syndicat *m.*
synonym synonyme *m.*
system système *m.*

T

table table *f.*
tablecloth nappe *f.*
tailor tailleur
take prendre
take advantage of, to profiter
take along emener
take care of s'occuper de
take off, to (aviation) décoller
talent talent *m.*
taste goût *m.*
taste, to goûter
tax impôt *m.* taxe *f.*
taxi taxi *m.*

tea thé *m.*
teach, to enseigner
teacher professeur *m.*
technique technique *f.*
telegram dépêche *f.*
telephone, to téléphoner
telephone téléphone *m.*
telephone book annuaire,
bottin *m.*
telephone booth cabine
téléphonique *f.*
telephone call coup de
téléphone *m.*
telepone operator
téléphoniste *m., f.*
tempest tempête *f.*
tempt tenter
ten dix
tendency tendance *f.*
tender tendre
tennis tennis *m.*
term terme *m.*
terminal terminus *m.*
terrace terrasse *f.*
terribly terriblement
thank, to remercier
thanks merci
that ça, cela, ce, cette
the le, la, les
theater théâtre *m.*
theirs le leur
them eux, elles
then puis
there là
there is, are voilà
therefore donc
thermometer thermomètre *m.*
these ces, ceux
they ils, elles
thing chose *f.*
think penser, croire, réfléchir
third troisième
third tiers *m.*
thirst soif *f.*
thirteen treize
thirty trente
thirty-seven trente-sept
this ça, celui, celle, ceci, ce, cet,
cette
thought pensée *f.*
thousand mille

thread fil *m.*
three trois
throat gorge *f.*
throw, to lancer
thunder tonnerre *m.*
Thursday jeudi *m.*
thus ainsi
ticket collector controlleur *m.*
ticket office guichet *m.*
ticket window guichet *m.*
tight étroit,-e, serré,-e
time temps *m.*, fois *f.*
time table horaire *m.*
tip pourboire *m.*
tire pneu *m.*
tire, to fatiguer
tired fatigué,-e
to à
toast toast *m.*
tobacco tabac *m.*
tobacco store bureau de
  tabac *m.*
today aujourd'hui
together ensemble
toilet toilette *f.*, cabinet *m.*
tomato tomate *f.*
tomb tombeau *m.*
tomorrow demain
tongue langue *f.*
too aussi
too much trop
tooth dent *f.*
toothache mal aux dents *m.*
toothbrush brosse à dents *f.*
tooth paste pâte dentifrice *f.*
toothpick cure-dent *m.*
top haut *m.*
torture, to torturer
touch, to toucher
tough dur,-e
tour tour *m.*
tournament tournoi *m.*
toward vers, envers
towel serviette *f.*
tower tour *f.*
town ville *f.*
town hall mairie *f.*
toy jouet *m.*
track voie *f.*
traffic circulation *f.*
traffic jam embouteillage *m.*

tragedy tragédie *f.*
train train *m.*
trait trait *m.*
transaction transaction *f.*
transatlantic transatlantique
travel, to voyager
traveler voyageur,-euse
travelers check travelers
  chèque, chèque de
  tourisme *m.*
tray plateau *m.*
treat, to traiter
tree arbre *m.*
trimming garniture *f.*
trip voyage *m.*
trolley tramway *m.*
trouble peine *f.*
trousers pantalon *m.*
truck camion *m.*
true vrai,-e
trunk malle *f.*
truth vérité *f.*
try, to tâcher, essayer
Tuesday mardi *m.*
turn, to tourner
turret tourelle *f.*
tuxedo smoking *m.*
twelve douze
twenty vingt
twenty, about vingtaine *f.*
twice deux fois
twin beds lits jumeaux *m.*
two deux
type sorte *f.*, genre *m.*
typewriter machine à écrire *f.*

U

ugly laid,-e
umbrella parapluie *m.*
unaware of, to be ignorer
uncle oncle *m.*
under dessous, sous
understand comprendre
underwear linge de corps *m.*
undo, to défaire
undress, to se déshabiller
unforeseen imprévu,-e
unfortunate malheureux,-euse
unfortunately
  malheureusement

unhealthy malsain,-e
uniformity uniformité f.
union, workers' syndicat m.
United States Etats-Unis m.pl.
university université f.
unknown inconnu,-e
unpacking déballage m.
unpleasant désagréable
until jusqu'à
up there là haut
upset contrarié,-e
upstairs en haut
urgency urgence f.
urgent urgent,-e
us nous
usages usages m. pl.
use (custom) usage m.
use, to se servir de
useful utile
useless inutile
usher, to annoncer
utilize, to utiliser

V

vacancy vide m., lacune f.
vacant libre
vacation vacances f. pl.
vaguely vaguement
valley vallée f.
valuable précieux,-se
value, to estimer
veal veau m.
vegetable légume m.
vehicle véhicule m.
velvet velours m.
very très
vest gilet m.
vicinity environs m. pl.
view vue f.
vinegar vinaigre m.
visa visa m.
visit, to visiter
visit visite f.
visitor visiteur m.
vizor visière f.
voice voix f.

W

waist taille f.
wait attendre

waiter garçon m.
waiting room salle d'attente f.
wake up se reveiller
waken, to reveiller
walk, to marcher
walking marche f.
wall mur m.
wall clock pendule f.
want, to vouloir
war guerre f.
wardrobe armoire f.
warm chaud,-e
warm, to chauffer
warn, to prévenir
wash, to laver
wash basin (fixture) lavabo m.
wash basin cuvette f.
watch montre f.
watchmaker horloger m.
watch out gare à vous
water eau f.
wave onde f.
wave hair, to faire onduler
  (les cheveux)
we nous
weak faible
wear, to porter
weather temps m.
Wednesday mercredi m.
week semaine f.
weigh peser
well! tiens!
west ouest m.
wet mouillé,-e
what quoi, quel,-e
wheat blé m.
wheel roue f.
when quand
where où
whereas tandis que
which que, quel,-e
white blanc, blanche
who qui lequel, laquelle
whom qui
why pourquoi
wicket (gate) portillon m.
wide ample
wife femme f.
willingly volontiers
win, to gagner
window fenêtre f.

window display étalage
wine vin *m.*
wing aile *f.*
wish souhaiter, désirer
with avec
without sans
witness témoin *m.*
witty spirituel,-le
wolf loup *m.*
woman femme *m.*
wonder, to se demander
wonderful merveilleux,-euse
wood bois *m.*
wool laine *f.*
word mot *m.*, parole *f.*
work ouvrage *m.*, œuvre *f.*
work, to travailler (people)
   marcher (machines)
workshop atelier *m.*
world monde *m.*
worldly mondain,-e
worry souci *m.*
worse pire, pis
worth, to be valoir
worthy digne
wrap up, to envelopper
wrench clef *f.*
wrinkle, to froisser

wrist watch bracelet-
   montre *m.*
write écrire
writer écrivain *m.*
writing paper papier à
   lettres *m.*
written écrit,-e
wrong tort *m.*
wrong, to be avoir tort,
   se tromper

Y

year an *m.* année *f.*
yellow jaune
yes oui, si
yesterday hier
yet encore
you tu, vous
young jeune
your vos, votre
yours vôtre
youth jeunesse *f.*

Z

zero zéro *m.*
zipper fermeture éclair *f.*